Psychology and Community Change

Psychology and Community Change

Challenges of the Future

Kenneth Heller
Indiana University

Richard H. Price
University of Michigan

Shulamit Reinharz
Brandeis University

Stephanie Riger
Lake Forest College

Abraham Wandersman
University of South Carolina

with the collaboration of
Thomas A. D'Aunno
University of Michigan

Second Edition
1984

The Dorsey Press
Homewood, Illinois   60430

ISBN 0-256-02860-5
Library of Congress Catalog Card No. 83-73092

Printed in the United States of America

1 2 3 4 5 6 7 8 9 0 MP 1 0 9 8 7 6 5 4

To our children
  whose lives will be affected by
  the way we create our communities.
  Carolyn, Daniel & Emily
  Richard, Margaret & Daniel
  Yali & Naomi
  Matthew
  Seth & Jeffrey

Preface

This book is about the contribution of psychology to the understanding of social and community change. The traditional concern of psychology has been the study of individual behavior. This book presents an alternative view and shows how psychology is being used to understand groups, organizations, and communities. We will present the knowledge that already has been developed in the field and also will chart some of the challenges community psychology will face in the future as our society changes.

Explaining how communities function and change is of interest to a number of academic disciplines. For example, economics is concerned with economic cycles, sociology with class conflict, anthropology with shared rituals and meanings, and political science with government organization and power distribution in communities. Psychologists are relative newcomers to the study of community phenomena, entering the field in the 1960s with the recognition that individual behavior and psychological well-being, the traditional concerns of psychology, could not be fully understood in isolation from broader social issues. Initially only an orientation, community psychologists found themselves using ideas from other disciplines (for example, sociology, political science, and public health) as well as from other areas of psychology, such as environmental, applied social, and organizational psychology. Accounting for social and environmental factors increases the complexity of psychological theories, but brings us closer to developing more useful and meaningful intervention programs.

Individual, organizational, or community change are not simple processes, and it is important to remember that people's lives are affected by the assumptions and values that often are implicit in intervention programs. That is why, throughout the book, we have tried to clearly articulate theoretical assumptions and values, including our own. There is a fair degree of congruence among the authors in personal values. In general terms, we are distressed by the social inequities that continue to plague our society and believe that the social sciences should be more active in the search for solutions to these problems. We would like to see a continued thrust toward properly evaluated social innovation. Empirical data on the effects of social policies should be important for citizens as well as government decision makers. An individual's political persuasion—whether "conservative" or "liberal"—should not determine the need for or willingness to use verified data. We are not advocating a society ruled by a "social science priesthood." In a democracy, any proposal for social action should be debated freely and ultimately decided by the people through the electoral process and community action. We believe that these decisions would be improved if they were based on evidence. We recognize that social policy decisions often involve an accommodation to competing political pressures. Such political responsiveness is necessary in a pluralistic democracy. However, we feel that it is socially irresponsible to suggest that such decisions should be made without evidence. It is our obligation to develop the best possible scientific evidence and to actively disseminate our results.

While each of us initially was attracted to community psychology by its underlying values and social concerns, we recognize that ideology alone cannot sustain a field during shifts in the social and political climate. We believe that the future of community psychology lies in its contribution as a field of inquiry. Our value as a field is in our ability to provide knowledge about social and environmental influences that can be used by citizens to improve their lives. That is why we have emphasized research and demonstration projects whenever possible in the substantive chapters of this book.

We have been heartened to note that since publication of the first edition of this book in 1977, there has been a veritable explosion of sound empirical work in community psychology. In 1974, Rappaport and Chinsky[1] described community psychology as a new orientation or point of view, rather than as a new substantive body of knowledge. Over the last decade, this initial stage in the development of the field has changed. There is now a greater commitment to empirical work and theory development which has given the field new vitality.

The process of preparing this book has involved the authors in a stimulating exchange of ideas that has been of value to us all. Heller, the senior author of the first edition, chose colleagues for the revision who he believed had established expertise in substantive content areas and who also demonstrated superior writing skills. The initial exchange of chapter outlines and preliminary drafts was supplemented by a planning meeting at an A.P.A. convention in Washington, D.C. In December of 1982, the authors were invited by the Department of Psychology at the University of South Carolina to present a day-long symposium on their research. This allowed the authors to spend an intensive weekend together in discussion and debate that helped shape the final chapter drafts. We are indebted to the University of South Carolina for the support provided and to the Wandersman family (Abe, Lois,

---

[1] J. Rappaport and J. M. Chinsky, Models for delivery of service from a historical and conceptual perspective, *Professional Psychology,* 1974, 5, 42–50.

Seth, and Jeffrey) for their hospitality in opening their home to us. All chapter drafts were circulated among the co-authors for comment, which often resulted in extensive revision. So while each of us bears primary responsibility for specific parts of the book, we consider the book to be a truly collaborative undertaking.

Each of the authors would like to acknowledge the help received from colleagues, students, and co-workers. Thomas D'Aunno collaborated with Price in writing Chapters 3 and 4. His substantive contribution to these chapters is acknowledged by the appearance of his name as first author on both chapters. D'Aunno also provided critical comments on several of the chapters as did Jean Ann Linney and Mac McClure. Leonard Jason and Dan A. Lewis provided important feedback on Chapters 5 and 6. Dan's thoughtful, substantive comments and unwavering support and encouragement are particularly appreciated. The chapter on citizen participation benefited from comments by Paul Florin, Richard Rich, Don Unger, and several graduate students in the clinical-community psychology program at the University of South Carolina. Lois Pall Wandersman and David Chavis reviewed several drafts of this chapter. Lois helped shape the chapter, and David provided important information in the area of community organization. Jean Marvel and members of the Wildflower Bakery enabled Reinharz to study the dynamics of an alternative setting. Some of the material retained from the first edition of the book initially was written by John Monahan. His encouragement to undertake this revision is appreciated.

Assistance in manuscript preparation was provided by Sharon Miller, Shari Pruett, Susan Markancek, and Lana Fish at Indiana University; Barb Strane and Patti Fuhst at the University of Michigan; Marilyn Aaron and Evan Harriman at Brandeis University; Janet Soule at Northwestern University; and Jerlean Barber at the University of South Carolina. Their work represented secretarial professionalism at its best. In addition, Charles Kieffer located references for Chapter 9, and Perilou Goddard completed the author index for Chapters 1, 2, 7, 8, and 11. Assistance in copy editing for all of the chapters was provided by Audrey Heller, whose support throughout this project is deeply appreciated.

Kenneth Heller
Richard H. Price
Shulamit Reinharz
Stephanie Riger
Abraham Wandersman

Contents

PART ONE

The Development of a Community Orientation

Introduction*

---

* This chapter was written by Kenneth Heller.

Almost everyone has heard about Love Canal, but not many people know what it is all about. The Love Canal story is about a thousand families who lived near the site of an abandoned toxic chemical waste dump. More important, it is a warning of what could happen in any American community. We have very little protection against the toxic chemical wastes that threaten to poison our water, our air, and our food. . .

When we moved into our house on 101st Street in 1972, I didn't even know Love Canal was there. It was a lovely neighborhood in a quiet residential area, with lots of trees and lots of children outside playing. It seemed just the place for our family. We have two children—Michael, who was born just before we moved in, and Melissa (Missy), born June 12, 1975. I was 26. I liked the neighborhood because it was in the city but out of it. It was convenient. There was a school within walking distance. I liked the idea of my children being able to walk to the 99th Street School. The school's playground was part of a big, open field with houses all around. Our new neighbors told us that the developers who sold them their houses said the city was going to put a park on the field.

It is really something, if you stop and think of it, that underneath that field was poisons, and on top of it was a grade school and a playground. We later found out that the Niagara Falls School Board knew the filled-in canal was a toxic dump site. We also know that they knew it was dangerous because, when the Hooker Chemical Corporation sold it to them for one dollar, Hooker put a clause in the deed declaring that the corporation would not be responsible for any harm that came to anyone from chemicals buried there. That one-dollar school site turned out to be some bargain! (Gibbs, 1982, pp. 1 and 9)

How would you react if you woke up one morning and found yourself living in a home that was declared unsafe to your health and the health of your family members? This dilemma faced homeowners at Love Canal in Niagara Falls, New York, and is likely to be repeated at numerous locations throughout the country as chemical dumpsites and other man-made disasters are discovered. What action can an individual citizen take to protect home and family? What role should government agencies have in protecting the public interest, and how can citizens activate slow-moving government bureaucracies so their needs can be speedily addressed? Questions of this sort might seem perfectly appropriate in a government or political science textbook, but why raise them in a book about psychology?

THE SCOPE OF COMMUNITY PSYCHOLOGY

Community psychologists are interested in the health and well-being of all members of a community. They are concerned about deleterious environmental conditions and the impact of such problems on behavior. Their concern is not just to spotlight dangers but also to reinforce helpful practices that aid in the development of psychological competence. The work of community psychologists is focused on improving community life for all citizens, in preventing disorder, and in promoting psychological well-being in the population. Unlike most clinical psychologists, community psychologists do not restrict the scope of their concern to those with established disorders.

Return, for a moment, to the Love Canal example. Is there anything that psychologists can do when the health and well-being of community members are threatened as they were at Love Canal? In actuality, the mental health professions serving the Love Canal area did very little that was of value to community residents (Gibbs, 1983). The local mental health center offered counseling and therapy services, but community members resented the implication that they needed mental health services. Accepting such help was interpreted by community members as implying that they were becoming "crazy" (Gibbs, 1983). Indeed, the frequency of long-term personality disorders which might have required intensive psychotherapy was no different among them than among any group of citizens. Many residents did display negative psychological effects from the prolonged stress they were experiencing, for which crisis intervention procedures (discussed in Chapter Seven) might have been helpful. However, becoming a mental health "patient" or "client" to receive such services could have had negative political consequences. It would have reinforced the claims of their detractors that the aroused citizens were simply a bunch of distraught housewives who had conjured up imaginary illnesses. Accepting psychological help could have been used as evidence that they were exaggerating the harmful effects of the chemical pollution.[1]

Mental health professionals like to think of their work as politically neutral, yet here was an instance in which neutrality would not have been possible. Accepting psychological help could have been harmful to the residents' cause.

If counseling and psychotherapy were not appropriate in this situation, were there other ways that psychologists might have been helpful? We hope that the answer to this question will become clear after examining the con-

---

[1] Lois Gibbs, the citizen who organized residents at Love Canal, believed that mental health professionals could have been helpful by coming to the office of the Homeowners Association and simply sitting around until they became trusted "insiders." Discussions then could have been organized "so that residents could receive the help they needed as well as learning how to help themselves and assist their neighbors" (Gibbs, 1983, p. 123). However, doing so would have involved major shifts in conceptual orientation and style of operation by the mental health professionals. Typical mental health work is office-bound, with the professional "waiting" for the client to appear and ask for help (Rappaport & Seidman, 1982). Mental health professionals are not accustomed to going to other organizations and "sitting around." It also would have involved them in social and political problems, like how to get financial reimbursement for now worthless homes—topics not typically included in their training.

The above comments should not be seen as an "attack" against clinical psychology but as a comment on the limitations of traditional clinical perspectives. While community psychology developed, in part, as a reaction against prevailing attitudes and practices within clinical psychology, in actuality both fields have been changing over time. There has been a fair degree of fusion among clinical and community psychology training programs (described in more detail in the Appendix) so that advances in community psychology now are welcomed by many clinical practitioners. For example, some clinicians now are trained to offer consultation and crisis intervention to community groups experiencing stress. Still, as an aid to conceptual clarity and to emphasize contrasting intervention implications, the differences between clinical and community perspectives will be highlighted in the material that follows.

tents of this book. At this point, we will outline the possibilities that will be discussed in more detail in subsequent chapters.

A psychologist might conduct research on the psychological effects of different environmental conditions. Knowledge of research about the psychological aftereffects of disasters (e.g., Baum, Gatchel, & Schaeffer, 1983; Gleser, Green, & Winget, 1981; Cohen & Ahearn, 1980) might have helped the residents of Love Canal cope better with the disaster they faced, because they would have been able to anticipate and prepare for the effects of exposure to prolonged stress and uncertainty. Hence, a role for a community psychologist might be not only to conduct environmentally relevant research but to disseminate the research in forms that can be accessed and used by community residents (Chavis, Stucky, & Wandersman, 1983). (A discussion of different types of community relevant research can be found in Chapter Four.)

There are other possible roles for a community psychologist as well. These include helping citizens organize to more effectively accomplish their goals (discussed in Chapter Ten) or serving as a consultant to government agencies attempting to meet the demands of aroused citizens (Chapter Eight). The decision about which side of a controversy to be on involves judgments about values and perceived effectiveness. Is a psychologist likely to be more effective by helping citizens organize or by helping responsible officials deal with new situations where prior procedures or guidelines no longer apply? Questions of this sort cannot be answered in the abstract, only in specific situations; but what is required is an explicit recognition of the value choices involved. In the Love Canal example, officials initially were more interested in cooling citizen anger and avoiding financial responsibility for the disaster (Levine, 1982), so consultation with officials in the early stages of the controversy probably would have contributed to minimizing the pollution dangers. Only later was there a serious attempt to find an effective solution that would help citizens deal with relocation problems.

The roles we have described for a community psychologist involve both research and action—research on the effects of environmental conditions on health and well-being, and action to help citizens and officials improve those conditions. The details of how these tasks are accomplished actually are complicated by a number of questions that can be difficult to resolve. For example, how should health and well-being be assessed to determine the impact of environmental conditions? In the Love Canal example, most of the citizens felt fine and would not have known of the existence of any problem had it not been for the action of an investigative reporter who exposed what had been up until then scattered complaints of individual citizens (Levine, 1982). There were complaints for over 20 years about oil and fumes in backyards and basements, but the seriousness of the problem was not recognized. There were other significant clues, such as a high incidence of birth defects and miscarriages in the neighborhood, but citizens did not learn about this pattern until *after* they had organized and began to compare notes. Since birth defects can come from a variety of sources, the link between birth defects and the chemical dumping that had occurred 20 years earlier was not immediately apparent. Nor were there readily available statistics, which could be used for comparison purposes, about the frequency of birth defects in the Buffalo–Niagara Falls area, where chemical plants were quite common, or in the population at large.

If health effects are difficult to assess, determining the *psychological* impact of environmental events can be even more difficult. One could look at the rates of treated cases of mental disorder in a community, or at the incidence of new admissions to the local mental hospital, but these statistics are not likely to be very useful in assessing the impact of specific environmental conditions. Negative events can have a cumulative impact, so their effects may not be seen immediately but only years later. Furthermore, increases in subjective distress or problems in coping effectiveness may not be picked up by treatment statistics. Many individuals in distress do not seek treatment. Furthermore, treatment rates not only reflect the number of distressed individuals in a community but also fiscal policies and the availability of alternative services. For example, we will show in the next chapter that, historically, institutionalization rates for mental disorders often varied as a function of the social climate of the times and fiscal policies concerning payment for inpatient versus outpatient services.

What this means is that the information collected about the psychological effects of environmental events may not present a "tight" case that directly links events and their impact. The data from research may vary considerably in quality or usefulness, depending upon the variables assessed, the ease of measurement, and the methodologies employed. (See Chapters Three and Four for a discussion of research methodologies in community psychology.) Thus, data will need to be interpreted by those familiar with the limitations of the methodologies employed in their collection. Important roles for psychologists could be to help in data collection, interpretation, and dissemination of findings. Whether that help should be provided to citizen groups or to responsible officials will be discussed later in the book. Also to be discussed are the different ways that social change could occur. How can individuals—whether citizens or officials—contribute to meaningful improvements in community life?

THE MULTIFACETED NATURE OF COMMUNITY PSYCHOLOGY

The description of the activity of community psychologists provided thus far does not do justice to the complex and multifaceted nature of the field. It is true that community psychologists are interested in improving the health and well-being of community members through research and action oriented toward producing significant social change. But there is much more to be said about the values, orientation, and research foci of those who identify with this field. An appreciation of the multifaceted nature of the discipline can be obtained by understanding its scope and diversity. The community point of view in psychology took form as part of the social reform movement of the 1960s. Thus, reformist *values* are important to the field and, for some community psychologists, these values mark the field's uniqueness. Community psychology also was part of a professional critique of the intra-psychic orientation brought to clinical psychology by psychoanalytic perspectives. So community psychology also can be described in terms of a *conceptual orientation* to psychological theory and practice. As community psychology matured, it became an area of research and scholarship highlighting specific topics in psychology. Since community psychologists were particularly interested in the action implications of their research, examples of the interaction between research and practice also increased. Thus, there now is a growing body of literature that would allow us to describe community psychology as opening new areas for *research and practice*. To properly understand community psychology and the diversity among its proponents, one must understand these different facets.

COMMUNITY PSYCHOLOGY VALUES

Any field whose practice touches the lives of others is confronted with value choices. Such decisions are not always apparent to the professional in day-to-day work, but they are implicit in what he or she does. The choice of problems considered legitimate for study and the imposition of intervention technologies to solve these problems reflect social values, not just "scientific" findings (Rappaport, 1977a). For example, the private practitioner may not be aware of any particular value decision on his or her part, but implicit in clinical work is the value that individuals should be helped to adjust to the goals and norms of the groups and organizations of which they are a part. Implicit also is the expectation that social institutions are basically benign, and that improved adjustment follows from individual change.

The social reform movement that began in the 1960s increased awareness in society at large of the tragic effects of social problems, such as poverty and racial discrimination. Psychologists were among those who recognized the urgency of these concerns. Many wanted to increase the scope and relevance of their activities, but found that the conceptual framework which guided their work was not adequate for the task. Despite the fact that behavior is best understood as an interaction between persons and their environments, the bias in psychological research is on "person-centered" characteristics. When psychologists investigate social problems, they are more likely to focus on variables within the individual (intra-psychic variables), while ignoring situationally relevant factors. What this leads to is a "person-blame" causal attribution; that is, "the tendency to attribute *causal* significance to person-centered variables found in statistical association with the social problem in question" (Caplan & Nelson, 1973, p. 199). The implications of the Caplan and Nelson position is that it is not enough to be interested in social problems. The bias that a discipline's conceptual framework imposes on natural phenomena also must be recognized.

Thus, one factor leading to the development of community psychology was an increased concern for the deleterious effects of social environments, and the recognition that standard psychological and psychiatric theories did not adequately deal with the complexity of these phenomena. This led a number of community psychologists to adopt an *ecological orientation* to their work, one that emphasized the interactions of persons and their environments (described in detail in Chapter Five).

As was true in the 1960s, current-day community psychologists also are concerned with inequities in social life. Today, we are still faced with the legacy of society's unfinished business. The social issues that were discussed so eloquently in the 1960s are still with us in full intensity. The complex and multidimensional problems of the poor are no less a cause for concern now than they were during the era when we declared a national "War on Poverty." Unfortunately there is a tendency in this country to think that solutions are best achieved by throwing money at a problem. Often we are unwilling to work on complex social problems that are not amenable to quick solutions. Interest lags, giving the appearance of either insolvability or of diminished need for concern. In actuality, the problems remain at full strength, perhaps capable of solution if only we would approach our task more systematically and with sustained commitment.

Campbell (1971) has described an ideal stance that society should take in working toward solutions of its major social problems. His "experimenting society" captures *a value commitment to social innovation and its evaluation* that many community psychologists would endorse.

> The experimenting society will be one which will vigorously try out proposed solutions to recurrent problems, which will make hard-headed and multi-dimensional evaluations of the outcomes, and which will move on to try other alternatives when evaluation shows one reform to have been ineffective or harmful. (Campbell, 1971, p. 1)

The experimenting society is committed to properly evaluated action research as a way of solving pressing social problems. It should be one in which there is public access to the records on which social decisions are made. Recounts, audits, reanalyses, and reinterpretation of results all should be possible. Citizens, not part of the government bureaucracy, should have the means to communicate their disagreements with official analyses and to propose alternative experiments. Within limits determined by the common good, the experimenting society should be voluntaristic, providing for and encouraging citizen participation, but not mandating participation by those who freely choose to remain uninvolved.

The experimenting society implies a close collaboration between citizens and scientists (Chavis, Stucky, & Wandersman, 1983). Sound public policies based on the best data available are important for all citizens. Social scientists working alone lack the power to influence or implement change. Citizens working alone often lack the information they need that can provide the basis for corrective action. Citizen–scientist collaboration is motivated by the democratic ideal of active participatory democracy (Newbrough, 1980).

Other values with which many community psychologists identify might include the following:

Empowerment—enhancing the possibility that people can more actively control their own lives (Rappaport, 1981; Riger, 1980).

Promoting a psychological sense of community—increasing the supportive links among citizens so that isolation and alienation can be reduced (Sarason, 1974).

A respect for cultural diversity and enhancing the potential and capabilities of all citizens (Serrano-Garcia, Costa, Perfecto, & Quiros, 1980).

The values listed above represent goal statements that many citizens could endorse. They do not belong to any political camp, in that both liberals and conservatives should be interested in facilitating individual and community self improvement. In this sense, they could become part of a "social agenda for the 80s," and could serve as a guide to citizen–scientist collaboration.

What is required to achieve an improved "sense of community" among citizens? We agree with Sarason (1974) that a community as a geopolitical entity may perform many of its functions well and yet its citizens may feel little kinship for it. They may work in the community, pay taxes, and vote and yet feel repelled by its other characteristics. Most important of all, citizens may feel impotent in shaping its characteristics. In contrast, an ideal community is one that maximizes citizen input by providing opportunities for individuals to participate and contribute to the welfare of the group.

The psychological sense of community does not require that the population of a community be homogeneous, nor does it imply that communities should be conflict-free. Differences among people and conflicts of interest are part of group life and cannot be wished away. The crucial issue is how differences are handled. Are they suppressed or accepted? Are there attempts to achieve constructive resolution of differences, or are alienated groups isolated from others? Are there community structures for conflict resolution to which all have access, or is conflict allowed to smolder unresolved, causing the further erosion of group solidarity and the development of schisms between community groups? Differences between groups, such as cultural heterogeneity, add to the level of strain experienced by community members. It would be naive to think otherwise. But the key to optimizing community life and gaining a psychological sense of community resides in the availability of community structures for building group cohesion and allowing for conflict resolution.

The avenues for improving community life by increasing citizen participation and control can take place by improving what have been called "mediating structures"—the family, neighborhood, church, and voluntary organizations—that link the individual to the larger society (Newbrough, 1980).

These social organizations allow a sense of cohesion to develop, based on the ability to work toward the fulfillment of common aspirations. We do not minimize the problems involved in creating or maintaining community settings, or the frictions that can be generated by heterogeneous societies; but many community psychologists believe that communities can deal more adequately with problems of group living if citizens are provided adequate opportunities and structures to do so.

THE CONCEPTUAL REORIENTATION PROVIDED BY COMMUNITY PSYCHOLOGY

According to Kuhn, science is not simply the accumulation of facts; scientific activity also involves attempts "to force nature into conceptual boxes supplied by professional education" (Kuhn, 1962, p. 5). Usually, scientists work toward elaborating and refining existing theories. However, since conceptual templates are only approximations of nature, much remains that is unknown or unaccountable by existing theory. Occasionally, a field undergoes a sudden transformation as a new way of looking at natural phenomena is discovered. When this occurs, there is a "paradigm shift" (Kuhn, 1962) as older ideas are rejected and new paradigms, or conceptual models, are adopted.

New paradigms allow one to "reframe the question" (Rappaport & Seidman, 1982); that is, they allow us to think about problems in new ways before solutions are attempted. Reframing the question opens the door to alternative solutions that otherwise would have been ignored. Consider the following example.

Some years ago, one of us provided consultation to a school system in a large city. A common practice at that time was for practitioners in mental health clinics to accept referrals from schools and social agencies and to write lengthy reports about the psychological deficits found in children so referred. It was dismaying to see that such reports were written routinely even when the clinic was not prepared to offer follow-through consultation to help the referring agent or parent deal more constructively with the child's officially diagnosed psychological problem. It seemed to be assumed without question that diagnosis without treatment was an ethically acceptable and professionally valuable enterprise.

Unfortunately, clinic reports written to schools were used to deny children access to regular classroom contacts. The schools were required to provide an educational opportunity for all children, but the law allowed special arrangements to be made for children officially diagnosed as "emotionally disturbed." In the school system in question, emotionally disturbed children who disrupted regular classroom routine and who could not be placed in the few special classrooms available were provided with one hour a day of individual home tutoring. Tutoring met the educational requirements of the law, but it was hardly an appropriate substitute for the educational and socialization experiences available in the regular classroom.

Without providing therapy or consultation that could eventually aid in returning the children to full participation with their peers, the clinics became part of a procedure that eventually hurt the children whom the reports were written to help. Restricted to one hour a day of individual tutoring, the children fell behind both educationally and socially. However, for clinic professionals to become aware of the problem would have required basic reorientations in theoretical perspective and work styles. As long as their model of practice suggested that effective psychological change could come about only through intensive psychotherapy, there was no point in their talking to teachers of children not in treatment or to parents of children for whom long-term intensive therapy was neither acceptable nor appropriate.

Consider the following case of a nine-year-old boy for whom home tutoring was provided. The child's official diagnosis was "school phobia." The parents did not follow through on the clinic's offer of intensive psychotherapy, dropping out after one session. From information provided by a home visit, a fresh perspective could be gained about the situation, one in which it would appear that, despite the official diagnosis of the child's "problem," he may have been responding reasonably well to an unfortunate family situation. An elderly and sick grandmother lived in the home, while economic circumstances forced both parents to assume full-time jobs. The parents were very worried about leaving their sick mother alone all day and freely communicated their concern to family members. They would say things like: "Grandma could fall downstairs and be killed if she were left alone with nobody to care for her." Was it any wonder that a child in this family developed fears of going to school, anticipating what might happen to a beloved grandmother in his absence?

What sort of "therapy" should be provided for a school "phobia" of this sort? Should the helping professionals in this case sit by impotently because the parents did not accept the plan for intensive psychotherapy—knowing all the while that the child was a victim of a situation he did not create? Not acting—that is, not providing an alternative treatment plan—is as much a value decision as would be a strategy that would call for putting greater pressure on the parents to remedy the situation. Should a treatment be devised to desensitize the child's fear so that he would feel less responsible for his grandmother's fate and could accept a possible accidental death without guilt? Desensitization techniques to accomplish such a goal already exist; their use again requires a value decision. Should an attempt be made to convince the family to hire a companion for the grandmother—a move they had already considered but unfortunately could not afford. Whether to divert funds from food to home care or whether to apply for welfare assistance again are value choices.

Up until now, the choices presented have stressed person-centered interventions of a kind that might be consistent with the usual operating styles of many mental health professionals. However, other alternatives can be suggested that would require greater conceptual shifts. For example, communities could devise better ways to provide for elderly citizens that would encourage more constructive pursuits in the "golden" years. There is no reason why grandmothers need sit at home, lonely and useless. Constructive work that could be accomplished through group effort can be provided for senior citizens. A somewhat feeble grandmother might still help out in a community nursery school where she could read to small groups of children, while at the same time being "supervised" herself. If the grandmother was completely immobile, she could still be involved in a neighborhood-based helping network—visited and cared for by other elderly citizens, while she in turn might have responsibility to maintain phone contact with others in similar restricted circumstances. Strategies such as these require a shift in conceptual analysis to give greater emphasis to the importance of group support and usefulness to others as key ingredients in maintaining psychological well-being. They require us to recognize that the problem is not simply due to the incapacity of frail grandmothers ("person blame") but that it also results from a dearth of useful social roles available to our elderly citizens. Reframing the question from "How should this grandmother be cared for?" to "Can we provide more useful social roles for the isolated elderly?" allows us to think of new possibilities.

The Origins of the Conceptual Changes

The 1960s saw the beginning of a major conceptual reorientation in clinical psychology. Treatment facilities had become overcrowded, and there was a growing belief that traditional forms of psychotherapy were lacking in social utility. Too many troubled individuals did not meet the "entrance requirements" for treatment and, for one reason or another, were not seen as appropriate candidates for psychotherapy. Patients were being warehoused in public mental hospitals; and even for those discharged, little was provided to help in the resumption of normal community living.

The need for change was in the air, and new ideas came from a number of quarters. Traditional theories in the mental health fields were predominantly psychoanalytic, and a major challenge to them came from the behaviorists. In 1952, Hans Eysenck began an attack on the effectiveness of traditional psychotherapy that was to continue throughout the decade (Eysenck, 1952; 1961). The general form of Eysenck's argument was to assert that the base rate for spontaneous improvement (i.e., improvement without therapy) among neurotic patients was about 66 percent. Since psychotherapy outcome studies generally reported a similar two-thirds improvement rate, Eysenck claimed that traditional psychotherapy did not have more beneficial effects than that obtained from the base rate for spontaneous improvement.

There were many early attempts to refute Eysenck's argument (DeCharms, Levy, & Wertheimer, 1954; Luborsky, 1954; Rosenzweig, 1954), for he was attacking the very heart of psychological and psychiatric activity, but these presentations were never given the publicity of Eysenck's original claim, which over time became part of the accepted lore of the field. It was not until 1971 that the original data upon which Eysenck based his arguments were systematically reanalyzed. That herculean task was performed by Alan Bergin (1971), who was able to show the ambiguity of the original data and how Eysenck ordered the data according to his own biases. Bergin was able to show deficiencies in Eysenck's claim that neurotics generally showed a two-thirds spontaneous improvement rate, and he presented new data to indicate that the median spontaneous remission rate "appears to be in the vicinity of 30 percent" (Bergin, 1971, p. 241).

The point of this discussion is to indicate that, while the effectiveness of psychotherapy is still an open question (Landman & Dawes, 1982; Rachman, 1971; Smith & Glass, 1977), Eysenck's attack on psychotherapy was generally accepted as valid. Eysenck was believed, not because he presented the field with impeccable data, but because many in the field were looking for evidence to bolster their skepticism about traditional psychotherapy. There was a growing dissatisfaction with an exclusive reliance on this treatment modality for solving the country's mental health problems.

The 1960s saw the development of a number of new helping modalities, most of which adopted an increasingly environmental focus. The growing movement in behavior modification led to the suggestion that clinicians de-emphasize the importance of past traumatic experiences and focus instead on reinforcing contingencies in the individual's current environment that serve to maintain maladaptive behavior. Similarly, family therapists looked at the manner in which dysfunctional behavior was developed and maintained by family systems. This also was the period for the development of crisis theory (Caplan, 1964), which led to a number of new intervention techniques to deal with the impact of sudden negative life events, such as death of a spouse or the impact of natural disasters.

The New Emphases: Prevention, Competence, and an Ecological Focus

The initial development of community psychology was part of the conceptual reorientation occurring within clinical psychology. In May of 1965, a conference was held in Swampscott, Massachusetts, that has been described as the event that marked the official birth of community psychology. The conference reflected the unrest in psychology that had been brewing for at least a decade. The majority of conference participants were "converted clinicians" (Bennett, 1965)—clinically trained psychologists who saw the conceptual inadequacies of their field.

One change advocated by the Swampscott participants was in orientation—from treatment to prevention. The point of intervention for most clinicians occurs *late* in the development of a psychological disorder, since clients tend to come to clinicians primarily when their problems are well entrenched. Could interventions be developed at earlier points in time to prevent or avoid the occurrence of later problems?

The prevention model, which was well accepted in public health practice, seemed particularly appealing. As used in that field, prevention involves lowering the rate of new cases of disorder "by counteracting harmful circumstances before they have a chance to produce illness" (Caplan, 1964, p. 26). The intent is to reduce the risk for disorder for whole populations, not just for specific individuals, by designing interventions to ameliorate harmful environmental conditions or to support the resistance of populations when harmful experiences are unavoidable.

Prevention activity can take place at a number of ecological levels, focusing either on persons or on broader community-wide factors. As a matter of fact, a second theme of the Swampscott conference was the need to focus on broader ecological levels. Thus, psychological-prevention-oriented activities could include techniques for strengthening the resistance of persons, such as anticipatory guidance (e.g., preparing patients for the stress of surgery), or techniques aimed at environmental modification (e.g., program consultation in schools, the development of citizen-run alternative facilities, or community organization; see Chapters Eight, Nine, and Ten of this book).

An ecological focus produced a conceptual shift that brought community psychologists closer to the concerns and interests of environmental psychologists, sociologists, and political scientists. At the second major conference on community psychology held in Austin, Texas, in 1975 (Iscoe, Bloom, & Spielberger, 1977), community psychology was said to emphasize the amelioration of situational and social forces that contribute to problem behavior. There was a call for psychologists to give up their exclusive focus on the individual and to learn more about processes of community change.

Participants at the Austin conference also sought to shift the focus from pathology to an emphasis on psychological strengths and competencies. The traditional concerns of clinical psychology were in the assessment and treatment of problem behavior. Some theorists wanted to define normality in more meaningful ways than simply as the absence of disorder (Shoben, 1957; Smith, 1959; Wallace, 1966); yet it was difficult to talk about *positive* mental health because of the inevitable disagreement as to what "normality" should encompass. It proved easier to circumvent this value-laden question by concentrating on pathology—after all, everyone could agree that the grosser forms of psychological disorder were "evils" to be avoided (Smith, 1959). Traditional therapists were more comfortable describing their work in terms of removing symptoms and reducing discomfort. It was assumed that increased productivity and competence would automatically result from a lifting of pathological processes.

An alternative to a deficit or pathology emphasis is one that focuses more directly on psychological *strengths* and *competencies*. This change is not simply a semantic shift but has implications for how one conceptualizes behavior and designs helping interventions. The conceptual shift toward an emphasis on skills and competencies was part of the movement toward the application of learning concepts to clinical problems. For example, operant psychologists emphasized that desired behaviors could be shaped through positive reinforcement, and behaviorists focused on teaching assertion skills in anxiety-arousing situations.[2] Since competency measures were found to predict psychopathology later in life (McFall & Dodge, 1982), it was expected that competency training initiated early might *prevent* the occurrence of later problems (competency as a prevention strategy is discussed in Chapter Seven). Competency training programs were developed in a number of different contexts. Competency training was provided to individuals (e.g., parent training) and to organization members (teachers, police officers) to improve organization functioning. Competency programs also were developed to reach members of the community at large via media programs that encouraged the learning and performance of desired behaviors (e.g., programs like "Sesame Street" or "Mister Rogers' Neighborhood" teach educational and interpersonal skills).

The conceptual reorientation encouraged by community psychology can be summarized in the following ways: a movement away from treatment and toward prevention; an emphasis on strengthening competencies rather than removing deficits; and a focus on the interaction of persons and environments (an ecological orientation). The conceptual shifts mandated that greater attention be given to the environmental determinants of behavior, and opened the possibility of organizational and community level interventions.

In the early stages of the development of community psychology, these themes were championed and discussed, but research on these topics did not appear immediately. This is because, in the early stages of any major conceptual shift, attention to paradigm development is required—how questions should be phrased so they can be realistically answered, and what methodologies are most appropriate to answer these new questions. Only when sufficient interest has been generated in the new orientation is it likely that new substantive knowledge will be produced.

COMMUNITY PSYCHOLOGY AS AN AREA OF INQUIRY, RESEARCH, AND PRACTICE

Some of the fields of greatest interest to community psychologists have an active research base, while others are much less well developed. For example, while environmental psychology was considered a new field in 1970, lacking in theoretical structure (Proshansky, Ittleson, & Rivlin, 1970), since that time there has been an explosion of environmentally relevant research (e.g., see Baum, Singer, & Valins, 1978; Fisher, Bell, & Baum, 1984; Canter, 1975; Holahan, 1982; or Russell & Ward, 1982). Similarly, research on problem solving and competency training as applied to prevention, which had a modest beginning in the school training programs designed by Ojemann and his colleagues (Ojemann, 1969), became a substantive area of research in the 1970s after publication of studies by Spivack and Shure

---

[2] McFall and Dodge (1982) provide a historical overview of the development of the skills concept in clinical psychology.

(1974) and by Goldfried and D'Zurilla (1969; D'Zurilla & Goldfried, 1971). On the other hand, other areas of inquiry were less intensively studied. For example, research on organizational and community change often depended on anecdotal, case study evidence in which a consultant or community organizer reflected upon his or her field experience (Alinsky, 1946; 1972; Argyris, 1970; Caplan, 1970; Eugster, 1974). Thus, it would be fair to conclude that a research base for community psychology, while not fully developed, is slowly beginning to accumulate.

Ideally, research should be used to solve community problems. However, the issue is complicated because the action implications of relevant research are not always apparent. For example, if noisy environments are associated with decrements in learning among children, how can those environments be modified? Schools in some cities are being built directly over busy highways. Other schools find themselves in the flight paths of newly expanded airports. Tenements in some cities are extremely close to elevated train lines. Should these buildings be torn down, or are other solutions possible? For example, can train tracks be modified to reduce noise levels? Can interested citizens prevent future school development near highways or convince airport authorities to change airplane approach patterns? Furthermore, how should these change attempts be undertaken to maximize the likelihood of success? In moving from research to action, publication of research findings is not enough. Research also is needed on the best approaches to the dissemination of research information (Davis & Salasin, 1975; Havelock, 1969; Rogers & Shoemaker, 1971). Community psychologists found that they needed to become more aware of public policy issues. Whether any particular innovation is adopted does not depend upon its research base alone. There are numerous public and professional interest groups that have a stake in most plans of action. Social policy decisions reflect these competing political pressures. Thus, the task is not only to develop the best possible scientific evidence but also to learn how to deal effectively with the political process of community decision making.

The current research activity of community psychologists is extremely diverse and not easily summarized in a short topical list. This is because the concerns of community psychologists touch upon so many different substantive areas. To illustrate, psychologists interested in primary prevention in schools should know the literature on child development and learning in children; but they also should be familiar with the organization change literature particularly as it might apply to schools as organizations. Similarly, psychologists interested in community organization should be familiar with the sociology of communities and the related topics in political science and anthropology. One of the reasons that community psychology is such an exciting field is that it touches upon and brings together so many different research traditions. To be sure, no one community psychologist is likely to be an expert in all of these areas—it is no accident that this book has five authors—but the recognition of the importance of diverse areas of research opens the door to interdisciplinary consultation and collaboration. We hope that, in the chapters of this book, the reader will capture some of the flavor of the diversity in content and styles of research relevant to community psychology.

A TERMINOLOGICAL NOTE: COMMUNITY PSYCHOLOGY AND COMMUNITY MENTAL HEALTH

A brief word should be said about the labels that can be applied to the subject of this book. To some, the labels "community psychology" and "community mental health" are synonymous and interchangeable. Others have a strong preference for one or the other.[3] While conceptual advances are not likely to hinge on a semantic issue, we consider the nuances and implications of the various terms sufficiently important to warrant a brief discussion.

Community mental health was the original term applied to this field, since some of the initial concerns were to change patterns of service delivery to increase access to mental health services for persons in need. The passage of the Community Mental Health Centers Act of 1963 (discussed in Chapter Two) established an alternative to state hospitals and private clinics for needy and troubled people. Many community mental health practitioners shared in the search for a new orientation toward psychological helping.

Over time, dissatisfaction with the community mental health system grew because its services often remained clinical in nature. The provision of psychotherapy in a store-front ghetto clinic expands the reach of service to otherwise underserved groups, but the service provided still is clinical—individualistic and rehabilitative. Community psychologists emphasizing the social determinants of behavior wanted to build social and institutional level interventions that could be used in a preventive sense—before patienthood occurred. Furthermore, it was not at all clear that problems in living were best conceptualized in "mental health" terms, since they involved complex social and psychological determinants. Therefore, a number of psychologists chose to distinguish between community psychology and community mental health (Goodstein & Sandler, 1978; Rappaport, 1977b).

We will use the term *community psychology* in this book to emphasize the new academic discipline that has evolved to study the effects of social and environmental factors on behavior as it occurs at individual, group, organizational, and societal levels. We are less concerned with *current* practice in community mental health centers and hope that the study of community psychology will lead to new modes of practice that can be adopted by individuals in a variety of settings. We hope to influence community mental health practice because mental health centers provide the most prominent

---

[3] Some of the leaders of the community mental health movement were psychiatrists and referred to their work as "community psychiatry" or "social psychiatry" (Bindman & Spiegel, 1969; Caplan, 1964; Plog & Edgerton, 1969). While we recognize their contribution, for simplicity's sake we will not discuss developments in psychiatry in this book.

practice base for community psychology (Elias, Dalton, Franco, & Howe, in press). Thus, community mental health practitioners might benefit by perusing the work covered in this book, but so could any citizens interested in improving their neighborhoods or communities. By aligning ourselves with community psychology, we are not abandoning community mental health, but are avoiding the constraints of current practice. We hope that our review will lead to new forms of intervention—"what could be" rather than "what is."

CONCLUSION

In this chapter, we have described the contribution of community psychology in terms of *values, conceptual orientation,* and *research focus.* These themes will appear throughout this book, since we take the position that the orientation and values of a researcher determine the questions of interest and the methodologies chosen for collecting data. They also influence the models of professional practice that are adopted. Also, we will see how orientation and values play a role in the definition of psychological problems and in the intervention methods chosen to deal with such problems.

Table 1–1 illustrates how theoretical orientations are linked to change strategies. The traditional orientations in psychology can be characterized in deficit terms. For example, the clinician's job is to remedy existing deficits or problems as they occur in individuals. Interventions beyond the small group or family levels rarely are considered.

One major shift in conceptual orientation has been to focus on psychological competencies. This change was initiated by behaviorally oriented clinicians who began to stress the teaching of social skills. Until that time, clinicians assumed that competent behavior would appear spontaneously once the underlying causes of existing problems had been rooted out. The behaviorists were able to demonstrate that, in many cases, it was more effective to focus on skills and competencies than on cathartic discussions of inhibitions and problems. Still, the work of most behavior therapists remains at the individual level.

In initially adopting a public health model, community psychologists challenged the assumption that individual office practice for distressed clients was the only effective helping modality. The public health model stressed environmental determinants of behavior and prevention rather than therapy and remediation. The term *prevention* had intuitive appeal—it made sense as a mental health goal—and yet it had no specific psychological meaning before the 1960s.

Once the concept was accepted, interest turned toward its operationalization. Prevention research gained considerable momentum, and today, prevention advocates may attend an annual conference on the topic (the Vermont Conference on the Primary Prevention of Psychopathology) or read scholarly summaries of newly published research (Felner, Jason, Moritsugu, & Farber, 1983; Price, Ketterer, Bader, & Monahan, 1980). Still, much of

TABLE 1-1
Strategies for Change as Determined by Theoretical Orientation and Level of Analysis

Theoretical Orientation	Level of Analysis		
	Individual	*Organizational*	*Community*
Deficit	Somatic therapies to correct biochemical or physiological imbalance Traditional psychotherapy to uncover and work through early traumatic events	Group psychotherapy or sensitivity training to correct interpersonal problems Special education and remedial reading programs	Institutionalization or special facilities built for the handicapped or emotionally disturbed
Competency	Most forms of behavior therapy particularly skill training Prevention programs for high-risk persons	Training and consultation to increase job competencies of organization members Prevention programs to reduce organizational stress and increase coping	Creating new settings and alternative programs Facilitating citizen participation and community organization Community-wide prevention programs to reduce environmental stress and increase citizen competencies

this research has remained concentrated on individual level factors—teaching interpersonal competencies to at-risk individuals (e.g., ghetto children, persons at risk for heart disease, workers facing unemployment or retirement, and the like). Since individual change programs are easier to develop and administer than programs aimed at environmental modification, they are more the norm in the literature.

The ecological perspective, which highlights the importance of environmental determinants of behavior in interaction with person characteristics, was another conceptual shift championed by community psychologists. Since environmental determinants can occur at a number of levels, the study of social settings (e.g., organizations and communities) became of crucial importance. Organizational and community level interventions had always existed, but the ecological analogy suggested that these might be more consciously utilized. For example, group psychotherapy programs for prison inmates had been in existence for a number of years, as had special education programs for intellectually deficient children. Institutional programs or special facilities for the mentally or physically handicapped were society's traditional response to those considered defective in some way. These programs emphasized custodial care and correction, but rarely was there an expectation that approaches to normal social intercourse were possible. The stigma of "mental patient," "retardate," or "cripple" highlighted the deficit and seemed to preclude competent self-care. (A fuller critique of institutionalization and its problems is presented in Chapter Nine.)

In describing the impact of conceptual models, Price (1972) distinguishes between scientific and social utility. While it might be of value scientifically to do research on schizophrenia as if it were a disease or defect, it is quite another matter to treat schizophrenics as if they are diseased. The social utility of a conceptual model has profound implications for how society behaves toward those who are different. Suppose that, instead of describing persons in terms of their deficits, we focused on their capabilities. While some patients might be capable of schizophrenic behavior, they might be capable of other behavior as well. This would suggest that a psychologist should study the *situations* that seem to differentially call forth schizophrenic and nonschizophrenic behaviors in order to maximize the occurrence of the latter.

The ecological perspective combined with a focus on competencies suggested that strategies for change could be developed at organizational and community levels to enhance competencies and produce more effective functioning. Many organizations (e.g., schools, religious groups, businesses and work organizations, and so on) perform psychological and social functions for their members. They provide opportunities for learning and performing important social roles that can be sources of considerable psychological satisfaction. Improving the atmosphere of such organizations and the competencies of their staff can have considerable impact on large numbers of persons. For example, if teachers, ministers or police officers become better trained, they should provide better service to the community. Similarly, if the work atmosphere improves at an industrial plant, stress experienced by workers might be reduced considerably.

At the community level, the possibility exists for citizens to organize to more effectively meet their own needs. By doing so, they can develop a greater "sense of community" and become more attached to their neighborhoods. They could develop new settings or alternative programs, if existing community programs were unsatisfactory, or they could learn how to organize and pressure community authorities to be more responsive to their needs.

The themes that we have just described can be found in the chapters that follow. We will attempt to document what has been done and what still can be done to improve community life. There is reason for optimism since adopting new paradigms allows questions to be asked in new ways and allows new solutions to be considered. Still we must caution that social change occurs slowly and under less than ideal conditions. Social problems are not solvable in any final sense, but must be solved repeatedly in succeeding decades (Price, 1982; Sarason, 1978). This is because they contain value dilemmas that are responded to differently depending on the social context. The next chapter will illustrate how the social context influences our ideas and practices.

References

Alinsky, S. D. *Reveille for radicals*. Chicago: University of Chicago Press, 1946.

Alinsky, S. D. *Rules for radicals*. New York: Vintage Books (Random House), 1972.

Argyris, C. *Intervention theory and method: A behavioral science view*. Reading, Mass.: Addison-Wesley Publishing, 1970.

Baum, A., Gatchel, R. J., & Schaeffer, M. A. Emotional, behavioral and physiological effects of chronic stress at Three Mile Island. *Journal of Consulting and Clinical Psychology,* 1983, *51,* 565–572.

Baum, A., Singer, J. E., & Valins, S. *Advances in environmental psychology* (Vol. I: *The urban environment*). Hillsdale, N.J.: Lawrence Erlbaum Associates, 1978.

Bennett, C. C. Community psychology: Impressions of the Boston conference on the education of psychologists for community mental health. *American Psychologist,* 1965, *20,* 832–835.

Bergin, A. E. The evaluation of therapeutic outcomes. In A. E. Bergin & S. L. Garfield (Eds.), *Handbook of psychotherapy and behavior change: An empirical analysis.* New York: John Wiley & Sons, 1971.

Bindman, A. J., & Spiegel, A. D. (Eds.). *Perspectives in community mental health.* Chicago: Aldine, 1969.

Campbell, D. T. *Methods for the experimenting society.* Paper presented at the meetings of the Eastern Psychological Association, Washington, D.C., April, 1971.

Canter, D. (Ed.). *Environmental interaction: Psychological approaches to our physical surroundings.* New York: International Universities Press, 1975.

Caplan, G. *Principles of preventive psychiatry.* New York: Basic Books, 1964.

Caplan, G. *The theory and practice of mental health consultation.* New York: Basic Books, 1970.

Caplan, N., & Nelson, S. D. On being useful: The nature and consequences of psychological research on social problems. *American Psychologist,* 1973, *28,* 199–211.

Chavis, D. M., Stucky, P. E., & Wandersman, A. Returning basic research to the community: A relationship between scientist and citizen. *American Psychologist,* 1983, *38,* 424–434.

Cohen, R. E., & Ahearn, F. L. *Handbook for mental health care of disaster victims.* Baltimore, Md.: The Johns Hopkins University Press, 1980.

Davis, H. R., & Salasin, S. E. The utilization of evaluation. In E. L. Struening & M. Guttentag (Eds.), *Handbook of evaluation research* (Vol. I). Beverly Hills, Calif.: Sage Publications, 1975.

DeCharms, R., Levy, J., & Wertheimer, M. A note on attempted evaluations of psychotherapy. *Journal of Clinical Psychology,* 1954, *10,* 233–235.

D'Zurilla, T. J., & Goldfried, M. R. Problem solving and behavior modification. *Journal of Abnormal Psychology,* 1971, *78,* 107–126.

Elias, M. J., Dalton, J. H., Franco, R., & Howe, G. W. Academic and nonacademic community psychologists: An analysis of divergence in settings, roles, and values. *American Journal of Community Psychology,* 1984, in press.

Eugster, C. Field education in West Heights: Equipping a deprived community to help itself. In F. M. Cox, J. L. Erlich, J. Rothman, & J. E. Tropman (Eds.), *Strategies of community organization: A book of readings* (2d ed.). Itasca, Ill.: F. E. Peacock Publishers, 1974.

Eysenck, H. J. The effects of psychotherapy: An evaluation. *Journal of Consulting Psychology,* 1952, *16,* 319–324.

Eysenck, H. J. The effects of psychotherapy. In H. J. Eysenck (Ed.), *Handbook of Abnormal Psychology.* New York: Basic Books, 1961.

Felner, R. D., Jason, L. A., Moritsugu, J. N., & Farber, S. S. *Preventive psychology: Theory, research and practice.* New York: Pergamon Press, 1983.

Fisher, J., Bell, P. & Baum, A. *Environmental Psychology* (2d ed.). New York: Holt, Rinehart & Winston, 1984.

Gibbs, L. M. *Love Canal: My story.* Albany, N.Y.: State University of New York Press, 1982.

Gibbs, L. M. Community response to an emergency situation: Psychological destruction and the Love Canal. *American Journal of Community Psychology,* 1983, *11,* 116–125.

Gleser, G. C., Green, B. L., & Winget, C. *Prolonged psychosocial effects of disaster: A study of Buffalo Creek.* New York: Academic Press, 1981.

Goldfried, M. R., & D'Zurilla, T. J. A behavioral-analytic model for assessing competence. In C. D. Spielberger (Ed.), *Current topics in clinical and community psychology* (Vol. I). New York: Academic Press, 1969.

Goodstein, L. D., & Sandler, I. Using psychology to promote human welfare: A conceptual analysis of the role of community psychology. *American Psychologist,* 1978, *33,* 882–892.

Havelock, R. G. *Planning for innovation through dissemination and utilization of knowledge.* Ann Arbor, Mich.: Institute for Social Research, 1969.

Holahan, C. J. *Environmental psychology*. New York: Random House, 1982.

Iscoe, I., Bloom, B. L., & Spielberger, C. D. *Communinty psychology in transition: Proceedings of the National Conference on Training in Community Psychology*. Washington, D.C.: Hemisphere Publishing, 1977.

Kuhn, T. S. *The structure of scientific revolutions*. Chicago: University of Chicago Press, 1962.

Landman, J. T., & Dawes, R. M. Psychotherapy outcome: Smith and Glass' conclusions stand up under scrutiny. *American Psychologist*, 1982, *37*, 504–516.

Levine, A. G. *Love Canal: Science, politics and people*. Lexington, Mass.: Lexington Books, D. C. Heath and Company, Copyright 1982, D. C. Heath and Company.

Luborsky, L. A note on Eysenck's article "The effects of psychotherapy: An evaluation." *British Journal of Psychology*, 1954, *45*, 129–131.

McFall, R. M., & Dodge, K. A. Self-management and interpersonal learning. In P. Karoly & F. Kanfer (Eds.), *Self-management and behavior change: From theory to practice*. New York: Pergamon Press, 1982.

Newbrough, J. R. Community psychology and the public interest. *American Journal of Community Psychology*, 1980, *8*, 1–17.

Ojemann, R. Developing a program for education in human behavior. Cleveland, Ohio: Educational Research Council of Greater Cleveland, 1969.

Plog, S. C., & Edgerton, R. B. (Eds.). *Changing perspectives in mental illness*. New York: Holt, Rinehart & Winston, 1969.

Price, R. H. *Abnormal psychology: Perspectives in conflict*. New York: Holt, Rinehart & Winston, 1972.

Price, R. H. Cooperation dilemmas. In A. Furnham & M. Argyle (Eds.), *Social behavior in context*. New York: Allyn & Bacon, 1982.

Price, R. H., Ketterer, R. F., Bader, B. D., & Monahan, J. (Eds.). *Prevention in mental health: Research, policy and practice*. Beverly Hills, Calif: Sage Publications, 1980.

Proshansky, H. M., Ittleson, W. H., & Rivlin, L. G. The influence of the physical environment on behavior: Some basic assumptions. In H. M. Proshansky, W. H. Ittleson, & L. G. Rivlin, *Environmental psychology: Man and his physical setting*. New York: Holt, Rinehart & Winston, 1970.

Rachman, S. *The effects of psychotherapy*. London: Pergamon Press, 1971.

Rappaport, J. From Noah to Babel: Relationships between conceptions, values, analysis levels and social intervention strategies. In I. Iscoe, B. L. Bloom, & C. D. Spielberger (Eds.), *Community psychology in transition: Proceedings of the National Conference on Training in Community Psychology*. Washington, D.C.: Hemisphere Publishing, 1977a.

Rappaport, J. *Community psychology: Values, research and action*. New York: Holt, Rinehart & Winston, 1977b.

Rappaport, J. In praise of paradox: A social policy of empowerment over prevention. *American Journal of Community Psychology*, 1981, *9*, 1–25.

Rappaport, J., & Seidman, E. Social and community interventions. In C. E. Walker

(Ed.), *Handbook of clinical psychology*. Homewood, Ill.: Dow Jones-Irwin, 1982.

Riger, S. *Toward a community psychology of empowerment*. Paper presented at a symposium, "Community psychology in times of scarcity," Midwestern Psychological Association, St. Louis, May 1980.

Rogers, E. M., & Shoemaker, F. F. *Communication of innovations: A cross-cultural approach*. New York: Free Press, 1971.

Rosenzweig, S. A transvaluation of psychotherapy: A reply to Hans Eysenck. *Journal of Abnormal and Social Psychology*, 1954, *49*, 298–304.

Russell, J. A., & Ward, L. M. Environmental psychology. *Annual Review of Psychology*, 1982, *33*, 651–658.

Sarason, S. B. *The psychological sense of community: Prospects for a community psychology*. San Francisco: Jossey-Bass, 1974.

Sarason, S. B. The nature of problem solving in social action. *American Psychologist*, 1978, *33*, 370–380.

Serrano-Garcia, I., Costa, S. M., Perfecto, G., & Quiros, C. *The University of Puerto Rico position paper*. University of South Florida Community Psychology Conference, Tampa, Florida, 1980.

Shoben, E. J. Toward a concept of the normal personality. *American Psychologist*, 1957, *12*, 183–189.

Smith, M. B. Research strategies toward a conception of positive mental health. *American Psychologist*, 1959, *14*, 673–681.

Smith, M. L., & Glass, G. V. Meta-analysis of psychotherapy outcome studies. *American Psychologist*, 1977, *32*, 752–760.

Spivack, G., & Shure, M. B. *Social adjustment of young children: A cognitive approach to solving real-life problems*. San Francisco, Calif.: Jossey-Bass, 1974.

Wallace, J. An abilities conception of personality: Some implications for personality measurement. *American Psychologist*, 1966, *21*, 132–138.

CHAPTER TWO

Historical Trends in Mental Health Beliefs and Practices*

---

* This chapter was written by Kenneth Heller.

U nless one adopts an historical perspective, it is difficult to understand that ideology in mental health is very much influenced by social and political events. A hallmark of current community orientations is a concern for the effects of environments on behavior. Yet, there were two previous periods in which American mental health practitioners expressed this same orientation. The first, the era of "moral therapy," occurred during the first part of the 19th century (Bockoven, 1963; Caplan, 1969). The second, the era of reform between 1890 and 1914, saw a number of human service innovations, including the settlement house movement (Levine & Levine, 1970). In this chapter, we will review these earlier innovations and describe the factors that led to their popularity and then later to their abandonment. We will describe the factors that led to the community mental health legislation of the 1960s, the accomplishments of the community mental health movement, and the fate of social reform efforts during conservative swings in the socio-political climate.

Community psychologists are interested in the psychological well-being of all members of a community, yet the examples we will use in this chapter will refer to the treatment and care of mental patients. There are several reasons for this emphasis. To begin with, we believe that ideas about the treatment and care of mental patients often reflect the dominant theories of the day concerning the development of personality and psychopathology. If this is true, then clinical examples can highlight historical theories and orientations in psychology more generally. A second reason to chronicle clinical views is that these were used to explain the development of normal behavior as well. Emphasizing psychological strengths and competencies are relatively new ideas in psychology. Most often in the past, positive mental health simply was considered an absence of problems, or at best a mastery over pathological processes. For example, Freud viewed artistic creativity as motivated by "regression in the service of the ego" (Schafer, 1958) in which the individual artist through his or her medium manages to express unconscious conflicts in socially acceptable ways. Finally, a historical review of the treatment of mental patients can tell us about historical views of other problems as well. Distinctions often were not made between persons with different problems. Mental patients, the retarded, the poor and others seen as somehow "different," often were described in similar ways and were treated by society in the same manner. For example, "the poorhouse" included as residents not only paupers but mentally retarded and psychotic individuals as well.

In describing the cyclical changes that have occurred in mental health beliefs and practices over the last two centuries, it is useful to think of the thesis developed by Levine and Levine (1970): that mental health theories emphasize environmental determinants during periods of political or social reform, while intrapsychic theories that assume the "goodness" of the environment are prominent during periods of political and social conservatism. If the Levines are correct, good ideas may be abandoned, not because they are disproved but because they are no longer considered fashionable. Studying history helps us recognize these forces and encourages us to think about ways to enable useful ideas and practices to survive during periods in which they are politically unpopular.

THE RISE OF "MORAL TREATMENT"

During the first half of the 19th century, "moral treatment" was the dominant influence in American psychiatry, and there was great optimism concerning what could be done for mental patients by changing their milieu. The basic procedures used by the moral therapists involved arranging environmental conditions to maximize normal behavior. They believed that patients could be cured by a return to a way of life guided by moral principles. They emphasized regular habits, personal cleanliness, occupational therapy, religious practices, reading, amusements, and sports. The superintendent or his assistant spoke to each patient daily (Levine, 1981) and conveyed the expectation that patients were to conduct themselves as "proper" ladies and gentlemen. Patients who behaved inappropriately were asked to regain their composure, and, if necessary, were excused from group activity until the behavior in question was once again under control. Visitors to these hospitals, accustomed to thinking of asylums for the insane as "bedlams," marveled at the lack of restraints, shackles, or use of force. Moral therapists (like Phillippe Pinel, who is cited in abnormal psychology texts for removing the chains from mental patients, see Davison & Neale, 1982) apparently were able to produce decorum through the use of positive expectations and the reinforcement of positive behaviors, the very same procedures that were to be rediscovered more than a century later by contemporary milieu therapists.

Consider for a moment the research of Fairweather and his associates (1964) who developed a modern-day milieu therapy program on the ward of a large mental hospital. In this program, patients lived in small, self-governing group units. Members were required to take care of one another and to make realistic decisions about their own lives and those of other group members. Patients were expected to develop their own leaders, make sure that they and their fellow group members participated in work activities, and handled ward privileges appropriately. The entire group was rewarded for the constructive behavior of its members, while rewards and privileges were withheld if appropriate member behavior was not forthcoming. Thus, the special program depended upon two main factors: increased group interaction with group norms established for cooperation and responsibility; and the encouragement of prosocial behavior and group interaction through social and monetary reinforcement. The usual effects of mental hospital living—namely, dependency on staff and hospital routine, squelching of initiative, and the reinforcement of bizarre and pathological behavior—were clearly discouraged in this program.

The results of this study indicated that the small-group treatment milieu had a significant impact on patient activity in the hospital. Compared with a control group that received the traditional mental hospital routine, members of the treatment group were more socially active in the hospital, had higher morale, were more involved in helping other members of their group, and had higher expectations for the future. The active participation of even the most chronic patients was impressive (Fairweather, 1964, p. 283). The morale of the staff also improved because they were no longer responsible for housekeeping and ward maintenance and now could function as patient counselors, supervisors, and helpers.

The similarities between Fairweather's milieu treatment ward and the regime imposed by the moral therapists should be apparent. Both emphasized the expectation and reward of constructive behavior. But there also were differences. Fairweather's group was more explicit and systematic in its use of reinforcement contingencies and placed greater emphasis on patient responsibility for their own affairs, peer pressure, and the development of patient group norms. Their ward was much less staff-centered. Still, there was remarkable similarity between Fairweather's procedures and what had been developed over a century earlier.

Fairweather followed his patients very carefully and tested their adjustment at several intervals. While patients did improve *in* the hospital, recidivism rates after discharge (i.e., rates of return to the hospital) remained high. Many patients were unable to live in the community on their own. Fairweather concluded that continued support in the community was needed, and he went on to develop a community lodge for mental patients (Fairweather, Sanders, Maynard, & Cressler, 1969) that was to become the prototype for the halfway houses and group homes that have become common in many communities today.

The moral therapists of a previous era, using a similar program, also reported impressive results. Bockoven (1963) presented data indicating that, during the decade of 1833 to 1842, the records of Worcester State Hospital indicated that 78 percent of hospital patients were discharged as either ''recovered'' or ''improved.'' However, these improvement rates were to become a source of considerable controversy. The supporters of moral therapy accepted the figures as valid and argued that recidivism was not a problem since patients at that time were most likely returned to the care of their families and could be integrated easily into an essentially agrarian economy. The critics, who were to include many mental hospital administrators of a subsequent decade, questioned the validity of the improvement rates reported by the moral therapists. They charged that patients were not successfully integrated into the community and that the recidivism problem simply was ignored by the moral therapists. By the second half of the 19th century, the influence of the moral therapists declined, not because their claims were investigated objectively and discredited but because conditions in the country were no longer favorable to their continued practice.

FACTORS LEADING TO THE DECLINE OF MORAL THERAPY

Moral treatment depended upon an empathic and close working relationship between doctor and patient. This type of rapport was possible during the first half of the 19th century, when the population of the United States was relatively homogeneous in culture and background. During the second half of the 19th century the United States moved from an agrarian to an industrial economy. Sharp increases in immigration led to growth in population, which swelled the cities and at the same time engulfed meager social and helping services. The newcomers, speaking "strange" dialects, with unfamiliar cultural and religious practices, and often economically destitute, did not enjoy the sympathy of the native population. The economic and social stresses associated with their arrival left them little understood or appreciated by the majority of the native populace. Even the helping professionals could not accept them. As was true of most native Americans, the psychiatrists of that period viewed foreigners as genetically inferior, lacking in moral fiber, and unwilling to attempt self-improvement. In such a climate, moral treatment failed, but probably because it was no longer appropriately implemented. Social integration was as difficult in the hospitals as it was in the community.

Immigration was a major source of social strain in the last half of the 19th century. During this period, about 25 million immigrants came to this country, most of whom were Catholics who settled in the cities and became the backbone of a new labor force. As the Catholic immigrants became assimilated and increased their political power in the larger cities, a steady rise in anti-Catholic feeling also occurred. The contention that the assassination of Lincoln had been a Catholic plot was one rumor that became widely circulated after his death. National leaders spoke out against the Catholic menace, and anti-Catholic secret societies were formed in the major cities.

The number of foreign-born patients in state mental hospitals increased dramatically during this period. For example, figures available from Worcester State Hospital indicate that, while the number of new admissions in 1893 was double that of 50 years earlier (in 1844), the number of foreign-born admissions increased sixfold (Bockoven, 1963). Since these immigrants usually were financially destitute, the name "foreign insane pauperism" was given to the problem of mental illness in the immigrant population (Bockoven, 1963, p. 25). Irish-Catholic patients in particular were castigated by hospital administrators, who saw them as "neglecting all the rules of health and preferring the solace of rum and tobacco to the quiet, intelligent influences of well-ordered homes" (Bockoven, 1963, p.24).

Hospitals were overwhelmed by the economic burden of caring for so many indigent patients. As the quality of treatment deteriorated, physicians had to confront and somehow explain their lack of success. They began to adopt the view that insanity was incurable and used the new advances in chemistry and histology to argue, by analogy, that just as physical diseases were traceable to biochemical anomalies, mental disorders ultimately would be found to be caused by brain defects. Treatment attempts were abandoned as hospital administrators became convinced that insanity, particularly among foreign paupers, was incurable. However, a distinction was made between those of foreign and those of native stock. Profound pessimism was reserved for the "foreign insane." For example, Caplan (1969) quotes from an 1887 article in the *American Journal of Insanity* as follows:

> [The "curable" class of patients] . . . is not composed of the world's drifting, unstable, ill-conditioned populations, including the modern tramp, but of the settled, industrious, home-loving and stable classes . . . [they] represent more nearly than any other . . . the average population of half a century ago, before the great influx of foreign blood and character, often bearing the germs of weakness, poverty and disease. It is therefore characterized by a higher average of good and sound heredity and power of resistance to disease, as well as freedom from the vices and habits which are demoralizing both physically and mentally. (Caplan, 1969, p. 294)

THE INFLUENCE OF SOCIAL DARWINISM

In society at large, increasing urbanization combined with immigration brought accompanying social disorganization and growing class antagonism. Rapid changes in population led to an increased burden on social welfare agencies and, at the same time, to fears of "national degeneracy" by foreign stock. It was this context of rapid social and economic change that encouraged the development and popularization of Social Darwinism as a theory to explain social relations. Social Darwinists borrowed concepts from evolutionary theory, such as the "struggle for existence" and "survival of the fittest," and applied them to social life. It was believed that, to improve the human species, those members who were not capable of meeting the demands of existence should be left to die out according to "natural laws." In this way only the physically and mentally superior would be able to reproduce, and over generations the quality of the human species would continually improve. According to Social Darwinism, the mentally disturbed and the retarded were seen as members of an inferior race that should be left to wither in accordance with the law of natural selection. Social assistance offered to this group was viewed as misguided charity that would only perpetuate the problem it was attempting to solve (Sarason & Doris, 1969). Learned professors toured the country speaking out against attempts to reintegrate the mentally disordered into the community. It was argued that it was better to keep society's misfits locked up in institutions to live out their years in peace rather than allowing them to return to the community, breed, and weaken the stock. This was the origin of the sterilization laws that appeared in a number of states. In 1907, the Indiana State Legislature passed the first eugenic sterilization law providing for the prevention of the procreation of "confirmed criminals, idiots, imbeciles and rapists" (Kanner, 1967). Indiana was followed by seven other states (Washington, California, Connecticut, New Jersey, Iowa, New York, Nevada) over the next seven years. By 1936, 25 states had eugenic sterilization laws on their books, and some have remained in effect ever since.

In this climate, hospital administrators were extremely reluctant to release mental patients back into the community. Family members were discouraged from visiting and were told that, since the patients were "comfortable" but incurable, the best that the family could do was to "forget" their hospitalized relatives and go about the business of normal living. Hospitals became increasingly isolated from the community, with the policy of segregation justified as a kindness to the family and as a protection of society. Caplan summarizes the influence of Social Darwinism on American psychiatry as follows;

> The insane were seen as an alien influence, creatures of another kind, now classed once more with other species of "degenerates": criminals, paupers, deaf mutes, retarded, and so on. All the groups were to be treated in the same way, by isolation and sterilization. Custodial asylums thus became instruments to segregate the mentally ill from the community; and laws were enacted to stop the insane from having children, who would, in turn, burden society by their dependency and might further pollute the blood of the community. This ideology dehumanized the insane, as it did other classes of dependents and a number of racial minorities. It further discouraged support of custodial asylums and reinforced the old prejudices of fear and shame. (Caplan, 1969, p. 301)

THE REEMERGENCE OF ENVIRONMENTAL CONCERNS

In the late 1880s and early 1890s other voices began to be heard in American psychiatry, stimulated by greater social concern expressed in society at large. The abuses associated with early industrialization were noted with increased frequency. A new era of reform was developing (Levine & Levine, 1970) in opposition to the Social Darwinists. There was interest once again in the environmental determinants of behavior. This was the era of the muckrakers, those enterprising journalists who exposed political corruption, industrial abuses, and the terrible conditions to be found in urban tenements and sweatshops. In 1889, the first of several exposés of mental hospitals was published when a newspaper reporter infiltrated a mental hospital as a patient and later reported on the cruelty and abysmal conditions he had observed.

The new reformist social climate encouraged the development of a number of social programs to help families overcome debilitating environmental conditions. For example, the period from 1890 to 1914 saw the start of a number of human service organizations, many of which are still active today. According to Levine & Levine (1970) this list includes:

The first psychological clinic, 1896.

Juvenile courts in Denver and Chicago, 1899.

The visiting teachers movement, 1906, which was the forerunner of current school social work programs.

National organization of the YWCA, 1906.

National Committee for Mental Hygiene, 1909, which became the current Mental Health Association.

Campfire Girls, 1910.

Boy Scouts, 1910.

Family Service Association, 1911.

Girl Scouts, 1912.

THE SETTLEMENT HOUSE MOVEMENT

At the same time, the concern for helping the poor and less fortunate led to the establishment of settlement houses in some of the major American cities. The founders, most often, were upper- and middle-class women who were imbued with a sense of responsibility to help immigrants improve their family life (see Rothman, 1978). Settlement houses (described in fascinating detail by Levine & Levine, 1970) provided a stepping-stone to the New World for thousands of immigrants who were helped to become acculturated by its various activities. The settlement house also was important because it provided community organization functions, helping citizens improve their lot through organized self-help projects.

The early settlement house workers were women of social conscience who turned their backs on their own upper-class upbringing to live and work among the poor. They took apartments in poor neighborhoods and began offering whatever helpful services would be accepted by their neighbors. Some started with child care and babysitting services, others reading letters for immigrants who did not know English, and still others offered skilled nursing care to families who could not afford medical treatment. The settlement house workers did what was needed and in this way gained the confidence of the people who initially could not understand why obviously well-bred young women would choose to live amongst them in poverty. In a sense, the settlement house workers were similar to urban missionaries or Vista workers, with some major differences. They preached a gospel of organized self-help and received no pay or government support for their efforts. They were not sent by any organization or agency and, therefore, were very much on their own in what proved to be extremely demanding work.

The settlement houses gradually shifted their focus to campaigns for neighborhood self-improvement and legislation to enhance the rights of the poor. Settlement house workers and local residents joined with other interest groups to help pass legislation establishing compulsory education, workers compensation, the juvenile court system, special education classes, and restrictions on the use of child labor. In other words, settlement houses changed from providing services to the poor to becoming effective community organizations with political muscle.

As much as possible, activities were conducted in groups, with members being given a great deal of responsibility in planning and managing the group's activities. The unit of organization within the settlement house was the club (Levine & Levine, 1970). In developing clubs, members followed the principles of democratic organization, elected their own officers, and decided on their own activities. Clubs were available both for youth and adults. The youth clubs were credited with helping to curb neighborhood delinquency, while the adult clubs often were educational and social in nature, with some, over time, developing political action agendas.

The Settlement House Workers and the Political Machine

Before the industrial revolution, local government leaders came from "patrician families" or were prominent local businessmen. After the industrial revolution, when the major cities saw an influx of large numbers of foreign immigrants, the balance of power often shifted to charismatic ethnic leaders, who used the political machine as a basis for political power. In some cities, political leaders were chosen from the predominant ethnic group. In others with a greater diversity of ethnic composition, the political machine became a vehicle for compromising the demands of various groups by distributing jobs and patronage among them. In several of its functions, the political machine served as an early form of community organization, in that social and economic services were provided for members as well as help in negotiating a "hostile system." For example, ward leaders provided help in such emergencies as relocating after a tenement fire, helping husbands get jobs, and getting sons out of jail. At times, the ward leader served as a broker between the poor and official administrative agencies. The immigrant told his or her problem to the local leader who was willing to send the message through the party apparatus to various offices for appropriate action (Aiken & Mott, 1970). To be sure, these services were provided at a steep price—the toleration of corruption that benefited the politician more than his constituents. But when the poor could find help in no other quarter, there was no choice but to turn to the sympathetic machine politician.

Levine and Levine (1970) present the following quote from a Tammany Hall leader, George Plunkitt. It shows the method he used for holding the allegiance of his constituents.

> There's only one way to hold a district; you must study human nature and act accordin'. You can't study human nature in books. Books is a hindrance more than anything else. If you have been to college, so much the worse for you.

You'll have to unlearn all you learned before you can get right down to human nature, and unlearnin' takes a lot of time. Some men can never forget what they learned at college. Such men may get to be district leaders by a fluke, but they never last.

To learn real human nature you have to go among the people, see them and be seen. I know every man, woman and child in the Fifteenth District, except them that's been born this summer—and I know some of them, too. I know what they like and what they don't like, what they are strong at and what they are weak in, and I reach them by approachin' at the right side.

For instance, here's how I gather in the young men. I hear of a young feller that's proud of his voice, that he can sing fine. I ask him to come around to Washington Hall and join our Glee Club. He comes and sings, and he's a follower of Plunkitt for life. . . . You'll find him workin' for my ticket at the polls next election day. . . . I don't trouble them with political arguments. I just study human nature and act accordin' . . . .

What tells in holdin' your grip on your district is to go right down among the poor families and help them in the different ways they need help. I've got a regular system for this. If there's a fire in Ninth, Tenth, or Eleventh Avenue, for example, any hour of the day or night, I'm usually there with some of my election district captains as soon as the fire engines. If a family is burned out I don't ask whether they are Republicans or Democrats, and I don't refer them to the Charity Organization Society, which would investigate their case in a month or two and decide they were worthy of help about the time they are dead from starvation. I just get quarters for them, buy clothes for them if their clothes were burned up, and fix them up till they get things runnin' again. It's philanthropy, but it's politics, too—mighty good politics. Who can tell how many votes one of these fires bring me? The poor are the most grateful people in the world, and, let me tell you, they have more friends in their neighborhood than the rich have in theirs. . . .

Another thing, I can always get a job for a deservin' man. I make it a point to keep on the track of jobs, and it seldom happens that I don't have a few up my sleeve ready for use. I know every big employer in the district and in the whole city, for that matter, and they ain't in the habit of sayin' no to me when I ask them for a job. (Levine & Levine, 1970, p. 110–12. Quoted from W. L. Riordan, *Plunkitt of Tammany Hall,* New York: McClure Phillips, 1905)

If party machines provided human services to ward constituents in the larger cities, it is not surprising that, at the turn of the century, political leaders felt threatened by the rise of settlement houses in their districts. Both groups provided services, with the eventual goal of increased political participation. The political bosses were content to trade votes for services. The settlement workers wanted to build a more active responsible constituency through community organization. In districts in which political leaders were benevolent and honest, the settlement workers tended to cooperate with the established leadership. It was not too difficult to show these politicians that community improvement was best for their own political interest. In other districts, the settlement workers supported reform candidates who hoped to overthrow the party machine. This tended to be a dangerous undertaking because the political boss sometimes had enough power to close the settlement house (e.g., through zoning violations) or make it difficult for its members to find employment. Moreover, if the reform candidate won, the people who supported him still expected him to provide them political favors—as the previous ward leader had done. As Levine and Levine note, the settlement house workers discovered that the system of political favors served important functions in the newly expanded cities—"functions which impartially administered laws could not provide for the people" (Levine & Levine, 1970, p. 114).

THE DECLINE OF SETTLEMENT HOUSES AS VEHICLES FOR SOCIAL CHANGE

The settlement house movement continued to grow until World War I, when the mood of the country once again moved in a conservative direction. As the United States entered the 1920s, political withdrawal and isolation increased. There was increased intolerance of deviance and dissent and foreigners once again were met with suspicion. For example, Jews, being the newest immigrants, were the most visible targets. Lipset and Raab (1970) report that in 1920 the *Christian Science Monitor* printed a lead editorial entitled "The Jewish Peril," in which the troubles of the world were blamed on a Jewish power conspiracy. That same year, the *Chicago Tribune* contended that Bolshevism was a tool for the establishment of Jewish control of the world. From 1920 to 1927, Henry Ford regularly attacked "The international Jewish conspiracy" in the newspaper the *Dearborn Independent*. The flavor of these articles can be seen from some of the titles: "Jewish Gamblers Corrupt American Baseball"; "How the Jewish Song Trust Makes You Sing"; "Jew Wires Direct Tammany's Gentile Puppets"; and, "The Scope of Jewish Dictatorship in America." That Ford's views had wide appeal can be seen in the short-lived campaign to nominate him for President in 1924. William Randolph Hearst, then publisher of the largest newspaper chain in the country, announced in 1923 that he was prepared to back Ford for President. Also in the same year, *Collier's* magazine reported that Ford led all other candidates in their presidential preference poll.

It was not just immigration that was producing social strain. America had just passed through an era of reform that ended in 1914 with the advent of a major European war. During this period, the country had seen the imposition of an income tax, minimum wage, and maximum hour laws, and federal appropriations for fledgling programs in education, rehabilitation, and public health. Organized labor reached a peak membership of 5 million in 1920 and the country had been steadily moving its power base toward the more secular and cosmopolitan cities. The extremist movements of the 1920s, such as the Ku Klux Klan, which were to experience their greatest growth in membership and influence during this era, hoped to return to the simpler values of a Protestant rural America. Theirs was a reaction against "modernism," which meant a waning church influence, the breakdown of parental control, and "loose" moral values as evidence by short skirts, public dancing, smoking, and drinking. Although the Klan eventually lost its grip on American politics, partially due to sex scandals from within its own ranks, it was still able to manage a measure of victory (Lipsett & Raab, 1970). By the end of the 1920s, the issues with which it had been most concerned were settled at least partially in its favor. New legislation placed severe limitations on immigration; prohibition seemed firmly established; the effort to bring the United States into the League of Nations had failed; and the country, in Presidents Calvin Coolidge and Herbert Hoover, was again in the control of a very conservative Protestant America.

The settlement house workers as champions of poor immigrants now found few receptive audiences. As the early settlement house workers became older and retired, they were replaced by a younger more conservative group who no longer championed social action agendas. Settlement houses continued to evolve, this time becoming primarily educational and recreational centers in response to the new conservative social climate.

THE RENEWED INTEREST IN THE ENVIRONMENT POST-WORLD WAR II

For the most part, few mental health or social service initiatives were proposed in the period between 1930 and 1945. The federal government, under Franklin Delano Roosevelt, was involved in massive attempts at economic revitalization. The Roosevelt administration believed that the problems of the 1930s required economic, rather than psychological or social service solutions. Human service programs were considered the responsibility of state and local governmental units, which had little interest or financial capability to mount major new programs. In the Great Depression years, all but the most crucial local services were curtailed. State mental hospitals fell into neglect and remained this way throughout World War II. The war not only drained economic resources away from domestic priorities but left many programs with severe manpower shortages, which, in turn, further aggravated poor conditions.

After the war, there were new pressures to upgrade treatment facilities as large numbers of veterans returned to civilian life with some form of physical or psychological impairment. Exposés of mental hospitals once again appeared. Most prominent of these were articles by newspaper reporter Albert Deutsch, later published as a book, *Shame of the States* (Deutsch, 1948). The public became aware of the problem most graphically in the novel and later the film *The Snake Pit*, which was nominated for an Oscar award for best picture in 1948, along with a nomination for best actress for its star, Olivia De Havilland (Michael, 1972). The public finally became aware of its neglect of hospitalized mental patients, and calls for action once again became prominent.

But what action should be taken? The simplest answer was to spend more money on upgrading facilities and personnel at the state mental hospitals. According to one estimate, per capita expenditures for patients in state mental hospitals in the late 1940s and early 1950s was one seventh that spent in community general hospitals and about two thirds less than comparable psychiatric facilities administered by the Veterans Administration (Joint Commission on Mental Illness and Health, 1961). State governments recognized the importance of upgrading the care and treatment of mental patients, but were extremely reluctant to bear the financial burden on their own (Levine, 1981).

If the federal government was to become involved, as many now thought that it should, what role should it play? Before 1960, the federal government sought only to aid the states in administering human service programs; no attempt was made to design or implement independent federal programs (Price & Smith, 1983). But times had changed, and mental health programs were beginning to be seen as requiring a national solution.

A major problem was that the treatment and care of mental patients had not advanced much since the time of the moral therapists. If anything, it could be argued that, over the years, American psychiatry pre-1955 had become *less* competent in dealing with chronic mental disorders. This is because psychoanalytically oriented therapy had become the dominant treatment philosophy in American psychiatry. This method was designed to deal with problems of inhibited neurotics and was most suited to this relatively small group of distressed individuals. Freud believed that psychotics were untreatable by psychoanalysis, and until the work of Harry Stack Sullivan (1956), psychoanalytically oriented therapy with psychotics rarely was attempted. Sullivan's major works, which were published after his death, became popular in the 1950s and early 60s and sparked a resurgence of interest in the dynamics of schizophrenic family life. Even so, Sullivanian treatment was expensive and extremely time-consuming. Ironically, despite the impracticality of psychoanalytic methods, psychoanalysis became the dominant point of view in American psychiatry between 1930 through 1960. The theory was intensely interesting, and appealed to many mental health professionals because it was comprehensive and seemed to have broad explanatory power. As long as there was an adequate supply of neurotic and mildly disturbed psychotic patients available, it was not uncommon for therapists to choose patients to fit the method, leaving the vast majority of patients essentially untreated.

Thus a dilemma for the mental health professions in the 1940s and 1950s could be stated as follows: after World War II, there was a general optimism that this country was capable of solving its major social problems (Levine, 1981). There was increased public awareness and interest in improving the treatment of mental patients. However, the mental health professions were not equipped, conceptually or technically, to deal with the problem effectively. New theories and treatment methods were needed.

By 1946, there was sufficient political support for Congress to pass a National Mental Health Act, which gave the United States Public Health Service (USPHS) broad authority to combat mental illness and to promote mental health. The USPHS was empowered by the act "to support training, research and demonstration projects, and research in universities, medical schools and research institutes" (Levine, 1981, p. 43). In 1948, that work became centralized in a National Institute of Mental Health (NIMH), and from that time to the present, NIMH has become the dominant federal agency supporting research, training, and service programs in mental health. The federal government, now for the first time, had assumed the mandate of improving psychological well-being.

By the early 1950s major breakthroughs began to occur in the development of psychoactive drugs to control the major symptoms of psychiatric disorders. Reserpine, whose potential for reducing blood pressure had been known for at least 20 years, now received fresh attention because of its sedative effects, "reducing tension and anxiety without inducing stupor" (Levine, 1981, p. 45). Similarly, chlorpromazine (marketed under the name Thorazine) was found to be useful in reducing schizophrenic symptomatology, making many patients much more manageable. Still, while the tranquilizing drugs revolutionized the care of psychotic patients by reducing the need for physical restraints, electroshock therapy, and lobotomy operations, other treatment alternatives were needed. The drugs did not cure and often were associated with their own distressing side effects, including tardive diskinesia (involuntary movements), drooling, tremors, facial grimacing, and shuffling gait. Patients had become controllable, but they still were far from normal.

In 1955, Congress passed a resolution for a nationwide reevaluation of the problems associated with mental illness. That task was conducted by the Joint Commission on Mental Health and Illness, a private nonprofit corporation. Several of the commission's studies were extremely forward-looking and influential, such as the national survey, *Americans View Their Mental Health,* published in 1960 by Gurin, Veroff, and Feld. This survey found that physicians and ministers were more likely to be called upon to help with personal problems than were mental health caregivers. This finding provided fuel for those who argued that consultation to these primary caregivers was an important but neglected mental health activity. However, the board of directors of the Joint Commission was heavily influenced by professional groups representing traditional mental health interests. Their final recommendation, shaped by what was thought to be politically expedient, was fairly conservative. The report concluded that the central mental health problem facing the country was the care of the severely mentally ill. Its essential thrust was to recommend a revitalized state hospital system.

A U.S. PRESIDENT LINKS SOCIAL CONDITIONS TO MENTAL HEALTH

In 1960, just as the Joint Commission was submitting its final report to Congress, a new president took office for whom improvement in the mental health system was part of an agenda for general social reform. President Kennedy saw psychological distress as linked to such social conditions as cultural and educational deprivation. By attacking poverty, he hoped to reduce its negative psychological and social concommitants. In calling for a "bold new approach" that emphasized prevention, Kennedy was accepting the proposition that environmental conditions were (in some still unspecified way) causally related to the development of mental disorder (Levine, 1981). Kennedy linked the prevention of mental disorder to the improvement of social conditions in the following way:

> Prevention will require both selected specific programs directed especially at known causes, and the general strengthening of our fundamental community, social welfare, and educational programs which can do much to eliminate or correct the harsh environmental conditions which often are associated with mental retardation and mental illness. (Kennedy, 1963, p. 2)

Reducing "harsh environmental conditions," such as poverty, requires a massive reordering of social priorities, an extremely difficult task in our pluralistic society. What made the problem even more difficult for Kennedy was that he had not been elected with a broad mandate for social change. Still, the Kennedy reformers were aware of the abuses and neglect to be found in mental hospitals. They believed the charges made by critics of mental hospitals: that hospitals had a role in perpetuating disorder by encouraging passivity and other symptomatic behaviors. Their goal was to bypass the existing state hospital system with a new network of federally funded centers.

POLITICAL COMPROMISE, COMMUNITY MENTAL HEALTH LEGISLATION, AND CHANGES IN MENTAL HEALTH PRACTICES

Opposition to plans to revamp the mental health system came from several sources. The American Medical Association initially opposed any federal involvement in health care delivery, viewing such efforts as undermining the traditional private practice model of medicine and as initial steps toward "socialized medicine." Also opposed were hospital employees and their unions, who feared losing their jobs if mental hospitals were phased out, and local officials in towns where mental hospitals were important sources of employment. Ironically, opposition also came from groups of mental health professionals either employed at mental hospitals or in private practice who feared that federally subsidized mental health services would diminish their income. These groups lobbied Congress arguing that patients needed a "protected" institutional environment and that communities would not tolerate mental patients in their midst.

The legislation that finally passed Congress as the Community Mental Health Centers Act of 1963 represented a series of compromises between competing interests. The bill authorized funds for construction of mental health centers; but, in deference to opposition from the medical profession, omitted funds for staffing (Levine, 1981). Staffing grants were to come later, as was a broadened mandate for service. Initially, five essential services were required to qualify for federal construction funds. Local groups requesting funds had to demonstrate that they could provide: inpatient services, outpatient services, partial hospitalization services (e.g., patients receiving treatment during the day and going home at night), 24-hour emergency services, and consultation and education programs.

The services on this list, for the most part, were not likely to revolutionize mental health care. Three of the five already were being performed by mental hospitals or community clinics (inpatient, outpatient, and partial hospitalization services). Prevention was to be accomplished through consultation and education services, but as will be described in Chapters Seven and Eight, prevention and consultation were such new ideas that it took over a decade for the field to learn how these concepts could be operationalized in specific programs. In the 1960s and early 1970s, when mental health centers were being built throughout the country, prevention and consultation were seen as interesting ideas; but less than 5 percent of mental health center budgets were devoted to these activities.

The most dramatic changes in mental health practices occurred as centers attempted to implement the requirement for 24-hour emergency services. This seemingly innocuous requirement initially was inserted in the legislation to increase the availability of service. Mental health clinics previously had operated on a 9-to-5 work schedule, which made it extremely difficult for people who worked similar hours to use their services. The reason this requirement jolted the mental health professions is because most psychotherapies were reflective procedures requiring the patient to analyze current difficulties in terms of their origin in the past. Psychotherapists were not prepared to deal with current crises and, as a matter of fact, believed that to do so would encourage neurotic "acting out." It was felt that, without engaging in a thorough life review, an individual would never learn to see repetitive neurotic patterns.

The requirement for emergency services promoted the development of crisis intervention strategies (discussed in Chapter Seven) and other short-term behavioral and interpersonal interventions. Thus, the requirements of the Community Mental Health Centers Act did contribute to gradual changes in practice.

PROBLEMS ASSOCIATED WITH THE COMMUNITY MENTAL HEALTH CENTERS ACT

Each community mental health center was designed to serve a geographic "catchment area" whose population was to be no less than 75,000 and no more than 200,000. The purpose of this requirement was to design centers of manageable size—large enough to be financially viable but not so large (as some state hospitals) that continuity of care between the patient and caregivers in the home community could not be established. The catchment area concept also meant that all individuals within the boundaries of the area were entitled to service. The centers could not openly discriminate against any group needing service.

These benign ideals were not always met, particularly in urban areas where a population of 200,000 might be encompassed in less than a square mile. The act did not preclude horse-trading or gerrymandering among competing centers for favorable neighborhoods. Thus, catchment area boundaries in urban areas sometimes violated natural neighborhood boundaries. Rather than serving an entire ethnic or racial neighborhood, for example, it was more likely that mental health catchment areas cut across different racial or ethnic neighborhoods. When this happened, it was difficult for any group to feel that the center was "theirs." The power of indigenous community groups to shape mental health programs to fit their needs was lessened, while the control of center programs by professional groups was enhanced.

Another problem was that the services performed in the mental health centers remained mostly clinical. While staffing grants for the centers eventually were forthcoming, there were no funds provided for training, nor were there any incentives to move services in a more community-oriented direction. Clinical services were perpetuated, in part, because staff had little training or experience in administering community oriented services; they acted in the professional roles they knew best.

Some critics claimed that the centers simply represented "old wine in new bottles," and were strikingly similar to the hospitals they were supposed to supplant. In some communities, mental health centers were located on the grounds of the local mental hospital and were staffed by mental hospital personnel. This occurred because any group capable of providing the essential services mandated by law could apply for mental health center funds. Mental hospitals, primarily run with state money, found it financially advantageous to tap into this new source of federal funds. Since monies initially were earmarked for center construction, there was a rush for new buildings, without too much thought or planning as to how mental health activities might be changed to become more prevention-oriented—the original hope of the Kennedy reformers.

A final problem is that, over the years, as new political pressure groups formed and became vocal in demanding federal programs for their constituents, it became expedient for Congress to respond to that pressure by subsequent amendments to the mental health act. Mental health centers became responsible for aftercare for psychotics, alcohol detoxification and drug abuse problems, rape counseling services, problems of the elderly, child abuse programs, and problems of minority and underserved populations generally. In each case, it was not difficult to posit a psychological or mental health component to the problem, so it seemed reasonable for mental health centers to become responsible for their amelioration.

However, there were clear disadvantages if all problems in living were to be treated as if mental health were their primary component. Many of these problems had complex determinants, including social, economic, and political factors. In all instances, a psychological solution might not be best. For example, if spouse and child abuse were associated with unemployment, would the best approach be individual counseling to determine the historical roots of temper outbursts in early childhood? Surely psychological factors contribute to the problem in this example, since not all unemployed men are wife-beaters and some employed men are. However, placing the responsibility for the solution of this problem with the mental health establishment can lead to other important components being ignored. In dealing exclusively at the individual level, the broader, and more difficult to change, social and economic components of the problem were avoided. In a similar manner, funding mental health solutions to social problems led to an underfunding of other community services. Education and vocational training programs, self-help projects, or community development efforts did not receive the same levels of consistent funding as did mental health. Although not always the most appropriate choice, the mental health center often became the community's "mega-agency."

ACCOMPLISHMENTS OF THE COMMUNITY MENTAL HEALTH LEGISLATION AND SUBSEQUENT RETRENCHMENT

In sponsoring the Community Mental Health Centers Act, President Kennedy hoped to halve the population residing in state institutions. That goal was accomplished by a combination of psychiatric tranquilizing drugs and community mental health aftercare. As a result of the widespread adoption of tranquilizing medication, the resident population of state mental hospitals began a slow but steady decline in 1956. The Community Mental Health Centers Act accelerated this trend because patients could be released into the community and still receive careful supervision and follow-up. The population of state mental hospitals declined from a high of 559,000 in 1955 to about 160,000 in 1978 (Levine, 1981).

A major accomplishment of the last two decades was the development of research programs that made community-based care a viable alternative for many patients (Kiesler, 1982; Levine, 1981). While chronic mental patients still are not likely to be "cured," community care was developed so the need for hospitalization could be minimized. For example, in various studies, the components of successful programs have included proper medication and support provided to families of patients (Pasamanick, Scarpitti, & Dinitz, 1967), structured living arrangements in a group lodge or halfway house (Fairweather, Sanders, Maynard, & Cressler, 1969), careful control of the halfway house environment so prosocial behavior can be learned and consistently maintained (Paul & Lentz, 1977), and aggressive outreach attempts to motivate patients to assume greater responsibility for independent living (Test & Stein, 1977).

Despite the successes of demonstration projects such as those just mentioned, in many cases the process of deinstitutionalization did not proceed smoothly. In some instances, what happened could be described simply as "dumping" chronic patients into the community to fend for themselves and be preyed upon by unscrupulous landlords and shopkeepers. This happened when state governments saw deinstitutionalization as an easy way of saving money, and they did not provide adequate community support and follow-up. While technically no longer living in an institution, these patients were not always better off on their own, particularly those who drifted into the unsupervised transient hotels and rooming houses that had sprung up as a new federally supported industry.

To some extent, deinstitutionalization was oversold by its proponents. There were claims in the 1960s that mental disorder would be eliminated because its florid manifestations were being reinforced and maintained by custodial institutions. There also were claims that institutions could be closed and that patients would get jobs to support themselves. What was found was much less than this ideal. With proper medication, training, and support, many patients were significantly less symptomatic and were employable. But some chronic patients could not live on their own and regressed when pushed to do so. There also were some who were so impaired that hospitalization was the only alternative, so some form of institution still was required. Since running a small institution is only slightly less expensive than maintaining a large one (there is economy in large scale) the financial savings realized were not as great as had been hoped. Finally, while employment for the marginally adjusted was possible during periods of business expansion, it was much more difficult for mental patients to compete in a recessionary market with few job opportunities. What this all meant was that having patients live in the community was a mixed benefit. Most did not need institutions and, despite initial fears by community members, did not pose a threat to community safety.[1] Some were a nuisance to have around because they acted inappropriately and looked "different" (sometimes as a side effect of their medication). Furthermore, their maintenance in the community, while providing a financial savings, did not eliminate the need for some form of secure hospital facilities.

Ironically, despite a legislative policy of deinstitutionalization, the trend in mental health care in the last decade has involved an increased use of hospitalization (Kiesler, 1982). This trend is not the result of a decision that institutionalization is in the best interests of most mental patients, but is the inadvertent result of other policies and practices. Once centers were established, the Community Mental Health Centers Act was designed to shift the financial cost of caring for patients from the federal to the state government. However, what happened was that, as federal community mental health funds were phased out, states attempted to use other federal programs to pay for the care of mental patients. Medicare, Medicaid, and Supplemental Security Income programs, initially designed to provide care for the elderly

---

[1] See Chapter Nine for a fuller discussion of community resistance to alternatives for mental patients.

and the disabled, were used to pay for psychiatric care (Levine, 1981; Price & Smith, 1983). The overall result was increased hospitalization rates, since inpatient treatment was a reimbursement requirement for the Medicare and Medicaid programs as well as for the major private insurance carriers, such as Blue Cross/Blue Shield. Kiesler (1982) presents data to indicate that the care of mental patients in general hospitals rose dramatically in the last decade as the use of state hospitals declined. In his words: "Medicare, Medicaid, Blue Cross/Blue Shield and other private insurance plans provide disincentives for outpatient care" (p. 1323). Increasingly, mental patients received hospital care, not because they needed it but because inpatient services were more easily fundable.

The use of outpatient mental health services by the population at large did increase as a result of the community mental health legislation. Units of outpatient care (the number of therapeutic interviews, not the number of patients) rose from 379,000 in 1955 to 4.6 million in 1975, a 12-fold increase over a period of 20 years (Kiesler, 1982). This increased use of mental health professionals for personal problems rose for all segments of the population (Veroff, Douvan, & Kulka, 1981; Veroff, Kulka & Douvan, 1981).

The original 1957 national survey, *Americans View Their Mental Health,* found that lower-income, less-well-educated individuals did not usually view their problems in psychological terms or use mental health resources (Gurin, Veroff, & Feld, 1960). In 1976, the survey was repeated, and the researchers found increased use of mental health professionals by all segments of the population. During the period from 1957 to 1976 there probably were changes in public attitudes toward personal problems (Price & Smith, 1983). Going to see a psychiatrist or psychologist may have become more acceptable due to TV and media exposure. However, Veroff and his colleagues believe that it was the increased availability of mental health centers that was the primary factor in increasing the use of these facilities.

We conclude this section by noting that the social legislation of the 1960s produced more complex results than the Kennedy planners had envisioned. In the case of mental health, the legislation was imposed on a system of care that was already established. Practices changed as a result of the legislation, but, in turn, professional groups acted in ways that subverted the original intent of the legislation. The mental health professions in many cases used the legislation to fund and expand existing services and only changed gradually toward a more environmental and preventive focus. States used the legislation to shift their responsibility for mental health services to the federal government, postponing and, in some cases, resisting active planning for the shift back to state control once the federal legislation had run its course. Also unanticipated was a change in the climate and events of the day, which reduced concerns for social welfare as a national priority.

In the mid-1960s, the United States entered into what was to become a protracted and unpopular war that left the country discouraged and divided. The legacy of Vietnam and then later Watergate was to increase suspicion of national leaders and distrust of government intervention. Many believed that the federal government itself had become the villain, and there was a call for retrenchment in government activities. Whereas 1960 saw a President elected who wanted to increase the activity of the federal government in domestic affairs, in 1980 a President took office whose platform was to decrease the role of the federal government as much as possible.

EBB AND FLOW: THE SOCIAL CLIMATE AND RESOURCE AVAILABILITY AS DETERMINANTS OF IDEOLOGY AND PRACTICE

If history is a guide, we can anticipate that the 1980s might see a return of individually focused or biologically oriented theories in psychology. The reascendance of theories that focus on individual level factors might occur in the following way. If social and community programs are phased out as too expensive or unworkable, the distress level among individuals served by these programs probably would increase. The problems of the poor, the elderly, or the psychologically troubled do not evaporate simply because they are ignored. As these individuals reach the limits of their ability to cope, and continue to experience difficulty, they are likely to display increased levels of socially undesirable behaviors. As society reaches the limits of its toleration for deviance, institutionalization rates probably will increase, particularly when other alternative care facilities are not available. As institutions become overcrowded, funds, always difficult to obtain, will become even more scarce. Institutional personnel, frustrated by their inability to offer proper treatment, may begin to view the problems of their charges as incurable. This was the sequence of events that occurred toward the end of the 19th century, and it could be repeated again, now 100 years later.

Is such a series of events inevitable? Are we fated to repeat the mistakes of the past? There are some who believe that periods of ebb and flow—movement and countermovement—are characteristics of decentralized pluralistic democracies. According to Marris and Rein (1967) the American system of government is designed to guard against the excesses of control by any one group. The system of checks and balances and divided authority among federal, state, and local governments helps guard against the domination by any segment of society, or by a centralized government itself, for that matter. But we pay a price for our form of decentralized democracy. It is difficult to sustain a consistent direction when constituencies with different philosophies of government and diverse social agendas vie for power and succeed in replacing one another every four or eight years. Long-range planning and sustained effort to solve social problems become nearly impossible to maintain. The dilemma is that complex social problems rarely are resolved by short-term, quick-fix solutions, yet short-term programs are all we have been willing to tolerate thus far. In the case of the community mental health programs described in the last section of this chapter, mistakes were made and we clearly know how to provide better mental health services than we did in the early 1960s when the community mental health programs were first initiated. A new generation of mental health professionals has been educated who now have some understanding of crisis intervention, consultation, prevention, and community development. Also, we now have a greater respect for the role of indigenous citizen-initiated efforts in maintaining psychological well-being. Often, the best "help" one can provide is to develop an environment in which people are encouraged to help themselves. Each of the above concepts has a rapidly expanding body of research that can provide more informed guides to practice. However, with periodic changes in national priorities, one can question whether these or any other new ideas ever will be fully explored and tested.

Can we develop a long-term commitment to solve our social and psychological problems? We can, if we decide as a nation to give high priority to attempts at their solution. Such attempts can take the form of research and demonstration projects, with appropriate follow up and dissemination of results to citizens to determine whether and in what ways the new information should be utilized.[2] Sustaining such an effort involves a long-term policy commitment that will require an informed and organized constituency willing to advocate and support consistent research and dissemination efforts. Hence, it is important for citizens to understand why the continuous ebb and flow of psychological and social practices produces so little forward movement. Social, political, and economic factors always will affect the fate of social innovations, regardless of their effectiveness. However, without taking seriously the need for analysis, evaluation, and the subsequent accumulation of verified knowledge, it is not likely that innovative ideas will survive the vicissitudes of history.

References

Aiken, M., & Mott, P. E. (Eds.). *The structure of community power.* New York: Random House, 1970.

Bockoven, J. *Moral treatment in American psychiatry.* New York: Springer, 1963.

Caplan, R. B. *Psychiatry and the community in nineteenth century America: The recurring concern with the environment in the prevention and treatment of mental disorder.* © 1969 by Basic Books, Inc., Publishers. Reprinted by permission of the publisher.

Davison, G. C., & Neale, J. M. *Abnormal psychology: An experimental clinical approach* (3d ed.). New York: John Wiley & Sons, 1982.

Deutsch, A. *Shame of the states.* New York: Harcourt Brace Jovanovich, 1948.

Fairweather, G. W. (Ed.). *Social psychology in treating mental illness: An experimental approach.* New York: John Wiley & Sons, 1964.

Fairweather, G. W., Sanders, D. H., Maynard, H., & Cressler, D. L. *Community life for the mentally ill: An alternative to institutional care.* Chicago: Aldine, 1969.

---

[2] Citizen involvement in the planning and utilization of research is a theme that can be found in several chapters of this book.

Gurin, G., Veroff, J., & Feld, S. *Americans view their mental health: A nationwide survey.* New York: Basic Books, 1960.

Joint Commission on Mental Illness and Health. *Action for mental health.* New York: John Wiley & Sons, 1961.

Kanner, L. *A history of the care and study of the mentally retarded.* Springfield, Ill.: Charles C Thomas, 1967.
Kennedy, J. F. *Mental illness and mental retardation.* Message from the President of the United States relative to mental illness and mental retardation. House of Representatives, 88th Congress, 1st Session, Document No. 58, February 5, 1963.
Kiesler, C. A. Public and professional myths about mental hospitalization: An empirical reassessment of policy-related beliefs. *American Psychologist,* 1982, *37,* 1323–1339.

Levine, M. *The history and politics of community mental health.* New York: Oxford University Press, 1981.
Levine, M., & Levine, A. *A social history of helping services: Clinic, court, school and community.* New York: Appleton-Century-Crofts, 1970.
Lipset, S. M., & Raab, E. *The politics of unreason: Right-wing extremism in America, 1790–1970.* New York: Harper & Row, 1970.

Marris, P., & Rein, M. *Dilemmas of social reform: Poverty and community action in the United States.* New York: Atherton Press, 1967.
Michael, P. *The academy awards: A pictorial history.* New York: Crown Publishers, 1972.

Pasamanick, B., Scarpitti, F. R., & Dinitz, S. *Schizophrenia in the community: Experimental studies in the prevention of hospitalization.* New York: Appleton-Century-Crofts, 1967.
Paul, G. L., & Lentz, R. J. *Psychosocial treatment of chronic mental patients.* Cambridge, Mass.: Harvard University Press, 1977.
Price, R. H., & Smith, S. S. Two decades of reform in the mental health system (1963–1983). In E. Seidman (Ed.), *Handbook of social intervention.* Beverly Hills, Calif.: Sage Publications, 1983.

Rothman, S. M. *Woman's proper place: A history of changing ideals and practices: 1870 to the present.* New York: Basic Books, 1978.

Sarason, S., & Doris, J. *Psychological problems in mental deficiency.* New York: Harper & Row, 1969.
Schafer, R. Regression in the service of the ego: The relevance of a psychoanalytic concept for personality assessment. In G. Lindzey (Ed.), *Assessment of human motives.* New York: Holt, Rinehart & Winston, 1958.
Sullivan, H. S. *Clinical studies in psychiatry.* New York: W. W. Norton, 1956.

Test, M. A., & Stein, L. I. A community approach to the chronically disabled patient. *Social Policy,* 1977, *8,* 8–16.

Veroff, J., Douvan, E., & Kulka, R. A. *The inner Americans: A self-portrait from 1957 to 1976.* New York: Basic Books, 1981.
Veroff, J., Kulka, R. A. & Douvan, E. *Mental Health in America: Patterns of help-seeking from 1957 to 1976.* New York: Basic Books, 1981.

PART TWO

Approaches to Community Research

CHAPTER THREE

The Context and Objectives of Community Research*

---

* This chapter was written by Thomas D'Aunno and Richard H. Price.

INTRODUCTION

- Imagine that a close friend of yours announces that he has joined a religious group whose central belief is that the world is coming to an end within two months. You are, of course, immediately shocked and worried, and, at the same time, determined to find out more about this group: Is the group "for real?" How did they "convert" your friend? What happens at group meetings?

- After visiting a psychiatric hospital you are convinced that the treatment of mental health problems can and should be improved. Suppose that you are committed to the principle that people should live as independently as possible in their homes and at work. What treatment program would you develop? How would you attempt to demonstrate its effectiveness relative to traditional approaches?

Each of these examples poses questions about community phenomena that may be answered by means of systematic research. It is unlikely that the same approach can be used in all cases, and it may be that the researchers' relationship to community members participating in the study would differ in each case as well.

A major objective of this and the next chapter is to introduce approaches to research that can effectively meet the needs of psychologists and other social scientists concerned with a wide range of community phenomena. There is, of course, much more to the enterprise of social science research than being familiar with and using different approaches to research. Thus, in addition to discussing approaches to community research, we will examine several other key aspects of social science research. The first section of this chapter provides an overview of the social context of research, emphasizing the importance of researchers' values and relationship to the individuals and communities they wish to understand. The second section examines characteristics of social and community phenomena that influence the design of community research. The third section discusses issues in the process of conducting research, and the chapter concludes with an introduction to different approaches to research in the community.

THE CONTEXT OF SOCIAL SCIENCE RESEARCH

Textbooks concerned with social science research often neglect a critical component of the research enterprise: the researcher. More specifically, little attention is given to the influence of the role that the values and biases of researchers have in each phase of a research project, including the selection of phenomena to study, choice of research method, and choice of audience for the results. Similarly, we often fail to discuss important dimensions of the relationships between researchers and the persons, organizations, and communities they study. Sometimes people who participate in studies are seen only as "subjects," and it is suggested that their relationship to a researcher must be distant and impersonal, and further, that participants can contribute little to the design or conduct of research. In this section we will discuss the importance of researchers' values in the research enterprise. We will describe some key aspects of the relationship between researchers and their social world, which includes, among others, participants in studies and the audience or "consumers" of research findings.

Science and Values

The past two decades have witnessed growing recognition among social scientists of the profound impact that personal values have on our research efforts (Myrdal, 1969). Further, we have come to realize that the values and biases of social scientists are heavily influenced by the societies and historical eras in which they live. Social scientists are not immune to the social and historical forces that shape individuals' behavior (e.g., Rappaport, 1977). Rather, it is becoming clear that social scientists are influenced by the very processes they study.

On the surface, acknowledging that the world views, theories, and methods of social scientists are not value-free may not seem startling. For many years, however, social scientists tenaciously argued that they were dedicated only to advancing scientific knowledge free from personal biases. There are at least two reasons why social scientists worked to preserve the idea that social science was value-free. First, they were eager to place the relatively young, developing social sciences on an equal footing with the more well-established and widely accepted physical and natural sciences, such as chemistry and mathematics. Second, social scientists were vying for support from the public at large who seemed to view their pursuits as something less than "scientific."

Recent analyses of the behavior of social scientists, and physical scientists for that matter, suggest the numerous and often subtle ways in which values, preferences, and biases can influence their work. Albee (1982) summarizes this position well:

> Instead of facts being useful as the objective building blocks of theories, rather it is more accurate to say that people, and especially social scientists, select theories that are consistent with their personal values, attitudes, and prejudices, and then go out into the world, or into the laboratory, to seek facts that validate their beliefs about the world and about human nature, neglecting or denying observations that contradict their personal prejudices (p. 5).

There are several fields of research in which the effects of the values of social scientists on the interpretation of research data are well documented. One of these areas involves the relationship among intelligence, heredity, and ethnic origin. Kamin (1974a), for example, illustrates how several leading American psychologists became involved in efforts to limit the immigration of certain ethnic groups to the United States in the 1920s.[1] Under the direction of Robert M. Yerkes, a committee of psychologists attempted to "take the national debate over immigration 'out of politics' and place it on a 'scientific basis.' " Researchers analyzed the results of intelligence tests administered to people of various ethnic origins by the Army in World War I to draw conclusions concerning the desirability of allowing certain groups to enter the United States.

One psychologist, Carl Brigham, found that immigrants who had been in the United States for 16 to 20 years were as intelligent as native-born Americans. Those who had arrived more recently, however, were likely to be classified as "feeble-minded." Brigham concluded that the difference was due to the fact that new immigrants were from Southeastern Europe, while those who had resided here longer were from England, Germany, and Scandinavia. He argued that the decline in scores was due to a decrease in "Nordic blood." Completely ignoring the influence of the environment on culturally defined judgments of intelligence, he went on to say,

> We are incorporating the negro into our racial stock, while all of Europe is comparatively free from this taint. . . . *The steps that should be taken must of course be dictated by science and not by political expediency* . . . the really important steps are those looking toward prevention of the continued propagation of defective strains in the present population. (Carl Brigham, cited in Kamin, 1974a; italics added)

Clearly, our values and biases can affect our choice of research problem, how we frame our questions, conduct our research, and interpret our findings. Rather than continue to deny the importance of social forces and personal values in the conduct of social science, we believe that we must begin to recognize that science and values are not incompatible. It is inevitable that social scientists have values that can influence their research. We believe that this obliges us to make our biases and values as explicit as possible and to attempt to understand their origins and impact on our work.

The Relationship between Researchers and Community Members

An often overlooked but nonetheless critical aspect of social science research is the relationship between researchers and the individuals, organizations, and communities they study. The quality of the relationship that researchers establish with participants of a study is crucial to the researchers' success in collecting data and making observations that will enable him or her to draw reliable and valid conclusions concerning the phenomena of interest. Community members are relatively free to cooperate or refuse to cooperate with researchers. Researchers must come to some implicit or

---

[1] This section of the chapter is based on Rappaport's (1977) excellent discussion of science and values.

explicit agreement with community members concerning their terms for participation in a study.

It is useful to view the relationship between researchers and community members as a partnership in which each party makes a contribution to the other. In other words, the relationship is based on an *exchange* of resources. In some studies, for example, college students are offered small sums of money or "extra credit" in a course in return for their time and effort. In other instances, people volunteer to participate in studies in exchange for the knowledge or experience they expect to gain. In this case, the exchange between researcher and participant involves resources which, though not "concrete," are highly valued by both partners.

A common difficulty in establishing a partnership between researchers and community members is negotiating terms of exchange that are acceptable to both parties. The complexity of community settings contributes to this difficulty. There may be several persons in a setting with authority or power who act as "gatekeepers" to the phenomena of interest. In studying public schools, for example, researchers must negotiate with boards of education, superintendents, principals, parent-teacher organizations, research committees, and so on. Each of these groups, of course, has legitimate concerns and responsibility for protecting the welfare of students by shielding them from potentially harmful research or from research that simply wastes their time. At the same time, each group is concerned with defending its prestige and maintaining its position relative to other groups that have a stake in the management of the school. In short, in negotiating exchanges, researchers can become entangled in complex political relationships that exist among members of organizations and communities. So it is that negotiating exchanges is a political as well as technical task.

Negotiating exchanges also is made difficult because the values and needs of each party may differ: what is a valued resource for one partner is not necessarily valued by the other. On the one hand, researchers value highly the opportunity to test hypotheses and build theories. In addition, they must contend with practical constraints, such as limited funds for data collection. On the other hand, community organizations and neighborhoods are relatively unconcerned with the world of theory; they value action taken to improve conditions that effect their daily lives. Far too often, researchers have failed to recognize the needs of community members and, unfortunately, have succeeded in negotiating exchanges that are favorable to themselves at the expense of the community. That is, researchers have contributed little to communities in return for observing and altering community processes as they please.

We believe that such unbalanced exchanges have undesirable consequences for both researchers and community members. For community members, the products of research often are not useful. Though journal articles and books that contribute to building social science theory and knowledge are legitimate and worthwhile products of community research, they do little to directly address the needs and problems of communities.

With few exceptions, researchers have simply contributed little to developing community members' knowledge or capacity to improve the quality of community life.

The consequences of unbalanced exchanges for researchers also are severe, but insidious in the sense that researchers often are led to believe that they are getting the best deal possible. In fact, however, researchers lose when they shortchange community members. Because of their emergent dissatisfaction with the terms of exchange, participants may adhere strictly to the negotiated contract and refuse to provide more than a minimum of information or cooperation. If people feel that the results of research may be used against their best interests, there even may be attempts to sabotage a researcher's efforts by providing incorrect information. In addition, community organizations and groups that have been shortchanged by researchers are reluctant, and rightfully so, to participate in future research projects.

Furthermore, community members often are in a unique position to help researchers improve their methods and provide insight into the meaning of research findings. Researchers who fail to recognize these potential contributions of community members may be overlooking a valuable resource.

One approach to improving the relationship between researchers and community participants is to ensure that exchanges are mutually beneficial to both partners. Indeed, this is an ideal that is expressed by many psychologists and other social scientists. Building balanced exchange relationships will require researchers to broaden or change their traditional roles. Researchers must move from a position of exclusive concern for theory-building and knowledge development to a position that includes commitment to community development and well-being. In other words, researchers must maintain a stance of giving as well as taking from the field setting.

Chavis, Stucky, and Wandersman (1983) describe a research project on neighborhood participation that began as a study of the basic processes underlying citizen participation, but which developed into a series of collaborative efforts with neighborhood groups and agencies to use the information for community purposes. These researchers point out that returning basic research to the community in this way can *(a)* improve the quality of social science research, *(b)* increase the potential for the use of research findings, *(c)* encourage public support for social science research, and *(d)* help people to help themselves. In a later chapter of this book, Wandersman discusses the issue of citizen participation in detail and considers the role of research in that arena.

The Role of Community Researchers

Several characteristics of the role we are advocating for community researchers are summarized by Price and Cherniss (1977).

1.   Research issues or problems are stimulated by community needs. The formulation of a problem for study begins with the perception of a real need in a community setting—a need that is perceived by members of that

setting, by community researchers, or, more likely, by both. Rather than being just an exercise in hypothesis testing, the research enterprise can be an effort to use knowledge and skills to deal with the needs of community groups.

The stance implies that theory serves as a means as well as an end. The development of social science theory remains an important goal in and of itself; but when problem formulation is stimulated by community needs, theory also can become a tool for broadening our understanding of specific instances of problems and their larger implications. Even as we recognize that attempts to solve practical problems do contribute to theory development (Garner, 1972), so can theory in itself be a guide for anticipating future events, and a much needed framework for understanding complex situations.

2. Research is a tool for social action. Like theory, research can be a tool rather than an isolated pursuit. It is a practical means of assessing community needs and choosing the most effective available course of action. The community researcher recognizes that it is not enough to choose a "relevant" problem. Informed and effective action directed at relieving a specific problem requires the systematic collection of information.

3. The research yields useful products. Community research seldom should have a journal article as its sole product. The product may vary depending on the problem under consideration and the goals and values of the research. It may be a training manual, a new administrative or evaluation system, the development of a new role for professionals, a new set of skills for people working in a human service agency, or even a new kind of community organization. The important point here is that the product contributes to an attempt to solve a real social problem.

4. Evaluation of social action is an ethical imperative. There is a compelling ethical reason for community researchers who are involved in social change efforts to use their skills to evaluate the effects of change on individuals and groups. If the community researcher fails to provide a basis adequate for measuring the impact of an intervention, the well-being of people in the community can be significantly affected.

The role of the community researcher that we have briefly described above is certainly not without its limitations. The benefits associated with the role derive from working more closely with and gaining the acceptance of community members and organizations, as well as from immersing oneself in the phenomena of interest. At the same time, however, the commitment of the researcher's skills and knowledge to community development has several other implications. One of these is that community research projects will require more time to complete. As researchers attempt to meet community needs, they will become involved in processes that unfold slowly over time and which, consequently, may demand longitudinal rather than cross-sectional research designs. A study of a community's decision to build a new hospital, for example, would extend over a period of months or even years.

Another implication of the new role is that researchers will need to deal with the politics of community organizations and neighborhoods. Communities can be cauldrons of dissent, as well as collections of quiet residential neighborhoods. Individuals and groups form coalitions that continuously bargain with each other and realign themselves in efforts to gain control of community resources they desire. Communities are in many ways political-economic entities. Researchers may encounter people who perceive them as allies of an "enemy" and who will work to subvert their efforts. Further, researchers may be tempted to abandon their role as researchers in order to participate more fully in efforts to bring about social change.

Finally, for community researchers who are academicians, the role we have described is likely to bring conflict with persons who value highly the traditional role of researcher as detached scientist. University departments are not likely to reward researchers whose efforts yield products other than scholarly articles and books. Community researchers will be expected to produce not only manuals and innovative organizations, such as alternative services, for example, but also traditional products. Of course, such expectations place considerable demands on community researchers.

METHODOLOGY AND THE PROCESS OF COMMUNITY RESEARCH

Even though many researchers have strong preferences for a particular research method, there is no one right way to conduct research in the community. Some researchers may believe that the only way to develop a clear understanding of a social phenomenon is to conduct a true field experiment, while others believe that the richness and complexity of community phenomena can only be understood by careful observation over long periods of time with as little intrusion into the setting as possible. We believe that the choice of methodology depends on a great many factors including (1) how much you already know about the phenomenon in question, (2) the practical and ethical constraints confronting the community researcher, (3) the researcher's objectives in conducting the research itself, and (4) the choice of the level of analysis appropriate to the phenomenon you wish to study.

A variety of research methodologies is available to community researchers, and we will explore a number of them in the following chapter. These approaches range from large-scale surveys to field experiments, or may involve detailed interviews with informants designed to understand the culture of a particular community setting. How then does the researcher choose a methodology in the process of conducting a community research project?

Actually, the choice of a particular methodology should come at a relatively late stage in the planning of a research project, and a great many other decisions need to be made before the choice of method is made. More likely, the research process itself actually begins before the researcher becomes fully aware of it. This can happen in a variety of ways. For example, in working as a volunteer to develop a neighborhood watch program as a deterrent to break-ins, the researcher may discover that people in the neighborhood are reluctant to participate in the program, even though its benefits have been shown in a number of other studies and perhaps even in other neighborhoods in the same city. Or, perhaps, the city council in a community faces a decision about where to locate a new park and the researcher's help may be requested. In any case, at some point early in the process of inquiry a phenomenon begins to present itself for explanation, or a practical question presents itself in need of an answer.

Even as your attention is being drawn to the phenomenon, you are developing tentative hunches about the nature of the problem, and you will be well advised to see how much is already known about it. This can present dilemmas to the researcher, since there is seldom a simple and clear match between research literature on a particular problem and the way it presents itself to you in a community setting. One can begin to talk to other experts or to explore the research literature. For example, in the case of the neighbors who are reluctant to participate in a neighborhood watch program, an examination of the existing research literature on community participation may provide additional knowledge and insight. One's ideas about the nature of the problem and what research literature is most relevant will almost surely continue to evolve throughout the entire research process.

Still another set of questions that needs answering before one can choose a particular research methodology has to do with the ethical and practical constraints that confront the researcher. This requires a combination of ethical sensitivity on the one hand and pragmatic judgment on the other. It is our experience that a failure to consider practical constraints on the researcher's own resources or those of his or her community is a major cause of incompleted projects. Plans to conduct a major community survey without adequate resources and expertise will inevitably confront practical limitations before the researcher has gone very far. Similarly, a failure to be sensitive to the ethical problems involved—for example, in covert research in which a community group is unaware that it is the subject of the researcher's activity—can lead to serious consequences for everyone included.

Thus, a great deal goes on in the thinking of a community researcher and his or her initial exploration of the relevant research literature, discussions with other colleagues, and with community members themselves before one can consider the choice of a research methodology.

Some Objectives of Community Research

Let us examine in somewhat more detail the range of research objectives that a community researcher might consider in developing a research plan. As we suggested, these objectives can vary widely and greatly influence the choice of methodology chosen to actually conduct the research. It is helpful to be as clear as possible about one's objectives before beginning the research, even though this can be a painstaking and intellectually demanding experience. It is tempting to believe that you can achieve a great many objectives in the course of a research project. More typically, however, a focus on one or perhaps two such objectives is more reasonable and will help a great deal in the planning process.

One possible objective of community research is *exploration and hypothesis formulation.* Often it is the case that, at the outset of a research project, it is quite difficult to specify the boundaries of phenomena we are trying to understand. In our example of low neighborhood participation, the initial attention may focus on the participatory process itself. On the other hand, other factors, such as a history of conflict over collective action in the neighborhood in the past, may be part of the phenomenon to understand. If we are not sure, and we seldom are, then exploratory research to develop a hypothesis may be in order. Casual inquiries of a number of neighbors about their perceptions of the relatively low levels of participation would be useful. Knowing that one's objective in a research project is largely exploratory helps determine your course of action and may lead you to choose some methodologies, rather than others, in pursuing that objective.

A second very common objective in conducting community research is *to seek information as a guide to action.* If the question confronting a community researcher involves finding out which groups in a community are most in need of a call-in crisis hotline, then perhaps a community survey to seek that information will serve that objective best. If, on the other hand, the researcher is asked to design a study to decide which of two methods of community outreach are most likely to help community members to become aware of a new community service, then perhaps an evaluation that tests the relative effectiveness of several preferred methods is in order. Again, knowing that your objective is to seek information as a guide to choosing a course of community action helps focus the researcher, and importantly influences the choice of method.

In still other cases, the researcher may have theoretical interests, in which case his or her objective may be to *test a hypothesis and rule out alternative explanations* for a finding. For example, it may be of theoretical and ultimately of practical interest to decide whether job loss increases the likelihood of alcoholism in a particular population or, alternatively, whether persons with alcohol problems have a higher likelihood of losing their jobs. Testing hypotheses about the causal direction of this relationship is no easy matter, but its practical and policy implications may be very great. Knowing that one's research objective is to rule out one of these alternative hypotheses has direct implications for the type of data collected, whether one follows a population and observes behavior over several time periods, and what populations must be sampled in the first place.

Finally, a legitimate and important objective of community research may be to *develop and test new research methods.* For example, some researchers may question whether accurate and complete information can be obtained from community members using telephone interview techniques. Cannell and his colleagues (1981) have conducted a number of sophisticated studies testing different strategies for encouraging telephone respondents to give complete and accurate information. They have been able to show that simply asking respondents to commit themselves to give accurate information and having interviewers encourage frank and honest answers can greatly improve the quality of information obtained from telephone interviews.

The point of our discussion of research objectives is straightforward. Community research projects can have a wide range of objectives, and researchers are well advised to consider carefully *which* objectives they actually have in mind before they begin to make decisions about the type of research methodology they intend to use.

Reliability, Validity, and the Objectives of Community Research

By now, most, if not all, students will be aware of the requirements of reliability and validity in conducting research. Repeatable procedures and reliable test instruments are obviously desirable tools in conducting community research. Similarly, data-gathering techniques that provide valid measures of the phenomenon in question are often described as critical ingredients in all social science research. We certainly agree with this standard prescription—but only up to a point.

We wish to argue that the requirements of reliability and validity are not absolute but depend on the researcher's objectives. For example, if the researcher is in the process of exploration and hypothesis formulation, it may be necessary to sacrifice reliability for descriptive richness. In this case, unstructured interviews or case studies of admittedly low reliability may be more informative in the exploratory process than rigidly structured questionnaires or artificial laboratory experiments. Similarly, in seeking information as a guide to action, it may be important to sacrifice the unique and rich descriptive quality of a case study in favor of classifying members of a population into reliable categories for the purposes of estimating the relative frequency of a community problem. Thus, we may wish to establish highly reliable categories for describing different types of traffic offenses in order to estimate what members of the population are most likely to commit those offenses or where in the community they are most likely to occur. The point is a simple but critical one. As desirable reliable measurements and valid predictors of a community phenomenon may be, the importance of reliability and validity is not absolute, but must be judged relative to the community researcher's objectives.

The Choice of Level of Analysis

A subtle but critical issue to consider before choosing a particular methodology for community research involves the unit of analysis appropriate to the phenomenon of interest. Community processes may be investigated at several different levels, and some thought about this issue will have an important bearing on a number of other research decisions to be made. Consider the following example.

Suppose that you are interested in evaluating the effects of an educational program that has been established in several school districts in your state. You could compare reading achievement scores among individual students, whole classes, schools, or even school districts: Which of these units would you choose for analysis? The critical point underlying this question is that society can be thought of as consisting of several levels of social organization—individuals, groups, organizations, and communities. Community and social phenomena, such as family and work life, can be studied from the vantage point of one or several of these levels of analysis. Psychologists have historically concerned themselves with understanding behavior at only two levels of analysis—the individual and the group levels. Typically, sociologists and anthropologists have focused on the organizational and community levels.

This sort of division of labor among social scientists has had the unfortunate consequence of obscuring the important ways that various and multiple levels of social organization influence social behavior. In other words, we have paid too little attention to understanding behavior from multiple levels of analysis. Consider again the issue of children's reading achievement. Researchers who focus exclusively on the contribution that individual characteristics, such as a child's intelligence, make to reading achievement, fail to take into account potentially crucial variables that operate at other levels of analysis, such as peer group or family support for achievement, size of classrooms, and the amount and quality of resources possessed by a student's school and community.

Some recent research by Shinn and her colleagues (Shinn & Mórch, in press; Shinn et al., 1983) illustrates the value of studying a phenomenon at more than one level of analysis. Shinn studied the way youth workers and counselors coped with stressful events in their work settings. Often the work was demanding and unpredictable. The clients included foster home residents, emotionally disturbed children, learning disabled children, and others. Shinn assumed that a stressful event (e.g., managing an emotional outburst from a child) could be managed through individual efforts of the counselor, by help from a coworker (group level coping), or through administrative means (a new policy might be set by administration). She interviewed workers about stressful episodes and how they were handled. She found that efforts at all three levels were helpful in relieving the psychological consequences of stress, and that, after taking individual level efforts into account, efforts at the group and organizational level had an *additional* beneficial effect. Thus, by conceptualizing the coping process as a multilevel phenomenon, Shinn was able to show that human service organizations can take steps over and above those taken by individual workers to help counselors deal with work related stress.

In addition, there has been too little theoretical or empirical work concerning interaction and relationships among the various levels of analysis. A notable exception has been the work of Watzlawick, Weakland, and Fisch (1974) on change among individuals and families. Their work suggests there may be principles of behavior that are unique to each level of analysis; that is, characteristics of behavior or relationships among variables found at one level may be inappropriately translated to another level. This error has been called the "fallacy of the wrong level" or "ecological fallacy" (Robinson, 1950; Borgatta & Jackson, 1980). For example, individuals' job satisfaction is incorrectly translated into measures of group morale or group cohesiveness by adding the individual scores and assuming that they reflect some group process. Similarly, a relationship between socioeconomic status and reading scores found at the school district level is assumed to be similar for individual pupils; students from wealthier homes are assumed to be better readers than students from poorer homes. Note that the fallacy can be made whether one is translating from a lower level of analysis (e.g., individual) to a higher level (e.g., group) or vice versa.

Our understanding of community and social phenomena can be extended considerably by research that takes into account the complex interaction of variables operating at multiple levels of analysis. In short, there is a pressing need for research concerned with the interaction between individuals and their social environments. The social environment of individuals consists not only of other individuals but also of collections of various groups, organizations, and communities whose influence on behavior we are only beginning to adequately conceptualize and study.

Methodologies Are More than Data Collection Methods

Before we begin to consider actual approaches to conducting community research, there is a final distinction we wish to make. It is between data collection methods on the one hand, and methodologies on the other. Data collection methods are technical procedures for gathering, storing, and recording information. Data collection methods include questionnaires, tape recordings of interviews, aerial photographs, requesting people to write autobiographies, or such unobtrusive measures as counting the number of people who gather on a particular street corner at a particular time of day. As important as data collection methods are to community research, they are only technical procedures for gathering, storing, and recording information. They are, however, often confused with the broader strategic approach to research implied in the idea of a *methodology* (Reinharz, 1981).

A methodology is much more than a data collection method, though it may focus on one, or perhaps several, specific methods for data collection. From our point of view, a methodology includes a set of procedures and assumptions made or chosen by the researcher. The assumptions include *(a)* what the phenomenon of interest actually is, and *(b)* what the nature of the relationship between the researcher and the object of study should be.

Not only are methodologies more complex than data collection methods, but they can, in some sense, be said to embody a set of assumptions about the nature of what we wish to understand and how we stand in relation to those we wish to study. The phenomenon of interest may be the frequency of some event, such as arson, or the nature of a process, such as labor union negotiations, or successful resolution of family differences. Not only may the phenomenon of interest differ depending on the particular methodology in use, but the nature of the relationship between the researcher and what is being studied also may differ. Using some methodologies, the researcher may be a participant in the community process and a collaborator with community problem solvers. In other cases, the researcher may see him or herself as a detached, objective observer. And, using still other methodologies, the researcher may see him or herself as part of the phenomenon to be understood.

The important point is that, in the *methodologies* for community research that we will explore in the next chapter, there are implicit assumptions both about what phenomenon is actually of interest and what the nature of the relationship between the researcher and community individuals or groups is or should be. Obviously, these are not decisions to be taken lightly, and, in exploring the methodologies that we discuss below, these issues will arise frequently.

Collaboration, Control, and Action Orientation as Dimensions of Community Research

In the next chapter we will introduce a range of approaches available for the study of community phenomena. The approaches include epidemiology, social indicators, true field experiments, quasi-experiments, simulations, network analysis, participant observation, and ethnographic studies. It is useful to note that each of the approaches varies along three key dimensions. One of these dimensions reflects the degree to which a researcher *collaborates* or works with the participants of the study. With some research approaches, researchers have minimal contact with community members. For example, each participant in a social indicators study may be interviewed for only an hour or two. On the other hand, there are other approaches—such as action research, in which community members play a significant role in defining the problem to study, designing and conducting data collection methods, and interpreting data.

A second dimension along which approaches to community research vary is the amount of *control* that researchers have over the variables or phenomena of interest (Willems & Rausch, 1969). There are approaches, such as field experiments, in which researchers have a significant degree of control in, for example, assigning participants randomly to various treatment conditions. In contrast, there are approaches to research in which researchers exert no control over community members or events, but, instead, attempt to influence events as little as possible. In other words, researchers attempt to become "one of the group" and to behave as do other persons in the setting.

A third dimension along which methodologies can be classified has to do with whether they are primarily *analytic* or *action*-oriented. A number of the approaches that we will examine have analysis of a prevailing state of affairs as their primary goal. Others are oriented to action. They are aimed at changing some characteristic of an individual, group, or community. These action strategies may be oriented to change for the purposes of improving the quality of community life, or to understand a phenomenon more deeply, or both. In any case, as we shall see, the dimension of analysis versus action orientation can help clarify the role and purpose of various methodologies for community research.

These dimensions along which approaches to community research vary, the amount of control over variables of interest, and the degree of collaboration with community members and action versus analytic approaches are shown in Figure 3–1. That is, we can think of several general "families" or

FIGURE 3–1
Approaches to Community Research*

Degree of Collaboration with
Community Members

		Low	Moderate	High
Degree of Control over Phenomena	Low	• *Epidemiology* • *Social indicators*	• *Network analysis* • *Ethnography*	• *Participant observation*
	Moderate		• Quasi-experiments	• Action research
	High		• True field experiments	• Simulations

* Analytic approaches are shown in italics, action-oriented approaches are nonitalicized.

types of approaches to research. As we shall see, the dimensions of collaboration, control, and action orientation have both scientific and human implications when we examine examples of different approaches to the conduct of community research in the next chapter.

SUMMARY

We began this chapter by suggesting that community researchers are not immune to the social forces that they study. There has been increasing recognition that a value-free social science may be impossible to attain. The values, assumptions, and world-view of the researcher play an important role in what problems are chosen, how they are studied, and how findings are interpreted. Because social science research is infused, at least in part, by the values of the scientist, researchers are obliged to be as explicit as possible about their own values and how those values contribute to decisions about the conduct of research.

A second critical aspect of community research has to do with the researcher's relationships with community members. We view these relationships as partnerships, or exchanges, in which such valued resources as time, energy, and insight available to each party are exchanged to the mutual benefit of both. Thus, for example, a community member may contribute experience and insights in a collaborative effort with a researcher, while the researcher may contribute expertise and technical skills. When this exchange is negotiated openly in a context of mutual respect, the product should be both more scientifically sound and more useful to the community.

Both the value context and the exchange relations of the community researcher with community members have implications for the researcher's role. We suggest that community research ought, wherever possible, to be stimulated by community needs, and that it can be a tool for action as well as an opportunity to expand knowledge. Even if these role requirements are reasonably clear to the researcher, he or she is still faced with a question of which research approach is best for a particular community problem.

The choice of research approach depends on how much is already known about the problem, the practical and ethical constraints that exist in any particular situation, and the researcher's own scientific objectives. Research objectives can vary widely, from tentative exploration to formal hypothesis testing, or may include an attempt to test a new research method.

We argued that one could distinguish between technical procedures for collecting information, on the one hand, and "methodologies," on the other. Methodologies are broader research approaches that include assumptions about the phenomenon, the relationship between the community researcher and community members, and the nature of the researcher's objectives. These various methodologies each have traditions of their own, and we will examine a number of them in the chapter that follows. Each of these methodologies varies in three important ways, however. One has to do with the degree to which they promote collaboration with community members, a second has to do with the degree to which the researcher can actually control variables of interest in the research, and a third has to do with whether the methodology is oriented primarily to analysis or to action.

References

Albee, G. W. The politics of nature and nurture. *American Journal of Community Psychology,* February 1982, *10*(1), 1–36.

Borgatta, E. F., & Jackson, D. J. *Aggregate data: Analysis and interpretation.* Beverly Hills, Calif.: Sage Publications, 1980.

Cannell, C. F., Miller, P. V., & Oksenberg, L. Research on interviewing techniques. In S. Leinhardt (Ed.), *Sociological methodology.* San Francisco: Jossey-Bass, 1981.

Chavis, D. M., Stucky, P. E., & Wandersman, A. Returning basic research to the community: A relationship between scientists and citizens. *American Psychologist*, 1983, in press.

Garner, W. R. The acquisition and application of knowledge: A symbiotic relation. *American Psychologist*, 1972, *27*, 941–946.

Kamin, L. J. *Heredity, intelligence, politics and psychology.* Paper presented at the meeting of the Eastern Psychological Association, 1974a.

Myrdal, G. *Objectivity in social research.* New York: Pantheon Books, 1969.

Price, R. H., & Cherniss, C. Training for a new profession: Research as social action. *Professional Psychology*, May 1977, 222–231.

Rappaport, J. *Community psychology: Values, research and action.* New York: Holt, Rinehart & Winston, 1977.

Reinharz, S. *Dimensions of the feminist research methodology debate: Impetus, definitions, dilemmas and stances.* Paper presented at the meeting of the American Psychological Association, Los Angeles, California, August 1981.

Robinson, W. S. Ecological correlations and the behavior of individuals. *American Sociological Review*, 1950, *15*, 351–356.

Shinn, M., & Mórch, H., Robinson, P. E., & Neuner, R. A. *Coping with job stress:* (Ed.), *Stress and burnout in the human service professions.* Elmsford, N.Y.: Pergamon Press, in press.

Shinn, M., Mórch, H., Robinson, P. E., & Neuner, R. A. *Coping with job stress: Individual, group and organizational strategies.* Unpublished manuscript, New York University, March 1983.

Watzlawick, P., Weakland, J. H., & Fisch, R. *Change: Principles of problem formation and problem resolution.* New York: W. W. Norton, 1974.

Willems, E. P., & Raush, H. L. (Eds.) *Naturalistic viewpoints in psychological research.* New York: Holt, Rinehart & Winston, 1969.

CHAPTER FOUR

Methodologies in Community Research:
Analytic and Action Approaches*

* This chapter was written by Thomas D'Aunno and Richard H. Price.

INTRODUCTION

- You notice in your neighborhood that old people and women don't appear on the streets after dark anymore. Some inquiries lead you to conclude that many neighbors now remain in their homes with the door locked because they are fearful of street crime. Their fears have made them prisoners in their own homes and have changed the quality of community life in the neighborhood as well. Where people once sat on their front porches and greeted passers-by there are now only locked doors facing each other on the block.

  But what is it that is really changing in your community? Is it a real increase in crime or only the fear of crime? Do people have an accurate picture of the threat of crime to themselves? The answer could tell us a great deal about the psychology of the community and of what might be done to improve the quality of community life.

In the preceding chapter, we concluded by introducing a framework for organizing various approaches to community research and suggested that different approaches varied both in terms of the degree to which researchers had an opportunity to collaborate with community members and the degree to which the researchers could control at least some of the variables under study. In this chapter we will examine a number of different methodologies for community research and will organize our presentation by dividing the methodologies into two groups: (1) those approaches which are intended primarily to allow description and analysis of community phenomena, and (2) those approaches which are action-oriented.

We believe that discussions of research methodology are, too often, presented in abstract fashion without examples to clarify points and to bring the process of community research alive to the reader. We will present numerous examples of community research projects that show how community researchers have used a particular methodology to illuminate a problem or phenomenon. In the course of discussing the range of methodologies, we also will observe that each method is more or less useful depending upon the researcher's objectives. Some methods are ideal for a tentative exploration of a problem or phenomenon, while others are more appropriately suited to hypothesis testing. But whichever approach we discuss, we also will consider its strengths and weaknesses. Each approach to research will be considered in the context of the researcher's objectives and the degree to which the relative strengths and weaknesses of the approach make it suitable to those objectives.

Let us now turn to a consideration of the analytic strategies for community research.

ANALYTIC STRATEGIES FOR COMMUNITY RESEARCH

Participant Observation

"Participant observation" refers to inquiry in which researchers both systematically observe and participate in the day-to-day life of the communities, organizations, and groups they study. The critical feature of participant observation is the degree of involvement the researcher has with the "subjects" of the research (Selltiz, Wrightsman, & Cook, 1976, p. 263). Participant observers maintain face-to-face relationships with those being studied and share in their daily experiences. In other words, participant observers immerse themselves in the lives of the people they wish to understand.

There is a twofold purpose for participating in the phenomena one is studying. First, participation minimizes the social distance and language differences that typically exist between researcher and subject. Minimizing such barriers enables researchers to gain an intimate qualitative understanding of complex social phenomena. Second, participation enables a researcher to understand a social phenomenon from the perspective of a person who is experiencing it.

Participant observation has long occupied a strategic place in the methodological "tool-box" of community-oriented inquiry (Bell & Newby, 1972, p. 55). In some instances, it has enabled researchers to study phenomena accessible only through direct participation. The behavior of street gangs and religious cults, for example, is not open to inquiry by social scientists, but can be observed by "members" of such groups (e.g., Festinger, Schachter, & Riecken, 1956). Participant observation also contributes much to our knowledge of the processes involved in community phenomena.

Researchers using the participant observation approach typically begin to collect data with more tentative, less detailed hypotheses than in experimental research. And typically, researchers do not precisely define the geographic area in which data are to be collected (i.e., the field setting). The purpose of loosely defining hypotheses and field settings is to enable observers to take advantage of their firsthand experience of the phenomena being studied. Observers are typically free to develop, revise, and test hypotheses as they learn more about a setting. In the first few days in the field, for example, an observer may find that his or her ideas do not fit the setting. Participant observers may then begin to formulate new research designs or new tactics and begin to ask different questions. In some cases they will leave the setting for another (Bogdan & Taylor, 1975, p. 27). For example, in a study of a state institution for the profoundly retarded, a researcher intended to study residents' perspectives on the institution, but found that many residents were nonverbal and many others were reluctant to speak openly about the institution. He then shifted his attention to attendants' perspectives, which proved to be a fruitful line of inquiry (Bogdan & Taylor, 1975, p. 27).

At the outset of a participant observation study, researchers can choose either to reveal or not to reveal their identity to the members of a group or community (Gold, 1958; Junker, 1960). In the strategy termed *complete participation,* observers entirely conceal their identity as researchers as they attempt to become full-fledged members of the group under study. A classic example of this approach, discussed in more detail below, is the study of a small group of persons who predicted the destruction of the world (Festinger, Schachter, & Riecken, 1956).

The complete participant approach enjoys the major advantage of enabling inquirers to gain access to settings where they would not be accepted as "social scientists." However, there are two problems with the approach. First, it is difficult for observers to conceal their lack of experience in the setting. In addition, covert observers often find that they cannot control the anxiety that results from the fear of getting caught and of the guilt of misrepresenting oneself (Bogdan & Taylor, 1975, p. 30). Second, the ethics of complete participation have been questioned. Some social scientists have argued against conducting research which does not have the explicit consent of the persons being studied (e.g., Erikson, 1967). Others claim that the benefits of such research justify its continuation. Though there is not a universally accepted solution to the problem, researchers should weigh the consequences of covert research before they undertake it.

In the strategy termed *participant as observer,* observers make their presence as researchers known and attempt to form relationships with members of a setting. Because of the problems of complete participation, this approach is more commonly used for entering field settings, particularly in community studies (Denzin, 1978, p. 188).

One of the crucial tasks facing observers who reveal their identity is minimizing the effects of their presence on a community's usual behavior and social processes. This can be accomplished by becoming "one of the crowd"; that is, by participating in social events and by adopting the language and dress of a group. The observers, however, must strike a balance between too little participation and too much. On the one hand, researchers who remain passive and aloof may find that subjects are reluctant to share information. On the other hand, observers who participate fully in the life of a group may find that their activities severely limit their ability to collect data.

Participants as observers also find that subjects attempt to place constraints on when, whom, or what they can observe. For example, "in many organizational settings, an official is appointed to give tours. Although these tours may be valuable in certain respects, tour guides tend to offer a biased and selective view of the setting" (Bogdan & Taylor, 1975, p. 44). Participants as observers must therefore carefully resist being drawn into relationships, modes of dress, and patterns of behavior that are not conducive to their research.

Lofland (1971) has noted that, in participant observation, unlike many other research methods, data collection and data analysis go hand in hand.

Observers examine the notes they compile on the field on a daily basis to identify themes, revise hypotheses, and plan for further data gathering.

In addition, observers' accounts of their own behavior, emotional reactions, thoughts, and plans are an important source of data. The following excerpt is from an observers' notes in a study of a state institution: "Although I don't show it, I tense up when residents approach me when they are covered with food or excrement. Maybe this is what the attendants feel and why they often treat the residents as lepers" (Bogdan & Taylor, 1975, p. 67).

Finally, data collection techniques other than observation are frequently used to supplement the data collected by observers. The methods include interviews, archival records (e.g., newspapers), and questionnaires.

Application: When prophecy fails. Recall the "hypothetical" example posed at the beginning of the previous chapter concerning religious cults. Researchers have indeed studied one such group that predicted the destruction of the world by a cataclysmic flood. The researchers used the "complete participation" strategy, concealing their identities entirely from members of the group.

The purpose of the study was to test a specific hypothesis derived from cognitive dissonance theory (Festinger, 1957). The theory can be briefly summarized as follows: To the extent that a person's beliefs, knowledge, or opinions are inconsistent or dissonant, the person experiences discomfort. There will arise pressures to reduce or eliminate the dissonance. Attempts to reduce dissonance can take any or all of three forms. The person may try to: (1) change one or more of the beliefs or opinions, (2) acquire new information that will increase consonance among the beliefs, or (3) forget or reduce the importance of those thoughts that are in dissonance (Festinger et al., 1956).

The researchers hypothesized that members of the cult would attempt to reduce the dissonance caused by disconfirmation of their prediction, not by admitting they were wrong but rather by attempting to gain more support for their position. Of course, this hypothesis runs contrary to common sense: why would people increase their zeal for a belief after it was disproven? The reason, according to cognitive dissonance theory, is that attracting others to one's belief not only reduces dissonance but also is less painful than discarding the belief altogether. Hence, when the world was not destroyed by a flood, proselyting by group members should increase.

The researchers first learned about the central figure of the group, Mrs. Keech, from an article in a small-town newspaper. Two researchers posed as businessmen interested in her predictions and visited her at her home. From the initial meeting the researchers were convinced that the study could not be conducted openly: group members were secretive and hostile to nonbelievers. Thus, they choose not to reveal their identities.

At the outset two college students were hired as observers and supplied with similar stories of "psychic experiences," which included events similar to those discussed by Mrs. Keech. One student approached Mrs. Keech and the other called on the leader of a second group that had formed in a nearby town. The students told their "stories" and were eagerly welcomed by members of both groups. The researchers quickly found, however, that this strategy had an unintended consequence: the beliefs of the groups were unintentionally reinforced by the two new "recruits." Nonetheless, to collect data effectively it was necessary to have at least two more observers enter the settings. This time, the observers, also students, merely expressed passing interest in joining the group. They were well-received: in fact, the group members were inspired by the upsurge of membership in a few days. Once again, entry into the group had influenced its behavior.

Once they became group members, the observers were faced with many of the obstacles discussed above. Their objective was to collect as much data as possible without interfering with or influencing group behavior and processes. But, of course, group members wanted the observers to participate actively in the life of the group. One of the observers, for example, was asked to lead a group meeting. He suggested rather awkwardly that the group meditate silently and wait for inspiration. In another instance, observers were pressured to quit their jobs and to spend all their time with the group. Observers were also forced to answer phone calls from "outsiders" inquiring about the group and its beliefs. Unfortunately, other group members were occasionally present, making it difficult for observers to avoid "selling" the group. At other times, observers were asked to take stands on divisions of opinion in the group. In short, any behavior of the observers as group members had consequences: they could not be neutral.

Observers gathered the following data for each group member: his or her personal history, degree of belief in and contribution to the group, the extent to which he or she engaged in proselyting, actions taken as the day of prophecy neared, and, of course, his or her behavior and attitudes when the prophecy failed. In addition, data were gathered concerning group meetings and the development of group beliefs over time.

Whenever possible, observers would secretly take notes as events occurred—for example, while "hiding" in bathrooms. Most often, however, observers dictated notes, using tape recorders alone in their rooms some three to four hours after events occurred. The reports of observers filled roughly 65 hours of tapes (nearly 1,000 typewritten pages) and 100 typewritten pages of handwritten notes. The data varied from direct quotes from group members to summaries of lengthy group meetings.

The behavior of group members following disconfirmation of the predicted flood generally provided support for the dissonance hypothesis. Of the 11 members of Mrs. Keech's group, only 2 gave up their belief following disconfirmation of the prediction. The others substantially increased efforts to win supporters and "converts" to the group. These efforts took several forms, including personal proselyting, lifting the secrecy surrounding the group, and a dramatic change in attitudes toward the press: Mrs. Keech and others began phoning newspapers, holding news conferences, and making tapes for radio broadcasts. As the researchers noted, "the once rejected suitor was hotly pursued." In short, using the participant observation approach, researchers were able to provide evidence for a counterintuitive hypothesis derived from cognitive dissonance theory—a theory that, at least in this case, seems to account for the unusual behavior of people whose beliefs were not confirmed.

Strengths and weaknesses. The relatively high level of researcher involvement with community members and their collaboration in the process of participant observation research provides a sense of immediacy for the researcher and allows the phenomenon under study to be studied close-up. But this high degree of involvement produces problems as well.

A serious problem with participant observation is that it produces changes in the behavior of the group under study. Moreover, the effect that observers have on a group is difficult to determine. The effect may fluctuate over time as they interact with group members in various situations. To reduce the severity of this problem, data should be collected only after time has elapsed after the observer enters the field. In any case, observers should be sensitive to the effects of their presence on group life. Field notes, for example, should include observers' perceptions of how they are affecting others' behavior.

Critics of the approach note that there is danger in providing little structure for observers in the field setting. One danger is that observers' participation in a setting may unduly affect their ability to develop and test hypotheses. A researcher attempting to study the relationship between city government and a neighborhood with unemployment problems may become so involved with the plight of residents that "city hall" becomes an enemy. The term *going native* has been coined to refer to observers who abandon their role as researchers to become members of the settings they were studying (Gold, 1958). A few guidelines that can prevent going native were discussed above. Bogdan and Taylor (1975) provide an extended discussion of the problem.

Critics of the approach also claim that observers' data are subject to selective perception. That is, observers tend to focus on behaviors they want or expect to see, often disregarding unexpected aspects of a situation or behavior and sometimes overlooking the obvious. The observer's behavior as a participant in group affairs may also influence a sequence of events to occur as "predicted."

There are several ways to deal with this problem. One is to use more than one observer in order to determine interobserver reliability. A second strategy is to use more than one data-gathering technique. The convergence of data can be established using a multimethod approach. Finally, conducting pilot studies that are unstructured may also reduce observers' biases by allowing them to monitor behavior without guiding hypotheses.

The Ethnographic Approach

For the community researcher, in particular, it is important to recognize that the people he or she seeks to study have a way of life and a culture of their own. Students in a junior high school, patients on a quadriplegic ward, and even skid-row alcoholics not only live in different cultural worlds but see their worlds in strikingly different ways. The ethnographic approach (Spradley, 1979) has been largely developed by cultural anthropologists and recognizes the need to understand how other people see their own experience. The ethnographic method allows us to step outside our own narrow cultural backgrounds and to better appreciate the cultural diversity of our communities.

Spradley observes that the first step in ethnographic research is to set aside our own assumptions about what other people's world is like and begin to appreciate the meanings that members of a cultural setting attach to objects and events in their own world. Ethnographers make inferences from what people say, how they act, and various objects or "artifacts" in the cultural setting. The ethnographic approach focuses, in particular, on what people say about events in their setting and the meanings they attach to those events.

How can the ethnographic approach help us to gain this kind of understanding? Spradley suggests that the ethnographic interviewing approach is designed primarily to reduce the "translation competence" of our informants. By translation competence, Spradley means the tendency of an informant to translate his or her own experience into the language of the researcher rather than retaining the cultural meaning of the setting itself. The interviewing approach described by Spradley is specifically designed to ask informants, in detail, the meaning of the words they use and the actions that occur in their everyday life. For example, within a traditional social science framework, they might ask someone whether they are "employed" or not. However, the meaning of employment to an inhabitant of skidrow may differ dramatically from our own meaning of the term. An inhabitant of skid row may not be "employed" by our definition, but he may engage in a variety of ways of "making it" to find food, clothing, and shelter, which serve many of the same ends. Simply asking about "employment" may lead our informant to "translate" into our language, leaving us ignorant about critical features of his or her own cultural context.

In conducting ethnographic research, the focus is upon the cultural scene. Spradley observes:

> Our everyday lives are lived in different social situations, dealing with different problems, doing different things. The thousands of career specializations represent different cultural scenes. So do hobbies, clubs, service organizations and even different neighborhoods. Any single individual will have knowledge of many cultural scenes and could serve as an informant for them. One woman, for example, may have detailed knowledge of the local P.T.A., the local synagogue, midwife culture, and the culture of skiers. (p. 21)

A first step in doing ethnographic interviewing is to locate an informant—someone the researcher asks to speak in the native language of the setting in which the informant lives or works. In order to appreciate how the research relationship with an informant differs from other possible research relationships, Spradley contrasts it with other ways of thinking about those with whom one does research. Social scientists often describe such people as "subjects." Typically, social scientists work with subjects to test hypotheses, and have preconceived ideas about what one expects to find. With informants, on the other hand, the ethnographic interviewer begins with a stance of ignorance, assuming that the interviewer knows nothing about the meanings of events in the cultural scene of the informant. The researcher views the informant as an expert about the cultural scene from which a great deal can be learned.

In Spradley's framework, the ethnographic interview has three major elements that blend together to form a conversation between the ethnographer and the informant. The first of these is to state an explicit purpose to make clear where the conversation is to go. Thus, an ethnographer might say to a professor who is his informant, "I want to learn about how to get promoted in the university." A conversation may ensue between the informant and the ethnographer discussing "research programs," "publications," "refereed journals," "tenure committees," and still other events, actors, and meanings within the life of a university professor.

A second major element in ethnographic interviewing involves providing the informant with ethnographic explanations. The ethnographic interviewer must explain why he or she is asking the questions that are being asked. Explanations may have to do with the project ("I want to learn about beauticians"), or processes of recording answers ("I want to go over the tape later to make sure I get the details right"), or about why one wants to know about the native language ("What would you say if I were a customer in your store?"). Finally, ethnographic questions are used to help the interviewer to understand descriptive terms used by the informant, how they are related to each other, and how they differ.

Unlike normal conversations, an ethnographic interview may involve a good deal of repetition, asking again and again about the meaning of particular terms or ideas, and expressing ignorance about things that might otherwise seem obvious so as to obtain detailed explanations from the point of view of the informant about the cultural scene under investigation.

Application: An ethnography of the world of ex-mental patients. A recent example of the application of ethnographic method is offered by Estroff (1981), who studied the cultural world of clients recently released from a psychiatric hospital into a community program designed to provide them with a sheltered community living experience. She began her research studying a "program of assertive community treatment," with the goal of learning about the experiences of patients described as "mentally ill" as they lived outside a hospital setting.

Estroff explored this world in a variety of ways. She developed relationships with a number of informants who were patients and staff in the setting. She participated in the program as if she were a client in many of the treatment and nontreatment aspects of the clients' lives as was possible. Her concern was not to evaluate the effectiveness of the program directly, but instead to study the culture of the clients, their way of thinking, feeling, and believing in their current way of life.

In the process of conducting her ethnographic research, Estroff discovered that working in the role of the ethnographer is sometimes stressful. She concluded that she would work with a research partner in the future, since trying to be both part of the culture of mental patients and trying to work as a social scientist can produce considerable strain. Being a female in a world primarily of men also had its own complications, as did invitations to engage in drug and alcohol consumption with patients.

The results of her intensive study yielded a number of insights. One such insight had to do with the complicated meanings of medication in that world. Having to take "meds" tended to communicate to the patients the idea that they were disturbed and might never get well again. And yet, paradoxically, medication often kept people from being more disturbed. In addition, some of the side effects associated with the medication itself, such as tremor and shuffling gait, revealed to others that one was a mental patient taking medication.

Estroff also learned about the paradoxes inherent in income maintenance. Many patients received supplementary security incomes, which had both beneficial and unintended effects. While, on the one hand, these payments provided a guaranteed income for patients who were often unable to participate in the labor market, they also tended to undermine patients' confidence and motivation to seek work. Similarly, programs for sheltered employment tended to communicate to patients the idea that "you can only make it there," thus undermining their confidence in their own capacities while, in many cases, providing patients with the only work they could undertake at that time. Estroff concluded that "making it crazy" became an occupation for many of the participants of the program. Thus, the patient role had its own paradoxes and contradictions that made being a patient in the community problematic and frustrating.

Strengths and weaknesses. Perhaps the greatest strength of the ethnographic approach to community research is its ability to understand the social life of community participants on their own terms and to challenge our own assumptions and theories about the nature of the social reality of those we study. Another strength of the ethnographic approach is the capacity of the approach to capture the complexity and richness of the meaning of life circumstances for individuals living in subcultures in our own society. Anthropologists and other social scientists have used various forms of ethnographic interviewing to understand a variety of community phenomena including life in an old people's home (Hochschild, 1978), the experience of people on skidrow (Spradley, 1970), the social world of poor unemployed black neighborhood inhabitants (Liebow, 1967), the culture of medical school (Becker, 1961) and others.

A weakness of the approach, however, has to do with the generalizability of the findings. Because it is necessary to interview one or a few informants intensively over long periods in the ethnographic approach, one may be left with questions about whether they apply only to a small group or even a single individual, or whether they have broader cultural and social meanings. Similarly, since a great deal of interpretation is necessary using this approach, it is unclear whether different ethnographers using the same method with the same informant would obtain the same findings. Because ethnographic approaches require at least a moderate amount of collaboration by community members, developing several informants may be helpful in developing an accurate picture, but may greatly increase the size of the effort needed to complete the research project.

Data collected either by the participant observation or the ethnographic interviewing approach can lend themselves to analysis and reporting using the case study method. The case study is a familiar tool to researchers in a variety of fields, including legal scholars, clinical psychologists, psychiatrists, historians, and others. Typically, case studies involve the recounting of an event or episode in the life of an individual, group, or community as it unfolds over time. Indeed, the example described earlier of the group that predicted destruction of the world by flood was reported in case study fashion, as an example of the way people's beliefs may actually be solidified when their prophecy fails.

Network Analysis

When social scientists have considered the social environment of individuals, they have most frequently been concerned with relatively well-defined social structures or organizations (Mitchell & Trickett, 1980). But there is an alternative approach to conceptualizing the social environment that focuses on the network of social relations in which every person is imbedded.

A network can be portrayed as points connected by lines. The points most typically represent individuals, and the lines or interconnections represent social relations. Of course, the points could represent whole organizations or even communities; from the point of view of network analysis, the result is the same. The social environment is characterized as a web of interconnecting social relations among various nodes or points. Indeed, several observers (Sarason, 1976a) have noted that all of society can be viewed as a network, and, theoretically, each person could, through the existing web of relationships, ultimately establish contact with each other person in the society (Politser, 1980).

The concept of social network provides us with a way of viewing social relations and social environments, and it offers us a concept intermediate between that of the relationship between two people and the broader concept of social system. Furthermore, the links in a network are potential communication channels and, therefore, allow us to understand how a variety of different messages are sent and received in the context of social structures.

Network concepts have been used to explain how politicians mobilize support, how people find a job (Granovetter, 1973), and even how one member of a work group was able to win a dispute by developing alignments with his friends (Boissevain, 1974). Network analysis also has been used to explain how a community attempted to resist changes brought about by urban renewal (Granovetter, 1973). The point is, a variety of different processes involving support, communication, and transactions lend themselves to analysis using the network approach.

Network analysis has its earlier origins in the field of sociometry, which attempted to map the relations between individuals (Moreno, 1934). Recently, anthropologists, such as Bott (1957), Barnes (1954), and Boissevain (1974), have made effective use of the network approach in studying a variety of cultural groups. Similarly, community psychologists, such as Gottlieb (1981), and organizational psychologists, such as Tichy (1980), have begun to apply network concepts and measurement techniques to community and organizational phenomena.

Typically, as Boissevain (1974) and Mitchell (1969) observe, the characteristics of social networks have been divided into those that describe structural aspects of the network and those that describe the interactional dimensions. Interactional dimensions include multidimensionality, reflecting the number of different kinds of transactions or relationships that occur between two elements. Two sisters who are also business partners could be said to have a multidimensional relationship, for example. Other interactional dimensions include frequency of contact, emotional intensity of the relationship, and reciprocity.

Structural measures, such as density, reflect the degree to which members of a person's network have contact with each other independent of the person. Very dense networks possess many interconnections, and networks of low density possess relatively few connections among members. Size, as reflected in the number of network members, is another important structural dimension of networks, since in a sense size may reflect the "reach" of an individual's network or that of an organization.

For the community researcher interested in network analysis, the major question of interest involves asking about the impact of various structural or interactional dimensions of networks on the behavior of an individual, group, or organization. In the example below, we will examine the impact of various personal network characteristics on the mental health of women experiencing life transitions.

Application: Women coping with life transitions through their networks.
Hirsch (1980) has reported a study which examines the network characteristics of the personal support systems of 20 young widows and 14 mature women returning to college. Hirsch reasoned that these women were coping

with life transitions which required them to draw on the resources of their personal social networks in order to cope with everyday life tasks and to successfully negotiate transitions from their previous life circumstances to their new emerging roles. In order to understand the nature of the natural support systems of these women, Hirsch asked them to keep a daily log of their interactions with others in their network over a period of 14 consecutive days. In addition, the women were interviewed to gain additional information about the interactions that occurred within their networks to obtain information about their mental health and self-esteem.

Hirsch arranged the logs kept by the women so they would reflect several different kinds of supportive interactions, and he also calculated two structural measures to their networks: (1) density, and (2) ratings of the number of friendships in each woman's network that were multidimensional in nature. Hirsch wished to identify those characteristics of networks and network relationships that were associated with differences among the women in measures of mental health and self-esteem and which presumably aided in coping with life transitions. (See Figure 4–1.)

FIGURE 4–1
Two Types of Social Networks that Appear to Affect the Individual's Capacity to Cope with Life Transitions Differently

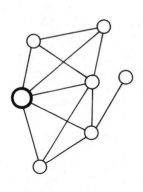
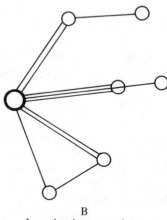

A
High-density network,
with unidimensional
relationships

B
Low-density network,
with multidimensional
relationships

Hirsch's results were both surprising and intriguing. He found, for example, that networks characterized by low density and by many multidimensional friendships tended to provide better support and were associated with better mental health outcomes than high-density networks with unidimensional relationships.

Hirsch interprets this finding in terms of the nature of the transitions being experienced by these women and the ways in which network characteristics aided in negotiating those transitions. For both groups of women, the family had become a less important source of rewards, and both widows and mid-career students were beginning to develop relationships in their occupational and social worlds outside of the immediate family setting. Dense networks linking families and friends may have actually constrained these women in coping with their transitions. Having a higher number of relatively independent relationships of a multidimensional nature, Hirsch reasoned, allowed smoother and less drastic reorganization of these women's lives. Women in lower-density networks with multidimensional relationships only have to change the extent of their already existing commitments or identifications with particular activities or relationships, rather than having to develop entirely new ones, as might the women in the very dense extended family network.

An interesting additional finding was that many women seemed to regard dense networks as more socially desirable, even though Hirsch's results suggested that these networks were associated with more negative mental health outcomes among women coping with transitions. There may be a cultural value associated with dense extended-family type of networks, suggesting that they are socially desirable even though other evidence suggests that such networks can be less helpful in coping with certain types of life transitions.

Strengths and weaknesses. While research on social networks has stimulated a great deal of interest among social scientists, there are a number of areas in need of further work before network analysis can begin to fulfill its promise as a major research strategy for conducting community research. For example, most research on social networks has been heavily dependent upon the perceptions of the respondent. Obviously, this means that it is unclear whether such investigations are studying social networks as they actually exist or only the respondents' perceptions of their social network.

An additional problem in need of clarification in network analysis has to do with the actual measures used to characterize both strutural and interactional properties of networks. Until some agreement about the standardized use of some measures is reached, progress in conducting studies in which findings can be directly compared will be slow (Mitchell & Trickett, 1980).

Still another limitation of social network research thus far is that most research has been conducted at the individual level of analysis. We noted earlier that it is possible to study the network connecting groups, organizations, or even whole communities. Unfortunately, however, with a few notable exceptions in community sociology (Turk, 1970, 1973, 1977), little work has been done to develop network studies at these higher levels of analysis.

Additional attention also needs to be paid to the interactional characteristics of networks. Until recently, structural characteristics have been more frequently studied in network analysis, and, even then, these structural measures have seldom been related to each other to assess how they may covary in various network configurations.

Despite these shortcomings, network analysis promises to be a powerful tool for the community researcher. The advantages of network analysis are several. First, because networks do not necessarily focus on any single community organization or institution, it is possible to understand the social environment of an individual or group across several different life spheres. Social scientists have tended to confine their research to the relatively arbitrary boundaries of different life spheres, such as work or the family. The advantage of a network approach is that it allows us to map interconnections between these life spheres and to understand how they may influence each other.

A second theoretical and methodological advantage of the network approach is that it allows us to connect individual and group or organizational level phenomena. Since network analyses allows us to map connections across different levels of social organization, it is possible to conduct studies in which the reciprocal influences between individual and community organization can be identified and their impact assessed. For example, using the network approach, it is possible to study how an individual community organizer may encourage relationships between different community organizations, which, in turn, may lead to improved services for other individual members of the community (e.g., Galaskiewicz & Shatin, 1981).

As Hirsch's study described above suggests, network analysis also has helped to illuminate our understanding of transitional life events, the role of supportive relationships in modifying the stressful nature of those events, and how network relationships may affect more enduring mental health outcomes.

Finally, an important feature of network analysis is that it helps clarify our understanding of how individual and group ties are related to access to resources in the community. By analyzing social interconnections among individuals and groups possessing different material and symbolic resources, we may begin to develop a more sophisticated understanding of the meaning of the structure of opportunity and equality in communities (e.g., Liebert & Imershein, 1977).

Studies of Community Populations

In the previous chapter we discussed the importance of studying phenomena from multiple levels of analysis, including the individual, group, and community levels. The methodologies we present in this section—epidemiology and social indicators—are particularly useful for studies at the community level of analysis. The purpose of these approaches is to examine the distribution of phenomena among entire populations of persons. In other words, researchers using these approaches typically are concerned with describing and analyzing events or behavior in a community or subgroups of a community.

Though social indicators and epidemiologic research have a similar purpose, they have historically been viewed as distinct approaches to research.

Perhaps the most significant difference between the approaches is that they have been used to study different phenomena. Epidemiologists, on the one hand, typically examine the distribution of behavioral problems or health disorders (e.g., schizophrenia, depression) in various populations. In contrast, researchers using the social indicators approach often focus on factors that influence the quality of individuals' lives and societal well-being (e.g., Campbell, Converse, & Rodgers, 1976). Thus, in this section we discuss the approaches separately and provide examples of each.

Epidemiology. Epidemiology is the study of the frequency and causes of physical and mental disorders. Epidemiologists count the cases of disorder in a population to determine if there are fluctuations in rates of disorder, and to identify groups of persons, if any, that have relatively high rates of disorder. Such groups are termed *high risk* or *at risk*. Researchers then attempt to identify particular socioeconomic or demographic conditions that may contribute to the development of disorder in such groups. Epidemiologic inquiry, for example, has indicated that there is a higher rate of schizophrenia among members of lower socioeconomic classes (e.g., Hollingshead & Redlich, 1958).

Medical scientists originally developed epidemiologic research methods in the mid-19th century to understand and to control such epidemic diseases as typhoid and cholera (MacMahon & Pugh, 1970). In the early 20th century, social scientists began to "borrow" the method to study phenomena other than infectious diseases, including, for example, accidents and behavior disorders.

As noted above, an epidemiologic inquiry consists of two sequential phases: first, determining the frequency of a disorder in a population (termed *descriptive epidemiology*); second, isolating variables that contribute to the development of a disorder (*analytic epidemiology*). We discuss each phase briefly in this section.

Two techniques are commonly used for counting cases of disorder in a population: measuring *incidence* and *prevalence*. Incidence is the number of new occurrences of a disorder within a specified interval. The interval under study can vary from a day, week, or month to a year or longer. "New occurrences" are defined as the first occurrence of a disorder within an individual's lifetime (Zax & Spector, 1974). Meaningful comparisons between populations or communities that vary in size are made possible by expressing incidence as a rate per 1,000 or 100,000 persons. Hence, incidence rate is the ratio of the number of cases found in a specified interval to the number of people in the population under study, multiplied by a constant. Consider, for example, the incidence rate of serious mental health disorder in the United States for the year 1979–80. In that year approximately 2.5 million Americans were hospitalized for the first time with mental disorders; thus, the incidence rate equals:

$$\frac{\text{Number of newly reported cases in 1979–80}}{\text{Population of the U.S. in 1979–80}} = \frac{2.5 \text{ million}}{220 \text{ million}} \quad \text{(K)}$$

where $K = 1,000$. Thus, the incidence rate equals 11.36 per thousand, or roughly one person per hundred. Note that the numerator and denominator of a rate must be defined in the same terms: if the numerator refers to a specific age, sex, or racial group, the same must hold for the denominator.

Prevalence, on the other hand, is the total number of cases of a disorder in a population at a given point in time. Consider, for example, the prevalence rate of mononucleosis among students at the University of Michigan for the month of October 1982. Prevalence rate equals:

$$\frac{\text{Number of known cases in October 1982}}{\text{Number of U. of Michigan students in October 1982}} = \frac{300}{30,000} \quad (K)$$

where $K = 1,000$; thus, prevalence rate equals 10 per thousand.

The number of cases of a disorder at any given point in time is dependent on two factors: (1) the number of *new* cases that develop during the interval under study, plus (2) the number of cases that continue to exist prior to the interval under study. In the example above, 50 students may have contracted mononucleosis in September 1982. Since they still had the disease in October, they are counted as cases along with the 250 new cases that occur in October itself.

Thus, the important difference between prevalence and incidence is that the former is a more inclusive measure. Because prevalence is a more inclusive measure of the frequency of disorder, it is usually easier to calculate than incidence: prevalence rates can be obtained by simply counting all cases of a disorder within a population at a given point in time.

There is a disadvantage, however, to using prevalence rates. They are difficult to interpret because they reflect both the incidence and duration of a disorder (Zax & Spector, 1974; Davison & Neale, 1978). Consider, for example, research concerning the relationship between social class and schizophrenia. Suppose we determine from prevalence data that there is a correlation between low social class status and high rates of schizophrenia. Is there a higher prevalence rate among lower social classes because they tend to recover less rapidly from schizophrenia (and, thus, there are more existing cases when a study begins)? Or does the correlation reflect the occurrence of a greater number of new cases of schizophrenia during the interval under study? Using prevalence data alone it is impossible to answer such questions. When one is studying phenomena whose duration may vary considerably (e.g., as a function of social class status), it is useful to calculate incidence as well as prevalence rates.

Once prevalence and/or incidence rates for a disorder have been determined, epidemiologists attempt to isolate variables that contribute to the development of the disorder. To achieve this, they compare socioeconomic or demographic groups that are similar to each other with respect to several significant characteristics but one. Consider a simplified example concerning the relationships between gender and mental health. If one wanted to learn if gender contributed to the onset of mental health problems, one could compare the incidence rate of disorder in a group of young white females from middle-class backgrounds to a similar group of young white males from middle-class backgrounds. If gender is indeed related to the occurrence of mental health problems, one group would show a significantly higher rate of disorder. A series of such comparisons, often using multivariate statistical techniques, enables epidemiologists to establish a correlation between a variable and the occurrence of disorder.

Application: Economic change as a cause of behavior disorder. In the early 1970s epidemiologic research was extended by the work of Brenner (1973) and others who began to examine the relationship between economic change and the incidence of behavioral problems. Brenner, for example, found that change in employment rates in manufacturing was highly associated with mental hospitalization and other health-related problems. In this section we summarize one study in a line of research conducted by Dooley and Catalano (cf, Dooley & Catalano, 1977; Catalano & Dooley, 1977; Dooley & Catalano, 1980) that further examines the relationship between economic change and physical and mental health.

Interviews were conducted with 1,173 adults (persons of age 18 and older) randomly selected from households in the Kansas City metropolitan area. The interviews, approximately one hour long, covered a wide range of issues. Individuals completed a scale assessing physical complaints; they also indicated which, if any, of several life events (e.g., change in residence, illness of spouse) they had experienced in the past few months. In addition to interview data, the researchers gathered data concerning economic conditions in the Kansas City area. Among the key indicators of economic conditions were monthly unemployment and inflation rates.

Two other methodological characteristics of the study should be noted. First, data were collected over a 16-month period, enabling the researchers to determine both immediate and long-term effects of economic change and other life events on individuals' well-being. Most epidemiologic research has been cross-sectional (i.e., data collected at one point in time) due to the expense of longitudinal studies. Cross-sectional research, of course, has the twofold limitation of yielding no information about the processes involved in phenomena, and, most often, the causal sequence of events cannot be determined.

Second, the study assessed the physical and mental health of individuals who were not receiving treatment for health problems. Much of previous epidemiologic research had calculated incidence and prevalence rates only by counting cases of disorder recorded by private and public health practioners. Thus, individuals who had health problems but were not receiving professional treatment had not been included in calculations of rates of disorder.

The results indicate that fluctuations, either increases or decreases, in rates of inflation have no effect on individuals' mental or physical health. On the other hand, four to eight weeks following an increase in unemployment there were significant increases in reports of psychophysical symptoms.

Thus, individuals' health does seem to be influenced by community unemployment rates. Further, analyses show that low-income groups and women were much more negatively influenced by economic changes than other subgroups of the population. The authors note that, as womens' participation in the work force has increased, they have become more vulnerable to stress caused by changes in the economy. Low-income groups have, of course, the fewest economic resources to "cushion" short-term economic setbacks.

Finally, the results indicate that increases in unemployment rates for the community were related to increases in the number of life events or transitions that people experienced. As unemployment increased, individuals were, for example, forced to change residences or to sell property.

Strengths and weaknesses. A major difficulty in conducting epidemiologic research is to obtain reliable estimates of prevalence and incidence. At first glance, it might seem simple to record frequencies of disorder from existing records of treated cases kept by public and private human service agencies. But, as noted above, this approach fails to take into account persons with health problems who are not, for a variety of reasons, receiving professional treatment. The Midtown Manhattan study (Srole, Langer, Michael, Opler, & Rennie, 1962) as well as the study reviewed above, demonstrate that many individuals with behavioral problems never receive professional treatment. Hence, it is necessary to establish community-wide prevalence rates, that is, prevalence rates which include samples of persons not receiving professional treatment.

Though establishing community-wide prevalence rates is a significant improvement in counting cases of disorder, it is difficult to reliably measure psychological disorder in persons who are not receiving treatment. That is, interviews and tests given to assess psychological well-being do not consistently identify individuals with disorders. As a result, 40 to 50 epidemiological studies of mental disorder have calculated prevalence rates that vary from less than 1 percent to a high of 64 percent (Dohrenwend & Dohrenwend, 1974). The problem of reliable diagnosis is not, of course, unique to epidemiologic research—clinicians face the task of reliably recognizing cases of disorder when they encounter them. Further research on the development of reliable diagnostic tools is needed to improve the accuracy of counts of disorder.

Despite the problem of reliability, epidemiologic inquiry can provide vital information for community planners, practitioners, and researchers. It can improve the delivery of mental health services by providing an estimate of the nature and severity of psychological problems in a given community. That is, descriptive epidemiology provides data on the frequency of various types of disorder that enable decision makers to plan accordingly: geriatric services are not emphasized in a "new town" composed largely of young married persons, nor does one open a day-care center in a retirement village.

Another advantage of epidemiology is that it can be used to study complex questions, such as the relationship between social class and psychological disorder. Such questions simply cannot be studied with laboratory or experimental methods of inquiry: one cannot randomly assign children to a certain social class and then raise them in a controlled "laboratory analogue" of society. Analytic epidemiology does nothing to disturb the usual behavior of a community. Furthermore, it enables researchers to establish correlations among factors involved in the development of a problem or disorder.

Finally, epidemiologic studies can provide an outcome measure of the effectiveness of mental health services. The effects of services on preventing and reducing the frequency and severity of behavioral disorders can be determined by descriptive epidemiologic surveys.

Social indicators. Social indicators are measures of community and societal well-being. Examples of social indicators include figures on rates of crime, divorce, mental hospitalization, and unemployment. An important characteristic of social indicators is that they are measured at regular time intervals, enabling one to determine trends and fluctuations in rates (Land & Spilerman, 1975). For example, one could monitor changes in rates of divorce between 1965 and 1975. Social indicators are also capable of being broken down or disaggregated by attributes of the persons or conditions being measured, such as age, race, sex. For example, one could determine if unemployment rates differ between men and women.

During the years 1949–69, the United States enjoyed steady economic growth: its gross national product doubled, as did the median income of American families. At the same time, however, there was an explosion of social turmoil, including increases in crime rates, racial unrest, and student demonstrations. These conditions prompted social scientists to doubt that economic growth and social progress were equivalent (Parke & Seidman, 1978). They called for increases in gathering and interpreting data on social well-being. The whirlwind of social change which swept through the 1960s thus gave rise to research on social indicators. The goal of social indicators research is to measure, analyze, and report on social conditions that affect well-being.

One of the major methodological concerns in social indicators research is to relate measures of well-being to each other. Single isolated statistics cannot contribute much to our understanding of social well-being. Consider, for example, the fact that the percentage of all adult women in the labor force has changed from 30 percent in 1940 to over 50 percent in the 1970s (Land & Spilerman, 1975). It is difficult to determine the implications of this single indicator for societal well-being. What effects has the movement of millions of women into the labor force had? What changes have occurred in the relationship between women's skills and the kinds of occupations they are entering? How have women's salaries changed in relation to men's?

To answer such questions we need to analyze relationships among a number of social indicators (Land & Spilerman, 1975). Suppose, for example, that we are interested in the relationship between citizens' involvement in community activities and their level of well-being. One could develop a measure of individuals' involvement in and satisfaction with community activities, such as volunteer work, voluntary associations (e.g., Lions Club), religious organizations, and political parties. After careful analyses of the interrelationships among several measures of participation, one would have informative indicators to relate to measures of well-being.

In fact, social indicators currently are classified as either descriptive or analytic. Descriptive indicators are measures of general social conditions (e.g., the number of physicians in the country); they are not integrated into theoretical frameworks specifying their relationships to each other. Analytic indicators are measures of social well-being with specific interrelationships as components of models of social systems.

Application: The fear of crime. Between the years 1964–75, the rate of violent crime in the United States increased by an estimated 336 percent (Skogan, 1978). This startling increase made "crime rate" one of the more well-known and widely cited of social indicators. The rate of crime, like other social indicators, is measured at regular time intervals and can be broken down for different groups of people. In 1976, for example, the chances of being a victim of violent crime were greater for men than for women.

A similar social indicator of the quality of individuals' lives is the rate of *fear of crime*. There has been an increase in the fear of crime that roughly parallels the increase in crime rates. The fear of crime, however, is not distributed across the population of the United States in a pattern that parallels rates of victimization: women and the elderly consistently report the most fear of crime, despite the fact that they have the lowest chances of being victims. The study described below is one in a series by Riger and her associates (1981) that examines the causes and consequences of women's fear of crime.

Researchers conducted telephone surveys of approximately 5,000 people living in the city limits of Philadelphia, San Francisco, and Chicago. In addition, 367 persons were invited to participate in a more intensive personal interview. The telephone survey and personal interviews included a wide range of questions concerning people's fear of crime, perceived risk of being victimized, perceptions of physical speed and strength, and degree of attachment to the community.

The results concerning rates of fear among various subgroups of the population were similar to those of previous studies. More specifically, young women (i.e., those least fearful among females) had about the same level of fear as elderly men, who were the most afraid of all men. In other words, women's fear of crime is at least twice as great as men's fear of crime. Older women reported much more fear than young women: 62 percent of women over age 50 reported that they were afraid to walk alone in their neighborhoods at night. Among both women and men, blacks and Hispanics reported more fear than whites, and respondents with low incomes were more afraid than those with high incomes.

The results also indicate that women's level of fear is related to several psychological variables. Women who believe that they are likely to be victims of crime were more fearful than other women. In fact, the perceived risk of being a victim was the strongest predictor of fear of crime.

Women who perceived themselves as less physically strong were also more likely to say they were afraid. Finally, women who felt less attached to their neighborhoods were more likely to report a high level of fear. The strength of one's attachment to neighborhood was measured in a series of questions asking, for example, if respondents could distinguish a stranger in their neighborhood from somebody who lived there.

In short, the results of Riger's research provided some understanding for the relationship between the social indicators of crime rate and fear of crime. Psychological and social factors so influence women's fear of crime that, though they are not likely victims of crime, they may behave as if they were. The research contributes to the development of analytic social indicators of crime and individuals' responses to crime. How actual rates of community events and changes in perceptions of those events occur in various groups can illuminate a variety of community processes.

Strengths and weaknesses. Many of the early reports on the development of social indicators shared an interest in providing data that could be used in public policymaking. Social scientists were interested in data that could be used to evaluate social programs and to set national goals and priorities for social well-being.

Other proposals for social indicators have focused on their use to monitor the impact of large-scale social change on the quality of life (e.g., Campbell, Converse & Rodgers, 1976). Closely allied to this "social change" rationale is a "social reporting" rationale that has emphasized the importance of regular, systematic reports on general social conditions (possibly as a means of predicting social events and well-being).

Of the rationales for developing social indicators, those with public policy implications have been the most widely debated. In regard to setting goals and priorities, "indicators must be regarded as inputs into a complex political mosaic" (Sheldon & Freeman, 1970, p. 169). That is, they are potentially useful in contributing to decisions about social program planning and development. At the same time, however, they can be subject to the political whims of decision makers: "advocates of policy can strengthen their position by citing hard data and so can critics of those policies" (Sheldon & Freeman, 1970, p. 169).

There also have been excessive claims about the utility of indicators in the evaluation of specific service programs. On the contrary, such tasks fall much more readily in the domain of "evaluation research," a rapidly developing discipline whose purpose is to provide decision makers with data on the development and outcome of service programs (Wortman, 1983).

Though these are useful caveats on the utility of social indicators in public policymaking, it should be acknowledged that the social indicators perspective is still in its infancy. Its full promise is yet to be seen. It appears that indicators can be immediately useful in: improving descriptive reporting of social conditions, analyzing social change, and predicting social events and patterns of social life. Sheldon and Freeman (1970) have noted that these three tasks are interdependent: "Adequate descriptive reporting is essential for the development of improved investigations of social change and correspondingly increased understanding of past social changes is required for better prediction of future events . . ." (1970, p. 172).

Regardless of the rationales that spur future efforts in social indicator research, it is important that we continue to build models of social phenomena which can relate indicators to each other in a meaningful manner. However, in calling for researchers to focus on interrelationships among indicators, we are not advocating that they wait for more refined social theories before they conduct empirical studies. Indeed, a comprehensive theory may never exist unless attempts are made to approximate it by making the most of available data.

SUMMARY

Table 4–1 (see pages 92–93) summarizes the analytic approaches to community research that were introduced in this section of the chapter. As we can see, there is considerable variation among these approaches in terms of their purposes, strengths, weaknesses, and distinctive characteristics. The critical point that we wish to emphasize, once again, is that researchers should select research approaches that meet their particular needs, objectives, and values. Community researchers should recognize the strengths and weaknesses of a variety of different approaches and use them accordingly rather than relying on a single approach.

The examples that we use to illustrate these various approaches provide us with an opportunity to illustrate the diversity of community phenomena that can be understood using these approaches. We considered a study of the pattern of beliefs in a religious cult, the culture of ex-mental patients in the community, the social networks of women experiencing life transitions, the relationship between economic change and psychological well-being in the community, and, finally, the relationship between crime rates and fear of crime among various community groups. In a number of cases, the phenomenon studied could not have been understood using any method but the one used in that particular case. This illustrates, yet again, the need for researchers to match their method to the problem they wish to explore.

ACTION-ORIENTED STRATEGIES FOR COMMUNITY RESEARCH

The Action Research Tradition

So far we have examined approaches to community research that were designed primarily to provide clearer descriptions of community phenomena or to examine the relations between community characteristics. While some of the approaches, such as participant observation, have the potential for inadvertently altering the phenomenon under study, they were designed primarily for description and analysis rather than to produce community change.

There is a second group of methodologies, however, that is designed both to increase our knowledge and to produce change. These methodologies are action-oriented and, compared to those discussed so far, allow the researcher to exercise more control over some of the variables under study.

From the community researcher's point of view, this feature of control has two advantages. First, by actually controlling a variable under study, such as a community's knowledge of the effects of smoking on heart disease, we are in a much better position to discover whether increases in the variable can have a *causal* effect on some other variable of interest, such as coronary disease rates. Second, in many cases, it is possible to control a variable, such as community health knowledge, by providing a specific program, such as an educational campaign. Using action-oriented methodologies and proper evaluation designs allow the community researcher to assess the effectiveness of the program and to draw conclusions about its potential usefulness in other communities. This action-oriented approach to community research often is described as the action research tradition.

The action research tradition can be traced to the early work of Kurt Lewin (1951), whose career was largely devoted to an attempt to integrate science and practice in action research. Cartwright (1978) has noted that Lewin believed that theory and practice as dual goals could stand in a fruitful relationship to one another. Lewin once observed that a close cooperation between theoretical and applied psychology can be accomplished, "if the theorist does not look toward applied problems with highbrow aversion or with a fear of social problems as a good theory" (Lewin, 1951, p. 169).

Ketterer, Price, and Politser (1980) have drawn on Lewin's earlier work (1946, 1947) to identify the key features of action research in Lewin's model. From Lewin's point of view, action research involved a cyclical process of fact-finding, action, and evaluation. In this approach, fact-finding methods are used to structure community goals, and these goals are converted into community action strategies or programs. The results of the action strategies or programs are then evaluated, and the process begins the cycle again.

Through the process of change itself, Lewin believed new understandings could emerge and that researchers and community members could collaborate in the change effort. Thus, Lewin argued that any research program set up within the framework of an organization or community should be guided by the needs of the group itself. Furthermore, Lewin believed that collaboration could produce new insights for the researcher not easily obtained in a more detached role.

Despite the fact that much of social science still advocated a value-free orientation in Lewin's time, Lewin had no illusions of the role of power and social values in action research, and he recognized that problems of power and values were interwoven with many of the questions the social scientist

TABLE 4–1
Summary of Key Characteristics of Analytic Strategies for Community Research

	Participant Observation	Ethnography	Network Analysis	Epidemiology	Social Indicators
Distinctive features	Researchers share in daily experiences of people, groups, etc., they wish to understand	Researchers set aside assumptions of what the informant's world is like and attempt to learn about culture of informant in his or her own words	The social environment is analyzed as a network of relationships among individuals, groups, or organizations	Researchers count cases of a phenomenon in a population and population subgroups, attempting to determine causes of the phenomenon	Measures of community and societal well-being are taken at regular intervals and are capable of being disaggregated for various groups of persons
Degree of collaboration	High	Moderate	Moderate	Low	Low
Level of control	Low	Low	Low	Low	Low
Major purposes	Exploration and hypothesis formulation Seek information as guide to action	Exploration and hypothesis formulation Seek information as guide to action	Information as a guide to action Hypothesis testing	Information as a guide to action Hypothesis testing	Information as a guide to action Hypothesis testing

Weaknesses	Disturbs behavior of group under study Problem of selective perception "Going native": role of researcher is restricted or abandoned altogether	Findings may lack generality Reliability between interviewers may be low	Measures of network characteristics are not standardized It is difficult to verify respondents' perceptions of network characteristics Too much focus on individual level of analysis and structural characteristics of networks	Difficult to obtain reliable estimates of number of "cases" Processes involved in phenomena often remain obscure	Limited use in policy-making decisions Currently there are few models of relationships among indicators
Strengths	Enables one to study phenomena accessible only through direct participation Increases knowledge of community processes Allows understanding of phenomenon from perspective of person experiencing it	Captures complexity and richness of life circumstances in subcultures of our society Improves understanding of social life from perspective of community member	Enables analyses of complete social environment of individuals Enables cross-level or multi-level analysis of events	Can provide information needed to design health and mental health services Can determine correlates of complex phenomenon disturbing community processes	Improves descriptive reporting of social conditions Can be used to analyze social events at other than individual or group levels of analysis

FIGURE 4–2
The Action Research Cycle

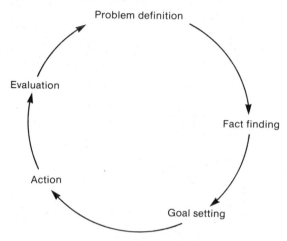

would study. Since Lewin's early work on action research, a variety of different forms of action research have developed, in both the United States and England. In addition, recent interest in evaluation research reflects some of the concerns of the action research tradition.

The action research approach is not confined to a single data collection method or to a particular theoretical orientation, and we can find examples of action research in environmental psychology (Holahan, 1980), research on organizations (Clark, 1976), community psychology (Price & Cherniss, 1977), education (Chesler & Flanders, 1967), and still other fields.

In the remainder of this chapter we will examine several action-oriented strategies for community research, including simulation studies, true field experiments, quasi-experiments, and time series. We will note that they vary both in the degree to which they afford control over variables of interest to the researcher and the degree to which they encourage collaboration with community members.

Simulation

To simulate an event or a social system is to reproduce as many of its essential characteristics as possible. Simulations attempt to capture critical features of phenomena as they unfold over time. The goal is to reproduce a social system in action, thereby enabling observers of and participants in the simulation to experience a series of outcomes that resembles the actual phenomena (Duke, 1964). Consider, for example, the use of simulation in the design and testing of spacecraft: with the aid of computers the conditions of space flight are replicated as carefully as possible to test the fitness of the craft and the ability of astronauts to deal with various conditions, such as weightlessness.

As phenomena are simulated, researchers gather data about participants' behavior and relationships among events by various methods, including observation, questionnaires, and interviews. In some simulations, for example, activity is periodically halted and researchers interview participants to learn about their reactions and plans. To the extent that a simulation accurately captures key aspects of the actual phenomena, these data are useful to both community members who wish to develop ideas about how to change real world conditions and to researchers who want to understand complex social events. In fact, the use of simulation in social science research has increased considerably in the past few decades, so much so that by 1965 it had become a widely used methodology in several disciplines (Dutton & Starbuck, 1971).

One important dimension along which simulation research varies is the extent to which a simulation relies on human actors. Simulations can vary from all-person simulations to person-computer combinations, or be all-computer simulations. All-person simulations rely solely on human actors who, operating within certain predetermined role definitions and rules, participate in a multifaceted role-playing experience to clarify what regularities are involved in the system being studied. The best known example of such all-person simulations in psychology is the Prisoners' Dilemma game (Rappoport & Orwant, 1965) that was developed to explore the conditions under which interpersonal negotiation will become competitive or collaborative.

Other simulations are built around a combination of human participants and computers. In this case, the humans are decision makers; the computers respond from a predetermined data base to the human decisions and track the quantitative tabulations resulting from those decisions. A widely known example of the combination person-computer approach is the InterNation Simulation (INS) developed by Guetzkow, Kotler, and Schultz (1972) to explore the dynamics of international conflict management.

The INS has many of the features of national and international politics: three or more nations, each with its voters, national resources, military capability, polls, channels of communication, advisors, trade, and elections. The players act as chiefs of state, diplomats, and cabinet members. Relationships among some components of the model are expressed mathematically and programmed into the computer. For example, if players decide to increase the military capability of their nation, the computer is programmed to indicate a decrease in certain national resources. As the model operates, changes in one component produce changes in others according to previously established equations. The advantage of the computer to INS is its ability to monitor interplay among numerous variables, involving calculations that would be prohibitive for humans.

In all-computer simulations, as in the mixed person-computer approach, researchers program computers with equations expressing relationships among several variables. The values of the variables are then systematically changed. The result is a series of outcomes or configurations that are useful to researchers attempting to understand the dynamics of a system. All-computer simulations have been used, for example, to gain insight into the economic problems of developing countries (e.g., Holland, 1972). Computers were first programmed with formulas relating such variables as prices and wages, rates of inflation, consumer demand, import and export levels, and capital investment. A series of computer "runs" was then completed, in which different values were assigned to the variables. It was then possible to analyze the impact of economic policy decisions (e.g., lowering capital investment) on a number of indicators (e.g., rates of inflation). The computer simulation enabled Holland to examine interaction among aspects of economies that are typically studied in isolation from each other. He noted that, in the past, such research has led to erroneous conclusions.

As knowledge increases about any specific set of interrelated variables, the logical progression of simulation would be from a preponderance of all-person or combination person-computer versions to an increasing reliance on all-computer simulations. The limiting factor is whether relationships among variables are sufficiently understood to be expressed in quantitative terms and fed into the computer. At present, few relationships are so well-analyzed; thus, the bulk of simulations involve human actors, sometimes with an assist from computer technology.

Application: The community action simulation. Klein (1975) has developed a useful simulation, in which community members' knowledge of real world conditions plays an important part. The community-action simulation (CAS) revolves around actual community groups that are attempting to achieve specific objectives (e.g., a coalition of Spanish-speaking groups seeking bilingual education in the public schools of their city). The community or action group helps to create the simulation by identifying other groups—allies, opponents, or significant neutrals—which are relevant to their situation. Such groups become part of the simulation and interact with the action group as it attempts to achieve its objective. For example, a simulation of an attempt of a community mental health center to form a coalition to work on the problem of drug abuse included an adolescent drug user, a suburban parent, an ex-addict, and a nondrug-user senior high school student (Klein, 1975).

The CAS also includes three social-psychological variables that can affect the nature of interaction among community groups: trust, social distance, and power. *Trust* refers to the extent to which one group feels that another group's motives are beneficent and that its agreements will be honored. Each group rates the others on a scale from 0 to 9. A rating of 0, for example, implies that no trust exists and communication between the two groups is restricted in terms of both nature and amount of contact.

Social distance refers to the ease with which community groups can contact each other. "In real life, opportunities for direct contact between groups vary according to such factors as socioeconomic status of group members, location of leaders' and members' residences, extent of member-ships in overlapping social groups, and political and social values'' (Klein, 1975, p. 361). Ratings of social distance between groups are used to deter-mine how many contact points a group must use to make contact with any other group.

Power in CAS is defined as "the ability of a group to realize its will in a communal action despite resistance from others participating in the situa-tion'' (Klein, 1975, p. 362). In the CAS, the formula by which power points are assigned to each group is not made known to them; neither is any group told the number of power points it possesses. Instead, as in real life, groups are left to operate as best they can on the basis of their own judgments about their ability to influence others.

Data are collected in the CAS in several ways. Researchers typically observe the behavior of participants and, of course, it is possible to deter-mine the extent to which they agree on their observations. There are also "critique sessions" during which participants, no longer in role, are de-briefed: they complete questionnaires that assess their satisfaction with life in the simulated community; they also rate trust, perceived power, and social distance among the groups, and the extent to which they believe group goals are being achieved. In addition, participants compare conditions in the simulation to conditions in "real life" to help researchers understand the phenomena being simulated.

The CAS has been used successfully with a variety of action groups including, for example, a community mental health center, a school/commu-nity council, and a group ministry working on race relations in a suburban county (Klein, 1975). Participants' post-simulation evaluations of the method have been highly favorable. By involving actual community groups, the CAS has a unique advantage: the results it generates can be compared to real world outcomes to determine whether and how realistically it repre-sented the essential characteristics of a community.

Strengths and weaknesses. The critical test for a simulation is how well it reproduces real world conditions. In other words, does the simulation enable one to make valid generalizations to actual social phenomena? Most directors of community simulations are convinced that participants' behav-ior in simulations is an authentic reflection of what would happen in real life (Sheperd, 1970). There is, however, a clear risk of making invalid generaliza-tions to real social phenomena. Researchers and participants may get drawn into playing the game for its own sake, creating a mass of data having to do with that game but possibly with little else in the real world.

Devising a good simulation is like devising a good portrait. How do we know whether the portrait is a good likeness of the subject? The answer lies in the agreement of those who know the subject best. Similarly, it has been suggested that, in community simulation, "the crucial tests . . . are evalua-tions of professionals whose competence includes the phenomena that are being modeled. They are likely to know the most about the working of the real world'' (Meier, 1964, p. iii). The test of "knowing" can also be extended to include a variety of other participants in that real world of which the simulation is, at best, an analogue—namely, community leaders, representatives of various constituencies, and government officials. The Community Action Simulation discussed above is an example of a simulation that increases its validity by involving community members.

Simulation involving human actors with or without computers seems especially well suited to community inquiry. Because of the community's multi-systemic nature, it is difficult, and usually impossible, to carry out direct observation of the multiple and often simultaneous phenomena involved in any sequence of events deemed worthy of study. One available substitute for direct observation of or participation in actual phenomena is a simulated version.

Advantages of the approach for the study of community complexities include (Raser, 1969): (1) *Economy:* running a model is usually far less expensive in terms of time, energy, and money than studying the "real thing." Complex space and extended time can be collapsed into manageable packages, sometimes involving little but game boards (e.g., Community Land Use Game; Feldt, 1966), and other times involving one or more rooms full of charts and diagrams, players' locations, and reams of printout material from well-fed computers (e.g., Metropolis; Duke & Meier, 1966). (2) *Safety:* "laboratory analogues" of dangerous phenomena protect the health and safety of human participants. (3) *Staging the future:* researchers can explore alternatives within a future that has not yet transpired. (4) *Studying processes in ways that nature prohibits:* it is possible to explore conditions that rarely occur (e.g., wars and riots); to replicate events that occur only once in nature (e.g., a specific international situation); and to start or stop events at will. (5) *Accessibility:* inquirers can gain access to events that occur "behind closed doors" (e.g., military strategy meetings, political decision making).

Field Experiments in the Community

There are times when a community researcher is confronted with decisions or questions concerning which of two or more programs, policies, or practices is most effective in accomplishing some goal or aim. The question may be a practical one requiring information as a guide to action, or the question may have theoretical implications and aid the researcher in choosing between theoretical hypotheses, or both. The best way for a researcher to ask the question or to test the hypothesis is to conduct a true field experiment which compares the effects of programs and asks which is superior in achieving a particular outcome.

Unfortunately, the social world seldom arranges itself so it is easy to conduct a true experiment to decide unequivocally whether differences in the outcome between two programs or policies actually are due to differences between the programs rather than some other unknown factor. The only way to test the effects of the two programs so we can be reasonably sure the programs actually are producing the observed effects is to randomly distribute the people across the various programs. In this way we are sure that whatever differences we observe are due to differences between the programs and not to some systematic difference between the people receiving them.

In the laboratory, it is relatively easy to control systematic differences between people receiving different experimental treatments by random assignment. In the relatively well-controlled world of the laboratory experimenter, true experiments are commonplace, and reliable answers to experimental questions often are possible. When one takes the community for one's laboratory, however, arranging circumstances to take advantage of the great strength of random assignment in ruling out alternative hypotheses is considerably more difficult. For example, even if it is possible to establish two models of health care delivery, one using nonprofessional personnel and one a more traditional service, it may be quite difficult to arrange to have physicians randomly refer patients to each service. They may believe that they already "know" which service is superior, or less costly, and may be concerned about the consequences of referring patients to the alternative that they see as less desirable.

Nevertheless, there are notable examples of true field experiments conducted in the community that do capitalize on the power of random assignment, and these have provided us with relatively clear-cut answers to questions about the relative effectiveness of different programs or policies. One set of such experiments has been conducted by Fairweather and his colleagues (Fairweather, 1964, 1967; Fairweather, Sanders, & Tornatzky, 1974).

Fairweather calls his approach "experimental social innovation." In this approach, he tests an innovative program, practice, or policy experimentally in the community, often comparing it with some alternative approach that already exists in common practice. Fairweather and Tornatzky (1977) observe:

> when a society is unable to solve a particularly pressing social problem, it becomes necessary for someone in that society to innovate new social programs that might alleviate the problem. The new social models that are created to solve the problem represent the *innovative* aspect of experimental social innovation (p. 27).

For example, one could test open admission policies in educational institutions and compare them with more typical closed admission policies to evaluate their relative effectiveness. Or, one could compare new health delivery systems that make much broader use of paramedical persons for treatment of routine problems, with more traditional approaches that make heavy use of highly trained and expensive medical personnel.

Fairweather and his colleagues make the important point that experimental tests of this kind should be longitudinal in nature. That is, they should follow people receiving the alternative programs over relatively long time periods to avoid premature conclusions about the relative effectiveness of one approach versus another. Such conclusions could lead to premature and unfortunate policy decisions. In addition, a solution found to be successful at one point in time may lose its effectiveness as the cultural environment of the community changes or as the criteria for success shift with changes in the social environment. In periods of high employment, for example, the most important criterion may be job satisfaction rather than employment; but, in periods of high unemployment, these criteria could be reversed in importance.

Application. Recall the example that appeared at the beginning of the previous chapter on community research. If you were committed to the idea that ex-mental patients should live as independently as possible after discharge from the hospital, what program would you develop? How would you know if your alternative was more effective than existing practice?

Fairweather and his colleagues conducted a series of experiments that nicely illustrate their approach to this problem. Their studies were designed to discover what could be done about the problem of increased chronic hospitalization, in which large numbers of patients who enter psychiatric hospitals, remain there, and find it difficult to return to a productive life in the community.

After a series of preliminary studies, Fairweather and his colleagues compared two major approaches to community placement. The first linked small groups of patients, who had worked with each other closely in the hospital in a small group therapeutic context, to community health agencies whose goals were to aid the community adjustment of patients with whom they worked individually. The second, which Fairweather described as the social innovation, linked the small group program within the hospital to a newly created "small society" run by ex-patients "so that hospital training permits the continuation of cohesive small group membership in the community" (1977, p. 37). Fairweather and his colleagues called this innovation the "Community Lodge." In the community lodge approach, a group would be moved out of the hospital as a unit rather than individually so the supportive relationships developed in the hospital could be transferred to the community lodge setting to aid patients in adaptation to their new life circumstances.

The researchers developed a number of administrative agreements with community agencies, the hospital itself, and a large university so that random assignment of patient groups to one of these two social models was possible. The experiment was longitudinal in nature and took place over a period of five years. In evaluating this social experiment, Fairweather and his colleagues found that the employment rate for the community lodge residents was significantly greater when compared with the more traditional program, and the return rate to the hospital was significantly lower as long as patients continued to reside in the lodge. In addition, patient costs were reduced to a small fraction of the cost of hospitalization, and the adjustment of those assigned to the community lodge was more adequate than those who participated in the traditional community mental health program.

As Fairweather and Tornatzky (1977) observe:

> the major variable manipulated in this study, of course, was the social role and status structure that historically exists in mental health organization between patients and mental health workers. Rather than mental health professionals supervising patients' behaviors, they helped them attain and sharpen their own decision-making processes and thus participated in liberating rather than controlling them (p. 39).

Strengths and weaknesses. The major strength of field experiments, in general, and Fairweather's experimental social innovation approach, in particular, is associated with the fact that it is a true experiment. Since patients had been randomly assigned to each of the two approaches, great confidence can be placed in the conclusion that the difference observed between the two programs were differences due to the programs themselves and not just some other characteristic of the patients receiving each of the programs.

Limitations of the field experiment approach exist as well. One of them simply has to do with the fact that conducting a field experiment presumes substantial prior knowledge about the problem being studied and the possible effects of the alternative treatments. Thus, as Fairweather and his colleagues observe, field experiments are best conducted once one has done a considerable amount of preliminary field research using other methods to sharpen our understanding of the problem and the probable effects of the treatment.

A second limitation of field experiments is practical. There are times when developing administrative arrangements to randomly assign patients, students, or health care recipients to one form of treatment versus another is very difficult no matter how persistent or clever the experimenter may be, even assuming that the ethical consequences of assigning people to one treatment versus another are not problematic. If there is good reason that one treatment may produce negative side effects, for example, then practical problems are compounded by ethical dilemmas, since we must decide whether the benefit of the knowledge gained outweighs the risk to participants. Because of these difficulties, experimenters often must settle for various quasi-experimental field research approaches, which we will discuss below.

Quasi-Experimental Approaches

In many field studies it is possible to approximate key features of the experimental method that enable researchers to establish causal relationships among variables. The term *quasi-experimental* refers to a collection of research designs that approximate, in varying degrees, the conditions of true experiments. This approach to research has been developed in the work of

Campbell and Stanley (1963, 1966) and Cook and Campbell (1979), who have identified two types of quasi-experiments: nonequivalent control group designs and time series designs. Distinctive features of each type of quasi-experiment are discussed below.

Nonequivalent control group designs. As we indicated in the previous section, one of the most salient characteristics of laboratory research is the random assignment of participants to either control groups or experimental groups that are exposed to an "independent variable" manipulated by the researcher. Random assignment, of course, typically insures that control or comparison groups are, on the average, similar to experimental groups. As a consequence, any differences in performance between an experimental group and a control group can be attributed to the effects of an independent variable.

In community research, however, it is often impossible, for a variety of ethical and practical reasons, to randomly assign persons, organizations, or communities to experimental and control conditions. In many instances, an intervention affects every person in a setting, precluding the possibility of randomly assigning persons to a control group. For example, a program to improve reading achievement in a classroom would affect all children in the class. But, it is possible for researchers to identify groups that are similar to an experimental group exposed to a treatment or independent variable. In other words, a control group that *is not* formed by random assignment can be used to make comparisons with the behavior of an experimental group. Such research designs are termed *nonequivalent control group* designs.

The effective use of nonequivalent control group designs depends, to a great extent, on the researcher's ability to find or arrange suitable control groups. Selecting control groups that are as equivalent as possible to experimental or treatment groups requires researchers to consider a wide range of variables that may make two groups differ from one another. If researchers are attempting to match individuals in two groups, for example, such factors as socioeconomic status, race, sex, and age are important to consider. Or, consider a unit of analysis, such as a school or classroom. In this case, a comparison group should be selected on the basis of similarity in the demographic characteristics of students and teachers, size of setting, curriculum methods, organizational patterns, and type of community (Linney & Reppucci, 1982).

The task of insuring equivalence between groups is made easier to the extent that researchers have control over the introduction of the independent variable and other aspects of the social systems under study. Mulvey and Reppucci (1983), for example, introduced a conflict resolution training program in a community police department using a simple nonequivalent control group design. Half of the police officers were trained in a two-week session, while the remaining officers served as a nonrandomly selected control group. Eight weeks later the second group was trained, and effects of the training were assessed for both groups.

Nonequivalent control group designs can involve much more than a simple comparison of the performances of two groups. The use of multiple groups, time lags, and various pre and post tests can be introduced to strengthen the ability of a design to rule out alternative explanations for differences between control and experimental groups. At the same time, there remain many threats to the validity of such designs that have been discussed in detail in the excellent volume by Cook and Campbell (1979). A more detailed example of the use of a nonequivalent control group design is given below.

Time series designs. Time series designs consist of a sequence of observations of behavior or events over time. Observations can be made of the same units or on different but similar measurement units. For example, to monitor performance on the Scholastic Aptitude Test (SAT) over time, the scores of different people each year would be examined. On the other hand, one could observe the achievement scores of a particular group of children over a number of years.

The logic of the time series design is relatively straightforward. The introduction of an independent variable (e.g., treatment or intervention) is expected to produce a change in the persons, groups, or social systems under observation. The intervention or treatment "interrupts" a series of observations at a specified point or points in time. If an intervention does indeed have an effect, the time series preceding it should differ from the time series consequent to it. Delaney, Seidman, and Willis (1978), for example, used a time series design to assess the impact of a crisis intervention service on admissions to a psychiatric hospital. Rates for admission to the hospital before the introduction of the service were compared to rates following the start of the service. A graph of hospitalization rates showed a significant decline in the number of admissions following the introduction of the service.

It is important to emphasize that a simple time series design is relatively weak in ruling out alternative explanations for a change in the variable of interest. The changes in admission rates reported in the Delaney et al. study, as pointed out by Linney and Reppucci (1982), might have been the result of long-term trends in the region, seasonal fluctuation, or the opening of a new factory in the area providing jobs for residents. The design as it stands does not enable one to rule out these alternative explanations for the results. Hence, several methodologists have pointed out the desirability of combining time series with nonequivalent control group designs (e.g., Cook & Campbell, 1979; Linney & Reppucci, 1982). An example of such a combination is given below.

Application: The Stanford Heart Disease Prevention Study. It is possible to develop a mass media campaign to reduce the risk of heart disease? How should such a program be evaluated? These questions were actually addressed by researchers evaluating the effects of a three-year community-wide public health campaign in northern California.

The researchers conducted a quasi-experiment that had characteristics of both time series and nonequivalent control group designs. Three communities were selected for the study: one community received health education messages via radio, television, and newspapers; a second community received the same media messages in conjunction with intensive instruction given to a randomly selected group of persons who were considered to be "at risk" for heart problems; the third community received no treatment. It is important to note that the communities were selected on the basis of their similarity along key dimensions, such as total population, geographic location, age of population, and the like. In other words, the researchers attempted to insure that the communities were as alike as possible.

Data were collected at four points over a three-year period, producing a time series of observations. Prior to the interventions, baseline data were gathered in interviews and medical examinations involving a random sample of people (aged 35 to 59) from each of the communities. Data were then collected at yearly intervals from the same groups of people to determine if changes had occurred in their behavior.

Data, such as age, sex, plasma cholesterol concentration, systolic blood pressure, relative weight, smoking rate, and electrocardiologic findings, were used to calculate a score indicating each person's risk of developing coronary heart disease. This method for estimating the likelihood of heart disease had been developed in previous research. In addition, surveys assessed community members' knowledge of factors related to heart disease as well as their dietary habits and levels of physical activity.

Results showed that both the media campaign and the media campaign plus intensive instruction reduced the risk of heart disease compared to the no-treatment community. After two years, the level of estimated coronary disease risk decreased by 17 to 18 percent for persons living in the communities exposed to interventions, but risk actually increased by at least 6 percent in the untreated community.

It is important to note, however, that the media campaign alone was not as effective in reducing the risk of heart disease as the media campaign plus intensive instruction. The intensive treatment approach produced more significant and long-lasting change in a broader range of individuals' behavior (Meyer et al., 1980).

More detailed analyses showed that declines in risk for heart disease were due primarily to changes in smoking, in dietary practices, and in blood pressure. Dietary changes, for example, included significant reduction in individuals' consumption of cholesterol and saturated fat. Finally, the more participants learned from the media and instruction, the more they altered their behavior, thereby reducing the estimated risk of heart disease.

Strengths and weaknesses. At best, quasi-experiments enable researchers to make inferences about the causes of differences in the behavior of two

FIGURE 4–3
Survey and Campaign Sequences in the Three Communities*

	1972	1973		1974		1975	
Watsonville (W)		Baseline survey (S1)	• Media campaign • Intensive instruction (II) for ⅔ of high risk participants	Second survey (S2)	• Media campaign • Intensive instruction (II) for ⅔ of high risk participants	Third survey (S3)	• Maintenance (low-level) Media campaign • II: Summer follow-up	Fourth survey (S4)
Gilroy (G)		Baseline survey (S1)	• Media campaign	Second survey (S2)	• Media campaign	Third survey (S3)	• Maintenance (low-level) Media campaign	Fourth survey (S4)
Tracy (T)		Baseline survey (S1)		Second survey (S2)		Third survey (S3)		Fourth survey (S4)

* From Fahrquar, 1978.

or more groups, organizations, or communities. In other words, quasi-experiments can have some of the advantages of true field experiments, even though random assignment is, as noted above, often impossible for both ethical and practical reasons.

There are, however, relatively few instances in which one can have as much confidence in the results of quasi-experiments as true experiments. It is often the case that various circumstances conspire to limit researchers' ability to design "ideal" quasi-experiments. For example, an obvious problem with nonequivalent control group designs is that researchers simply may not be able to find or arrange control groups that are very similar to an experimental group. There are, of course, several more subtle problems that severely restrict the conclusions that can be drawn from comparisons between experimental groups and nonrandomly formed control groups. Consider, for example, instances in which people in a control group know that they are not receiving a desired treatment or intervention: the control group as an "underdog" may be motivated to reduce or reverse the expected effect of the treatment (Cook & Campbell, 1979). On the other hand, members of a control group may be demoralized in knowing that they are not receiving a desired treatment, and there may be a decrement in their performance. These possibilities exist for control group members in either true experiments or quasi-experiments. However, they can cause a more systematic bias in the results of quasi-experiments. Control group subjects in true experiments, because they were chosen randomly, may not know one another or have much close contact. On the other hand, nonequivalent control groups often are intact groups (e.g., a fourth-grade class, residents of a particular block or neighborhood and the like). Their proximity increases the likelihood that they will act in concert or develop similar perceptions of the experiment.

Demoralization and compensation are but two of several factors that can influence the results of quasi-experiments and limit their usefulness for the purpose of testing hypotheses and ruling out alternative explanations for phenomena. The important point is that researchers using quasi-experimental designs must proceed with caution, attempting to identify threats, such as demoralization, before conducting a study.

SUMMARY

In this last section of the chapter we discussed four action-oriented approaches to community research, and Table 4–2 (see pages 108–109) summarizes some of the important similarities and differences among these approaches. We observed that there is considerable variation among the action-oriented approaches and the degree to which researchers collaborate with community members. And we noted that the distinctive characteristics, strengths, and weaknesses of each approach also varied considerably. For example, the action research approach typically involved close collaboration with community members, while field experiments may involve little or no interaction with community participants.

On the other hand, the action-oriented approaches are similar in that the researchers exert at least a moderate degree of control over the variables or phenomenon of interest. In many instances, researchers using these approaches combine social action or intervention with research. We have noted, for example, that field experiments often are conducted to determine which of two or more service programs is superior in achieving a particular outcome. Of course, when researchers exert control over variables or events, they are more likely to be able to make inferences about cause-and-effect relationships.

It is important to recognize, however, that having moderate or even high degrees of control over variables is not always useful or desirable. Researchers whose purpose is to develop hypotheses and explore a phenomenon may find control unnecessary, or even misleading, if it involves disturbing the usual pattern of community processes. In addition, a high degree of control does not guarantee that we will be able to make valid inferences about causal relationships. In simulation research, for example, researchers have a great deal of control over the variables and events that are being simulated; but there remains a clear risk of making invalid generalizations to real world situations because of the artificial conditions in which the simulations are conducted.

We have now considered a broad array of community research approaches and, in the second half of this chapter, we have observed a variety of different ways in which community action can have the potential of improving community well-being. The wise application of community research methods provides us with an opportunity not only to develop new knowledge but also to assess the degree to which our research actually contributes to the well-being of community members.

TABLE 4-2
Summary of Key Characteristics of Four Action-Oriented Approaches to Research

	Action Research	Simulation	Field Experiment	Quasi-Experiment
Distinctive features	Researcher attempts to understand phenomena by changing them in close collaboration with community members	Researcher attempts to reproduce as many essential characteristics of phenomena as possible to learn about them in a controlled setting	Random assignment of participants to experimental and control conditions	Comparisons are made between experimental groups and control groups *not* randomly formed, or a single group's performance is observed at several intervals (i.e., time-series)
Degree of collaboration	High	High	Moderate	Moderate
Level of control	Moderate	High	High	Moderate
Purposes	Hypothesis testing Information as a guide to action Exploration and hypothesis formulation Develop and test new research techniques	Exploration and hypothesis formulation Information as a guide to action	Hypothesis testing Information as a guide to action Develop and test new research methods	Hypothesis testing Information as a guide to action Develop and test new research methods

Weaknesses	Researcher's involvement in social action may limit effectiveness as social scientist Difficult to establish causal relationships without adequate control groups	There is a risk of making invalid generalizations to real world events; can oversimplify events in unknown ways	Sometimes difficult for practical and/or ethical reasons to randomly assign participants to various conditions	Results are not always as interpretable as those of true experiments because there is no random assignment
Strengths	Ideally, contributes to social science theory and social change simultaneously Collaboration with community members leads to many insights for researchers	More economical than field study Allows the study of "future" events and those typically inaccessible Allows the study of processes in ways that nature prohibits	Enables one to make inferences about cause-effect relationships Combines intervention with research in many instances	Well-designed quasi-experiments enable causal inferences without the constraints sometimes associated with random assignments

References

Barnes, J. A. Class and communities in a Norwegian island parish. *Human Relations,* 1954, *7,* 39–58.

Becker, H. S. *Boys in white.* Chicago: University of Chicago Press, 1961.

Bell, C., & Newby, H. *Community studies.* New York: Praeger Publishers, 1972.

Bogdan, R., & Taylor, S. J. *Introduction to qualitative research methods: A phenomenological approach to the social sciences.* New York: John Wiley & Sons, 1975.

Boissevain, J. *Friends of friends: Networks, manipulators and coalitions.* Oxford, England: Blackwell, 1974.

Bott, E. *Family and social networks.* London: Tavistock, 1957.

Brenner, M. H. *Mental illness and the economy.* Cambridge, Mass.: Harvard University Press, 1973.

Campbell, A., Converse, P. E., & Rodgers, W. L. *The quality of American life: Perceptions, evaluations and satisfactions.* New York: Russell Sage Foundation, 1976.

Campbell, D. T., & Stanley, J. C. Experimental and quasi-experimental designs for research and teaching. In N. L. Gage (Ed.), *Handbook of research on teaching.* Skokie, Ill.: Rand McNally, 1963.

Campbell, D. T., & Stanley, J. C. *Experimental and quasi-experimental designs for research.* Skokie, Ill.: Rand McNally, 1966.

Cartwright, D. Theory and practice. *Journal of Social Issues,* 1978, *34,* 168–180.

Catalano, R., & Dooley, D. Economic predictors of depressed mood and stressful life events in a metropolitan community. *Journal of Health and Social Behavior,* 1977, *18,* 292–307.

Chesler, M., & Flanders, M. Resistance to research and research utilization: The death and life of a feedback attempt. *Journal of Applied Behavioral Science,* 1967, *3,* 469–487.

Clark, A. W. (Ed.). *Experimenting with organizational life: The action research approach.* New York: Plenum, 1976.

Cook, T. D., & Campbell, D. T. *Advanced level quasi-experimentation: Design and analysis issues for field settings.* Skokie, Ill.: Rand McNally College Publishing Co., 1979.

Davison, G. C., & Neale, J. M. *Abnormal psychology: An experimental clinical approach.* New York: John Wiley & Sons, 1978.

Delaney, J. A., Seidman, E., & Willis, G. Crisis intervention and the prevention of institutionalization: An interrupted time series analysis. *American Journal of Community Psychology,* 1978, *6,* 33–46.

Denzin, N. K. *The research act: A theoretical introduction to sociological methods.* New York: McGraw-Hill, 1978.

Dohrenwend, B. P., & Dohrenwend, B. S. Social and cultural influences on psychopathology. *Annual Review of Psychology,* 1974, *25,* 417–450.

Dooley, D., & Catalano, R. Money and mental disorder: Toward behavioral cost accounting for primary prevention. *American Journal of Community Psychology,* 1977, *5,* 217–227.

Dooley, D., & Catalano, R. Economic change as a cause of behavioral disorder. *Psychological Bulletin,* 1980, *87,* 450–468.

Duke, R. *Gaming simulation for urban research.* Lansing, Mich.: Institute for Community Development and Services, Michigan State University, 1964.

Duke, R., & Meier, R. Gaming simulation for urban planning. *Journal of the American Institute of Planners,* 1966, *32,* 3–17.

Dutton, J. M., & Starbuck, W. H. (Eds.). *Computer stimulation of human behavior.* New York: John Wiley & Sons, 1971.

Erikson, K. T. A comment on disguised observation in sociology. *Social Problems,* 1967, *14,* 366–373.

Estroff, S. E. *Making it crazy.* Berkeley: University of California Press, 1981.

Fahrquar, J. W. The Community-Based Model of Life-Style Intervention Trials. *American Journal of Epidemiology,* 1978, *108,* 103–111.

Fairweather, G. W. (Ed.) *Social psychology in treating mental illness: An experimental approach.* New York: John Wiley & Sons, 1964.

Fairweather, G. W. *Methods for experimental social innovation.* New York: John Wiley & Sons, 1967.

Fairweather, G. W., Sanders, D. H., & Tornatzky, L. G. *Creating change in mental health organizations.* New York: Pergamon Press, 1974.

Fairweather, G. W., & Tornatzky, L. G. *Experimental methods for social policy research.* New York: Pergamon Press, 1977.

Feldt, A. Operational gaming in planning education. *Journal of the American Institute of Planners,* 1966, *32,* 17–23.

Festinger, L., Schachter, S., & Riecken, H. W. *When prophecy fails.* Minneapolis: University of Minnesota Press, 1956.

Festinger, L. *A theory of cognitive dissonance.* New York: Harper & Row, 1957.

Galaskiewicz, J., & Shatin, D. Leadership and networking among neighborhood human service organizations. *Administrative Science Quarterly,* 1981, *26,* 434–448.

Gold, R. L. Roles in sociological field observations. *Social Forces,* 1958, *36,* 217–223.

Gottlieb, B. H. (Ed.) *Social networks and social support.* Beverly Hills, Calif.: Sage Publications, 1981.

Granovetter, M. S. The strength of weak ties. *American Journal of Sociology,* 1973, *78,* 1360–1380.

Guetzkow, H., Kotler, P., & Schultz, R. L. (Eds.). *Simulation in social and administrative science.* Englewood Cliffs, N.J.: Prentice-Hall, 1972.

Hirsch, B. J. Natural support systems and coping with major life changes. *American Journal of Community Psychology,* 1980, *8,* 159–172.

Hochschild, A. R. *The unexpected community: Portrait of an old age subculture.* Berkeley: University of California Press, 1978.

Holahan, C. J. Action research in the built environment. In R. H. Price & P. E. Politser (Eds.), *Evaluation and action in the social environment.* New York: Academic Press, 1980.

Holland, E. P. Simulation of an economy with development and trade problems. In Guetzkow, Kotler, & Schultz (Eds.), *Simulation in social and administrative science.* Englewood Cliffs, N.J.: Prentice-Hall, 1972.

Hollingshead, A. B., & Redlich, F. C. *Social class and mental illness.* New York: John Wiley & Sons, 1958.

Junker, B. H. *Field work: An introduction to the social sciences.* Chicago: University of Chicago Press, 1960.

Ketterer, R. F., Price, R. H., & Politser, P. E. The action research paradigm. In R. H. Price & P. E. Politser (Eds.), *Evaluation and action in the social environment*. New York: Academic Press, 1980.

Klein, D. C. Macrosystem simulation for community research and problem-solving. *American Journal of Community Psychology*, 1975, *3*, 353–366.

Land, K. C., & Spilerman, S. (Eds.) *Social indicator models*. New York: Russell Sage Foundation, 1975.

Lewin, K. Action research and minority problems. *Journal of Social Issues*, 1946, *2*(4), 34–46.

Lewin, K. Frontiers in group dynamics: Part II, Social planning and action research. *Human Relations*, 1947, *1*, 143–153.

Lewin, K. *Field theory in social science*. New York: Harper & Row, 1951.

Liebert, K. J., & Imershein, A. W. *Power, paradigms and community research*. Beverly Hills, Calif.: Sage Publications, 1977.

Liebow, E. *Tally's corner*. Boston: Little, Brown, 1967.

Linney, J. A., & Reppucci, N. D. Research design and methods in community psychology. In P. C. Kendall and J. N. Butcher (Eds.), *Handbook of research methods in clinical psychology*. New York: John Wiley & Sons, 1982 (pp. 535–566).

Lofland, J. *Analyzing social settings: A guide to qualitative observation and analysis*. Belmont, Calif.: Wadsworth, 1971.

MacMahon, B., & Pugh, T. *Epidemiology: Principles and methods*. Boston: Little, Brown, 1970.

Meier, R. Preface in R. Duke (Ed.), *Gaming simulation for urban research*. Lansing, Mich.: Institute for Community Development and Services, Michigan State University, 1964.

Meyer, A. J., Nash, J. D., McAlister, A. L., Maccoby, N., & Farquhar, J. W. Skills training in a cardiovascular health education campaign. *Journal of Consulting and Clinical Psychology*, 1980, *48*, 129–142.

Mitchell, J. C. (Ed.). *Social networks in urban situations*. Manchester, England: Manchester University Press, 1969.

Mitchell, R. E., & Trickett, E. J. Task force report: Social networks as mediators of social support: An analysis of the effects and determinants of social networks. *Community Mental Health Journal*, 1980, *16*(1), 27–44.

Moreno, J. L. *Who shall survive? A new approach to the study of human relations*. Washington, D.C.: Nervous and Mental Disease Publishing, 1934.

Mulvey, E. P., & Reppucci, N. D. Police crisis intervention training: An empirical investigation. *American Journal of Community Psychology*, 1983, in press.

Parke, R., & Seidman, D. Social indicators and social reporting. In C. Taeuber (Ed.), *America in the seventies: Some social indicators*. Philadelphia: The American Academy of Political and Social Science, 1978.

Politser, P. E. Network analysis and the logic of social support. In R. H. Price & P. E. Politser (Eds.), *Evaluation and action in the social environment*. New York: Academic Press, 1980.

Price, R. H., & Cherniss, C. Training for a new profession: Research as social action. *Professional Psychology*, May 1977, 222–230.

Rappoport, A., & Orwant, C. J. *Prisoner's dilemma: A study in conflict and management*. Ann Arbor: University of Michigan Press, 1965.

Raser, J. *Simulation and society: An exploration of scientific gaming*. Boston: Allyn & Bacon, 1969.

Riger, S., & Gordon, M. T. The fear of rape: A study in social control. *Journal of Social Issues*, 1981, *37*(4), 71–92.

Sarason, S. B. Community psychology, networks, and Mr. Everyman. *American Psychologist*, 1976a, *31*, 317–328.

Selltiz, C., Wrightsman, L., & Cook, S. *Research methods in social relations*. New York: Holt, Rinehart & Winston, 1976.

Sheldon, E. B., & Freeman, H. E. Notes on social indicators: Promises and potential. *Policy Sciences*, 1970, *1*, 97–111.

Sheperd, C. *Simulation games: Potential sociological utilization*. Unpublished paper, University of Cincinnati, 1970.

Skogan, W. G. Crime in contemporary America. In H. Graham and T. R. Gurr (Eds.), *Violence in America* (2d ed.). Beverly Hills, Calif.: Sage Publications, 1978.

Spradley, J. S. *You owe yourself a drunk: An ethnography of urban nomads*. Boston: Little, Brown, 1970.

Spradley, J. S. *The ethnographic interview*. New York: Holt, Rinehart & Winston, 1979.

Srole, L., Langner, T. S., Michael, S. T., Opler, M. K., & Rennie, T. A. *Mental health in the metropolis: The midtown Manhattan study*. New York: McGraw-Hill, 1962.

Tichy, N. M. Networks in organizations. In P. C. Nystrom & W. H. Starbuck (Eds.), *Handbook of organizational design* (Vol. II). London: Oxford University Press, 1980.

Turk, H. Interorganizational networks in the urban society: Initial perspectives and comparative research. *American Sociological Review*, 1970, *30*, 1–19.

Turk, H. *Interorganizational activation in urban communities: Deductions from the concept of system*. Washington, D.C.: American Sociological Association, 1973.

Turk, H. *Organizations in modern life*. Englewood Cliffs, N.J.: Prentice-Hall, 1972.

Wortman, P. M. Evaluation research: A methodological perspective. *Annual Review of Psychology*, 1983, *34*,

Zax, M., & Spector, G. A. *An introduction to community psychology*. New York: John Wiley & Sons, 1974.

PART THREE

Basic Concepts

CHAPTER FIVE

Ecological and Environmental Influences on the Individual*

---

* Stephanie Riger was the primary author of this chapter. Abe Wandersman wrote the sections on "community."

COMMUNITY AS RELATIONSHIPS AND RESOURCES
Neighboring and Networks
Neighboring Functions
The Social Organization of Neighborhoods

THE ATTACHMENT BETWEEN THE INDIVIDUAL AND THE COMMUNITY: SENSE OF COMMUNITY

SUMMARY OF ECOLOGICAL CONCEPTS

INTRODUCTION

W hy does a student fail at one college but flourish at another? Is it simply a question of personal skills, effort, and maturity, or can the college environment itself influence whether one will succeed or fail? One study which took the latter point of view assumed that college environments exert pressures, practices and policies intended to influence the development of students, and that these environments vary in different colleges (Pace & Stern, 1958). Environmental influences were measured with a scale called the College Characteristics Index which asked for true/false answers to statements about college life. The results of administering the scale to students and faculty at several colleges indicated that significant differences existed in the college environments. For example, the climate at one college emphasized social activity, helping others, and civic responsibility, while at another the intellectual life and the pursuit of understanding for its own sake were paramount. A student with a high need for order might find this need satisfied by the climate of one school but frustrated by another. He or she might fail, or find few friends in one school and be perfectly contented in another. Thus, it is the pattern of congruence between personal needs and the environment, rather than characteristics of either alone, that determine achievement and growth in college.

This study is typical of an *ecological* approach to psychology, an approach which emphasizes the relationship between people and their environments rather than examining the characteristics of either in isolation. In this chapter we will briefly examine the origins of the ecological perspective as they are found in biological ecology and as first applied to community settings by early sociologists (known as "human ecologists"), and then consider the ways psychologists define and measure environments. We will look at the impact of environmental and community fluctuations on people in order to understand the ways in which these influences can affect behavior and psychological well-being. Finally, we will consider different aspects of the meaning of "community."

BIOLOGICAL AND HUMAN ECOLOGY

Ecological theory has its roots in a tradition dating back to 19th-century biologists such as Charles Darwin. Darwin (1859) explained the diversity of plants and animals as the outcome of a natural process of adaptation, instead of attributing it to a divine master plan. "In the Galapagos Islands, off the west coast of South America, Darwin noted that slight environmental differences between islands only a few miles apart had produced recognizably different varieties of turtles from the same ancestral species" (Catalano, 1979, p. 17). Certain species characteristics survived while others died out because of their lack of usefulness in the struggle for survival within a particular environment. Ultimately the survival of a species depends on the fit between the organism and the environment. To understand differences among species, then, one must examine the features of the habitat, and how these features change over time.

Species compete for desirable (i.e., resource-rich) land areas, resulting in invasion, succession, and eventual dominance of a land area by one species after another (Catalano, 1979). Ingredients in the environment, such as soil, moisture, and temperature, determine which types of plants and animals will best thrive there; these plants and animals will in turn affect the environment's capacity to support them. In a stable ecosystem, these elements change slowly, and organisms appear able to adjust to changes in the environment in a self-regulating process. Catastrophic or sudden changes in the environment can radically alter this process. As we have learned to our dismay through such examples as chemical dumps which pollute a town's water supply, human intervention sometimes can irreversibly—albeit unintentionally—damage the ecosystem.

Ecological theory focuses on the fit between an organism and its environment, and how that relationship changes over time. Biologists were so successful in explaining change in subhuman populations by using this theory that, in the 1920s, sociologists and geographers adopted it to explain change in human populations as well (Bernard, 1973; Catalano, 1979).

THE APPLICATION OF ECOLOGICAL THEORY TO SOCIAL ENVIRONMENTS

The French sociologist Emile Durkheim is considered the first social scientist to trace systematically the relationship between individual abnormal behavior and variations in the social environment. In his study, *Suicide* (1897), he demonstrated that different social groups (e.g., males and females; married and unmarried people) have different rates of suicide. Therefore, an act as seemingly private as suicide is not only a matter of the individual's decision but also of group influence.

The use of ecological theory as a tool for understanding human behavior is a hallmark of the early "Chicago school" of sociology. As indicated in the chapter on historical trends, the last half of the 19th century and the beginning of the 20th century in the United States was a time of rapid industrialization and urbanization, marked by the arrival of waves of rural and foreign-born immigrants to rapidly expanding cities. Chicago was an archetypal case, and sociologists at the University of Chicago attempted to explain patterns of growth in the city and the behavior of these new urbanites by borrowing several concepts from biological ecology and applying them to human communities (Bernard, 1973; Catalano, 1979). According to these "human ecologists," such as Robert Park and Ernest Burgess, cities developed in predictable patterns. Links among people producing goods and services and the materials needed for the production process were analogous to the biologists' notion of the "web of life" in an ecosystem. The desire to increase security paralleled subhuman species' drive for survival.

Human ecologists emphasized the spatial distribution of populations and activities in the city. Land use followed patterns of competition, invasion, and succession. Limits on urban space intensified that competition for land use, and led to the segregation of activities in different districts, ideally described as five concentric zones ranging from the central business district to the outer residential rings. The low-rent zone lying between the central business district and workingmen's homes (called the "zone in transition") attracted new urban migrants and those whose behavior did not match the requirements of the setting (i.e., "misfits"). These people either had not yet learned or were unable to learn the skills and behavioral expectations optimal for the new setting. Thus, ecological theory predicted that rates of abnormal behavior would be highest in this zone. This hypothesis was partially supported in a study conducted by Warran Dunham (1937). He identified the home communities of Chicago psychiatric patients who were hospitalized between 1922 and 1934, and found that patients diagnosed as schizophrenic were likely to come from this area.

Much of the work of the Chicago school of sociology consisted of chronicling the behavior of people living in the zone in transition, as reflected in the titles of such classic works as *The Gang, The Hobo,* and *The Gold Coast and the Slum.* By the early 1940s, several challenges were mounted to the Chicago school's findings and to the ecological paradigm itself. If the zone in transition was populated by the least "fit" people, by whose standard were they unfit? For example, in the study mentioned above of psychiatric patients in Chicago, richer patients were more likely to be diagnosed as manic-depressive, while the poor were more likely to receive a diagnosis of schizophrenia. This suggests a social class bias in labeling forms of mental illness. Was fitness simply a function of competition, or did such factors as fluctuating labor markets and racism affect the standards of "fitness?" Ecological theory is based on a free market model, in which economic rationality is the prime mover. In fact, we do not operate under a free market, since corporate monopolies and government regulations affect economic decisions.

Ecological theory remains useful today in that it directs us to look at the complex interrelationship between organisms and their environments, and to consider problems of behavior as dysfunctional adaptations to a particular set of environmental circumstances.

ELEMENTS OF AN ECOLOGICAL PERSPECTIVE

James Kelly (1966, 1968, 1971, 1975, 1979; Mills & Kelly, 1972; Trickett, Kelley, & Todd, 1972) has been a prolific pioneer in the application of concepts derived from biological and human ecology to the area of community intervention. For Kelly, the ecological perspective "provides a dynamic frame of reference which analyzes changes in terms of the particular setting in which they occur" (Mills & Kelly, 1972). Kelly proposes four principles, derived from biological ecology, as a guide to the planning of community interventions:

1. Interdependence. Whenever any component of a natural biome (or "ecosystem") is changed, there are alterations between all other components of the system as well. Intervention in one community problem, or with one community agency, invariably will have an effect (for better or worse) on other community problems or agencies. Changes in the mental health system (e.g., closing state hospitals) have ramifications that will be felt by law enforcement and welfare agencies, and vice versa. Releasing large numbers of mental hospital patients in order to "deinstitutionalize" the mentally ill has vastly increased the cadres of the homeless who wander the streets in large urban areas, putting a strain on social service agencies. This principle suggests that a narrow attention to traditional "mental health" problems— without viewing them in relation to other problems—is a doomed effort. The notion of interdependence implies that we must take the community as our unit of concern (Kelly, 1966) and intervene at multiple levels and in roles not traditionally identified with the mental health professions.

2. The cycling of resources. A traditional research activity in biological ecology is the measurement of energy as it is transferred from the sun to plants, and from plants to animals. Trickett, Kelly, and Todd (1972) suggest that the transfer of community resources ("energy") is an important aspect of community functioning. An analysis of the existing definition and utilization of community resources is considered to be an essential prerequisite for devising an intervention that will modify the way in which resources are distributed. A community with a high proportion of families in which both parents work outside the home might mobilize elderly residents to be child-care workers, or might encourage local businesses to provide drop-in day-care facilities for children while parents shop.

3. Adaptation. For an organism to survive over time, it must be able to cope effectively with environmental changes. Those organisms that cannot adapt to environmental change (e.g., dinosaurs) become extinct. The manufacturers of buggy whips disappeared with the advent of the automobile; similarly, typewriter manufacturers may disappear if they cannot incorporate computer-based word-processing technology into their machines. Existing community resources should be strengthened so that those people in transition—those in the process of adapting to new roles and new environments—will find the necessary supports (Kelly, 1966). Self-help groups for widows or for new parents, for example, could ease the transition into these new roles.

4. Succession. Odum (cited in Trickett et al., 1972) defines the concept of succession in terms of three parameters: "(1) It is the orderly process of community changes; these are directional, and therefore, predictable; (2) It results from the modification of the physical environment by the community; (3) It culminates in the establishment of as stable an ecosystem as is biologically possible on the site in question." The "gentrification" of urban neighborhoods appears to follow a predictable pattern of succession in many cities. First, young single people without children move into an area, undeterred by the local crime problem or poor schools and willing to make the effort to renovate housing. Renovations make an area charming and attractive, thus drawing in wealthier residents who have sufficient political clout to get local city services, such as garbage collection and schools, upgraded. The area may become so desirable (and therefore expensive) that the original "ungentrified" residents can no longer afford to live there, completing the turnover from one economic group to another. The wealthy new residents' large economic stake in the area will prevent them from leaving easily, slowing the rate of population exchange and stabilizing the neighborhood at a higher socioeconomic level.

The principle of succession suggests that the direction in which a community is already changing must be taken into account in the planning of new intervention strategies. In planning for mental health services for children, for example, the principle of succession suggests that, rather than simply obtaining an estimate of the number of children currently in need of service, an estimate of the *rate of change* in the need for service would be needed. Given the same number of children currently in need of service, it would make a great deal of difference in planning if this number were 50 percent higher or 50 percent lower than the previous year.

In a more colloquial vein, Barry Commoner (1968) proposes that the four "laws of ecology" are:

1. Everything is connected to everything else.
2. Everything must go somewhere.
3. Nature knows best.
4. There is no such thing as a free lunch.

Commoner's first law is clearly the same as Kelly's principle of "interdependence." That everything must go somewhere reminds us that, if a problem is simply moved, it is not thereby solved. The assertion that nature knows best leads one to exercise caution whenever a "planned intervention" is attempted. The absence of free lunches likewise alerts the intervener to the possible unintended and hidden costs of intervention.

THE ROOTS OF THE ECOLOGICAL TRADITION WITHIN PSYCHOLOGY

Interest in an ecological approach has a long history in psychology, starting with Henry Murray's (1938) view that behavior was determined by both an individual's needs and the demands of his or her environment (the "environmental press"). This is perhaps best summarized by Kurt Lewin's (1951) classic formulation that human behavior is a function of the interaction of person and environment: B = f(P, E). The "person" side of the person-environment equation has received a great deal of attention from psychologists. Specifying what we mean by person is easy, since a person is a concrete entity with identifiable boundaries. Specifying what we mean by the environment is more problematic because we have few guidelines indicating what aspects of the environment are important for human behavior, and what the boundaries of the environment are.

Pioneering work on identifying environments was done by Roger Barker (1968) and his colleagues at the Midwestern Psychological Field Station of the University of Kansas. Although the Field Station looked like a quaint 19th century newspaper office complete with oak furniture and oscillating overhead fans, its establishment in 1947 marked a significant departure in psychology (Holahan, 1982; Price, 1976; Wicker, 1979a). Barker and his colleagues studied ordinary people as they engaged in everyday activities in a small Midwestern town, a radical shift from the traditional psychologists's interest in behavior within carefully controlled laboratory settings. Barker's goal was to record the "stream of behavior" as it is experienced by people— walking to school, shopping in a drugstore, attending a basketball game, and so on. He used the term *behavior setting* to refer to the naturally occurring spatial and temporal features that surround behavior and the appropriate behavioral match. The behavior setting is the basic environmental unit of ecological psychology. Barker and his colleagues set out to identify and describe such behavior settings in the town they called Midwest (Oskaloosa, Kansas) and to examine how settings influence people who inhabit them. To do so, they described specific places, the physical objects, the pattern of behavior, and the events that occurred in those places in order to understand the relationship between behavioral and nonbehavioral factors.

Barker identified the ecological environment of a behavior setting by "blotting out" the person and observing the events that occur around him or her. Suppose we want to understand the ecological environment of a first baseman in a ball game. Observing only the player's behavior would never let us understand the "game" that gives meaning to the player's actions, nor would learning the attitudes and aspirations of individual players. By blotting out the player and observing the game around him or her, the ecological environment of the player is made visible (Barker, 1968). This ecological environment has considerable coercive power over the behavior which occurs within it; that behavior can remain in a stable pattern for generation after generation within the same setting.

Barker and his colleagues produced detailed descriptions of behavior settings in the Midwest, and compared them with those in Laybourn, Yorkshire, England (which he called "Yoredale"). Although the American town had a considerably smaller population than Yoredale, it had many more behavior settings. Thus, residents in the American town had to take on more positions of responsibility if the behavior settings were to be maintained, and to include more people who were only marginally qualified to function in those settings. Barker argued that the behavior settings of the Midwest were *undermanned* (a term intended to apply to both males and females), pushing its inhabitants into participation in a wider variety of settings than those with a higher ratio of people to settings, and making them feel that they serve in valued and important roles. Barker and Gump (1964) found support for the undermanning hypothesis in a comparison of big and small high schools. While the big school might appear at first to offer more opportunities for its students, close examination of its behavior settings revealed otherwise:

> The large school has authority: its grand exterior dimensions, its long halls and myriad rooms, and its tides of students all carry an implication of power and rightness. The small school lacks such certainty: its modest building, its short halls and few rooms, and its students, who move more in trickles than in tides, give an impression of a casual or not quite decisive educational environment.
>
> These are outside views. They are illusions. Inside views reveal forces at work stimulating and compelling students to more active and responsible contributions to the enterprises of small than of large schools. (Barker & Gump, 1964, p. 195)

Compared to students in large schools, those in small schools participated in a much wider range of behavior settings, were active performers twice as frequently, and received direct rather than vicarious satisfactions from their personal competencies.

Wicker (1979b) has extended Barker's work on undermanning. He suggests that the critical feature is not the size of the behavior setting or the number of occupants but the ratio of three factors; (a) the number of people who seek to participate in a setting relative to (b) the capacity of the setting to accommodate people and (c) the minimum number of persons required for the setting to be maintained. Whether a setting is undermanned, adequately manned, or overmanned depends on this ratio. If more people seek to participate than the setting can accommodate, the setting is overmanned. The setting is undermanned if there are too few people than needed to maintain it. Undermanning generates pressure on its inhabitants to keep the setting going, and in response the occupants take up a wider range of tasks, encourage others to participate, and become more involved in the setting. These effects have been generally confirmed by research in such diverse settings as schools, churches, and work stations of Yosemite National Park rangers (Wicker, 1979b). In the latter, the number of people entering the park per day was used to calculate the manning level. Heavier work loads (the under-manning situation) were associated with greater feelings of challenge and being needed on the job. However, this positive relationship declined over the course of the summer: "By the end of the season, days when work loads were heavy were characterized more by feelings of physical and emotional fatigue than by job involvement" (Wicker, 1979b, p. 760). Wicker is using these and other studies to explore the consequences of inadequate manning levels in service institutions on the quality of workers' experience, and to devise ways to combat burnout, the emotional disengagement of staff from clients.

Research on the manning of behavior settings can have important implications for the study of overpopulation. Zlutnick and Altman (1972) suggest that how one defines excess population determines how he or she will seek to deal with it. Conceptualizing population in terms of density (e.g., number of people per acre) leads one to suggest two types of solutions: (1) reduce the number of people, or (2) increase the amount of space. Conceptualizing overpopulation in terms of overmanned behavior settings, however, leads to a broader range of strategies. Wicker (1973) gives the example of an over-manned high school play where more students sought to be in the cast than there were acting parts available. One solution suggested by behavior setting theory would be to set up an additional cast ("double casting") to perform on a different night so that twice as many people could serve as actors. Likewise, an overmanned chamber music group can reorganize to become an orchestra. In both examples, overpopulation is dealt with not by reducing the number of people but rather by changing the nature of the behavior setting.

Of special relevance to community work, research on the manning of behavior settings has important implications for how social systems handle psychological deviants or marginal members. Barker (1968) suggests that, in optimally manned settings, occupants who perform at a substandard level are dealt with by "vetoing mechanisms" (i.e., by removing them from the setting). This is because the costs involved in replacing deviant persons are generally less than the costs of modifying the deviant behavior. In under-manned settings, however, the cost of replacing deviants, or of maintaining the behavior settings without them, is generally greater than the cost of modifying their behavior. Undermanned settings are more likely to accept deviants, while optimally manned settings will reject them in favor of some-one more qualified. Willems (1967) presents data to support this relationship between manning the marginal persons. He gave students from large and small high schools lists of extracurricular behavior settings (dances, plays, basketball games, and the like) and asked them to report any external pressure for attending these activities. Subjects had been selected on the basis of their being "regular" or "marginal" students. Regular students had average or better IQs and grades and were from middle-class families. Marginal students had below-average IQs and grades and were from lower-class families. Willems found that students from the small schools reported twice as many pressures to participate as did students from the large schools. More importantly, in the small schools, the pressure on marginal students to participate was nearly as great as the pressure on regular students. In the large schools, however, marginal students reported only one fourth as many pressures as regular students, strongly confirming Barker's original hypothesis. Willems' work suggests that under- and overmanned settings may have their greatest impact on marginal individuals. "It is these people who could most benefit by the adaptive skills potentially provided by optimally manned settings and who could also perhaps most benefit by the motivational forces generated by undermanned settings" (Price, 1974).

Not only the number, but also the types of people in a setting may be important. Kanter (1977) suggests that certain dynamics prevail when "tokens" are present in a group, regardless of the basis of their token status. The only man in a group of women, the only black in a group of whites, and the only Protestant in a group of Catholics are likely to be subject to similar pressures to side with the majority against their own kind, are expected to conform to stereotypes, and are scrutinized more closely than nontokens. Moving from the level of the group to that of society, Guttentag and Secord (1983) argue that the ratio of women to men accounts for a society's gender roles and patterns of relationships between the sexes. When women are scarce, a protective morality surrounds them, encouraging them to be domestic and monogamous. When men are scarce, however, these protective attitudes toward women disappear and men become less willing to commit themselves to a lasting relationship with one woman. Thus, sex ratios can have a profound effect on family stability and sexual mores, creating predictable patterns of strain in a society.

APPROACHES TO ENVIRONMENTAL ASSESSMENT

Behavior Settings

Despite the promise of research in ecological psychology, very few surveys of behavior settings have been conducted on entire communities (aside from the work done by Barker and his colleagues). Identifying and describing all the behavior settings in a particular community requires an enormous amount of time-consuming, detailed work. "Barker's survey procedures required 13 data sheets, approximately 230 data entries, for each behavior setting identified and there were more than 800 settings in the Midwest in a single year" (Wicker 1979b, p. 757). In order to make this task manageable, researchers have attempted to identify the important dimensions of settings and to use those dimensions to classify settings into distinct types. Price and Blashfield (1975) analyzed 455 settings identified by Barker in the Midwest. Their goal was to isolate major dimensions upon which behavior settings vary, and to classify settings based on their similarities and differences on those dimensions. They found 12 distinct clusters or types of settings in the Midwest, such as youth performance settings, men's and women's organizations, and religious settings. Age and sex variables of inhabitants were particularly useful in classifying settings, as was the role of the inhabitant as member, performer, or target of action. The findings suggest that a small number of attributes can be used to classify settings, simplifying the researcher's task considerably.

Price and Blashfield (1975) believe that settings can be clustered according to their similarity of attributes. Krupat and Guild (1980) used this idea to develop a classification system for distinguishing cities. They identified six factors which described the social climate of cities: (1) warmth and closeness, (2) activity and entertainment, (3) alienation and isolation, (4) good life (e.g., the people are intellectual, affluent, and so on), (5) privacy, and (6) uncaring. These six factors successfully distinguished the large urban area from the medium-sized city, and the medium city from the small town. In a subsequent study, which asked subjects to compare among 14 major American cities, they found two dimensions that were useful in distinguishing among urban areas. The first dimension referred to interpersonal factors, such as warmth, intimacy, and solidarity. The most populous cities fell on the cold, impersonal end of this continuum (New York followed by Chicago) and the smaller Southwestern cities on the warm and intimate side. The second dimension referred to the style of life within cities, with West Coast cities like Los Angeles and San Diego rated as more "unconventional" than large East Coast cities. Midwestern cities like Columbus and Cleveland were rated by respondents as most "conventional."

Moos (1973; 1974) suggests five ways to conceptualize the environment in addition to Barker's concept of behavior settings:

Physical Factors

The first approach is to examine physical factors in the natural and built environment, such as architecture and design of space. This approach is characteristic of environmental psychology (see Stokols, 1978, and Holahan, 1982, for reviews) and is discussed further in the next chapter.

Group Characteristics

The second approach looks at the characteristics and behavior of the group of people inhabiting a setting. This approach essentially is the person-oriented emphasis of traditional psychology writ large; that is, the environment is considered to be the aggregate of the personal characteristics of a particular group of people. Thus, a school with a predominantly middle-class black population would differ from one with a predominantly working-class white population because the characteristics of the student bodies differ.

Organizational Structure

The third approach considers dimensions of organizational structure, such as the size of an organization, the distribution of power within it, the turnover rate, and so on. An organization which shares power equally among its members would present different environmental demands on its members than one in which power is concentrated among top-level administrators.

Reinforcement Consequences

The next approach looks at the reinforcement consequences for behavior within various settings. Fundamental learning processes, such as classical and operant conditioning, affect people's behavior in various settings. The application of the behaviorist perspective to community settings has led to the development of a subspecialty within community psychology—behavioral community psychology (see Glenwick & Jason, 1980, and Chapter Eight of this book).

Organizational or Social Climate

This approach considers the perceptions and beliefs of inhabitants of a setting. While the "group characteristics" approach described above looks at people's behavior and characteristics, the organizational climate includes people's subjective perceptions of their environments. Moos (1974) and his associates have developed scales to assess the perceived climates of different social organizations. Their work assumes that environments have unique "personalities" in the same way that individuals have personalities: some are supportive, others competitive, and so on. Their work demonstrates that a broad array of settings, ranging from psychiatric wards and community-oriented treatment programs such as halfway houses, to schools, work and family environments, all can be characterized along three basic dimensions.

1. The *relationship* dimension assesses the extent to which individuals are involved in the environment and help and support one another. Examples of the relationship dimension are involvement, affiliation, and peer support.
2. The *personal growth* dimension assesses the opportunity afforded by the environment for self-enhancement and the development of self-esteem, as reflected in, for instance, autonomy and achievement-orientation.
3. *System maintenance* and *system change* dimensions reflect the degree of structure, clarity of expectations, and openness to change that characterize the organization. Examples of this dimension are order and organization.

Moos and his colleagues have found that these dimensions have specific, demonstrable effects on individual and group behavior and health and well-being. In one study, the psychosocial climate of military basic training companies was related to enlisted men's moods and sick call rates. More anxiety and depression, and more frequent sick calls, occurred in companies that emphasized strict organization and control, deemphasized autonomy and personal status, and lacked positive relationships among enlisted men and between men and the officers. A subsequent study of college student residence halls found more frequent use of the health center and more physical symptoms of distress among those living in residences that were seen as academically and socially competitive. Moos (1981, p. 4) summarizes the findings of these and other studies: "Indices of illness and dysfunction are higher in settings characterized by a strong competitive orientation and time pressure, by restrictive organization and control, by a lack of emphasis on personal choice and autonomy, and by ambiguity about the rules and policies governing the environment. Not surprisingly, supportive interpersonal relationships among individuals and between individuals and their supervisors (officers, teachers, and managers) seem to provide some protection against dysfunctional health outcomes." Yet some people are much more affected than others by the characteristics of environmental settings, a phenomenon that we shall discuss in the next chapter where we consider factors such as individuals' coping abilities.

SUBJECTIVE AND OBJECTIVE MEASUREMENT OF THE ENVIRONMENT

The scales devised by Moos and his colleagues measure the subjective perceptions that inhabitants have about an environment. An environment can be measured objectively also (Krupat & Guild, 1980). Objective information includes events and objects that can be counted in the same way by different observers. Such data include crime statistics, city population size, average income, and so on, as well as Barker's descriptions of behavior settings (since those settings should be described in the same way by different observers). Subjective data rely directly upon the perceptions, evaluations, and opinions of people, and may vary considerably depending on who is providing the data. Such information might include people's beliefs about whether their city is a good place in which to live or whether they feel a part of their neighborhood.

While both objective and subjective data can be useful for assessing environments, the perceptions that people have of a particular setting and the "objective" evaluation of that setting may not always coincide. Research on fear on crime in urban neighborhoods has found that the safest neighborhoods according to crime statistics are not always the ones perceived as safe by their inhabitants. People rarely see a crime occurring, and so they calculate their extent of danger from the presence of such phenomena as graffiti, vandalism, and teenage boys hanging out on street corners

(Lewis & Maxfield, 1980). Although some of these phenomena are not illegal, they are thought to be associated with crime because they are interpreted to mean that local processes of social control have broken down. Thus, in order to understand people's reactions to various settings, we have to understand the meaning of environmental factors for them. Years ago, Kurt Lewin stressed that the environment of greatest relevance is the environment as it is experienced by the individual, not necessarily the so-called objective world. To him, the job of the psychologist is to understand how situations are perceived by the people participating in them. Krupat and Guild (1980) suggest that it is inappropriate to examine exclusively either objective or subjective data. "Rather, the job of social scientists at this point is to specify the particular behaviors that they are interested in, to note which perceptions each of those behaviors should be related to, and to examine the objective characteristics of the city that might influence these perceptions and behaviors" (p. 26). Thus objective and subjective data are complementary rather than mutually exclusive, and together may give us the best picture of environmental influences on behavior.

Once we have perceived and made inferences about an environment, we reconstruct and recall information about it when that environment is no longer present. This process is known as environmental cognition. Our images of the environment, and our knowledge about it can be shaped by such factors as familiarity. A famous cover of the *New Yorker* magazine draws the map of the United States from a typical New Yorker's perspective: 75 percent of the area consists of New York City, with the area west of the Rockies becoming smaller and smaller in size except for California, which is larger than the midwestern areas combined. Californians, of course, have retaliated with their own image of the United States, in which anything east of Las Vegas is miniscule in size except for New York and Chicago.

Such factors as age and sex can affect our ideas about the environment. Holahan and Holahan (1977, 1979) found considerable sex differences in descriptions of living environments from male and female college students. Women's images of their environments included more personal references than men's, while men's descriptions were more impersonal and objective. "One male student described his living environment in this way: 'Small, one-bedroom apartment, off campus, i.e. "efficiency," with kitchen, the usual furniture, high rent and utilities, roaches and no view.' A female student, in contrast, responded in highly personal terms: 'I'm living in an apartment on Lakeside Road with my sister, her best friend, and my best friend. We have a cat and lots of mostly dead plants! The apartment is colorful, with lots of posters of places we'd like to visit. We try to keep it pretty clean. I'm planning on getting married so it's got lots of stuff lying around" (Holahan, 1982, p. 73). The emphasis on social factors in women's ideas about the environment agrees with theories of female socialization, which propose that women are encouraged to develop a more personalized, relationship-oriented attitude toward the world, while men are encouraged to be impersonal and objective (see Chodorow, 1978).

Such factors as sex role status can affect not only our ideas about the environment but also our attitudes. Saegert (1981) compared attitudes toward city and suburban homes of men and women. She found that men generally found the suburbs to be more satisfying, while women had more options available to them in the city. Since women were forced to choose between the private world of the home and the public world outside, moving to the suburbs meant the loss of opportunities for work, leisure, and social relations found in the city. This choice was not demanded of men. A move to the suburbs increased their satisfaction with the home as retreat and recreation source, while it did not interfere with their access to city opportunities. Higher-density, mixed-use environments typical of city life afford more options to women, since the public and private worlds are not so spatially and temporally separated as between suburb and city. Thus, people living in the same environmental setting can vary considerably in their attitudes and reactions to that setting.

COMMUNITY AND THE ASSESSMENT OF ITS ATTRIBUTES

One of the most important environmental contexts for understanding human behavior and well-being is the community in which people live and work. Community is a term that is widely and ambiguously used in the social sciences. There are two major ways of discussing community: one is as a place and the other is as a set of relationships and resources.

COMMUNITY AS A PLACE

The early research of the Chicago sociologists mentioned at the beginning of this chapter used biological ecology concepts to divide cities into "natural areas." These areas, such as census tracts, catchment areas, or neighborhoods, can be described in terms of their population and the physical environment (type of terrain, types of housing). Hunter and Riger (in press) discuss three general typologies of community that are relevant to the area conception of community.

1.   *Demographic* typologies refer to basic social characteristics of the residents in a given area. For example, neighborhoods are often described according to the social class or race or ethnic origin of residents living there. Studies of urban neighborhoods have found that people tend to live in neighborhoods with others similar in socioeconomic status (e.g., income, education, and occupation), family or life-cycle stage (e.g., percent married, women in the labor force, presence of children), and racial/ethnic identity.

2.   A second set of typologies of communities focus on *land use and the quality of the housing*. For example, a neighborhood life cycle has been described that begins with sparse single-family homes, followed by increased development, such as apartment buildings, resulting in high density,

followed by decline and abandonment, and occasionally neighborhood renewal and revitalization.

3.   The third set of typologies focuses on the *institutional* and *organizational* composition of the community. The emphasis here is on the presence or absence of such institutions and organizations as schools, churches or civic groups.

Levels of community. A resident lives in a number of communities, as the following description illustrates:

> The micro-neighborhood is operationally defined as a next-door neighbor, the person in the next apartment, or the most immediate set of adjacent households. It is defined when a mother yells out the window to young people playing in the street, "Go play in your own neighborhood." That notion in turn leads us quickly into the notion of the residential block.
>   Beyond the residential block begins the walking-distance neighborhood. The administrative definition of a walking-distance neighborhood is usually the elementary school district. In our own research on neighborhoods, the elementary school district has been utilized because it is a compromise between the notions of the very small micro-neighborhood and larger definitions such as "the west side," the "black community," "my part of town," and so forth." (Warren, 1981, p. 63)

The levels of community that are contained in larger levels have been called "nested" communities.

Generally, we will be interested in three units of community: the block, the neighborhood, and the larger community. The block consists of the two sides of a street that face each other, with cross streets serving as block boundaries. It represents the immediate residential environment. The neighborhood is harder to define and has a variety of objective and subjective definitions. We will use Warren's definition of an elementary school district as a good approximation. The larger community refers to a region of a town or city that usually combines several neighborhoods (e.g., the middle-class area or the west side of town) or the entire city (e.g., Lynd & Lynd, 1937; Warner & Lunt, 1941). Most of the recent theory and research on community has focused on the neighborhood unit, and that will generally be our focus here.

COMMUNITY AS RELATIONSHIPS
AND RESOURCES

Neighboring and Networks

As technology, communication, transportation, and lifestyles have advanced and made the city "smaller," neighborhoods may be losing some of the importance they once had (Wellman & Leighton 1979). Many of the relationships people have, and many of the activities people engage in, can and do take place outside of a person's neighborhood. Relatives, friends, work settings, and associations are often located outside the neighborhood. "There may be a shift from a neighboring of *place* to a neighboring of *taste*" (Keller, 1968, p. 61), where friendship is based on affinity, not proximity. Keller (p. 123) has suggested that "more typical of the realities of this century are those individuals and families seeking more space, better jobs, higher status, or greater amenities. For these people local areas or neighborhoods are but stepping-stones—not necessarily devoid of sentimental value—in the pursuit of happiness." This view has increased the importance of understanding a person's informal social networks, which may not necessarily be located in one's neighborhood. Informal social networks refer to a person's relations with relatives, friends, neighbors, co-workers, and acquaintances. Social networks may have a significant impact on many aspects of an individual's life, such as health and general well-being, and ability to cope with life crises and transitions.

While extra-local networks can provide critical functions, local neighboring relations still have a very important place in many individuals' lives. (Unger & Wandersman, 1982). The close spatial location of neighbors makes them particularly unique to perform functions that other network members would find difficult, such as caring for children while parents are hospitalized or helping to extricate snowbound automobiles. Neighbors often serve as support systems for individuals providing emotional and material aid. They may foster a sense of identification and serve as a buffer from the feelings of isolation often associated with today's cities. Neighbors also may join together to exercise their political skills and to better the quality of their living environment. Participation in neighborhood organizations has frequently become a strategy to solve neighborhood problems.

Neighboring Functions

Neighbors are *simply* defined by proximity: the people who live next door, the people who live on the block. What characterizes a good neighbor depends on values (Keller, 1968). In some neighborhoods, a good neighbor is expected to mind his or her own business. In other neighborhoods a good neighbor is friendly, helpful, lends tools or food, and gives advice. Neighboring refers to the activities that people who live near one another engage in. Several roles of neighbors have been described (Keller, 1968; Warren, 1981).

1.   Neighbors have been viewed as natural (as opposed to professional) helpers. Neighbors can provide direct aid such as helping to watch children or lending tools. Neighbors can be referral sources—they can refer an individual to other helpers. This role has been called a *gatekeeper* role, in which a neighbor makes referrals to individuals, experts, or organizations that may be located inside or outside the neighborhood. Linkages outside of the neighborhood can provide access to a wide variety of resources.

2.   Neighbors provide a sociability function. The extent to which neighbors are willing to greet and visit with each other can serve as a source of social belonging and reduce feelings of social isolation fostered in cities.

3.   Neighbors are a source of interpersonal influence. Neighbors can provide subtle and overt norms on a range of behaviors, such as how to decorate your house and lawn, to how to punish your child.

The Social Organization of Neighborhoods

Warren and Warren (1975; 1977; Warren, 1981) have developed a typology of neighborhoods based on the social organization of a population residing in a geographically proximate location. It is based on three dimensions:

A.   *Interaction.* The degree of social exchanges within a neighborhood (e.g., how often people in the neighborhood get together).
B.   *Identity.* The degree of individual identification with the neighborhood (e.g., the extent to which people in the neighborhood feel that they have a great deal in common).
C.   *Connections.* The degree to which the neighborhood is explicitly linked to the larger community (e.g., how many people in the neighborhood belong to political parties and other organizations outside the neighborhood).

Using these dimensions, the Warrens identified six types of neighborhoods.

1.   The *integral* neighborhood is high in interaction, connections, and identity.

> This neighborhood is like a vast radar network. It picks up resources and information from many outside points. Residents have influential jobs and links with many kinds of community groups. At the same time they are active within their neighborhood. Thus they are able to bring new information and techniques into the neighborhood and to let outside institutions, such as city government or professional groups, know what people in their neighborhood are thinking. In this way, they can heighten the sensitivities of outsiders to the concerns of their neighbors. (Warren & Warren, 1975, p. 78)

2.   The *parochial* neighborhood is high in interaction, high in density, and low in connections.

> In many ways the structure is identical to that of the integral neighborhood. People interact often and have a network of neighborhood groups. But unlike the integral neighborhood, it faces inward. Information seldom passes directly into the neighborhood; it is filtered and modified by key opinion leaders. These leaders have strong commitments to their neighborhood but are less likely than integral leaders to transmit to their neighborhood the concerns of the larger community. (Warren & Warren, 1975, p. 78)

3.   The *diffuse* neighborhood is low in interactions, high in density, and low in connections.

> Residents identify with this neighborhood because they find it a pleasant place to live; but they seldom get together as a basis for shaping or protecting their

lifestyle. Information flows slowly, and the neighborhood is often relatively slow in taking action even though there is a great deal of organizational potential. Basically, this is an underdeveloped neighborhood, in the sense that neighbors do not rely on each other for aide and support but go directly to outside sources. (Warren & Warren, 1975, p. 78)

4. The *stepping-stone* neighborhood is high in interaction, low in identity, and high in connections.

This neighborhood is somewhat like the integral neighborhood in that it has a high degree of internal organization as well as a large number of residents with outside connections. But the residents have no strong commitment to the neighborhood. Often they are mobicentric young executives who move out again for the next job. The neighborhood usually has formal mechanisms to integrate new residents quickly. As soon as their bags are unpacked, a welcoming committee greets them and tells them about the neighborhood groups they may join. But residents usually continue to be more active in outside than in local groups. (Warren & Warren, 1975, p. 80)

5. The *transitory* neighborhood is low in interaction, low in identity, and high in connections.

The population turnover is so great and the institutional fabric so restricted that there is little action in this neighborhood. It often breaks down into cliques of long-time residents who belong to the same groups and never allow newcomers in. Neighbors feel they have little in common and usually avoid local entanglements. There may be pockets of intense activity but there is no cohesion. (Warren & Warren, 1975, p. 80)

6. The *anomic* neighborhood is low in interaction, low in identity, and low in connections.

This neighborhood has virtually no leadership structure. A few residents may have connections to outside groups but remain inactive on their home turf. Individuals and families are on their own, confronting outside institutions without any kind of support from their neighbors. If they are poor, they will find little help in solving their problems. Usually they are distrustful of outside groups but almost never can they get help or guidance from anyone in their neighborhood. (Warren & Warren, 1975, p. 80)

Warren (1981) presents evidence which suggests that neighbors are important helpers (neighbors are used as direct helpers in over 25 percent of all helping transactions) and that the type of neighborhood is related to helping by neighbors (neighbors are used as helpers much more often in integral neighborhoods than in anomic ones) and to well-being.

THE ATTACHMENT BETWEEN THE INDIVIDUAL AND THE COMMUNITY: SENSE OF COMMUNITY

Now that we have discussed what a community is, we turn our attention to describing the *feeling* of the relationship—the "sense of community." Sarason (1974) suggests some of the ingredients of sense of community: "The perception of similarity to others, an acknowledged interdependence with others, a willingness to maintain this interdependence by giving to or doing for others what one expects from them, the feeling that one is part of a larger dependable and stable structure" (p. 157). Nisbet (1966) and Yankelovich (1981) discuss sense of community in somewhat similar terms. Sarason considers sense of community "as the overarching value giving justification and direction to community psychology" (1974, p. 15).

Despite the importance placed on sense of community by social scientists and the public, the definitions of sense of community are somewhat ambiguous, and there has been relatively little research analyzing the meaning of sense of community. For example, Yankelovich (1981) based his survey results about "hungering for community" on an aggregate of items; but no definition of community was provided in the survey to respondents, and it is unclear whether people had a common understanding of what they were rating. For Yankelovich, hungering for community is "an intense need to compensate for the impersonal and threatening aspects of modern life by seeking mutual identification with others based on close ethnic ties or ties of shared interests, needs, backgrounds, age or values" (p. 251). He defines community as "the feeling that here is where I belong, these are my people, I care for them, they care for me, I am part of them, I know what they expect from me and I from them, they share my concerns, I know this place, I am on familiar ground, I am at home" (p. 227).

There is a clear need for specification and analysis of key concepts like sense of community. Here we will discuss a theoretical conception of sense of community (McMillan & Chavis, in press) and research that used a variety of psychological approaches to explore it, and determine whether it is a shared definition (Chavis, Hogge, McMillan, & Wandersman, in press). McMillan and Chavis propose that there are four elements or principles of sense of community.

1.   *Membership* involves a feeling of belonging, a sense of relatedness. Membership has several attributes: (*a*) boundaries, which define who is in or who is out; (*b*) emotional safety, which involves the concept of security and can involve physical and economic security; (*c*) sense of belonging and identification, which involves the feelings, beliefs, and expectations that one fits in the group and is accepted by the group; (*d*) personal investment, which involves working for membership in the group; (*e*) common symbol systems, which involve the holding of similar language, rituals, ceremonies, or other signs of commonality.

2.   *Influence* involves whether an individual can affect the group and whether the group can exert some power in the larger systems that contain it. Reciprocally, the group has influence and can put pressures on an individual to perform tasks or to conform to some of its rules, or both.

3.   A *sharing of values with an integration and fulfillment of needs* involves the fulfillment of an individual's values by a group or community.

To the extent that the values are shared, there will be a greater sense of community.

4. *A shared emotional connection* is partly based on a shared history. People do not have to physically share that history, only identify with it. A shared emotional connection can be increased by interpersonal contact, the success of contact, and the importance of a shared event to individuals. In addition, there may be a spiritual bond or "community of spirit" (e.g., the concept of soul among blacks).

Chavis, Hogge, McMillan, and Wandersman (in press) used this definition to explore sense of community in a neighborhood. The major questions they confronted were: (*a*) Can we define a concept like sense of community? (*b*) Since the definition has a number of parts, can we develop a single score or index of sense of community? (*c*) Can we get agreement on the score which would indicate that the score is objective or shared?

According to McMillan and Chavis (in press), the description of sense of community by Sarason and its use by others indicates that the assessment of sense of community may be very subjective. Like beauty, it may be in the eyes of the beholder and different eyes may view it differently. If it is shared by many types of people, it can represent a concept that has objective reality (group's perception) as well as subjective reality (individual's perception) (e.g., Berger & Luckmann, 1966) and, therefore, be more amenable to scientific study.

Hogge, Fellendorf, Moore, and Wuescher (1979) developed a technique to form a single overall score, and which could be tested for the degree of agreement on the score. The technique draws on social judgment theory (Hammond, Steward, Brehmer, & Steinmann, 1975), which is based on Brunswik's theory of probabilistic functionalism and lens model (Brunswik, 1956). According to the lens model, the "true" level of a construct like sense of community cannot be directly observed. Instead, it can only be inferred from the judgments of a wide variety of information related to sense of community.

Chavis, Hogge, McMillan, and Wandersman (in press) explored whether the definition of sense of community proposed by McMillan and Chavis allowed a variety of judges to have a significantly high degree of agreement in their estimates of levels of sense of community. They used surveys of 1,213 people who lived in a neighborhood in Nashville, Tennessee, as the raw data for the study. Information from each individual was obtained on demographic characteristics, attitudes toward the block and neighborhood, neighboring activities, involvement in block and other community organizations, and so on. Several items were selected that fit each of the four principles in the definition of sense of community. A judge was then shown the answers to the selected items of an individual and asked to rate the overall sense of community of the individual on a scale of one to five, thus developing a single overall score of sense of community based on a variety of information that operationalized the conceptual definition. A variety of judges (social scientists, community service organizers and community professionals, local political and neighborhood organization leaders, and members of the general public) rated the same individual profiles. If the judges tended to give each profile a similar score, this would demonstrate that a single score of sense of community had been developed and that the score was objective (had a shared reality). The assessment of agreement among the judges resulted in an alpha coefficient of .97, which was interpreted as indicating a very high degree of agreement. It also was found that variables from each of the four principles in the definition of sense of community were significantly related to the overall sense of community score.

In summary, we have suggested that sense of community represents an important concept and value in our society and, perhaps, a central concept in community psychology. However, the study of its actual importance has been inhibited by its ambiguity and lack of operationalization. Using concepts from the social science literature and a psychological methodology, it was shown that an operational definition of sense of community can be formed and that there is agreement on what sense of community is. This will aid our understanding of what sense of community is and how it forms, and can help us test interventions to promote sense of community.

SUMMARY OF ECOLOGICAL CONCEPTS

We began this chapter with a discussion of the ways in which social scientists have adapted concepts of biological ecology to understand human behavior. Holahan and Spearly (1980) summarize the ecological perspective in psychology in four central concepts:

1.   *"Behavior as nested in a series of circumjacent contexts."* By "circumjacent" we refer to the various levels of the environment that simultaneously surround a person. Influences on behavior can stem from the immediate behavior setting, from the surrounding context in which that setting is located (such as the school or work organization), or from the larger society. Thus, in discussing "community," we have considered the local block, the walking-distance neighborhood, and the encompassing city as contexts which can separately or jointly exert an influence on behavior. Understanding the behavior of individuals, therefore, requires a broad vision of the larger arena in which that behavior takes place. This is similar to Kelly's principle of interdependence, or, as Barry Commoner (1968) puts it, "everything is connected to everything else."

2.   *"A phenomenological attitude."* The environment is not perceived directly; rather, psychological processes involved in perception affect the way that individuals interpret and then act on environmental information. A teenager involved in street-gang life may view a neighborhood block as safe because it is his gang's "territory", while an elderly resident may believe that the same block is dangerous and is to be avoided. Individuals' "perceptions, evaluations, and inferences" (Holahan & Spearly, 1980, p. 673) as

well as sociodemographic characteristics affect the way they experience the environment. Thus, male and female students may differ in descriptions of their living environments even though they occupy similar dormitory space. Not only the objective characteristics of the environment, but also the individual's subjective interpretation of those characteristics must be assessed in order to understand their impact on behavior.

3. *"An interactional perspective."* Ecological principles call attention not only to the characteristics of individuals and environments, but especially to the "goodness-of-fit" between those characteristics. As we mentioned in our opening example of the different climates on various college campuses, a school may be the ideal environment for one student but harmful for another. It is the match between the individual and environment that determines success. Thus a marginal student whose participation is demanded by an "undermanned" setting may flourish in that environment but become alienated and withdrawn in an adequately manned setting where his or her presence is less critical for the setting's survival.

4. *"Reciprocal action."* The ecological perspective assumes that "not only do events affect the behavior of individuals, but the individual is an active agent in influencing environmental events" (Holahan & Spearly, 1980, p. 675). As we will see in the next chapter, an ecological perspective emphasizes the active role that people take in coping with environmental influences on behavior, rather than seeing people simply as the passive recipients of those influences. Coping with environmental influences may involve acting in order to modify the environment.

In this chapter, we have stressed that there are many different ways of looking at environments: as behavior settings, as locales containing particular social climates, and so forth. All of these perspectives are enhanced by considering them within an ecological framework. The behavior setting of a high school, for example, might have had radically different norms in the years of student rebelliousness of the 1960s than in the "age of conformity" of the 1950s. The larger social context exerts an influence on the behavior setting, which can be a critical factor in determining people's actions.

Similarly, in discussing "community," we stress that people live not only within a particular block or neighborhood but also within a larger environment. Modern communication and transportation systems permit the inclusion of people who live in other cities or even other countries as members of one's social network. Thus one's "community" can consist of a particular geographical place, or it can consist of a nonterritorially based network of relationships that provide friendship, esteem, and tangible support.

The fit between the individual and the local neighborhood depends on both the individual's needs and the type of neighborhood. A parent who is home all day taking care of young children may welcome the cohesiveness of an "integral" neighborhood, while a person who spends many long hours at work may resent the expectation that he or she be part of a community group within such a neighborhood. A strong "sense of community" can sustain some people, while others feel stifled by such ties. Ecological theory suggests that we examine the fit between individuals' needs and community resources, rather than considering each of these separately.

Trickett, Kelly, and Vincent (in press) summarize the *spirit* of ecological inquiry by stating that "To think ecologically is: (1) to consider how persons, settings, and events can become resources for the positive development of communities; (2) to consider how these resources can be managed and conserved; (3) to approach research so that the effort expended will be helpful to the preservation and enhancement of community resources" (p. 1). The "preservation and enhancement" of communities can be achieved through a number of strategies described in this book, such as citizen participation in neighborhood organizations and the creation of alternative settings. The success of those strategies is likely to be determined partly by the extent to which they are based upon an ecological understanding of community settings. In sum, if our research continuously illustrates that environmental factors have deleterious individual consequences, psychologists will need to learn new behaviors to intervene in the environment. This is one of the achievements and challenges of psychologists working in community settings, as we will see in the following chapter.

References

Barker, R. *Ecological psychology*. Stanford, Calif.: Stanford University Press, 1968.

Barker, R., & Gump, P. *Big school, small school*. Stanford, Calif.: Stanford University Press, 1964.

Berger, P. L., & Luckmann, T. *The social construction of reality*. New York: Doubleday Publishing, 1966.

Bernard, J. *The sociology of community*. Glenview, Ill.: Scott, Foresman, 1973.

Brunswik, E. *Perception and the representative design of psychological experiments* (2d ed.). Berkeley: University of California Press, 1956.

Catalano, R. *Health, behavior and the community*. New York: Pergamon Press, 1979.

Chavis, D., Hogge, J., McMillan, D., & Wandersman, A. Sense of community through Brunswik's lens. *Journal of Community Psychology*, in press.

Chodorow, N. *The reproduction of mothering: Psychoanalysis and the sociology of gender*. Berkeley: University of California Press, 1978.

Commoner, B. *The closing circle*. New York: Basic Books, 1968.

Darwin, C. *On the origin of species*. London: John Murray, 1859.

Dunham, H. W. The ecology of the functional psychoses in Chicago. *The American Sociological Review*, 1937, *2*, 467–79.

Durkheim, E. *Suicide: A study in sociology*. Paris: Alcan, 1897.

Glenwick, D., & Jason, L. *Behavioral community psychology: Progress and prospects*. New York: Praeger Publishers, 1980.

Guttentag, M., & Secord, P. *Too many women? the sex ratio question*. Beverly Hills, Calif.: Sage Publications, 1983.

Hammond, K. R., Stewart, T. R., Brehmer, B., & Steinmann, D. O. Social judgment theory. In M. F. Kaplan & B. S. Schwartz (Eds.), *Human judgment and decision processes*. New York: Academic Press, 1975.

Hogge, J. H., Fellendorf, G. W., Moore, J. W., & Wuescher, M. L. A delivery service index based on evaluative judgments. *Evaluation Quarterly,* 1979, *3,* 643–660.

Holahan, C. J. *Environmental psychology*. New York: Random House, 1982.

Holahan, C. J., & Holahan, C. K. Sex-related differences in the schematization of the behavioral environment. *Personality and Social Psychology Bulletin,* 1977, *3,* 123–126.

Holahan, C. J., & Spearly, J. L. Coping and ecology: An integrative model for community psychology. *American Journal of Community Psychology,* 1980, *8,* 671–685.

Holahan, C. K., & Holahan, C. J. Effects of gender and psychological masculinity and femininity on environmental schematization. *Personality and Social Psychology Bulletin,* 1979, *5,* 231–235.

Hunter, A., & Riger, S. The meaning of community in community mental health. *Journal of Community Psychology,* in press.

Kanter, R. M. *Men and women of the corporation*. New York: Basic Books, 1977.

Keller, S. *The urban neighborhood: A sociological perspective*. New York: Random House, 1968.

Kelly, J. Ecological constraints on mental health services. *American Psychologist,* 1966, *21,* 535–539.

Kelly, J. Toward an ecological conception of preventive interventions. In J. Carter (Ed.), *Research contributions from psychology to community mental health* (pp. 75–99). New York: Behavioral Publications, 1968.

Kelly, J. Qualities for the community psychologist. *American Psychologist,* 1971, *26,* 897–903.

Kelly, J. *The ecological analogy and community work*. Paper presented to the International Society for the Study of Behavioral Development Biennial Conference, University of Surrey, England, 1975.

Kelly, J. G. (Ed.). *Adolescent boys in high school: A psychological study of coping and adaptation*. Hillsdale, N.J.: Lawrence Erlbaum Associates, 1979.

Krupat, E., & Guild, W. Defining the city: The use of objective and subjective measures for community description. *Journal of Social Issues,* 1980, *36,* 9–28.

Lewin, K. *Field theory in social science*. New York: Harper & Row, 1951.

Lewis, D. A., & Maxfield, M. G. Fear in the neighborhoods: An investigation of the impact of crime. *Journal of Research in Crime and Delinquency,* 1980, *17,* 160–189.

Lynd, R. S., & Lynd, H. M. *Middletown in transition*. New York: Harcourt Brace Jovanovich, 1937.

McMillan, D., & Chavis, D. A theory of sense of community. *Journal of Community Psychology,* in press.

Mills, R., & Kelly, J. Cultural and social adaptations to change: A case example and critique. In S. Golann & C. Eisdorfer, *Handbook of community mental health* (pp. 157–205). New York: Appleton-Century-Crofts, 1972.

Moos, R. H. Conceptualizations of human environments. *American Psychologist,* 1973, *28,* 652–665.

Moos, R. H. Systems for the assessment and classification of human environments: An overview. In R. H. Moos, & P. M. Insel (Eds.), *Issues in social ecology*. Palo Alto, Calif.: National Press Books, 1974.

Moos, R. H. The social climate scales: An overview. Palo Alto, Calif.: Consulting Psychologists Press, 1974.

Moos, R. H. *Creating healthy human contexts: Environmental and individual strategies*. Invited address, American Psychological Association convention, Los Angeles, August 1981.

Murray, H. *Exploration in personality*. New York: Oxford University Press, 1938.

Nisbet, R. A. *The sociological tradition*. New York: Basic Books, 1966.

Pace, C. R., & Stern, G. G. An approach to the measurement of psychological characteristics of college environments. *Journal of Educational Psychology*, 1958, *49*, 269–77.

Price, R. Etiology, the social environment and the prevention of psychological dysfunction. In P. Insel & R. Moos (Eds.), *Health and the social environment* (pp. 287–300). Lexington, Mass.: D. C. Heath, 1974.

Price, R. Behavior setting theory and research. In R. H. Moos, *The human context*. New York: John Wiley & Sons, 1976.

Price, R., & Blashfield, R. Explorations in the taxonomy of behavior settings: Analysis of dimensions and classification of settings. *American Journal of Community Psychology*, 1975, *3*, 335–351.

Saegert, S. Masculine cities and feminine suburbs: Polarized ideas, contradictory realities. In C. Stimpson, E. Dixler, M. J. Nelson, & K. B. Yatrakis, *Women and the American City*. Chicago: University of Chicago Press, 1981.

Sarason, S. B. *The psychological sense of community: Prospects for a community psychology*. San Francisco: Jossey-Bass, 1974.

Stokols, D. Environmental psychology. *Annual Reviews, Inc.*, 1978, *29*, 253–295.

Trickett, E. J., Kelly, J., & Todd, D. The social environment of the high school. In S. Golann & C. Eisdorfer (Eds.), *Handbook of community mental health* (pp. 331–406). New York: Appleton-Century-Crofts, 1972.

Trickett, E. J., Kelly, J. G., & Vincent, T. A. The spirit of ecological inquiry in community research. In D. Klein & E. Susskind (Eds.), *Knowledge Building in Community Psychology*. New York: Pergamon Press, in press.

Unger, D. G., & Wandersman, A. Neighboring in an urban environment. *American Journal of Community Psychology*, 1982, *10*, 5, 495–509.

Warner, W. L., & Lunt, P. S. *The social life of a modern community*. New Haven, Conn.: Yale University Press, 1941.

Warren, D. I. *Helping networks: How people cope with problems in the urban community*. Notre Dame, Ind.: University of Notre Dame Press, 1981.

Warren, D. I., & Warren, R. B. Six types of neighborhoods. *Psychology Today*, 1975, *9*, 1, 74–79. Reprinted from *Psychology Today* magazine, copyright © 1975, American Psychological Association.

Warren, R., & Warren, D. *The neighborhood organizer's handbook*. Notre Dame, Ind.: University of Notre Dame Press, 1977.

Wellman, B., & Leighton, B. Networks, neighborhoods and communities: Approaches to the study of the community question. *Urban Affairs Quarterly*, 1979, *14*, 363–390.

Wicker, A. Undermanning theory and research: Implications for the study of psychological and behavioral effects of excess populations. *Representative Research in Social Psychology*, 1973, *4*, 185–206.

Wicker, A. W. An introduction to ecological psychology. Monterey, Calif.: Brooks/Cole Publishing, 1979a.

Wicker, A. W. Ecological psychology: some recent and prospective developments. *American Psychologist*, 1979b, *34*, 755–765.

Willems, E. Sense of obligation to high school activities as related to school size and marginality of student, *Child Development*, 1967, *38*, 1247–1260.

Yankelovich, D. *New rules: Searching for self-fulfillment in a world turned upside down*. New York: Random House, 1981.

Zlutnick, S., & Altman, I. Crowding and human behavior. In J. Wohlwill & D. Carson (Eds.) *Environment and the social sciences: Perspectives and applications* (pp. 44–58). Washington, D.C.: American Psychological Association, 1972.

CHAPTER SIX

Coping with Stressful Environments and Events*

---

* Stephanie Riger was the primary author of this chapter. Abe Wandersman wrote the section on the physical environment.

People used to sit on their steps in the evening, doors were open. Now the streets are deserted early in the morning and after dark. My mother used to go to church every morning—she stopped doing it—she is afraid of having her purse snatched. Many church and social activities here have stopped—people won't go out at night. (South Philadelphia, November, 1976) (Skogan & Maxfield, 1981, p. 48)

This quote from a study of the impact of the fear of crime on city dwellers illustrates the harmful effects that environmental conditions can have on people. While the environment can affect people in many ways, the kinds of person-environment relations of particular interest to community psychologists are those which are likely to enhance or inhibit adaptation. Since environmental stress has been described as a risk factor leading to poor adaptation and to psychopathology (Dohrenwend, 1978), it is the stress-producing and stress-mitigating aspects of the environment that will be the focus of this chapter. More and more evidence is accumulating about the deleterious impact of environmental stress on a wide range of behaviors from school performance to eating habits to one's state of health (Insel, 1980). We will also consider life changes that produce stress, such as graduating from college or having a baby, and examine environmental factors that help or hinder people in coping with such events.

A STRESS MODEL OF PERSON-ENVIRONMENT INTERACTION

Monat and Lazarus (1977) propose that the term *stress* refers to "any event in which environmental demands, internal demands, or both *tax* or *exceed* the adaptive resources of an individual, social system, or tissue system" (p. 3). Stress exists when there is an imbalance between the demands of the environment and the individual's ability to respond adequately to these demands (Novaco, Stokols, Campbell, & Stokols, 1979). Thus, stress is neither an environmental condition nor an individual's response, but rather a person-environment transaction (Coyne & Holroyd, in press). Stress can arise from sudden, cataclysmic phenomena, such as war or an earthquake; from daily hassles, such as commuting on a crowded subway; or from radical changes in one's life situation caused by such occurrences as the birth of a child or the death of a spouse (Lazarus & Cohen, 1977).

In this chapter, we discuss three sources of stress: one's position in the social structure, major life changes, and stressful aspects of the physical environment. We then consider ways in which people resist stress, and discuss implications of a stress model for community intervention.

SOCIAL STRUCTURE AS A SOURCE OF STRESS

A long tradition of research in epidemiology supports the existence of a relationship between social class status and the incidence of abnormal behavior. One of the earliest studies in the United States, conducted by Edward Jarvis in 1855, concluded that "the pauper class furnishes, in ratio of its numbers, 64 times as many cases of insanity as the independent class" (cited in Dohrenwend & Dohrenwend, 1981). More recently, a random sample of 1,660 people living in downtown Manhattan were surveyed in order to ascertain the incidence of mental illness among the general population (Srole, Langner, Michael, Opler, & Rennie, 1962). The rates of abnormality were considerably higher among the lower socioeconomic class than among the upper class. Thirteen percent of the lower class residents showed some evidence of psychotic traits, as opposed to 4 percent of those in upper classes. Neurotic traits showed a similar pattern: almost twice as prevalent (20 percent) in the lower than in the upper classes (11 percent). While more disturbance was found in the lower classes, they did not receive more psychotherapy. Psychiatric services were disproportionately distributed to those who were wealthier, of later generations, and better educated. Other early studies (e.g., Hollingshead & Redlich, 1958) suggest that, when mental health service was provided, the type of service was significantly affected by the patients' economic situation, with the poor receiving physical treatment, such as medication, and the wealthy receiving introspective treatment modalities, such as psychoanalysis. Savage (1968) described the bulk of those seeking out (nonhospital) psychotherapeutic services as belonging to the YAVIS category: young, attractive, verbal, intelligent, and successful. These people have been overrepresented as clients simply because they are attractive to therapists. However, the historic bias in the distribution and use of mental health services appears to have disappeared in recent years, perhaps because of greater accessibility of those services in community mental health centers (see Chapter Two).

Social Class, Poverty, and Mental Disorder: Is There a Causal Connection?

In a review of studies of social class and mental illness, Dohrenwend and Dohrenwend (1974) found consistent evidence of the relationship between low socioeconomic status and schizophrenia and personality disorders (but not neurosis). In 28 of 33 studies of the prevalence of mental disorders, the highest rate of psychological disorders is found in the lowest social class. The crucial question concerns the direction of causality of this relationship. Does poverty cause mental disorder (and if so, how)? Or do people who are mentally disturbed tend to remain at the bottom or drift downward in the social structure? The first explanation assumes that social-environmental factors are more important than genetic or constitutional factors in the etiology of mental illness; that is, mental disorders are the consequence of adverse social circumstances. The stresses associated with living in poverty precipitate psychological breakdowns. The second explanation assumes the opposite: mental disorders, caused by genetic or constitutional factors, are the cause, not the consequence, of adverse circumstances and prevent people from bettering their social status. These two hypotheses, known as *social causation* and *social selection* (a derivative of the idea of natural selection) respectively, are not necessarily mutually exclusive, but they do point to radically different types of interventions for those interested in reducing the amount of mental illness. Yet, testing the two hypotheses is problematic (Dohrenwend & Dohrenwend, 1969). Simply identifying cases of mental illness among the general (i.e., nonhospitalized) population is difficult because researchers use different definitions and diagnoses of mental disorders.

Social Class, Stress, and Lack of Control

The question arises as to how social environmental conditions could produce mental disorder. A number of studies (summarized in Dohrenwend, 1973) have demonstrated that stressful life events, such as divorce, a death in the family, or job loss, produce psychological distress in individuals. Dohrenwend (1973) examined the distribution of stressful life events across the population, and found that members of lower classes and women were both exposed to a high rate of stressful changes in their lives. However, the relationship between life-change scores and symptom scores was strong in the lower class but not in the higher class; that is, respondents in the higher class tended to have low levels of symptoms of psychological disorder, regardless of the magnitude of their life change scores, while in the lower class symptom scores varied directly with life-changes scores. "One implication of these findings is that members of the lower class are more vulnerable to the impact of life change" (p. 231). The Dohrenwends (1981) suggest two possible class-linked sources of this vulnerability: personal dispositions or attitudes, such as feelings of helplessness and lack of control, and contemporary social conditions, such as lack of support from other people. In a book entitled *The Hidden Injuries of Class,* Sennet and Cobb (1973) argue that status inequalities have a psychological impact on people. For example, members of lower classes and women blame themselves for their lack of success, internalizing responsibility for their low social status. Low social class appears to be linked to the belief in the inability to control one's life, a belief that is both stimulated and reinforced by the lack of access to material goods, opportunities, and personal support that permit control.

Thompson (1981) suggests three ways in which actual control of aversive events can reduce the effects of stress. First, control can allow a person to predict the stressor. If we can anticipate certain events and the appropriate responses, then stress is less threatening. Second, control is beneficial because it reflects a self-image of competence and power. Lack of control may lead to feelings of incompetence. Third, control of a situation may enable one to determine outcomes of that situation. People whose life situations reduce the amount of control they have to begin with, such as the poor or the elderly, are likely to be most susceptible to the effects of environmental stressors, since pre-existing feelings of helplessness may be reinforced and the harmful effects of environmental stressors may be cumulative. Scarce resources could limit the amount of behavioral control people have over the environment, also, preventing them from buffering themselves from the negative effects of such environmental conditions as noise and crowding. During one heat wave in Kansas City, for example, the poor and the elderly were more likely to die than people from other groups because they were less able to afford to buy air conditioners and fans to keep body temperatures low (Holahan, 1982).

In an experiment which highlights the importance of control, Langer and Rodin (1976; Rodin & Langer, 1977) studied the impact on institutionalized elderly residents of increasing the amount of control they had. The difference in control was slight, giving some residents a plant to take care of and encouraging them to take responsibility in other areas of their life, such as arranging their room furniture. The impact, however, was powerful. Not only were short-term increases in happiness and activity level found three weeks later, but these differences persisted over 18 months. Most important, perhaps, was the difference in mortality rates among residents. Only 15 percent of the residents in the group which had more control had died in the intervening time span, compared to 30 percent of those in a similar group which had not received enhanced responsibility. The findings dramatically illustrate the importance of psychological factors, such as control over the environment, in determining people's physical and psychological health.

Other studies have demonstrated that not only actual control but simply *belief* in control can mitigate the effects of aversive circumstances. Glass and Singer (1972) exposed college students to loud and irritating noise. Half the students were told they could stop the noise by pushing a button, although they were asked not to do this. The other students were not told the button was available. Although none of the students actually pushed the button, those who believed it was available performed better on tasks and were less irritated by the noise than the group which did not know that the noise could be stopped.

An Example of the Relationship between Unemployment, Stress, and Lack of Control: Mental Health and the Economy

Some of the most important research on the way higher-order levels of the environment affect individuals has examined the relationship between changes in economic conditions and mental health. Brenner (1973) has conducted extensive investigations into the relationship between the economy and admissions to public mental hospitals in New York State. He found an inverse correlation between manufacturing employment and first admissions to mental hospitals. When the economy prospered, hospitalization rates generally decreased. During economic downturns, rates increased. A similar pattern held for readmissions, emergency admissions, and admissions to hospitals for the "criminally insane." The relationship holds for the entire

127-year period for which data are available and has become stronger in the past 30 years.

Brenner's findings are provocative. Yet because they are correlational in nature (indicating simply that two phenomena are likely to occur simultaneously) they cannot tell us why that relationship exists. Catalano (1979) suggests two alternative explanations of Brenner's findings. As ecologists would predict, economic change may increase the incidence of factors which precipitate abnormal behavior (i.e., stressful life events, such as divorce or job loss), and thereby increase rates of mental illness. Alternatively, the rate of abnormal behavior could remain relatively constant, but economic conditions might preclude home care and encourage the use of institutions as shelters for those who need help, thus "uncovering" existing cases of mental illness. In a study analyzing monthly data from Kansas City, Catalano and Dooley (1977) found support for the first explanation. Changes in the economy were associated with the monthly incidence of stressful life events and depressed mood of residents, giving support to an ecological interpretation of Brenner's findings.

A second problem with Brenner's findings is that they are based on aggregate (or group) level data. We do not know if those same people hard hit by a recession are also the ones who enter mental hospitals. We also cannot determine from these data if unemployment causes mental illness, or if it is those who are less mentally fit who become unemployed; that is, unemployment might be a response to rather than a cause of emotional strain. In order to examine these issues, we need longitudinal studies which follow the same individuals over a long time span. Liem and Liem (1979) conducted such a study by following approximately 40 blue-collar and 40 white-collar workers' families for a year following the husband's involuntary loss of his job. They found that emotional strain was a consequence and not a cause of job loss in this group of workers, and that not only the husband but also the entire family was affected. At both one and four months after loss of their job, the husbands exhibited higher levels of psychiatric symptoms, compared to a similar group of men who were employed. After several months, wives of unemployed men were more anxious and depressed than wives from employed families. Signs of stress were also evident in the children of these families—"moodiness at home, new problems in school, and strained relationships with peers" (Liem & Rayman, 1982, p. 1122).

Similar findings emerged from Rayman and Bluestone's (1982) study of the impact of unemployment among aircraft industry workers in the Hartford, Connecticut, area. In addition to financial hardships, serious emotional or physical strain occurred among many of these workers. "High blood pressure, alcoholism, increased smoking, insomnia, neurasthenia, and worry and anxiety were among the more commonly reported forms of strain" (Liem & Rayman, 1982, p. 1120).

Reactions to unemployment are affected by one's life circumstances. In the study of aircraft workers, middle-aged heads of households with young dependents were most severely affected. Catalano and Dooley (in press) found that fluctuations in the economy most affect middle-income workers. The poor and the rich remain so during good times and bad, while middle-income workers experience more undesirable job and financial events, such as a mortgage foreclosure or decrease in wages, during periods of economic contraction. For a lucky few, unemployment can be an opportunity rather than a disaster. A study of 100 technical professionals who had lost their jobs in defense-industry cutbacks found that a surprising 48 percent held favorable attitudes to their job loss (Little, 1976). Some workers make use of this time to further their education or switch to a new and more rewarding job field. One's life circumstances, coping abilities, and networks of social support all influence reactions to unemployment.

Implications for Community Interventions

The most straightforward implication of these studies for the prevention of psychological and physical disorder is to keep the national economy continually on an even keel. Obviously, such a solution is beyond the capabilities of mental health personnel working alone. Judging from the tremendous inflationary spiral around the world starting in the mid-1970s, it may also be beyond the capabilities of economists and politicians.

But there are many other things mental health personnel can do in the face of stress-inducing economic change. Where a social stressor is preventable (e.g., in the case of noise or maladaptive architectural design), we would urge mental health personnel to work toward its prevention. But where a social stressor (e.g., economic downturns) cannot be prevented, the role of mental health personnel lies in mitigating the adverse effects of social stress.

If an economic downturn were forecast for a given area, for example, the community mental health system could begin preparing the population for how to deal with the psychological ramifications of the downturn. Relying upon anticipatory guidance (Bloom, 1971) through the mass media, one could attempt to persuade the about-to-be unemployed that their situation, while very unfortunate, is not of their own doing. They did not cause their unemployment and should not feel personally responsible for it or guilty about it. Neither should their families view them as failures. Consultation with unemployment agencies to encourage treating clients with respect rather than condescension also would be advised. Other strategies may be advocated as well, such as encouraging workers to organize to buy out a plant rather than accept unemployment.

That such efforts at a preventive "attribution therapy" (Davison & Valins, 1969), where one attempts to mitigate the psychological effects of unemployment by attributing it, correctly, to societal rather than personal inadequacies—might be of some success is suggested by Brenner's data. During the Depression of the 1930s, the increase in mental hospitalization was not as great as would have been expected from the enormity of the economic decline. "The reason for this curious finding," Brenner speculates, "may be that a very large number of persons lost income and employment at about the same time, particularly within similar industries and occupations. It may be generally true, then, that the more an individual feels he is among a minority of the economically disadvantaged, or the closer he comes to feeling singled out by economic loss, the more likely he is to see economic failure as a personal failure, one due to his own incompetence" (1973, p. 236).

Attributing psychological difficulties to their actual social causes rather than to clients' personal disposition is the direct opposite of the traditional treatment approach, which deals with clients as if their difficulties sprang from characterological flaws rather than from a constellation of social forces (e.g., social intolerance of homosexuals or social limitations on the roles deemed "appropriate" for women). Such a change in orientation may be demanded for psychological—as well as moral—reasons if the stresses induced by social forces are to be attenuated. Lest passivity ensue from portraying the individual as a helpless victim of economic and social circumstances beyond his or her control, it may be important to separate responsibility for the cause of a problem from responsibility for its resolution.

Brickman and his colleagues (Brickman, Rabinowitz, Karuza, Jr., Coates, Cohn, & Kidder, 1982) differentiate among four models of helping and coping, distinguished by whether or not people are held responsible for causing their problems and whether or not they are held responsible for solving these problems (See Table 6–1). These four models are labeled moral, enlightenment, compensatory, and medical. The compensatory model holds that people are not responsible for the development of problems, but are responsible for solutions. Social or situational factors, not personal deficiencies, are the cause of problems, yet correcting them may require individual effort. While the individual should not feel personally responsible for being unemployed (or guilty if a homosexual, or anomic if a housewife), he or she should be encouraged to actively take responsibility for resolving the underlying problems (e.g., finding another job, campaigning for the repeal of antihomosexual laws, or beginning a new career, to mention only a few of the many options available). Helping people under this model may take the form of training them to deal more assertively or effectively with their environment. Control remains in the hands of the people affected rather than in the hands of experts or authorities. The compensatory model implicitly or explicitly underlies many community psychology interventions.

LIFE EVENTS AS A SOURCE OF STRESS

Stress may occur because of life changes which are simply a result of maturation across the life cycle. Holmes and Rahe (1967; Rahe, 1968) have found that the frequency of life changes is associated with the likelihood of becoming physically ill. They developed a Social Readjustment Rating Scale

TABLE 6–1
Consequences of Attribution of Responsibility in Four Models of Helping and Coping

Attribution to Self of Responsibility for Problem	Attribution to Self of Responsibility for Solution	
	High	*Low*
High	**Moral model**	**Enlightenment model**
Perception of self	Lazy	Guilty
Actions expected of self	Striving	Submission
Others besides self who must act	Peers	Authorities
Actions expected of others	Exhortation	Discipline
Implicit view of human nature	Strong	Bad
Potential pathology	Loneliness	Fanaticism
Low	**Compensatory model**	**Medical model**
Perception of self	Deprived	Ill
Actions expected of self	Assertion	Acceptance
Others besides self who must act	Subordinates	Experts
Actions expected of others	Mobilization	Treatment
Implicit view of human nature	Good	Weak
Potential pathology	Alienation	Dependency

From Brickman, P., Rabinowitz, V. C., Karuza, J. Jr., Coates, D., Cohn, E., & Kidder, L. Models of helping and coping. *American Psychologist,* 1982, *37,* 370. Copyright (1982) by the American Psychological Association. Reprinted/ Adapted by permission of the author.

to measure stressful life events. They asked respondents to rate a series of events requiring adaptation and change, such as divorce, job changes, residential change, and so forth, using as a reference the event *marriage,* which was arbitrarily given a weight of 50 (see Table 6–2). Death of a spouse received the highest mean rating (100 units), while minor violations in the law received the lowest (11 units). Those with a higher life events score were more likely to have experienced illness.

Considerable debate has emerged about the diversity of types of events included in the life events scale. Some events seem desirable, while others would generally be considered undesirable. Negative or undesirable events, such as incarceration, seem to involve more change than positive ones, although such positive events as marriage or the birth of a child can be stressful, also. For example, parents' delight in a new child may be confounded by the absence of sleep, the additional work, and the constant responsibility that parenthood brings. Critics of the Holmes and Rahe scale argue that some events may be within a person's control, while others may be unavoidable; some events may be expected or anticipated, while others come as a surprise; some events involve loss, while others involve gain (Eaton, 1980; Eckenrode & Gore, 1981). Unanticipated and uncontrolled

TABLE 6–2
Social Readjustment Rating Scale

Rank	Life Event	Change Score
1	Death of spouse	100
2	Divorce	73
3	Marital separation	65
4	Jail term	63
5	Death of close family member	63
6	Personal injury or illness	53
7	Marriage	50
8	Fired at work	47
9	Marital reconciliation	45
10	Retirement	45
11	Change in health of family member	44
12	Pregnancy	40
13	Sex difficulties	39
14	Gain of new family member	39
15	Business readjustment	39
16	Change in financial state	38
17	Death of close friend	37
18	Change to different line of work	36
19	Change in number of arguments with spouse	35
20	Mortgage over $10,000	31
21	Foreclosure of mortgage or loan	30
22	Change in responsibilities at work	29
23	Son or daughter leaving home	29
24	Trouble with in-laws	29
25	Outstanding personal achievement	28
26	Wife begin or stop work	26
27	Begin or end school	26
28	Change in living conditions	25
29	Revision of personal habits	24
30	Trouble with boss	23
31	Change in work hours or conditions	20
32	Change in residence	20
33	Change in schools	20
34	Change in recreation	19
35	Change in church activities	19
36	Change in social activities	18
37	Mortgage or loan less than $10,000	17
38	Change in sleeping habits	16
39	Change in number of family get-togethers	15
40	Change in eating habits	15
41	Vacation	13
42	Christmas	12
43	Minor violations of the law	11

From Holmes and Rahe, 1967, Table 3, p. 216.

events appear to be more stressful than those which are expected or can be controlled. Some stressful events, such as having an abortion or becoming a crime victim, do not appear on the scale.

Dohrenwend (1978) suggests that "stressful life events vary in the extent to which they are determined by the environment or by psychological characteristics of the central person in the event" (p. 3). People may be the "passive recipients" of some events but the "active creators" of others (Zautra & Reich, 1980). Losing a job because one is chronically late to work is likely to be a different experience than losing a job because a plant goes out of business. While the extent of actual control over events varies, perceived control may vary, too. The chronic latecomer sometimes blames the boss instead of himself or herself for the job loss. Furthermore, individuals differ in the amount of stress incurred by the same event (Eckenrode & Gore, 1981). As we have just mentioned in the previous section, unemployment can bring a welcome break in routine to a lucky few who can afford the absence of income, while others are devastated by the lack of a job.

Immediate reaction to a stressful life event may include the development of psychological symptoms, yet these symptoms usually are transient in nature (Dohrenwend, 1978). Psychological growth, no substantial change, or the development of persistent psychopathology, all are possible outcomes, depending on the context in which the stress reaction occurs. Psychological factors, such as one's coping abilities, and situational factors, such as the presence or absence of material and social support, affect the outcome of the transient stress reaction; we discuss these factors later in the section of this chapter titled "Coping with Stress."

Kobasa (1982) suggests that personality traits also determine one's reaction to stress. Her research assumes that "persons' general orientations toward life or characteristic interests and motivations would influence how any given stressful life event was interpreted and dealt with and, thereby, the event's ultimate impact on the physiological and biological organism" (1982, p. 6). She has identified a personality style of stress resistance or hardiness composed of three factors. *Commitment* to self and others and to one's work and interpersonal relationships provides a sense of community and purpose to life that buffers the harmful effects of stress. Belief in *control* leads one to interpret events as stemming from one's own actions, and, therefore, as subject to influence and modification, while *challenge* is an orientation that welcomes change as a natural part of life and a source of opportunity rather than threat. The hardy personality, incorporating aspects of commitment, control, and challenge, is less likely to become ill when faced with stressful life events.

While Dohrenwend (1978) emphasizes the role of discrete stressful events in the production of psychopathology, others believe that ongoing exposure to longstanding stressful conditions is the primary cause of stress reactions. In addition, chronic life conditions, such as quarreling parents or a sick mother, may precipitate the occurrence of stressful life events (Eckenrode & Gore, 1981). A study of low-income mothers found that the continual pressure caused by poverty, heavy responsibilities, and loneliness led to depression among this population group even if there was no single emergency or catastrophe (Guttentag, Salasin, & Belle, 1980). Others (Kanner, Coyne, Schaefer, & Lazarus, 1981; De Longis, Coyne, Dakoff, Folkman, & Lazarus, 1982) have found that relatively minor but irritating daily hassles, such as traffic jams or losing things or too many interruptions, also have an impact on health independent of life events. Indeed, research by Lazarus and his colleagues has found that the frequency of hassles were a better predictor of psychological symptoms (Kanner et al., 1981) and somatic illness (DeLongis et al., 1982) than life events. As a poem by Charles Bukowski illustrates:

> It is not the large things that
>   send a man to the madhouse. . . .
> No, it's the continuing series
>   of small tragedies that send
>   a man to the madhouse
> Not the death of his love
>   but a shoelace that
>   snaps with no time left.
> (Bukowski, 1980)

Catalano (1979) claims that the level of stress experienced by a population over time can be predicted by the age profile of the population and the prevailing economic conditions. He divides the list of stressors included in the life-events scale into three categories: life-cycle events, economic well-being, and random occurrences. The random occurrence events, such as death of a family member or personal illness, remain relatively constant over time for a population and form a "baseline" level of stress. The age profile of the population would indicate the frequency of life-cycle events, such as leaving home or being married, while fluctuations in the economy would predict the rate of financial stressors, such as unemployment or a new mortgage. Such estimates of rates of health and behavioral problems could be used for social planning and policy development.

THE PHYSICAL ENVIRONMENT AS A SOURCE OF STRESS

Environmental Stressors

In this section, we consider the role that stressors in the physical environment, such as poor air or noise, can play in people's behavior and coping. The air we breathe, the streets we walk on, and the environments we live and work in are generally inconspicuous. We tend to notice them only if something is wrong.

Low-quality environmental conditions, such as high population density, air pollution, heat, noise, and toxic chemicals, have received considerable attention from the public and from environmental psychologists (e.g., Wandersman, Andrews, Riddle, & Fancett, 1983). Since research on environmental conditions has proliferated sufficiently to fill its own textbooks in recent years (e.g., Holahan, 1982) we cover only selected topics here in order to illustrate environmental effects; for a more detailed discussion, see Wandersman et al., 1983.

Density. The largest number of psychological studies on environmental stress has been performed on population density, stemming in part from the relationship between crowded conditions and urban riots in the late 1960s (Harries, 1980). While *density* is an objective number of people in a given space, *crowding* is the negative psychological state which *may* result from high density.

The following studies illustrate some of the effects density can have on social environment, performance, and health. One study compared the behavior of students who had been randomly assigned by the housing office to live in doubles with those in triples (i.e., two people living in rooms designed for two people versus three people living in rooms designed for two people), due to a lack of dormitory space (Karlin, Epstein, & Aiello, 1978). At the end of the semester, students living in triples had lower grades and lower performance on complex tasks. Tripled women had more physical and psychological problems than women living in doubles or than tripled men, and all of the female triples dissolved by the end of the first semester. Baum and Valins (1977) found that students living in high-density conditions were more likely to withdraw from social interaction.

Another study looked at the effects of density on social climate, interpersonal relations, and health in a juvenile correctional institution (Ray, Wandersman, Huntington, & Ellisor, in press). Both the social environment and the treatment program deteriorated when density increased. Under high-density conditions, the social climate of the dorm was disorganized, hostile, and disruptive. For example, to the statement, "This unit is very well organized," 100 percent of the residents answered "false" during high density, while 42 percent answered "false" during low density. Additional studies on density in dormitories and prisons have found similar results to those described above (e.g., Baron, Mandel, Adams, & Griffen, 1976; Paulus, McCain, & Cox, 1978).

The simple hypothesis that high numbers of people always lead to crowding and negative effects has not been supported by research (e.g., Baum & Valins, 1979; Freedman, 1975). A number of *mediating* conditions, such as architectural features and feelings of control, have been found to moderate the effects of high density (Baum & Valins, 1979). Baum and Valins (1979, p. 138) propose that "crowding is experienced when high density inhibits individuals' ability to regulate the nature and frequency of their social interaction with others."

Noise. The distinction between sound and noise is somewhat similar to the distinction between density and crowding. Noise is a psychological concept defined as "sound that is unwanted by the listener because it is unpleasant, bothersome, interferes with important activities or is believed to be physiologically harmful" (Cohen & Weinstein, 1981, p. 38). Negative effects of noise have been demonstrated on cognitive abilities and social behavior.

Cohen, Glass, and Singer (1973) investigated the effects of highway noise on children living in high-rise apartments. Children on the lower (noisier) levels performed significantly more poorly on auditory discrimination and reading tests than did children on higher floors. A similar pattern of difficulties was found in children whose classrooms were next to a railroad, compared to those whose classes were on the other side of the building (Bronzaft & McCarthy, 1975). Cohen, Evans, Krantz, and Stokols (1980) investigated the effects of airplane noise on children's feelings of personal control, attentional strategies, and physiological processes related to health. They compared children attending schools under the airport corridor of a busy metropolitan airport versus children in quiet schools. The schools were similar in racial and social class composition. Students from the noisier schools had higher blood pressure, were more likely to fail on a cognitive task, and were more likely to give up before the time to complete the task had elapsed than the children from quiet schools. However, some expected differences (e.g., reading scores) were not found.

Social behavior is also affected by high noise levels (Glass & Singer, 1972; Page, 1977). Appleyard and Lintell (1972) studied streets which varied in the amount of traffic (and, therefore, traffic noise) they had. More casual social interaction took place on the light-traffic street, while residents on the high-traffic street reported that it was a more lonely place to live.

Toxic wastes. The danger of toxic chemicals has been brought to public attention by national media coverage of such events as the Three Mile Island (TMI) nuclear plant accident and local coverage of numerous toxic waste problems, such as leaking barrels in recycling dumps and the derailing of railroad cars filled with dangerous substances. The psychological implications of toxic wastes represents a new area of investigation for environmental psychologists. A study of the aftereffects of the Three Mile Island incident by Baum, Fleming, and Singer (1982) illustrates the role psychological research can play. The researchers compared residents living in four locations—living near TMI, living near an undamaged nuclear plant, living near a coal-fired plant, and not living near a power plant. They found that residents living near TMI reported more somatic and psychological problems (e.g., headache, nausea, depression, anxiety) and showed poorer task performance and higher levels of catecholamines (a biochemical measure of stress) in the urine than the three comparison groups. The difference between the TMI and other residents still existed a year and a half after the incident.

In summary, environmental factors have been found to affect performance, physical and mental health, and interpersonal behavior. However, from previously reported studies on various environmental stressors it is readily apparent that psychological factors play an important role in people's perception of the environment and resulting behavior. The necessity for distinguishing between objective stimuli and the psychological state (e.g., density versus crowding, sound versus noise) provides evidence for this assertion. For example, it is not clear in the case of the Three Mile Island accident discussed above whether the actual levels of radioactivity in the air were enough to be dangerous. Regardless of the actual radioactivity levels, the fear of what might happen, which was heightened by media coverage, added to the intensity of the stressor.

The Built Environment

Density, noise, and toxic wastes are conditions in the ambient (surrounding) environment which affect people. In addition, the design of buildings and spaces in which we live and work can have an impact on psychological well-being. In this section, we illustrate the relationship between the built environment, coping, and effects on behavior by discussing two examples: mental health treatment settings and urban environments.

Mental Health Treatment Settings

Several studies suggest that seating arrangements can affect social interaction. Sommer and Ross (1958) found that women in a geriatric hospital room engaged in limited contact when chairs were in a row along day-room walls. However, when seating was manipulated by the experimenters into small clusters of chairs, conversation was facilitated. Similarly, Holahan (1972) found that quality and quantity of conversation increased when small groups of male psychiatric patients were seated around a table, as opposed to being seated in rows around the wall.

While the preceding examples involve small-scale interventions into the problem of withdrawal, other research has focused on the effects of large-scale changes. Holahan and Saegert (1973) documented the effects of a large-scale manipulation of the environment: ward redesign. Remodeling of a psychiatric admissions ward was based on the preferences and dissatisfaction of patients and staff who were interviewed, and consisted of repainting, refurnishing, and creating areas on the ward which "afforded a wide range of social options." Another admissions ward of the hospital did not undergo the redesign and served as a control ward for comparison purposes. After the remodeling, patients on the experimental ward engaged in more social behavior and were thus less withdrawn than the patients on the control ward. In addition, the change in design affected a change in the ward social system. For example, new expectations and competencies developed among staff as they participated in the planning of the redesign, and the ward became a showplace for hospital administrators. Holahan notes that the increased feelings of competence during the process "generalized naturally to other role behaviors involving therapeutic planning, interpersonal staff relations, and more healthy contacts with patients" (1979, p. 226).

The Urban Environment

Popular views of the city conclude that it fosters negative behavior: Cities are places of stress, tension, fear, complexity, confusion, crime, pollution, and crowding (Fischer, 1976; Proshansky, 1978). Empirical evidence verifies that persons in cities are more likely to encounter environmental stressors (e.g., noise, density) which have negative effects on individuals in certain situations. Proshansky (1978) suggests, however, that many urban researchers have assumed that the city is undesirable and, thus, have focused on negative effects. He proposes that the effects of the urban environment are more complex and often more positive than the research has revealed.

Negative effects. Many stimuli identified as potential environmental stressors, such as noise, air pollution, and density, are more prevalent in cities than in nonurban areas. In addition, high traffic in the street on which one lives is related to less social interaction among neighbors and more territorial withdrawal and concerns about safety (Appleyard & Lintell, 1972). Fear of crime, prevalent in urban areas, is associated with emotional reactions (Lawton, Nahemow, Yaffe, & Feldman, 1976; Lewis, 1981) and with risk-management strategies that reduce people's opportunities for leisure activities and social interaction (Riger & Gordon, 1981). City dwellers are more likely to avoid affiliation with strangers (Milgram, 1970) and may be less willing to help others in need (Korte, 1978).

Positive effects. Proshansky (1978) implies that the structural diversity confronting the urban dweller promotes personal growth and ability. He argues that urbanites have the freedom and opportunity not only to expect environmental choices but also to make the choices. The urbanite also may learn more overlapping social roles and socially mediated coping techniques, which encourage the individual to respond positively to environmental change. Fischer (1976) proposes that the structural differentiation of cities results in highly supportive subcultures, which increase the likelihood that one will have friends like oneself, mutual assistance, and exposure to innovative ideas.

Urban areas, when compared to nonurban areas, reveal higher rates of crime (Harries, 1980), mental hospital admissions (Kirmeyer, 1978), and alcoholism (Fischer, 1976). But differences in rates may be attributable to more sophisticated reporting and service availability in urban areas. Fischer's (1976) review of the evidence suggests that, while urbanites are increasingly reporting lower life satisfaction, there is no consistent difference in the suicide rates between urban and rural areas; and surveys reveal community size is not associated with stress symptoms or expressions of powerlessness.

This brief review suggests that urban environments are complex and have a variety of effects, both positive and negative. The urban environment presents an individual with objective physical conditions. How a physical condition, such as graffiti on buildings, is perceived can be affected by individual differences. For example, urban newcomers from smaller communities are more adversely affected by urban stressors than long-time residents. Newcomers report sensing higher levels of noise, crowding, and awareness of crime and fast pace of life (Wohlwill & Kohn, 1973). Differences between long-term urbanites and newcomers tend to disappear within the first year on most dimensions (Ittelson, 1978). Urban effects also vary by degree of *control* perceived by the individual (Cohen, 1978). Since certain subpopulations, such as the elderly or the poor, may have generalized low control, these groups may be at higher risk of disorder induced by environmental effects.

The Significance of Personal Control

Perception of the environment is influenced by objective physical conditions and individual differences. Perception of the environment involves a number of processes and concepts, including control, risk, novelty and complexity, and territoriality and privacy (see Bell, Fisher, & Loomis, 1978, for a review). People judge whether the environment is in the acceptable or unacceptable range. The concept of control is perhaps the most significant element in understanding the effects of stressful environments on human behavior (Cohen & Sherrod, 1978). The person who can exercise control or believes that control is available is more likely to be mentally healthy since he or she can change an undesirable environment or can adapt positively to environmental stressors.

Privacy and social interaction are key concepts and concerns in the environments we have discussed, such as mental hospitals and urban settings. In these settings, people do not seem to want too much or too little social interaction. Altman (1975; Altman, Vinsel, & Brown, 1981) has crystallized this issue by discussing privacy as a dialectic which involves *control* over social interactions with others. Sometimes people want to be with others. When they do not achieve their desired state of interaction (e.g, they have too much privacy), feelings of social isolation result. When there is more interaction than the person wishes, then the person feels crowded. The key issue, then, is *control* over the amount of interaction itself. Control or lack of control influences whether a person feels crowded, or one's territory is infringed, or one feels overloaded with stimuli, and so on.

COPING WITH STRESS

Not everyone reacts to stressors in the same way. Lazarus's (1966) model of stress, centered on a two-step appraisal process, helps us understand individual differences in reaction to stressors. First, people evaluate the nature and extent of danger from a stressor. For a stimulus to be experienced as a stressor, it must be a signal to people of some possible future harm. Psychological factors mediate the way that stressors are perceived (McGrath, 1977; Lazarus & Launier, 1978): What is a threat to some people may be perceived as a challenge or even of no consequence to others. People then appraise the extent of their resources to cope with a threat and select a particular coping strategy. For example, people living in a dangerous urban neighborhood may attempt to minimize their contact with street crime by going out of the house as infrequently as possible, or they may reduce stress by denying that the neighborhood is dangerous for them. Finally, reappraisal involves a change in the original perception of the situation, since coping may change the conditions under which the stressor was originally assessed. If one leaves the house frequently without encountering danger, then the neighborhood may be reappraised as safe.

Coping Strategies

Lazarus and his colleagues (Folkman & Lazarus, 1980) have identified two general coping strategies: problem-oriented and emotion-oriented. Problem-focused strategies attempt to deal directly with the source of stress, while emotion-focused techniques seek to reduce stress by regulating one's emotional reactions. While people use both types of coping in all types of stressful situations, they may vary in the amounts of each type employed. Thus, one study found that people "used relatively more problem-focused coping at work and in situations they appraised they could change, and more emotion-focused coping in health situations and ones they appraised that they must accept" (Aldwin, Folkman, Schaefer, Coyne, & Lazarus, 1980, p. 2).

Factors in the environment can exert a "pull" for particular modes of coping. If the environment is seen as intractable, then people may adopt emotion-oriented coping strategies rather than attempt to modify or change the environment. In addition, resources available to people may affect their choice of coping strategy. Moving from a dangerous neighborhood may be the most effective way to deal with threat of crime, but this option is not available to people of limited means.

Riger and Gordon (1981) have studied the strategies that women use to cope with crime in urban areas. Although women are not the most frequent victims of violent crime, with the exception of rape, they are more afraid of crime and limit their lives more than men do in a quest for safety. Women use two types of coping strategies to minimize their likelihood of attack (see also Skogan & Maxfield, 1981). The first, isolation, reduces danger by avoiding risks. Not going out alone at night and staying out of certain parts of town can reduce women's exposure to certain forms of street violence. The second strategy consists of "street savvy" tactics, which permit women to minimize risks in the face of danger. While the strategies that women use to cope with crime do not necessarily cost money, they do cost time, effort, and, in some cases, lost opportunities. For the women interviewed by Riger and Gordon, such necessary activities as work or school were sufficiently compelling to overcome the threat of danger, while optional social or recreational activities were those most likely to be foregone. Thus, crime had the effect of shrinking women's choices, affecting the quality of their lives, and reducing their freedom of movement through public areas.

The type of coping strategy employed can have serious consequences for the outcome of a stressful situation. Janoff-Bulman (1979) identified two modes of coping with rape. Some victims blamed their behavior for the rape, saying, for example, "I shouldn't have been in that neighborhood" or "I shouldn't have talked to that man." Others blamed their character, believing that in some way they deserved the attack because they were too trusting, too naive and gullible, unable to take care of themselves, and so on. Counselors reported that behavioral self-blame was much more common than characterological self-blame among rape victims, which Janoff-Bulman interprets as an attempt by victims to reestablish a sense of control. Assigning blame to specific behaviors permits the possibility of control in the future, since the behavior at fault can be changed. Blaming one's character offers no such possibilities of avoiding an attack in the future. Well-meaning helpers who tell the victim, "It wasn't your fault," inadvertently may increase his or her sense of powerlessness. Instead, control may be reaffirmed by discussing behavioral strategies to minimize the risk of victimization in the future.

Traditional psychology has emphasized the defense mechanisms used to ward off anxiety in coping with stress. Now we are beginning to see recognition of strategies that permit more positive forms of accommodation, such as seeking information in the face of serious illness (Hamburg, Coelho, & Adams, 1974).

The Role of Natural Support Systems in Coping with Stress

One of the most important resources in coping with environmental stress appears to be the presence of people who act as a "natural support system." A number of studies (reviewed in Gottlieb, 1981) indicate that the availability of a supportive social network can help people cope with situations ranging from job loss to serious illness to marital disruption. Those with a support network tend to have fewer symptoms of both physical and mental disorder in the face of stress. Although research findings in this area are promising, methodological and substantive questions remain to be explored. The concept of "social support" itself is not always clearly defined. What, exactly, do people receive from a social network? And how does this help them cope with stress? (See Chapter Seven for a further discussion of the problems with the support construct.)

Hirsch (1981) identified five forms of support: cognitive guidance, socializing, social reinforcement, tangible assistance, and emotional support. In studies of women undergoing life changes (e.g., widowhood and returning to college), Hirsch found that multifaceted friendships—ones in which the partners engaged in more than one kind of activity with each other (such as recreation and intimate discussion)—were associated with higher self-esteem and more satisfying social and tangible assistance. These relationships may have helped because they enabled these women to develop new contacts outside of the family. Hirsch conceptualizes the social network as "a personal community that embeds and supports critical social identities" (p. 160), and permits participation in society. During periods of life change, the presence of a social network can facilitate the difficult process of building a new identity structure.

While much of the research on social networks examines their effect on the outcomes of stressful situations, researchers are now beginning to examine the processes which mediate these outcomes. Descriptions of the coping processes that people use to reduce and moderate stress offer insight into the reasons behind individual differences in reactions to stress. A particularly rich description of the coping process utilizing social network support is provided by Carol Stack (1974). Her book, *All Our Kin,* portrays the strategies that poor black families use to ensure survival in a situation of chronic poverty. Coping with poverty in a black urban ghetto (called The Flats) required the exchange of goods and services among people that united them in a rich cooperative network of reciprocal obligations, illustrated by the following example:

> Cecil (35) lives in The Flats with his mother Willie Mae, his oldest sister and her two children, and his younger brother. Cecil's younger sister Lily lives with their mother's sister Bessie. Bessie has three children and Lily has two. Cecil and his mother have part-time jobs in a cafe and Lily's children are on aid. In July of 1970 Cecil and his mother had just put together enough money to cover their rent. Lily paid her utilities, but she did not have enough money to buy food stamps for herself and her children. Cecil and Willie Mae knew that after they paid their rent they would not have any money for food for the family. They helped out Lily by buying her food stamps, and then the two households shared meals together until Willie Mae was paid two weeks later. A week later Lily received her second ADC check and Bessie got some spending money from her boyfriend. They gave some of this money to Cecil and Willie Mae to pay their rent, and gave Willie Mae money to cover her insurance and pay a small sum on a living room suite at the local furniture store. Willie Mae reciprocated later on by buying dresses for Bessie and Lily's daughters and by caring for all the children when Bessie got a temporary job. (Stack, 1974, p. 37)

While participation in the resource exchange network enabled these families to survive, the obligations and duties that it entailed themselves could be a source of stress. Stack found that "close kin who have relied upon one another over the years often complain about the sacrifices they have made and the deprivation they have endured for one another" (1974, p. 36), yet continued exchange was a necessity given the scarcity of their resources.

Implications for Community Intervention

A stress model of person-environment interaction suggests several community-based strategies for reducing the amount of tension experienced by the population as a whole. The most obvious, but by no means the easiest, preventive programs would remove the stressor. Building more dormitories so that high density does not exist, creating regulations limiting noise or not building schools and airports near each other, passing legislation reducing air pollutants, or not building nuclear reactors represent large-scale prevention efforts that would eliminate stress and the potential effects that can follow. Someone familiar with the adverse effects of traffic noise on the reading ability of children living near a highway (Cohen, Glass, & Singer, 1973), for example, might want to use this knowledge to help a citizen's group prevent highway construction near a school. However, attempting to eliminate sources of stress in the environment may require social and political action that has not been considered part of the traditional domain of psychologists, and may bring the psychologists in conflict with possible vested interests. Testifying in court, lobbying a city council or participating in public demonstrations in one's role of psychologist (rather than citizen) is not part of the traditional model of the impartial, objective psychologist-as-scientist, and is the source of a great deal of controversy within the profession itself.

Instituting changes in the immediate environment may be easier for psychologists in their traditional roles. Several studies have found that high density and corridor architectural design in dormitories leads to crowding, negative affect, withdrawal, and behavior symptomatic of learned helplessness by affecting the degree to which an individual can control social contact. Baum and Davis (1980) experimentally investigated the effects of an architectural intervention which reduced the number of residents living on a long corridor from 40 to 20. The intervention converted three bedrooms in the middle of the corridor into a lounge, essentially bisecting the floor. They found that students living in the bisected dorm corridor had more positive interaction on the floor, more confidence in their ability to control events in the dormitory, and less withdrawal in both residential and nonresidential settings. This positive experience was equivalent to an unbisected *short* corridor dorm. The results show more symptoms of stress, withdrawal, and helplessness on the long corridor. The authors conclude: "Direct architectural intervention prevented crowding stress and post stressor effects. In the long run a preventive strategy of the kind taken in the present research may be more beneficial to residents of high-density settings than treatment programs instituted after the problem has been identified" (p. 480).

In addition to attempting to eliminate or prevent avoidable stressors, psychologists can help reduce the impact of those which are unavoidable. An example offered by Harshbarger (1976) in describing the psychological effects of a crisis suggests the need to consider the environment in planning treatment interventions. Harshbarger notes that, following the Buffalo Creek flood, in which hundreds of families suddenly lost their homes, priorities among emergency personnel were to (1) clear the debris, and (2) locate quasi-permanent shelter for persons who lost their homes. The Department of Housing and Urban Development provided mobile homes to the survivors. However, when families were assigned to mobile homes, no attempt was made to cluster residents according to their former neighborhoods; thus, social grouping among the survivors was further splintered. Harshbarger notes such action probably negatively affected the individual's adaptation to the stress. By planning the environment to accommodate existing social networks, adaptation problems might have been reduced.

The variables that mediate stress also can be the target of community interventions. In this chapter we have emphasized the importance of beliefs about control as a mediating variable. We have described above the process of "attribution therapy," in which one attempts to mitigate the psychological effects of a stressful situation by learning to attribute it to societal rather than personal causes. While care must be taken to prevent feelings of helplessness, such a shift in the process of attribution can reduce the intrapunitive effects of self-blame, and can help orient people to social and environmental factors which shape their lives. Consciousness-raising groups of the women's liberation movement in the 1960s and 1970s promoted the understanding among participants that women's common problems are due to societal expectations and influences, not personal deficiencies. Self-help groups among people in similar situations of adversity, such as crime victims or the unemployed, can encourage this viewpoint while offering emotional support and assistance to their participants.

Other mediating variables can be the target of intervention efforts. Lewis and Maxfield's (1980) research showed that signs of social disorder in a neighborhood, such as grafitti or teenagers hanging out on the street, increase citizen's fear of crime. Neighborhood groups can reduce instances of asocial behavior by removing grafitti or fixing abandoned buildings. While such efforts may not reduce the crime rate in a neighborhood, they may eliminate the cues that stimulate fear.

Since eliminating all stressors from our lives is impossible (and possibly undesirable), another way to reduce the harmful effects of stressors is to increase people's coping abilities. Training programs for homemakers displaced by divorce or widowhood may help them adjust to the strains of their new situation. Given the high divorce rate in the United States, anticipatory socialization for adults and children on the psychological effects of divorce might also be appropriate. These programs teach people strategies for coping effectively with specific stressful situations, while other programs attempt to enhance general problem-solving abilities. While the relationship between improved social competency and adjustment calls for further examination (discussed in the chapter on prevention), these interventions offer possibilities for developing techniques that can prevent future problems.

Two additional strategies are suggested by the stress model. First, we can increase the resources that people have to cope with problems. Linking people to social networks can be an effective helping strategy, instead of (or in addition to) providing professional care to those in distress. Silverman (Silverman, Mackenzie, Pettipas, & Wilson, 1974) has developed an innovative program of mutual aid groups among the newly widowed. By meeting with others in the same situation, those in distress can share effective coping strategies and information, and can provide support and reinforcement for each other. Furthermore, the "helper therapy principle" suggests that the act of providing help may be beneficial to the helper as well (Riessman, 1976). Although self-help groups are not likely to supplant professional services, they have grown quickly in recent years for a diversity of conditions ranging from terminal illness to cigarette smoking. The President's Commission on Mental Health (1978) estimated that over half a million self-help groups were operating in the United States. For those in distress the development of a social support network may be an important complement to professional help. In addition to providing emotional support, network members can act as "brokers" to help people get access to tangible resources, such as jobs and housing (Wellman, 1981).

Finally, community psychologists can help people develop skills which give them access to and control over the environment. Rappaport (1981) proposes empowerment as a guiding model for community psychologists, instead of traditional notions of prevention. By empowerment, he means "that our aim should be to enhance the possibilities for people to control their own lives" (p. 15). Many of the problems facing people are not "solvable" in the sense of having a final solution, but rather consists of ongoing dilemmas that are manifested differently depending on environmental conditions (Sarason, 1978). The ability to influence one's environment, therefore, becomes a critical survival skill.

References

Aldwin, C., Folkman, S., Schaefer, C., Coyne, J., & Lazarus, R. S. *Ways of coping: A process measure.* Paper presented at the annual meeting of the American Psychological Association, Montreal, September 1980.

Altman, I. *The environment and social behavior: Privacy, personal space, territory and crowding.* Monterey, Calif.: Brooks/Cole Publishing, 1975.

Altman, I., Vinsel, A., & Brown, B. B. Dialectic conceptions in social psychology: An application to social penetration and privacy regulation. In L. Berkowitz (Ed.), *Advances in experimental social psychology* (Vol. 14). New York: Academic Press, 1981.

Appleyard, D., & Lintell, M. The environmental quality of city streets: The residents' viewpoint. *Journal of the American Institute of Planners,* 1972, *38,* (2), 84–101.

Baron, R. M., Mandel, D. R., Adams, C. A., & Griffen, L. M. Effects of social density in university residential environments. *Journal of Personality and Social Psychology,* 1976, *34,* 434–446.

Baum, A., & Davis, G. E. Reducing the stress of high density living: An architectural intervention. *Journal of Personality and Social Psychology,* 1980, *38* (3), 471–481.

Baum, A., Fleming, R., & Singer, J. E. Stress at Three Mile Island: Applying psychological impact analysis. In L. Bickman (Ed.), *Applied Social Psychology Annual* (Vol. 3). Beverly Hills, Calif.: Sage Publications, 1982.

Baum, A., & Valins, S. *Architecture and social behavior.* Hillsdale, N.J.: Lawrence Erlbaum Associates, 1977.

Baum, A. & Valins, S. Architectural mediation of residential density and control: Crowding and the regulation of social contact. In L. Berkowitz (Ed.), *Advances in experimental social psychology.* Vol. 12. New York: Academic Press, 1979.

Bell, P. A., Fisher, J. D., & Loomis, R. J. *Environmental psychology*. Philadelphia: W. B. Saunders, 1978.

Bloom, B. Strategies for the prevention of mental disorders. In American Psychological Association (Ed.), *Issues in community psychology and preventive mental health* (pp. 1–20). New York: Behavioral Publications, 1971.

Brenner, J. *Mental illness and the economy*. Cambridge, Mass.: Harvard University Press, 1973.

Brickman, P., Rabinowitz, V. C., Karuza Jr., J., Coates, D., Cohn, E., & Kidder, L. Models of helping and coping. *American Psychologist, 1982, 37,* 368–384.

Bronzaft, A. L., & McCarthy, D. P. The effect of elevated train noise on reading ability. *Environment and Behavior, 1975, 7,* 517–528.

Bukowski, C. The shoelace. *Bukowski reads his poetry*. Santa Monica, Calif.: Takoma Records, 1980.

Catalano, R. *Health, behavior and the community*. New York: Pergamon Press, 1979.

Catalano, R., & Dooley, D. Economic predictors of depressed mood and stressful life events. *Journal of Health and Social Behavior, 1977, 18,* 292–307.

Catalano, R., & Dooley, D. The health effects of economic instability: A test of the economic stress hypothesis. *Journal of Health and Social Behavior,* in press.

Cohen, S. Environmental load and the allocation of attention. In A. Baum, J. Singer, & S. Valins (Eds.), *Advances in environmental psychology* (Vol. 1: *The urban environment*). Hillsdale, N.J.: Lawrence Erlbaum Associates, 1978.

Cohen, S., Evans, G. W., Krantz, D. S., & Stokols, D. Physiological, motivational and cognitive effects of aircraft noise on children. *American Psychologist, 1980, 35,* 231–243.

Cohen, S., Glass, D., & Singer, J. Apartment noise, auditory discrimination and reading ability in children. *Journal of Experimental Social Psychology, 1973, 9,* 407–422.

Cohen, S., & Sherrod, D. R. When density matters: Environmental control as a determinant of crowding effects in laboratory and residential settings. In L. Severy (Ed.), *Crowding: Theoretical and research implications for population-environment psychology*. New York: Human Sciences, 1978.

Cohen, S., & Weinsten, N. Nonauditory effects of noise on behavior and health. *Journal of Social Issues, 1981, 37,* (1), 36–70.

Coyne, J. C., & Holroyd, R. A. Stress, coping and illness. In T. Millon, C. Green, & R. Meagher (Eds.), *The handbook of health care clinical psychology*. New York: Plenum Press, in press.

Davison, G., & Valins, S. Self-attribution and the maintenance of behavior change. *Journal of Personality and Social Psychology, 1969, 11,* 25–33.

DeLongis, A., Coyne, J. C., Dakoff, G., Folkman, S., & Lazarus, R. S. Relationship of daily hassles, uplift, and major life events to health status. *Health Psychology, 1982, 1,* 119–136.

Dohrenwend, B. P., & Dohrenwend, B. S. Social and cultural influences on psychopathology. *Annual Review of Psychology, 1974, 25,* 417–452.

Dohrenwend, B. P., & Dohrenwend, B. S. Socioenvironmental factors, stress, and psychopathology. *American Journal of Community Psychology, 1981, 9,* 128–164.

Dohrenwend, B. P., & Dohrenwend, B. S. *Social status and psychological disorder*. New York: John Wiley & Sons, 1969.

Dohrenwend, B. S. Social status and stressful life events. *Journal of Personality and Social Psychology,* 1973, *28,* 225–235.

Dohrenwend, B. S. Social stress and community psychology. *American Journal of Community Psychology,* 1978, *6,* 1–14.

Eaton, W. W. The sociology of mental disorders. New York: Praeger Publishers, 1980.

Eckenrode, J., & Gore, S. Stressful events and social supports: The significance of context. In B. Gottlieb, *Social networks and social support.* Beverly Hills, Calif.: Sage Publications, 1981.

Fischer, C. S. *The urban experience.* New York: Harcourt Brace Jovanovich, 1976.

Folkman, S., & Lazarus, R. S. Coping in an adequately functioning middle-aged population. *Journal of Health and Social Behavior,* 1980, *21,* 219–239.

Freedman, J. L. *Crowding and behavior.* New York: Viking Press, 1975.

Glass, D., & Singer, J. *Urban stress.* New York: Academic Press, 1972.

Gottlieb, B. *Social networks and social support in community mental health.* Beverly Hills, Calif.: Sage Publications, 1981.

Guttentag, M., Salasin, S., & Belle, D. (Eds.). *The mental health of women.* New York: Academic Press, 1980.

Hamburg, D. A., Coelho, G. V., & Adams, J. E. Coping and adaptation: Steps toward a synthesis of biological and social perspectives. In G. V. Coelho, D. A. Hamburg, & J. E. Adams (Eds.), *Coping and adaptation.* New York: Basic Books, 1974.

Harries, K. D. *Crime and the environment.* Springfield, Ill.: Charles C Thomas, 1980.

Harshbarger, D. An ecological perspective on disaster intervention. In H. J. Parad, H. L. Resnick, & L. Parad (Eds.), *Emergency and disaster management: A mental health service book.* Bowie, Md.: Charles Press, 1976.

Hirsch, B. J. Social networks and the coping process: Creating personal communities. In B. Gottlieb, *Social networks and social support.* Beverly Hills, Calif.: Sage Publications, 1981.

Holahan, C. Seating patterns and patient behavior in an experimental dayroom. *Journal of Abnormal Psychology,* 1972, *80,* 115–124.

Holahan, C. J. *Environmental psychology.* New York: Random House, copyright 1982, reprinted with permission.

Holahan, C. J. Environmental psychology in psychiatric hospital settings. In D. Canter & S. Canter (Eds.), *Designing for therapeutic environments: A review of research.* New York: John Wiley & Sons, 1979.

Holahan, C., & Saegert, S. Behavioral and attitudinal effects of large-scale variation in the physical environment of psychiatric wards. *Journal of Abnormal Psychology,* 1973, *82,* 454–462.

Hollingshead, A. B., & Redlich, F. C. *Social class and mental illness.* New York: John Wiley & Sons, 1958.

Holmes, J. H., & Rahe, R. H. The social readjustment rating scale. *Journal of Psychosomatic Research,* 1967, *11,* 213–218.

Insel, P. M. *Environmental variables and the prevention of mental illness.* Lexington, Mass.: D. C. Heath, 1980.

Ittleson, W. H. Environmental perception and urban experience. *Environment and Behavior,* 1978, *10,* (2), 193–213.

Janoff-Bulman, R. Characterological versus behavioral self-blame: Inquiries into depression and rape. *Journal of Personality and Social Psychology,* 1979, *37,* 1798–1809.

Kanner, A. D., Coyne, J. C., Schaefer, C., & Lazarus, R. S. Comparison of two modes of stress measurement: Daily hassles and uplifts versus major life events. *Journal of Behavioral Medicine,* 1981, *4,* 1–39.

Karlin, R. A., Epstein, Y. M. & Aiello, J. R. Strategies for the investigation of crowding. In A. Esser & B. Greenbie (Eds.), *Design for community and privacy.* New York: Plenum Press, 1978.

Kirmeyer, S. Urban density and pathology: A review of research. *Environment and Behavior,* 1978, *10,* (2), 247–269.

Kobasa, S. C. The hardy personality: Toward a social psychology of stress and health. In J. Suls & G. Sanders (Eds.), *Social Psychology of Health and Illness.* Hillsdale, N.J.: Lawrence Erlbaum Associates, 1982.

Korte, C. Helpfulness in the urban environment. In A. Baum, J. Singer, & S. Valins (Eds.), *Advances in environmental psychology* (Vol. 1: *The urban environment*). Hillsdale, N.J.: Lawrence Erlbaum Associates, 1978.

Langer, E. J., & Rodin, J. The effects of choice and enhanced personal responsibility for the aged: A field experiment in an institutional setting. *Journal of Personality and Social Psychology,* 1976, *34,* 191–198.

Lawton, M. P., Nahemow, L., Yaffe, S., & Feldman, S. Psychological aspects of crime and fear of crime. In S. Goldsmith (Ed.), *Crime and the elderly.* Lexington, Mass.: D. C. Heath, 1976.

Lazarus, R. S. *Psychological stress and the coping process.* New York: McGraw-Hill, 1966.

Lazarus, R. S., & Cohen, J. B. Environmental stress. In I. Altman & J. F. Wohlwill (Eds.), *Human behavior and environment* (Vol. 1). New York: Plenum, 1977.

Lazarus, R. S., & Launier, R. Stress-related transactions between person and environment. In L. A. Pervin & M. Lewis (Eds.), *Perspectives in interactional psychology.* New York: Plenum, 1978.

Lewis, D. A. (Ed.). *Reactions to crime.* Beverly Hills, Cal.: Sage Publications, 1981.

Lewis, D. A., & Maxfield, M. G. Fear in the neighborhoods: An investigation of the impact of crime. *Journal of Research in Crime and Delinquency,* 1980, *17,* 160–189.

Liem, R., & Rayman, P. Health and social costs of unemployment: Research and policy considerations. *American Psychologist,* 1982, *37,* 1116–1123.

Liem, R., & Liem, J. Social support and stress: Some general issues and their application to the problem of unemployment. In L. Ferman & J. Gordus (Eds.), *Mental health and the economy.* Kalamazoo, Mich.: Upjohn Institute, 1979.

Little, C. B. Technical-professional unemployment: Middle-class adaptability to personal crisis. *Sociological Quarterly,* 1976, *17,* 262–274.

McGrath, J. E. Settings, measures, and themes: an integrative review of some research on social-psychological factors in stress. In A. Monat, & R. S. Lazarus (Eds.), *Stress and coping: an anthology.* New York: Columbia University Press, 1977.

Milgram, S. The experience of living in cities. *Science,* 1970, *13,* 1461–1464.

Monat, A., & Lazarus, R. S. (Eds.). *Stress and coping: an anthology.* New York: Columbia University Press, 1977.

Novaco, R. W., Stokols, D., Campbell, J., & Stokols, J. Transportation, stress, and community psychology. *American Journal of Community Psychology*, 1979, *7*, 361–380.

Page, R. Noise and helping behavior. *Environment and Behavior*, 1977, *9*, 311–340.

Paulus, P. B., McCain, G., & Cox, V. Death rates, psychiatric commitments, blood pressure and perceived crowding as a function of institutional crowding. *Environmental Psychology and Nonverbal Behavior*, 1978, *3*, 107–116.

President's Commission on Mental Health. Washington, D.C.: U.S. Government Printing Office, 1978.

Proshansky, H. M. The city and self-identity. *Environment and Behavior*, 1978, *10* (2), 147–169.

Rahe, R. H. Life-change measurement as a predictor of illness. *Proceedings of the Royal Society of Medicine*, 1968, *61*, 1124–1126.

Rappaport, J. In praise of paradox: A social policy of empowerment over prevention. *American Journal of Community Psychology*, 1981, *9*, 1–25.

Ray, D. W., Wandersman, A., Huntington, D. E., & Ellisor, J. The effects of high density in a juvenile correctional institution: A field test of spatial and social density. *Basic and Applied Social Psychology*, in press.

Rayman, P., & Bluestone, B. The private and social response to job loss: A metropolitan study. Final report of research sponsored by the Center for Work and Mental Health, National Institute of Mental Health, 1982.

Riessman, F. How does self-help work? *Social Policy*, 1976, *7*, 41–45.

Riger, S., & Gordon, M. T. The fear of rape: A study in social control. *Journal of Social Issues*, 1981, *37*, 71–92.

Rodin, J., & Langer, E. J. Long-term effects of a control-relevant intervention with the institutionalized aged. *Journal of Personality and Social Psychology*, 1977, *35*, 897–902.

Sarason, S. B. The nature of problem solving in social action. *American Psychologist*, 1978, *32*, 370–380.

Savage, C. Psychedelic therapy. In J. M. Shlien (Ed.), *Research in psychotherapy* (Vol. 3). Washington, D.C.: American Psychological Association, 1968.

Sennett, R., & Cobb, J. *The hidden injuries of class*. New York: Vintage (Random House), 1973.

Silverman, P. R., Mackenzie, D., Pettipas, M., & Wilson, E. W. (Eds.) *Helping each other in widowhood*. New York: Health Sciences, 1974.

Skogan, W. G., & Maxfield, M. G. *Coping with crime: Victimization, fear, and reactions to crime in three American cities*. Beverly Hills, Calif.: Sage Publications, 1981.

Sommer, R., & Ross, H. Social interaction on a geriatric ward. *International Journal of Social Psychiatry*, 1958, *4*, 128–133.

Srole, L., Langner, T. S., Michael, S. T., Opler, M. K., & Rennie, T. A. *Mental health in the metropolis: the midtown Manhattan study*. New York: McGraw-Hill, 1962.

Stack, C. B. *All our kin: Strategies for survival in a Black community*. New York: Harper Colophon, 1974.

Thompson, S. C. Will it hurt less if I can control it? A complex answer to a simple question. *Psychological Bulletin*, 1981, *90*, 89–101.

Wandersman, A., Andrews, S., Riddle, D., & Fancett, C. Environmental psychology and prevention. In R. Felner, S. Farber, L. Jason, & J. Moritsugu (Eds.), *Preventive psychology: Theory, research and practice.* Elmsford, N.Y.: Pergamon Press, 1983.

Wellman, B. Do networks support? A structural perspective. In B. Gottlieb (Ed.), *Social networks and social support in community mental health.* Beverly Hills, Calif.: Sage Publications, 1981.

Wohlwill, J., & Kohn, I. The environments experienced by the migrant: an adaptation-level view. *Representative Research in Social Psychology,* 1973, *4,* (1), 135–164.

Zautra, A., & Reich, J. Positive life events and reports of well-being: some useful distinction. *American Journal of Community Psychology,* 1980, *8,* 657–670.

Prevention and Health Promotion*

---

* This chapter was written by Kenneth Heller.

INTRODUCTION

There is considerable evidence that entry into high school can be a stressful event for many students. While some students adjust to the transition well, others do not. The latter are likely to do poorly in their academic subjects, become truants, or drop out of school altogether. Once these problems develop, they are difficult to treat because students become "turned off" to school. A communication barrier develops between students, and their teachers and counselors. Is there any way to ease the transition to high school so that problems such as these can be prevented? Should changes be made in school procedures or the classroom environment (for example, allowing students to stay in the same room rather than changing classes with each change in academic subject)? Can students become better prepared to deal with the new situations they are likely to face in high school?

Although not widely known by the general public, surgical procedures, such as open heart operations, can induce psychotic-like symptoms (hallucinations and delusions) in otherwise healthy adults. What seems to precipitate these reactions is the frightening atmosphere in some intensive care recovery rooms in which there is constant monitoring of heart functioning, often in direct sight of the patient. Constant light, interrupted sleep, restricted movement, and emergency procedures occasionally needed for other patients, also increase the likelihood of psychotic reactions. Since many of these procedures are necessary for maintaining vital life functions, can hospital recovery rooms be designed to reduce the psychological stress experienced by patients? Can nursing personnel be better trained to deal with the psychological impact of surgery so that the incidence of adverse reactions can be reduced?

This chapter is about a relatively new concept in psychology—prevention. Most simply stated, prevention workers attempt to reduce the incidence of psychological maladjustment. In the examples cited above, this means reducing the frequency of truancy and poor school performance or reducing the probability that psychotic reactions will appear during recovery from surgical procedures.

While the goals in these examples are clear, how these goals should be achieved is not always apparent. What complicates the picture is that the links between etiological factors and ultimate disorder are not clear-cut. There is a growing consensus among prevention workers that there is no direct correspondence between specific etiological factors and specific disorders (Bloom, 1979; Price, Bader, & Ketterer, 1980) and that psychological disorders result from a number of complex, interacting determinants (Price, 1974). Thus the proper design of prevention programs requires considerable research effort to determine the contributing factors.

In this chapter, we will review the literature on prevention and the issues that prevention programs raise. We will begin with a historical survey, in which we explain why prevention concepts are only now being investigated.

Prevention as a Public Health Concept

The prevention concept came to the mental health fields relatively late, having been borrowed from public health, a field in which prevention had a rich and distinguished history. Public health practice is characterized by a population orientation in that the health of entire communities is the major concern. The unit of focus is a population, not an individual, and the search in public health practice becomes one of finding ways to promote the well-being of populations while at the same time reducing the incidence of disease. The emphasis is on preventing the onset of disease rather than on finding cures once disease has occurred.

In modern public health theories, disease is seen as an end product of an interaction among a host, which is the person afflicted, a pathological agent, which is the disease carrier, and the environment (Bloom, 1965). Thus, effective prevention can occur through modification of any one of these factors. Disease can be prevented by strengthening or immunizing the host (e.g., immunizing an individual against smallpox), by removing the pathological agent (e.g., spraying mosquito-infested areas to reduce the number of disease-carrying mosquitos), or by environmental modification (e.g., encouraging the use of window screens or mosquito netting to reduce the incidence of bites from disease-carrying insects).

The prevention analogy, as it first was applied to mental health in the early 1960s, was compelling. It seemed logical that mental health professionals should be interested in the psychological well-being of community members generally, not just in their individual clients. And it certainly seemed more efficient to promote health and reduce the likelihood of disorder rather than treating dysfunctional behavior after it had become entrenched. The logic of prevention was easy to understand and was adopted by John F. Kennedy in his presidential message of 1963:

> Our attack must be focused on three major objectives: First we must seek out the causes of mental illness and mental retardation and eradicate them. Here, more than in any other area, "an ounce of prevention is worth more than a

pound of cure.'' For prevention is far more desirable for all concerned. It is far more economical and it is far more likely to be successful. Prevention will require both selected specific programs directed especially at known causes, and the general strengthening of our fundamental community, social welfare, and educational programs which can do much to eliminate or correct the harsh environmental conditions which often are associated with mental retardation and mental illness.

An implied mandate to engage in prevention activities became part of the Community Mental Health Center legislation of the 1960s; however, very little prevention activity actually occurred. The reasons for the scarcity of prevention research and demonstration projects are complex. One of the impediments was the historical neglect of prevention in the mental health fields. New points of view are difficult to introduce once existing ideas have become entrenched and form the basis for professional practice. Thus, in order to understand why prevention was talked about but not practiced after the passage of the Community Mental Centers Act in 1963, we will need to describe the dominant biases and values prevalent in the mental health fields.

The Developing Mental Health Professions: Pressures for Treatment and Neglect of Prevention

A concern for the psychological well-being of populations and an orientation toward prevention did not represent the historical stance of the mental health professions. This was true in 1963 and before, and is still true today. A field's conceptual orientation generally can be determined by noting the dominant activities of its members. Thus, as Cowen points out, ''If 90 percent of MH (mental health) activities are in psychodiagnosis, therapy, and institutional care, then that is the field's prevailing, if implicit, conceptual bias'' (Cowen, 1973, p. 429). Even at the present time, mental health activity primarily consists of the individual treatment of disordered behavior. This is so much the case that many mental health professionals do not have a language to adequately encompass population and prevention concepts, let alone a set of procedures that would allow them to develop practical applications.

How did it happen that the mental health professions developed a treatment rather than a prevention language and technology? To begin with, one should remember that, from a historical perspective, the mandate given the mental health professions by the public was treatment or incarceration—not prevention. Communities were concerned about the troubled and deviant members in their midst. The early mental health workers, mostly medical practitioners, were asked to treat or at minimum hold in custody those who were thought to be no longer capable of caring for themselves and whose behavior was judged to be frightening and unpredictable. The doctors who worked in mental hospitals accepted this mandate. Historically, American psychiatrists were mental hospital administrators. Note that the organization now called the American Psychiatric Association had its origins in the "Association of Medical Superintendents of American Institutions for the Insane" founded in 1844 (R. Caplan, 1969). The early pioneers and heroes of the mental health professions—Janet, Charcot, Freud, and Sullivan—are held in esteem primarily for their contributions to our understanding and treatment of the severe emotional disorders. Even today the status hierarchy in medicine gives highest prestige to those equipped to deal with complex and unusual disorders—though their occurrence may be relatively infrequent in the general population. The general practitioner or public health physician receives much less admiration from medical colleagues and much less pay than the more exotic specialist.

This same set of values can be seen in the status given psychiatric practitioners by their medical colleagues. Common problems in living are not considered as "real" and worthy of as much expert attention as are physical maladies. Common emotional disorders are considered malingering at worst or as involving simple suggestibility at best. This kind of attitude would lead to a status pressure within psychiatry to de-emphasize the milder disorders and to focus upon the severe disorders that clearly would be beyond the capabilities of most medical practitioners and that the latter would be all too willing to refer to their psychiatric colleagues.

But what of clinical psychology? Why did it develop a technology that was basically treatment oriented? It has been suggested that, as clinical psychology developed, it adopted a stance toward practice that emulated the private practice mode of service dominant in the field of psychiatry. The model was that of a practitioner offering a service to people referred because of the intensity of the disturbance they create among their associates. These clients are further preselected by their ability and willingness to pay and by their acquiescence to the definition of their problems in mental health terms.

That psychiatry became the model for the practice of clinical psychology should not be too surprising. The theories dominant in the mental health professions were psychiatric in origin, academic psychology had not developed its own helping procedures, and the facilities most interested in hiring the new fledgling psychologists were medical in orientation. One should remember that the growth of clinical psychology was accelerated after World War II, in part as a function of the government's response to the adjustment problems of returning veterans. Special grants were given to academic departments of psychology to develop clinical psychology programs, whose practicum facilities were to be the psychiatric institutions supported by the federal government through Veterans Administration and Public Health Service programs. As Albee suggested in 1970:

> If, 25 years ago, enormously increased amounts of federal support for training in psychological intervention had been funneled through the public school system, rather than through psychiatric facilities, the present nature of clinical psychology would have been altogether different. Or, if psychological manpower had been supported and trained through the welfare system, we would be a still different field today. (Albee, 1970, p. 1073)

The practice of psychiatry in America has followed the model of the private practice of medicine. While public health concepts have always been a part of medicine, except for a concern with communicable disease and sanitation, few physicians have ever taken seriously the public health mandate of promoting general health and well-being. The House of Delegates of the American Medical Association defines public health as "the art and science of maintaining, protecting and improving the health of people through organized community efforts" (B. S. Brown, 1969). Yet how many physicians are actively involved in or concerned with improving the health of persons outside their own specific office practice? So, too, for psychiatry and clinical psychology. Our chronology suggests that clinical psychology looked to psychiatry for a model of practice, while psychiatry in turn was most influenced by the prevailing private practice modes of operation dominant in general medicine. Both groups of mental health practitioners were reinforced in these views by increased status and greater financial remuneration associated with the private-practice therapy specialist model. The thinking associated with this model became so pervasive that, as Cowen points out, it is as if we automatically accepted the identity: "Helping people in distress = Psychotherapy" (Cowen, 1973, p. 424).

From the late 1940s through the 1970s there was an unquestioned acceptance of psychotherapy as the only psychological method available for helping people in distress. Conceptual alternatives were never seriously considered; and without a change in how one looks at a problem, a change in how one deals with that problem will not occur.

The Shift in Interest toward Prevention

While most training programs in psychiatry, clinical psychology, and psychiatric social work remained wedded to a treatment model, there were leaders in these fields who were urging a shift in orientation as early as the 1960s. Most of the initial work provided a conceptual reorientation—defining prevention (G. Caplan, 1964), linking it to its appropriate analogues in public health (Bloom, 1965), recognizing the role of environmental and institutional forces in the development and maintenance of disordered behavior (Reiff, 1966), and outlining the direction that work in prevention might take (Cowen, 1967, 1973). Over time, the potential utility of prevention as a mental health goal became increasingly accepted. So much so that by 1978 prevention was highlighted in a report from the President's Commission on Mental Health (Task Panel Report on Prevention, 1978). While prevention activities remained minimal during this period, acceptance of the concept had been established so that by 1979 Herbert (1979) was led to conclude that prevention "should by all rights be the glamour stock on the mental health market."

Unfortunately, prevention activity once again became threatened just as interest in the prevention concept was increasing. With a change in federal priorities in 1980, funds for human service programs began to shrink. Federal and state policies encouraged mental health providers to give priority to the most severe cases of disorder that were disturbing community tranquility, even though the help offered might only be palliative. With extremely tight budgets, few resources were left to develop prevention programs. Still, a small but significant Prevention Research Branch was established within NIMH in 1982.

Some mental health professionals have argued that the encouragement of prevention would threaten the funding of existing treatment programs (Lamb & Zusman, 1979). They view prevention as untried, conceptually ambiguous, and grandiose, and they caution that there is little evidence supporting the prevention rhetoric. As we shall describe more fully in a moment, the complaints about the "fuzziness" of prevention concepts do have some validity. But there is more to the resistance to prevention than concern about inadequate evidence. The very individuals who are most critical of prevention's research base are champions of treatment and of the continued funding of treatment programs. They are willing to discount the critical attacks on the effectiveness of treatment programs (Eysenck, 1952; 1961; Rachman & Wilson, 1980) and seem to be imposing a higher standard for the acceptability of prevention (Albee, 1981).

It may be that some of the criticisms against giving prevention researchers a chance to demonstrate what can be accomplished by prevention programs are motivated by professional self-interest. Simply put, if prevention were to succeed, it could reduce the therapy "business" available to treatment specialists. For example, the success of water fluoridation in reducing tooth decay significantly decreased the amount of tooth repair and restoration provided by dentists in most communities. However, we wonder whether professional self-interest is the major reason that prevention has not been embraced by the mental health professions. While one can point to the opposition of medical and mental health establishment organizations as obstacles to the widespread adoption of prevention (Albee, 1981), conceptualizing the conflict only in terms of political self-interest probably oversimplifies the nature of the opposition to prevention. We should recognize that there are major conceptual and methodological impediments to the development of a prevention technology, apparent even among prevention's philosophical supporters. Return to the fluoridation example for a moment. Once the value of fluoridation had been demonstrated, the American Dental Association and individual dentists nation-wide championed the use of fluoride in drinking water, despite the anticipated loss of dental business. We doubt that mental health practitioners are more conservative or self-serving than dentists, and suspect that they, too, would become prevention advocates if conceptual clarity could be achieved and a prevention technology developed. To be informed prevention advocates, we need to understand the nature of the difficulties involved. Thus, we now turn to a discussion of some of the conceptual ambiguities in prevention.

WHAT IS PREVENTION?

It is easier to say what prevention is not, than to be precise in specifying what meaning it should have. Prevention is not the extension of existing mental health treatment services to new populations formerly considered unreachable. Clearly such action, while desirable, simply extends the scope of existing services. Prevention is not training new mental health workers (paraprofessionals) to engage in remedial work that they might do more efficiently than overtaxed professionals. Again, such action serves to extend treatment facilities to new populations. Prevention is not the development of new treatment programs (e.g., community care for the mentally ill, milieu therapy, family therapy, behavior modification, and the like) no matter how sensible or in vogue such treatment programs may be. All of the above are not prevention activities, but have become associated with community mental health because they promise to make treatment more efficient—and because they are easily understood by clinic professionals who are most often treatment-oriented themselves.

Primary, Secondary, and Tertiary Prevention

The most widely accepted definition of prevention is contained in G. Caplan's (1964) concept of "primary prevention." Caplan distinguishes between three types of prevention in the following manner:

> the term preventive psychiatry refers to the body of professional knowledge, both theoretical and practical, which may be utilized to plan and carry out programs for reducing (1) the incidence of mental disorders of all types in a community (primary prevention), (2) the duration of a significant number of those disorders which do occur (secondary prevention), and (3) the impairment which may result from disorders (tertiary prevention). (G. Caplan, 1964, pp. 16–17)

Bolman amplifies on this definition as follows:

> Primary prevention attempts to prevent a disorder from occurring. Secondary prevention attempts to identify and treat at the earliest possible moment so as to reduce the length and severity of disorder. Tertiary prevention attempts to reduce to a minimum the degree of handicap or impairment that results from a disorder that has already occurred. From the standpoint of the community, these distinctions are equivalent to reducing incidence, prevalence and extent of disability respectively. (Bolman, 1969, p. 208)

Some writers believe that tertiary prevention and certain types of secondary prevention should not bear the label "prevention" at all. Cowen (1973) suggests that it is a misnomer to think of activities that are oriented toward reducing the residual effects of existing disorders as prevention. From this point of view, "so-called tertiary prevention" should be justified on grounds other than prevention, such as the need to minimize human misery and suffering. Similarly, Cowen notes that "secondary prevention" has been used in two quite distinct ways. Its first use involves identifying incipient dysfunction in the very young, and intervening to forestall further maldevelopment. A second use occurs in describing efforts to detect an acute psychotic episode very early in its development rather than after weeks or months, so it can be handled more effectively. This latter use increases the ambiguity of the concept, and we shall accept Cowen's (1973) point of view that a crisper conceptual alternative is presented if prevention is redefined to include only primary and early secondary activities.

Conceptual Impediments to Prevention Practice

Notice that, while the definition of primary prevention just presented seems straightforward and easy to understand, neither of the definitions specifies operations by which the goals of reduced incidence, prevalence, or lowered disability are to be achieved. Despite their apparent simplicity and appeal, prevention definitions are goal statements that do not include specific guidelines about how prevention goals should be operationalized.

Part of the problem is that the prevention metaphor borrowed from public health suggested a too-simple analogy as applied to psychological problems. The major successes in public health prevention had been for diseases with single specific causes, as in diseases of bacteriological or viral origin. In these cases, highly specific preventive procedures could be developed that were linked to these specific disorders. Thus, as Bloom (1979) notes, malaria could be prevented by spraying the breeding ground of specific types of mosquitos, but such action affected no other disorder. Similarly, one might reduce the incidence of dental caries by drinking fluoridated water, but such action prevented no other disease.

The problem in the mental health fields is more complex because clear links between precipitating factors and disorder are not likely to be found. As a matter of fact, advocates of prevention are in the uncomfortable position of recommending prevention when the specific causes of psychological dysfunction still are obscure. How can one mount prevention programs when etiology is unknown? Some would downgrade prevention attempts for this reason. However, prevention cannot be dismissed so easily for the same might be said of treatment activities. How can one expect to successfully treat mental disorders of uncertain etiology? Yet treatment activities flourish, with little apparent concern for the ambiguities of causation.

G. Caplan takes the position that, while full knowledge of etiology would be helpful, much can be done in both prevention and treatment with less than perfect knowledge. Pointing to the history of public health activities, he cites examples of successful programs of primary prevention that were instituted before valid knowledge was available concerning their etiology. He describes these examples as follows:

> Some of the most successful programs of primary prevention were instituted before we had valid etiologies of the illnesses which were prevented. The prevention of smallpox by vaccination and the prevention of scurvy by eating limes and fresh vegetables preceded by many years our knowledge of the causes of these illnesses. In fact, the major advances in the control of epidemics of infectious diseases in our cities in the latter part of the 19th century predated the germ theory and the discovery of the microbial agents responsible for disease. The sanitary programs were based on the belief of the hygienic reformers that dirt,

squalor, and congestion were "unnatural" and "unhealthy" and by a desire to introduce the "pure" conditions of country life into the towns.

Even the history-making preventive action of Snow in removing the handle of the Broad Street pump to halt the London epidemic of cholera in the 19th century was not based on knowledge of the existence of the cholera organism in the polluted water or of the significance of this microorganism in the etiology of the epidemic.

The public health practitioners in these and many other instances did not wait until they had etiological knowledge before instituting their preventive programs. They relied on the best current judgments of factors which seemed to be associated with the presence or absence of illnesses in various segments of the population. In each instance, the proponents of a preventive program based themselves on personal observation or popular impressions. Jenner was struck by the absence of smallpox in those members of a population who had previously contracted cowpox. The British Admiralty was impressed by the stories that sailors on ships well stocked with citrus fruits and fresh vegetables did not suffer scurvy. The 19th century hygienic reformers made the general observation that epidemics occurred in the big cities and not in the rural areas. And Snow carefully listed the addresses of persons contracting cholera and demonstrated that they all drew their water from the Broad Street pump, whereas those who obtained water from some other source were not infected. (G. Caplan 1964, pp. 29–30)

An implication of this position is that, while partial knowledge can lead to actions that might later prove to be wrong, more is to be gained by taking action based on incomplete causal information than by doing nothing. It is in this spirit that many preventive intervention programs are initiated. Even ineffective programs can lead to useful information if they are conducted in such a way that their results can be reliably assessed and the reasons for lack of success can be determined.

Still, a basic problem remains—how shall we proceed in designing prevention programs. One must adopt some working hypothesis about etiological factors in order to conceptualize prevention activities, yet views of the etiology of mental disorder are marked by considerable controversy. The matter is of some importance because, as Price (1974) points out, assumptions about etiology do strongly influence our notions of appropriate intervention.

ADOPTING A MULTIPLE-RISK FACTOR ORIENTATION TO ETIOLOGY AS A GUIDE FOR PREVENTION

Epidemiologists are moving away from a conception of disease that implies a simple unitary cause. Even for medical disorders in which etiology would seem clearcut, such as tuberculosis, the appearance of the actual illness can be related to psychological stress factors (Lemkau, 1969). Price (1974) makes the same point with regard to schizophrenia. Even for disorders whose predisposing etiology may have a strong genetic component, social factors in the form of psychosocial stresses may still determine whether disordered behavior actually occurs.

What this means is that we should now think in terms of "multi-factorial causation" (Price, 1974) or "risk factors" instead of simple causation. The best analogy from physical medicine might be how we currently view the risk factors associated with the likelihood of heart disorders. We know that the risk factors associated with the appearance of heart attacks include genetic and constitutional factors, such as the extent to which there is a history of heart attacks in the family, age of onset, weight, and cholesterol level; but also include lifestyle variables, such as diet, amount of smoking and exercise, pace of life, and type of reaction to stress. There is no single "cause" of heart disorders, but anyone who demonstrates a large number of the above risk factors is statistically more vulnerable to the appearance of heart disorder than is an individual with a low-risk loading. Similarly an individual can reduce the likelihood of a heart attack by reducing as many of the risk factors as possible—such as cutting down on smoking, increasing exercise, controlling diet, and so on.

What is particularly interesting about the heart disorder example is that, over the last decade, the incidence of heart disorder in the general population has indeed gone down. While the reasons for reduced incidence are not completely clear, it does appear that large numbers of people have adopted lifestyle changes that have addressed a number of risk factors simultaneously. Furthermore, reduced incidence did not occur because of improvements in treatment, or by increasing the number of treatment specialists, such as cardiologists. Thus, it is not the case that prevention necessarily is advanced by upgrading treatment.

The cancer example in medicine also presents some interesting analogies to mental disorders. The exact causes of cancer are not known, but a number of risk factors have been identified in epidemiological and laboratory research with animals. The relative contribution of such risk factors as noxious environmental agents and personal predisposition also are unknown. It does appear that, while not all individuals exposed to cancer-inducing conditions succumb, environmental contaminants do increase risk so that, given sufficient exposure, relative immune individuals also would succumb. What is particularly intriguing about the cancer analogy is that, as in mental disorder, the appearance of symptoms often is delayed.

In a similar manner, the appearance of psychological symptoms often occurs in adulthood, when reaction patterns learned earlier become habitualized and entrenched, not in childhood when exposure to risk may be greatest. In addition, what complicates discovery of exact risk factors for the development of psychological difficulties is that a single discrete exposure to noxious environmental events probably does not cause irrevocable later symptomatology. As Barbara Dohrenwend (1978) has suggested, competent functioning is influenced by patterns of stressful events interacting with personal predispositional factors that are moderated by protective relationships with significant others. Thus, the risk factors associated with psychological disorder will be difficult to tease apart.

Adopting a multiple risk factor orientation to the etiology of mental disorders means that one does not expect that a *single* factor functions as the sole cause of psychic dysfunction. The new orientation also implies that intervention to reduce the incidence of dysfunctional behavior can occur at a number of levels. Prevention efforts might be oriented toward reducing the impact of environmental stress at community, institutional, or familial levels; or intervention programs might be aimed at strengthening the capacity of vulnerable populations to deal with that stress. This is what Catalano and Dooley (1980) mean when they describe the distinction between proactive and reactive primary prevention. Whenever possible, prevention programs should attempt to eliminate or avoid environmental stressors (proactive primary prevention). However, if environmental stressors are unavoidable, individuals can be prepared to deal with stress more effectively (reactive primary prevention). Because environmental conditions are difficult to change, proactive approaches rarely are attempted. We hope that various chapters in this book (particularly Chapters Five and Six) will give the reader a realistic assessment of different approaches to environmental change. We agree with Catalano and Dooley that ignoring ecological (proactive) variables may miss the most important ingredients in the prevention of disorder.

TYPES OF PREVENTION PROGRAMS

Community-Wide, Milestone, and High-Risk Strategies

Bloom (1968) describes a typology of preventive efforts that distinguishes more clearly among types of intervention. Bloom describes prevention as involving either *community-wide, milestone,* or *high-risk* programs. In the first, all the residents of a community are the recipients of the program. Examples might be water purification to eliminate typhoid fever and cholera, swamp drainage to reduce the risk of malaria, and supervision of food and water processing. Mental health analogues might include community development programs in disorganized slum communities, or programs aimed at initiating community-wide support for better jobs, housing, education, or child development services. In the milestone approach, citizens are exposed to the program at specific periods in their lives. Psychological "milestones" might include critical developmental periods, such as birth of a sibling, initial school attendance, entry into adolescence, first semester away from home at college, first year of marriage, birth of the first child, job change, menopause, death of a spouse, and retirement. These nodal developmental events are chosen because they have the potential for being situations of high psychological risk. In the milestone approach, "residents of a specified area march as it were, past the program. Prior to reaching it they are not protected" (Bloom, 1968, p. 118). When they reach the program, they are exposed to its effects. An example of this type of program might be smallpox vaccination required upon admission to school. While the focus in the milestone approach is on situations or events, in Bloom's third type of prevention program—the high-risk program—the focus is on vulnerable populations. Groups vulnerable to specific disorders are identified and subject to special programs designed to reduce or prevent the incidence of dysfunction. An example might be a program for children to reduce the stress associated with surgery. Examples of high-risk populations might include: the children of alcoholics, drug addicts, or mental patients; children who experience death of a parent at an early age; children with physical handicaps, or those about to experience major surgery; and survivors of natural or manmade disasters, such as earthquakes, floods, plane crashes, and wars.

Each of the three types of prevention programs described by Bloom has both strengths and liabilities. High-risk programs can be focused to fit the specific suspected vulnerability. However, the early identification of high-risk groups poses some ethical dangers. The presumption of later disability from early signs of vulnerability is usually accompanied by an overprediction bias. More cases are tagged as needing remediation than eventually would become disabled if left alone. Furthermore, the identification of incipient disability can bring with it problems of stigma if the labeling of vulnerable cases is not done with sensitivity and tact.

Community-wide and milestone interventions avoid the problems of labeling particular groups, since no one is singled out as particularly needy. The intervention is provided for everyone. But there are disadvantages. The first is cost, because many more people get the program than actually need it. A second is that those who benefit most from a community-wide intervention generally are the most competent who need it the least. One of the controversies concerning the TV program "Sesame Street" concerns this very issue. The program was designed for the educationally disadvantaged, but critics have charged that children from educationally advanced homes are more likely to watch the program regularly than children from deprived homes (Cook et al., 1975).

There are no easy answers to the issues raised above. Any intervention has both costs and benefits, and both must be realistically assessed in any decision to implement a program. Programs can be designed to minimize financial and psychological costs, but this cannot be done without full awareness of potential program liabilities.

Environment and Person-Centered Interventions: Risk-Inducing Situations and Populations at Risk

Cowen (1973) described a distinction in the prevention literature between systems-centered and person-oriented approaches. A systems focus assumes that human development is primarily shaped by a small number of key social institutions and settings, and that prevention should be oriented toward institutional or setting change. Person-oriented interventions assume that the focus of prevention should be on early childhood intervention with the key individuals who shape the child's development (e.g., parents, teachers, and other primary caregivers). The focus is on people who inhabit settings, not on the settings themselves.

A similar distinction is made by Catalano and Dooley (1980) between macrolevel and microlevel primary prevention. Macrolevel interventions are those aimed at large social forces in the environment, such as community and organizational factors. Prevention efforts at this level, for example, "might involve community-wide transportation planning to prevent excessive automobile lead exhausts and airport noise from occurring near school playgrounds." Microlevel interventions are aimed at factors or persons within the individual's immediate environment, such as parents, teachers, co-workers, etc. At this level, prevention "might take the form of mental health education for expectant parents to prevent the occurrence of damaging parental practices" (Catalano & Dooley, 1980, p. 24).[1]

Price (1980) suggests that as a conceptual aid in initiating prevention research, it may be useful to adopt a situation orientation to risk groups. People are members of risk groups not only because of individual characteristics they may possess but because they may be faced with situations that place high demands on adaptive capacity. Altering some characteristic of the risk situation or event is at least as likely to reduce risk as is person-centered intervention, whose purpose is to strengthen the coping capacity of the affected individual. For example, cooperative housing for the elderly can mitigate some of the isolation resulting from conjugal bereavement; alternative employment possibilities for the retired can prevent many of the consequences resulting from mandatory retirement; providing alternative adult parent figures, as with Big Brothers and Big Sisters, can partially compensate for the inconsistent parenting offered by disturbed or absent parents. Price (1979) argues that the advantages of a situational orientation to risk groups are both conceptual and practical. Attributions of causality (person or situation) strongly condition how we view the affected groups and how we intervene. Furthermore, the situational approach to prevention has a greater likelihood of leading to a focus on "movable" variables—those that can be more easily manipulated for the purposes of intervention.

Price (1979) proposes that researchers can utilize environmental data to design programs to increase adjustment in three ways: by means of setting selection, setting change, and setting creation. Settings can be selected, changed, or created in order to better "fit" individual needs and goals with setting characteristics. For example, helping individuals find recreation, leisure time, self-help groups, or educational institutions that best meet their needs qualify as setting selection interventions. Setting change might be accomplished by consultation and organization development, while setting creation occurs when groups develop alternative structures (e.g., alternative

---

[1] Macrolevel factors are discussed more fully in Chapter Five. The examples of prevention programs that follow in this chapter are more likely to be microlevel interventions. This is because, as Catalano and Dooley point out, changes in microlevel variables are easier to implement by health professionals. However, it is important to emphasize macrolevel factors even though these tend to be neglected by many researchers. They can be modified during sympathetic periods in the political climate, and, in the long run, may prove to be more important for prevention.

schools) to meet their needs. Since much of the prevention literature is change-oriented, the possibilities of maximizing adjustive coping through setting selection often are overlooked. Most of us engage in setting selection naturally, on our own. That settings can be purposely selected as an intervention strategy comes as a surprise, because we tend not to select settings in any conscious or systematic way.

The Distinction between Proximal Programmatic Objectives and Distal Prevention Goals

The most popular way of thinking about prevention is in terms of "end-states" (Cowen, 1973) to be prevented. Yet, global end-state goals cannot be dealt with in research without a clear objective statement of the target behaviors to be reduced and a specification of the operations by which such goals are to be achieved. Furthermore, while reducing adverse end-states may be a distal (long-range) goal of social interest, most prevention programs have difficulty demonstrating an impact on such goals. To the extent that disorder develops over time in response to multiple interactive risk factors, other variables not accounted for in any specific prevention program also will influence the ultimate community-wide incidence of disorder.

If a prevention program that focuses on a single factor by itself is unlikely to influence incidence rates, how can researchers hope to demonstrate program effectiveness? Basically, we must recognize that prevention research is faced with two separate problems. The first is to determine the effects on behavior of specific intervention programs. The second is to link proximal (short-range) objectives, such as effective behavior change (if the program was successful), with the ultimate reduction in rates for the end-state goals in question. For example, if the distal goal involves a reduction in delinquency rates, a first step would be to determine the risk factors that are most likely to be associated with high delinquency. Several could be specified, among which might be included poor school performance, troubled family relationships, parental alcoholism, antisocial behavior patterns among peers, few employment opportunities, and so on. Choosing one risk factor as an example, school performance, a researcher might develop a program to improve poor school work through a tutorial reading program. However, is it likely that tutorial reading by itself will reduce delinquency rates? Probably not, and it would be misleading to expect that improved school performance alone would influence the distal goal of delinquency prevention. However, research on whether school performance can be improved by a tutorial reading program should be done because this knowledge about the influence of separate risk factors will put us in a better position to mount intervention programs that combine a number of interventions which would be likely to impact on the distal goal. Thus, the steps we are advocating in the design of prevention programs involve collecting data on the effectiveness of specific intervention programs in modifying specific risk factors, and, as a separate question, determining what combination of interventions is most effective in producing an impact on ultimate prevention goals.

EXAMPLES OF PRIMARY PREVENTION PROGRAMS

Preparing for Specific Unavoidable Stressors: Anticipating and Preparing for Recovery from Surgery

The effects of preparing patients for unavoidable surgical operations is well documented in the prevention literature. Compared to other areas of primary prevention, the research has a long history and is relatively unambiguous. The stressor is clearly defined—a surgical procedure—and the effects of the operation on both the medical and psychological state of the patient are not too difficult to assess. Psychological intervention cannot prevent the necessity for the operation, so intervention must be geared toward improving the patient's ability to cope with the anticipated stress.

In an early study, Egbert, Battit, Welch, and Bartlett (1964) prepared a group of patients for the stress of surgery by providing them with information regarding the impending operation and their possible reactions and experiences during recovery. Patients were visited the night before the operation by the anesthetist, who described the anesthesia, the time and duration of the operation, and told the patients that they would wake up in the recovery room. The control group received no further information. The experimental group patients received further instruction concerning postoperative pain. They were told about its severity and duration and were instructed in simple exercises that would help relax their abdominal muscles. Finally, they were encouraged to request medication should they find it difficult to achieve a reasonable level of comfort. The results of the study revealed that patients who received the special preparation, including permission to request medication, used *less* medication and were discharged earlier than patients in the control group who received contact from the anesthetist but no instruction in pain anticipation and control.

The Egbert et al. (1964) study did not separate the effects of anticipatory guidance from those of practice in muscle relaxation and related behavioral techniques. A clearer test of the influence of information per se on the recovery of surgery patients was conducted by Andrew (1970). Subjects in a Veterans Administration hospital about to undergo hernia surgery were classified according to coping style and then presented with taped information about the operation they were about to receive. Results indicated that the midgroup on the coping style variable improved most, recovering in less time and with least medication when instructed than when not instructed. Patients whose personality style was to avoid or deny threatening emotions required *more* pain-killing medication when instructed than when not, while those subjects who were sensitive to and readily acknowledged threatening feelings showed no effect due to instruction. Andrew suggests that this latter group of "sensitizers" had already prepared themselves for the operation so that the taped information did not provide them with incentive for additional preparation.

In providing information about anticipated surgery, another personality variable to consider is locus of control—the tendency of individuals to believe that they have personal control over the reinforcement they receive. In a study providing preparatory information to patients about to undergo dental surgery, Auerbach, Kendall, Cuttler, and Levitt (1976) compared the value of general or specific information. They found that subjects with an internal locus of control (i.e., those who believed that they could control the consequences of events to which they were exposed) were rated as better adjusted during and after surgery when they received specific rather than general information. On the other hand, "externals," those who believed that the consequences of events were outside of their personal control and were determined primarily by luck or chance, were rated as better adjusted if they received general information. The authors speculate that general information is not useful to "internals," because it does not provide enough specific data that would allow them to attempt to control the impending aversive event. Similarly, specific information is not useful to "externals," because they do not believe that they can influence the aversiveness of events even with appropriate information.

The studies by Andrew (1970) and Auerbach et al. (1976), when taken together (as well as other research reviewed by Averill, 1973), indicate that, while preparation for stress generally can be expected to produce more effective coping, positive results will not be obtained for all; some will not need the preparation, while others will be emotionally unprepared to use the information they receive. Thus, program developers should consider specifically designing preparatory information to match the individual's expectational style.

Another interesting surgery study indicates the need to think of prevention in terms of *specificity of effects*. Cassell (1965) provided preparation for cardiac catheterization through the use of a puppet theater to children between the ages of 3 and 11 who were about to undergo this diagnostic procedure. The operating room procedure that the child actually would see was acted out in puppet play, starting with changing the puppet into a hospital gown, then through the application of the EKG electrodes and anesthetic. After the initial enactment, role reversal occurred with the child playing the part of the doctor and the therapist the role of a frightened child eliciting reassurance from the patient-"doctor." At the end of the session, the therapist put on a surgical mask, encouraged the child to guess whether she was happy or angry, and allowed the child to take the mask back to his room. Questions and discussion were encouraged throughout the puppet sessions.

The results of the study demonstrate the specificity of effects that should be expected from intervention studies. Compared with a control group that did not receive the puppet intervention, children who received anticipatory guidance through puppet play showed less emotional upset during the catheterization procedure. Experimental group subjects also expressed a greater willingness to return to the hospital for further treatment. However, the groups did not differ in their general emotional disturbance following the procedure while they were in the hospital or in post-hospitalization adjustment at home as rated by parents. In other words, the patients in the experimental group were not distressed by the catheterization and were willing to return to the hospital, but their general adjustment in other areas of functioning was not affected.

The Cassell study demonstrates how hospital procedures can be changed to reduce the stress associated with hospitalization. Cassell's results have been confirmed by Melamed and Siegel (1975), who found that children observing a film of another child being prepared for surgery while coping with his fears also showed less anxiety preoperatively and during a post-surgery examination one month later. The value of preparation also can be seen in a series of studies concerned with recovery from open-heart surgery.

Recovery room procedures associated with open-heart surgery have been known to induce psychological symptoms in adults (Kornfeld, Zimber, & Malm, 1965), although not in children. The stress-related symptoms, although transitory, can assume psychotic proportions, including hallucinations and delusions. Precipitating factors include not only the preoperative state of the individual and the life threatening nature of the illness but also the frightening atmosphere of the recovery room with its constant monitoring, heart beepers, and visual displays of heart functioning. Constant light, interrupted sleep, and restricted movement further debilitate the patient and increase the likelihood of psychotic reactions (Lazarus and Hagens, 1968).

Kornfeld and Politser (1980) in their review of the effects of hospital environments on patient behavior suggest how the open-heart recovery rooms should be modified:

1. Nursing procedures should be modified to allow the maximum number of uninterrupted sleep periods. The usual day-awake, night-sleep cycle should be maintained whenever possible.
2. Patients should be placed in individual cubicles. There they would not be awakened or made more anxious by activity occurring around other patients.
3. Monitoring equipment should be maintained, when possible, outside the patient's room. Bedside monitors could be turned on whenever needed. This would reduce the anxiety in those patients who are aware of the significance of these signaling devices and the danger implicit with any change in their pattern.
4. Patients should be allowed increased mobility by removing as many wires and cables wherever possible.
5. The constant noise of oxygen and cooling tents should be modified or removed whenever possible.
6. Each room would be equipped with a large clock and calendar.
7. An outside window should be visible to the patient to allow for orientation.

There is an experimental study demonstrating that the incidence of acute psychosis following open-heart surgery can be reduced. Lazarus and Hagens (1968) gave a preparatory interview to patients prior to surgery and instructed nurses to increase contact with patients, provide support, and help the patient maintain a reality focus in the recovery room. The experimental group receiving the intervention showed a significant reduction in psychiatric symptoms compared to a control group at a comparable hospital in which operations were performed by the same surgeons but where patients did not receive the intervention.

Reducing the Negative Impact of Major Life Transitions

An important prevention approach can be seen in work which attempts to target interventions to specific "milestone events" (Bloom, 1968) that are likely to arouse stress, at least in part because of changing roles and expectations that occur as individuals enter new settings (Wandersman, Wandersman, & Kahn, 1980). As will be noted in the following examples, the intervention can be designed for specific high-risk populations or can be used more generally with any group likely to experience the specific stress-arousing event.

Beginning with birth as a major milestone event, there is clear evidence that poor maternal nutrition during pregnancy places infants at risk for later deficits in cognitive functioning (Eisenberg, 1979). Thus prevention questions can be asked early in development and should not ignore basic physiological and nutritional development. Can cognitive deficits be prevented by proper nutrition, and if so, when are nutritional supplements most important? These questions were investigated by Freeman, Klein, Kagan, and Yarbrough (1977), who worked in an extremely poor rural area of Guatemala. In this study, pregnant and lactating mothers and their infants were given a high protein-calorie dietary supplement, which also included vitamins and minerals. In two similar control villages, the protein-calorie supplement was cut by two thirds, but the same amount of vitamins and minerals were given. Results indicated that cognitive performance was significantly better for high protein-calorie supplemented children who were followed up and tested at ages three to four. The effects of nutrition on cognitive development were largest when the supplement was given to mothers during pregnancy rather than to the children themselves directly after birth. The work on the effects of severe malnutrition presents a clear example of the crucial role of prevention, compared to later treatment. While the poor level of mental development associated with severe protein-calorie malnutrition can be partially reversed by *later* dietary supplements and long-term mental stimulation, residual effects often remain (Grantham-McGregor, Stewart, Powel, & Schofield, 1979).

Another vulnerable infant group consists of prematurely born infants who are at risk not only because of retarded development and poorer health status but also because they tend to receive poorer parenting once they are discharged from the hospital (Minde, Shosenberg, & Marton, 1982). The exact reasons for the frequently cited instances of parental neglect of premature infants are not clear. One possible causal factor, inadequate infant/ mother bonding, has been suggested because mother/child contact can be severely restricted when the baby must be placed in an incubator immediately at birth. Other factors suggested as responsible for poorer parenting include guilt and shame at having produced such a small baby or fearfulness of damaging the infant further by unskilled contact. However, regardless of cause, inadequate contact and care have been documented to occur for premature infants in the hospital and at home. Several studies have attempted to reverse this tendency and prevent later infant neglect and/or abuse.

One such study by Minde, Shosenberg, Marton, Thompson, Ripley, and Burns (1980) examined the effects of a discussion-support group for parents of very small premature infants. Mothers of such infants were randomly assigned to a discussion group co-led by a nurse coordinator and a "veteran" mother of a premature infant, or participated as no-treatment controls. Some mothers initially were very hesitant and would not attend the group meeting until they had spent several sessions individually with the coordinator. Those mothers with the poorest attendance were those with the highest levels of pre-existing social or psychological difficulties (e.g., a husband in jail, being victims of physical abuse themselves, or with major psychiatric symptoms). The veteran mother was the group catalyst and "animator" who, by her example, gave parents the opportunity to talk about their depression, guilt, and fears. The authors state that only after these feelings were relieved was it possible for the mothers to attend to and comprehend instructions concerning the care of their premature infants.

The results of the study indicated that mothers who had participated in the groups visited their infants more often while in the hospital than did the controls. During these visits they touched, talked to, and looked at their infants more directly than did controls. At three months' follow-up, these same indices of increased involvement were apparent during a home visit by a trained observer. Mothers also rated themselves as more competent on a number of infant-care measures and showed greater concern for their babies' development. Support groups for new parents have been studied by others (e.g., McGuire & Gottlieb, 1979; Wandersman et al., 1980); however, what is particularly significant about the Minde et al. (1980), research was their clear specification of the type of intervention needed, and their use of behavioral observation measures in which effects could be demonstrated.

School transitions represent another milestone event whose negative effects can be ameliorated by appropriate prevention efforts (Bogat, Jones, & Jason, 1980; Jason & Burrows, 1983). For example, Signell (1972) provides an excellent case description of a discussion group program for parents, called "Preparing your child for kindergarten entry." Recognizing that some parents living in "suburban ghettos" often are isolated from others who could be used for reference, comparison, and support (e.g., family members and neighbors), Signell provided a discussion group for parents with concerns about their child's first experience in school. The groups were co-led by parents who themselves had successfully dealt with kindergarten entry problems in previous years. Signell's article provides rich detail concerning how problems associated with separation were handled. The groups were educational and cathartic and adopted an anticipatory guidance framework in which potential problems were elicited, elaborated in open discussion with the group, and in which alternative modes of coping were suggested.

Transition to high school also has been described as a stressful event. Felner, Primavera, and Cauce (1981) found that, while a single school transition due to residential mobility had little effect on later adjustment, repeated school transfers among low-income black children were associated with school failure. Since school transition can represent a risk event, Felner, Ginter, and Primavera (1982) developed a program to aid that transition. In entering a typical American high school, not only are there new students and teachers with whom one must develop new relationships but there is also an unfamiliar and constantly shifting environment. For each new subject class, the process of adjustment must be repeated since persons and classrooms shift with each subject period change. The intervention designed by Felner et al. was aimed at reducing the confusion and at increasing peer and teacher support in the high school environment. Students were randomly assigned to project or control groups, with the former staying together as a class unit for four of their academic subjects. Homeroom teachers were encouraged to be active in providing guidance to their class units, and homeroom and academic classes were kept in the same part of the building to further reduce confusion in adjusting to the new environment.

The data from this study indicate that, overall, project students were more successful in coping with the transition to high school than were control group students. Although experimental and control subjects were similar in academic achievement and self-concept scores at the beginning of the ninth grade, by the end of the year control group children declined significantly on both measures. The intervention did not improve the grades of project children, but it did prevent the decline evidenced by the control group. It was the worsening of the control group across all measures that was responsible for the post-test experimental-control group differences. It seems clear that the ability of the high-risk project students to maintain their school performance was associated with the changes in the structure of the school environment which they experienced. Project youngsters saw the school environment as having clearer expectations and a clearer organizational structure, and they reported higher levels of teacher support, compared with control group students. Furthermore, controls had higher rates of absenteeism than did project students, indicating that controls may have been withdrawing from what they perceived their high school environment to be—confusing and nonsupportive.

Problems of school entry at the college level were addressed in a study by Bloom (1971) at the University of Colorado. Bloom felt that college freshmen represented a high-risk group. Not only are they over-represented among patients at university health clinics but evidence suggests that college dropout rates are highest in the freshman year. The problem was to design a low-cost program to reach members of this population.

The method Bloom developed in a pilot project was to periodically administer a series of questionnaires about problems of adjustment to a group of freshmen and then to provide them written feedback about their entire group in terms of the percentages of males and females responding to the different questionnaire items. The students were thus able to compare their reaction to that of the entire group. In addition, occasional articles were distributed, dealing with such topics as mental health on the college campus and sexuality among college-age persons.

Reactions to the project among participating students seemed quite favorable. Of those who responded to the questionnaires at the start of their sophomore year: 94 percent said they enjoyed reading the articles that were distributed; 80 percent felt they had learned things about themselves by completing the questionnaires; 99 percent indicated a willingness to continue filling out questionnaires; and 96 percent wanted to continue to receive articles and progress reports.

Enrollment data for the sophomore year indicate that, while "survival rates" were quite high for freshmen in general, they still favored the experimental group. Eighty-five percent of that group reenrolled at the university, compared to 77 percent of a comparison group not in the program. What is more interesting is the fate of the nonenrollees. The groups did not differ in their dropout rate from college. However, they did differ in their rate of transfer to other schools. Only 3 percent of the experimentals transferred to another school, while 10 percent of the comparison group transferred. In other words, the program was successful in maintaining more students at the University of Colorado by affecting the transfer rate, not the dropout rate. Students who dropped out of school did so primarily because of academic difficulties or because of poor emotional adjustment. The program did not provide academic help and, apparently, was too minimal an intervention to help those with serious adjustment problems. Students who transferred did so because they felt the university was too large and impersonal, professors too distant, and their lives too socially isolated. These were the feelings that Bloom's program was effective in counteracting.

This study demonstrated that intervention effects often are quite specific. Getting feedback about the problems others are having that are similar to one's own can increase identification with others, reduce feelings of loneliness and estrangement, normalize problems of adjustment, and increase feelings of competency. But decreasing feelings of loneliness should not be expected to influence general problems of adjustment if more serious psychological problems are present.

Other studies of specific life transitions indicate that prevention programs could be effective at a number of points. For example, efforts could be made to reduce the stresses associated with marital disruption (Bloom, Asher, & White, 1978; Bloom, Hodges, & Caldwell, 1982); death of a spouse and widowhood (Barrett, 1978; Lindeman, 1976; Silverman, 1970); and nursing home relocation (Hughes, 1976; Rowland, 1977). In each instance the precipitating event may not be preventable, but negative psychological consequences may be. The intervention planned need not always involve a massive multifaceted program but may at times involve relatively simple procedures designed to enhance coping. Providing college freshmen with feedback about the adjustment difficulties of their fellow students (as in the Bloom, 1971, study just described) is one example of a relatively simple, low-cost intervention.

Prevention through Public Education: Heart Disease, Smoking, Alcohol, and Drug-Abuse Prevention Programs

If risk factors associated with adjustment problems and disorders are identified, can the effects of these factors be reduced by warning the public? Health education campaigns assume that an educated public will take the necessary steps to protect their health, and that education is an important component of prevention.

Unfortunately over the years, mental health education campaigns have developed a lackluster reputation. Davis, reviewing a group of early studies, came to the pessimistic conclusion that "mental health educators have little or nothing specific and practical to tell the public" (Davis, 1965, p. 138). Looking back at this early work, a possible reason for failure can be seen. Early workers in mental health education were not too clear about what they wanted the public to know or what people were expected to do with the information they received. When John and Elaine Cumming developed and attempted to implement a mental health educational campaign in a small Canadian community (Cumming & Cumming, 1957), their efforts met with so much resistance that they were invited by the mayor to leave town (Bloom, 1980). Apparently, the Cummings interpreted mental health education to mean educating the public "about the nature of those already ill." Their attempts at changing attitudes about "mental illness" frightened the residents into believing that the real goal of their project was to soften public attitudes to facilitate the building of a large government mental hospital in the community.

In more recent years, there has been a shift from general education about "mental illness" to more focused programs aimed at educating the public about specific risks, or providing concrete coping information to specific risk groups (Adler, 1982). A good example of how such a strategy might be implemented can be seen in the Stanford Heart Disease Prevention Program designed to reduce cardiovascular risks (Maccoby & Alexander, 1979;

Meyer, Nash, McAlister, Maccoby, & Farquhar, 1980).[2] Factors leading to increased risk for heart disease had been identified in previous research. In this study, three such factors—smoking, high serum cholesterol, hypertension—were chosen for modification through a public education campaign. The media campaign conducted in one town was compared with the same campaign, plus intensive instruction conducted in a second town, and with a no-intervention comparison group in a third town.

The media materials included radio and television programs and spot announcements, newspaper columns, billboard and bus posters, and direct mailings. The content of the campaigns was intended to increase awareness of cardiovascular risks and to provide knowledge and skills to accomplish changes in behavior. For example, dietary suggestions were made, and reduction in cigarette smoking and increases in physical activity were advocated.

The intensive instruction intervention was administered either in groups or through individual visits to subjects' homes. The content of the intervention was concerned with specific behaviors needed to achieve risk reduction, such as techniques for smoking reduction. Subjects were trained in self-monitoring, and in the steps needed to acquire desired alternative behavior, and were reinforced for successful performance.

Results indicated that the best overall risk reduction occurred for the media campaign plus intensive instruction group. This group experienced a 28 percent reduction in overall risk score, which was maintained throughout the follow-up period. The greatest reductions for this group occurred in smoking reduction, dietary modification, and blood pressure reductions.

The media campaign was successful in increasing *knowledge* of cardiovascular risk factors. Increased knowledge did not decay after the intervention was withdrawn but continued at the same level in both treatment communities over the three-year follow-up period. Media alone, without intensive instruction, were not as effective in producing behavior change, but some behavioral effects were noted. There were significant dietary changes and reduced blood pressure readings, but changes in smoking rates did not occur for the media-only group. Finally, none of the groups were successful in increasing leisure-time physical activity nor in maintaining weight reduction over the three-year follow-up period.

Overall, the study was successful in reducing some of the risks associated with heart disease, but important questions remained. This study concentrated on individual-level risk factors (smoking, diet, exercise, and the like). Could environmental and community-level risks for heart disorder also have been reduced (e.g., industrial pollutants, economic and cultural factors leading to poor diet, traffic congestion, noise stressors, and so on)? Leventhal, Safer, Cleary, and Gutmann (1980) believe that the ultimate payoff in

---

[2] Note that the methodology of this study was discussed in Chapter Four.

risk reduction for community-level factors is greater than the individual-level factors modified in the Stanford Heart Disease Project.

A second problem with this study is that morbidity and mortality data were not collected. Thus, we do not know whether the incidence of heart attacks or death rates from heart diseases were reduced by the intervention. This last step is needed in order to determine whether risk reduction leads to ultimate disorder reduction.

This study also raises the question about how much prevention benefit should be expected of media campaigns and mass education efforts. Maccoby and Alexander (1979) believe that media campaigns have been underrated as sources of behavior change, and provide useful suggestions for increasing their specificity and meaningfulness. In the Stanford Heart Disease Project, media alone were successful in increasing knowledge of risk and in producing some changes in behaviors. Unfortunately, other prevention programs that have relied exclusively on educational campaigns have produced less impressive results.

The clearest examples of failure of educational campaigns come from research on the prevention of smoking, alcohol, and drug abuse.[3] The assumption of many antismoking campaigns and alcohol and drug education programs is that disseminating information about the dangers involved will allow individuals to make an informed choice not to use these substances. Unfortunately, this strategy has not worked. Neither fear-arousing campaigns (scare tactics) or more neutrally toned "objective" information transmission has produced any significant reduction in smoking, alcohol, or drug practices. For these problems there appears to be no direct correspondence between information gains and changes in behavior. For example, Evans (1980) presents data that 85 percent of eighth-grade children who identify themselves as cigarette smokers know that smoking endangers their health. Similarly, Evans believes that most drug addicts are aware of the dangers of drugs before they begin using them, and many heart patients, even after their heart attacks, continue to take risks which can lead to further heart disease. The question then becomes how to decrease the frequency of behaviors that individuals "know" are bad for them.

Several approaches have been used in smoking and alcohol abuse programs to increase behavioral compliance. One approach is to emphasize immediate costs and benefits rather than dangerous outcomes far in the distant future. For example, Evans (1980) and his colleagues found that messages which stressed the short-term consequences of smoking (e.g., carbon monoxide in the breath and lungs, and "bad breath") were more effective deterrents against early experimentation with cigarettes than were messages that stressed more serious but far-off health consequences (e.g., cancer). Similarly, giving specific behavioral instructions (e.g., videotapes focusing on resisting peer pressure) also were more effective than merely

---

[3] The authors would like to thank Patricia S. Meek for stimulating their thinking about this topic with her review of the failures of drug-abuse prevention programs.

instructing subjects in the long-term dangers of smoking. Finally, practicing alternative behaviors and their reinforcement also is important. This factor was a component of the smoking cessation success of the intensive-instruction group in the Stanford Heart Disease program, and has been a key factor in other successful prevention projects as well (e.g., Bry, 1982; Bry & George, 1979). Thus, the most effective programs have not relied on educational campaigns alone but have followed up these efforts with opportunities for behavioral practice and reinforcement for alternative behaviors once they have been acquired.

There is an added dilemma for prevention programs aimed at reductions in smoking, alcohol, and drug use. The substances used are pleasurable and occur in a culture in which their use, particularly by teenagers, often is a prerequisite for socialization and peer acceptance. Given this social context, prevention programs that focus only on the dangers of substance use are not addressing the major reasons why teenagers smoke, drink, or use drugs. Helping teenagers learn how to resist peer pressure may be one answer, but more structural social changes should have greater effects. What are needed are meaningful social roles that are personally enhancing and that allow for the demonstration of competence as an alternative to "getting high." This point can be illustrated by a letter to newspaper columnist Ann Landers:

> Dear Ann Landers: I am a high-school teacher in the Fort Wayne public school system. Since 1967 I have watched sloppy, indolent, sassy, unmotivated students virtually sleepwalk through this school.
>
> I won't go into detail about the lack of respect for authority or the students I have seen stoned, spaced out, still drunk on Monday morning, glassy-eyed from Quaaludes, freaked out from PCP and depressed after coming down from a high. . . .
>
> A few weeks ago, an act of God opened my eyes. Fort Wayne experienced the worse floods in our history. . . .
>
> Like thousands of others, I went downtown to help—and what did I see? Hundreds of students whom I had written off as lazy, irresponsible goof-offs. They had come as volunteers to work in the sandbag lines, haul rubble and trash, help evacuate the elderly and stranded, do whatever needed to be done. Some were even ready to risk their lives if necessary. And were they having a great time? The best ever!
>
> I spoke with many at length and learned some lessons that aren't in the books. I discovered that trouble can bring out the very best in folks, and if we want our young people to amount to something we must give them a sense of purpose—of being needed, and most of all, something to do. (Ann Landers, Daily Herald-Telephone, April 19, 1982. Reprinted by permission of Field Newspaper Syndicate.)

Why should it take a natural disaster for teenagers to be seen as socially useful? In our society, the teen years are supposed to be a time of preparation for adult social roles; but too often training in responsible citizenship is not available. We attempt to train teenagers academically and vocationally, but leave the development of citizenship skills to happenstance. Teenage intrusions into community affairs often are resented. We are bothered by the seeming "immaturity" of teenagers and yet provide few opportunities for mature decision making. The lesson from Ann Landers is clear. We should not expect drug and alcohol use to decrease unless meaningful social participation increases.

The use of the media for prevention and health promotion is receiving growing research interest (Johnston, 1982; Keegan, 1982; Solomon, 1982). What we have learned from this research is that, while such mass communication devices as television have the potential for enormous positive influence, this potential for the most part remains unrealized. Prevention information on television generally has been limited to infrequent "public service" announcements. The impact of any one message is considerably diluted by the barrage of other messages with which it must compete. Solomon (1982) concludes that, because of the overload in what is transmitted, the message must be kept simple when television is used in health campaigns. Solomon believes that health campaigns on TV err when they attempt to present complex messages, "since very little of the information may penetrate to the audience's awareness." Viewers are so accustomed to "tuning out" commercials that they have a tendency to tune out messages of all sorts that are not an integral part of the particular program they are watching.

A major, still undeveloped, use of television for prevention purposes is in changing attitudes and social stereotypes. As will be described in more detail in the next section, a first step in effective coping is the adoption of an orientation or belief structure that action on a problem is possible—and is likely to succeed. It is in this sense that television can be helpful in priming action by contributing to the beliefs and expectations of viewers.

At the present time, the expectations conveyed by television often do not promote a sense of active coping, particularly for certain stereotyped groups. For example, a content analysis of television entertainment programs found that women were more likely to be portrayed in passive, non-problem-solving roles. On the other hand, men were more often seen as making plans for themselves and others, and having their plans eventuate in successful outcomes (Greenberg and Heeter, 1982). The research on the television series "Freestyle," aired on a PBS station in Los Angeles, indicated that social role stereotypes of this sort can be changed (Johnston, 1982). Not only can attitudes and expectations toward women be changed but similar changes can be induced in attitudes toward other stereotyped groups, such as the elderly (Keegan, 1982). The problem is that positive programming of this sort faces an uphill battle on TV because negative sex and age stereotypes appear on the majority of programs. What is required is more than token demonstration projects. A more substantial commitment to a review of program content is needed from an industry that, up till now, has not given sufficient attention to the psychological impact of its broadcasts.

Competency Enhancement and Interpersonal Problem Solving as Prevention Strategies: Does Training Have to Be Stressor Specific?

Recently, many clinical and community psychologists have adopted a competency orientation; that is, they have begun to conceptualize their task as helping individuals develop psychosocial skills that could be used in a variety of situations (Albee & Joffee, 1977; Bloom, 1979; Kent & Rolf, 1979). Prevention activities from this point of view would mean that programs could focus on building adaptive strengths, with the assumption that a strengthened individual would be able to deal better with any number of different stressors that eventually might lead to disability.

The development of prevention approaches to enhance competence received their greatest impetus from the work of George Spivack, Myra Shure, and their colleagues. Their initial work demonstrated that psychiatric patients were deficient in the ability to generate solutions to interpersonal problems (Platt & Spivack, 1972; Platt, Siegel, & Spivack, 1975). This deficit was found to apply in younger patients as well (Platt, Spivack, Altman, & Altman, 1974). Disturbed elementary school children were less likely to solve problems effectively, and were more likely to use impulsive and physically aggressive solutions regardless of social class and intellectual functioning (Shure & Spivack, 1972). Believing that cognitive problem-solving skills are a prerequisite for good adjustment, the research group shifted its focus and developed a program to train children in problem-solving skills as a primary prevention strategy (Spivack & Shure, 1974).

The basic findings of this research are that problem-solving skills can be enhanced through training. Teachers were shown how to train four- and five-year-old children from low-income day-care centers in interpersonal problem-solving skills. Improvement generally lasted at least one to two years beyond termination of training, and trained youngsters also improved in social behavior. Training was extended to low-income mothers, and again positive effects were found. Mothers could transmit interpersonal problem-solving skills to their preschool children and significant behavioral improvement occurred. The best predictor of improved adjustment was the ability to think of a number of alternative solutions to interpersonal problems. What is particularly impressive about this work was that generalization was reported to have occurred. Children trained in one environment, by their mothers at home, improved in their behavior as observed by teachers in school. Children previously rated as impulsive were less easily upset in the face of frustration and were better able to wait, share, and take turns. Previously inhibited children became more socially outgoing and were less fearful in entering social situations (Shure & Spivack, 1979).

What are the children learning that enables them to better meet the frustrations of daily living? The skill that correlates best with later adjustment is the ability to generate alternative solutions. Children were not taught specific solutions to problems but were encouraged to think of many different solutions to the same problem. For example, if the problem was how to play with a toy another child had, alternative solutions might include "Hit him" (force-attack); "Tell the teacher" (appeal to authority); "Can I hold it?" (ask-beg); "Snatch it" (force directed at object); "If you let me play with that *boat;* I'll let you play with my *car*" (trade-bribe) (Shure and Spivack, 1979.).

Working independently from the research literature in cognitive psychology, Goldfried and D'Zurilla (1969) developed a similar problem-solving model that they then applied to adult psychotherapy clients. While not adopting a prevention focus themselves, their problem-solving model was used by others for both psychotherapy and prevention. D'Zurilla and Goldfried (1971) synthesized the previous literature and proposed that effective problem-solving occurs in a series of five general steps. First, a *general orientation* is developed, which recognizes that problem situations are a part of everyday living, that they must be expected and recognized, that it is possible to cope with these situations effectively, and that the tendencies to act on impulse or to assume a helpless "nothing can be done" attitude must be inhibited. The second stage involves *problem definition and formulation.* All aspects of the situation are defined in operational terms. Major subproblems are identified, as well as important issues or conflicts that might impede problem resolution. The third step involves the *generation of alternatives* and is similar to the method of "brainstorming" (Osborn, 1963). The attempt is made to produce as many solutions as possible. To maximize uninhibited thinking, criticism is ruled out at this stage. Sheer quantity of alternatives rather than quality is important in this stage, so judgment and evaluation are deferred. Later in the fourth step, *decision making,* evaluation and the selection of the best alternative are attempted. The task is to predict the consequences of each of the alternatives previously generated, so the optimal alternative can be selected. In the final stage, *verification* is attempted. A particular solution is tried and its success is noted so that feedback and self-correction become possible.

The D'Zurilla and Goldfried model of problem solving was embraced by the growing movement in cognitive behavior modification (Mahoney & Arnkoff, 1978) and, along with the Spivack and Shure research, was applied to a variety of problem-solving situations. Work was conducted on enhancing social competency in both school-aged children and in adults.

Allen, Chinsky, Larcen, Lochman, and Selinger (1976) developed a problem-solving curriculum that was tested in a Connecticut school serving third and fourth graders only. The program included didactic material, videotape modeling, and role-playing exercises, and was organized into six steps following from the D'Zurilla and Goldfried model: developing a divergent thinking and problem-solving orientation; learning to identify and elaborate problems; generating alternative solutions; considering the consequences for each solution generated; elaborating the details of execution for the solutions generated; and finally, implementing, getting feedback, and integrating problem-solving behavior into the individual's regular response repertoire.

The results of the study indicated that the children learned the appropriate problem-solving behavior in the classroom and, when tested, did show increases in behaviors emphasized in the program—for example, increases in the number of alternative solutions generated and a richer elaboration of the solutions presented. Unfortunately, generalization to other situations in the classroom or in the natural environment outside the classroom was not achieved.

The difficulty of obtaining generalization of problem-solving behaviors in this age group has been reported by other investigators as well. Investigators at the University of Rochester's school-based Primary Mental Health Project designed a training program that integrated the elements from previous work into three core components. These included:

1. Defining the problem—a process of information gathering, clarifying, and goal setting.
2. Generating alternatives—the ability to think of a wide variety of potential solutions without regard for their quality.
3. Considering consequences—the ability to anticipate the impact of one's social acts on others and on oneself. (Gesten, Flores de Apodaca, Rains, Weissberg, & Cowen, 1979, p. 229)

The basic findings of the Allen et al. research were replicated by the Rochester group. Children trained in social problem-solving skills did show significant increases in the generation of alternative solutions and in evaluating their consequences (Cowen, Gesten, & Weissberg, 1980); but generalization to classroom or school adjustment produced mixed results. When the program was tested in both suburban and inner-city schools, the suburban children were found to show improved adjustment, but not so the inner-city school children. On some measures, the adjustment of the urban children declined (Weissberg, Gesten, Rapkin, Cowen, Davidson, Flores de Apodaca, & McKim, 1981). A clue to what may have been producing the negative outcome in the inner-city school can be obtained from teacher reports. Some teachers complained that, in their groups, brainstorming alternative solutions without regard to their quality encouraged the production of a large number of aggressive alternatives, which negatively affected class discipline. Furthermore, in neither group was there a direct relationship between gains in social problem-solving skills and adjustment. That is, it was not necessarily the case that youngsters who showed the highest levels of problem-solving skills also showed the best adjustment ratings.

Thus, the relationship between improved problem-solving skill and mental health is not as simple as it initially appeared. The success of Spivack and Shure with preschool children and the more ambiguous results from the Connecticut and Rochester groups with school age children may mean that social competency training must be initiated early, before school entry, for maximal effectiveness. But even this recommendation cannot be made with complete confidence, because maximum follow-up for the Spivack and Shure children was only two years. Thus, the value of social problem-solving training as a prevention strategy remains an open question. We still do not know whether long-term adjustment is affected or for whom social problem-solving training might be most effective.

A most intriguing prevention-oriented use of social problem-solving training with adults is reported by Novaco. As an extension of social problem-solving training he first developed for use with clinical problems of anger control (Novaco, 1975) a "stress-inoculation" approach was adopted in the training of police to handle similar problems—anger management (Novaco, 1977; Meichenbaum & Novaco, 1978). Stress-inoculation training as originally developed by Meichenbaum (1975) bears considerable similarity to the training in social problem solving already described. The added elements provided by Meichenbaum focus more directly on the role of cognitions in how situations are initially defined and reacted to. As a cognitive therapist, Meichenbaum believes that cognitions have a central role in the development of psychopathology. By expecting the worst from others, or evaluating their own behavior in negative terms, cycles of self-confirming negative expectations are generated from which clients find it extremely difficult to extricate themselves.

Stress-inoculation as designed by Novaco included cognitive preparation, skill acquisition, and practice of coping techniques during a series of role-played provocations. Police officers were encouraged to differentiate the various kinds of situations they found stressful. The cues in these situations that elicited anger were identified, along with the officers' own attitudes and expectancies concerning these situations. Practice was then given in positive "self-statements"—thoughts police officers should say to themselves in order to maintain control of the situation. Finally, alternative behaviors to deal with the provocation were role-played and then discussed. Novaco does not present data concerning the prevention potential of his training program, but its utility should be high, given that police constantly encounter anger-provoking situations and thus are motivated to manage these situations well.

The Evaluation of Problem-Solving Training as a Prevention Strategy

There are two major questions that can be raised about training in social problem solving as a prevention strategy. The proponents of this approach believe that a generalized problem-solving strategy can be learned that will be applicable across a wide variety of problem situations. However, we know that learning is most effective when it occurs in situation-specific contexts, which may be one reason why generalization of problem-solving training has been so difficult to attain in a number of studies. But we also know that learning sets can have an important influence on behavior; that is, there is research that demonstrates that both humans and animals can "learn how to learn" by adopting problem-solving strategies. Like any other learned response, whether learning sets are utilized depend upon a number of factors: the similarity between training and generalization situations, the motivation and prior experience of the learner, the potency of other competing responses in the learner's response repertory and so on. The conditions in which learning sets are *least* likely to generalize include an unmotivated learner who does not see the relevance of what is being taught and who has strong prior interfering habits that come into play almost automatically in real-life eliciting situations. Thus, we would predict that motivated police officers should do well in Novaco's training program, but that those who have a history of being quick to anger will need to work harder to overcome their predisposition to anger and aggression.

Is it likely that preschool or latency-age children will use problem solving learning sets in the various interpersonal situations they confront in daily life? Our analysis would suggest that the likelihood of their use depends upon the individual's motivation and the level of interfering habitual responses. For many children, motivation for popularity with peers and success in school is high, so they should be motivated to learn new problem-solving strategies to increase their skills. Unfortunately, school-age children also learn competing responses strongly reinforced by their peer culture (e.g., strength and cunning may be more immediately successful than polite asking or taking turns). Thus, our basic point is that, while training in social problem solving should be successful, we would not expect it to have universally positive effects. Whether any learning set is utilized depends upon a number of interacting factors.

The second major question about social problem-solving training programs concerns their long-range prevention potential. The issue is whether the basic assumption of this line of research is correct—that individuals whose basic competencies are increased are less vulnerable to later disability. Some have argued that the reduced incidence of mental disorder should not be the major goal of prevention programs (Danish & D'Augelli, 1980). These authors have adopted an "enhancement model," and suggest that the enhancement of human development is a "more constructive goal" for the development of intervention programs in mental health. Thus, it is argued that increased competency in meeting the stresses of everyday life is a worthwhile objective in its own right. From this view, competency enhancement alone would be considered a socially useful goal regardless of any reductions in later disability. The competency enhancement view has become extremely popular among prevention researchers (e.g., Bond, 1982). However, we believe that advocacy of competency enhancement or disorder reduction goals for prevention programs are value issues, not empirical ones. At this point, we still do not know what prevention activities society will be willing to support financially. We suspect that during an era of limited funds for human service programs, most citizens will be unwilling to support programs that are not in some way related to distal goals of disorder prevention. Thus, in our view, research still needs to be done to determine whether social competencies developed in intervention programs persist over time, and whether individuals whose competencies are improved are "immunized" and are demonstrated to be less vulnerable to later disorder.

EXAMPLES OF SECONDARY PREVENTION

The Issues Raised by Early Identification and Intervention

Several studies have demonstrated that it is feasible to identify children with emotional problems at an early age (much of this research is summarized by Zax & Specter, 1974, pp. 173–201). There is evidence that children so identified are more poorly adjusted years later, particularly if no intervention has been attempted. As Zax and Specter note, the available research suggests that the emotional problems of children are not ephemeral—something that the child will outgrow—but that they tend to endure. The best evidence for this point comes from the Rochester Primary Mental Health Project under the direction of Emory Cowen.

In a series of studies beginning in 1963, Cowen and his associates (Cowen, Izzo, Miles, Telschow, Trost, & Zax, 1963) screened youngsters for early signs of emotional disturbance soon after entry into the first grade. A "Red-Tag" was applied to the folders of all children showing incipient signs of maladjustment based on data obtained from the mother, teachers' reports, or direct observation. In various studies, the number of children so tagged was slightly over 30 percent of the total group.

By the end of the third grade, red-tagged youngsters were doing significantly less well than nontagged children on a variety of behavioral, educational, and adjustive indices (Cowen, Zax, Izzo, & Trost, 1966). They performed less well in school, obtained lower achievement test scores, showed greater indication of maladjustment on personality tests, and were rated less positively by their peers. Four years later, in the seventh grade, red-tagged children continued to be distinguishable from non-red-tagged children, scoring in a more negative direction on these same measures (Zax, Cowen, Rappaport, Beach, & Laird, 1968). In a further follow-up, these same early detected vulnerable children were found to have significantly higher appearances in a community-wide psychiatric case register, which is an index of use of psychiatric facilities (Cowen, Pederson, Babigian, Izzo, & Trost, 1973).

While emotionally vulnerable youngsters can be identified at an early age, should such identification take place? Are the effects of special attention harmful to the children involved? It is not just that children labeled as "disturbed" may be treated badly by teachers and peers, but some psychologists believe that children labeled as disturbed encounter a "hands-off" phenomenon (Sarason, Levine, Goldenberg, Cherlin, & Bennett, 1966). These observers note that labeled children are avoided by teachers, resulting in increased social distance and less frequent interaction with the very persons from whom they might otherwise encounter corrective social experiences. In other words, the early labeling of emotionally disturbed children can result in a decreased opportunity to learn prosocial adaptive behaviors. In the previously mentioned research by Cowen et al. (1973), it was found that, even without formal labeling, sociometric peer ratings in the third grade were successful predictors of appearance years later in a psychiatric case register. Young children in this study identified troubled peers early, and viewed them more negatively. If teachers and peers both adopt a "hands-off" policy toward troubled youngsters, it is not difficult to imagine the resultant social isolation that such youngsters must deal with in addition to their already manifest problems.

The issue is whether corrective intervention can reverse this negative trend so that early identification would be justified. Practitioners of secondary prevention believe that it can, but the evidence is far from conclusive. For example, Cowen et al. (1966) found that, in a school provided with a comprehensive mental health program, children generally showed more positive scores on measures of behavior, achievement, and adjustment than did children in a matched control school that did not receive the program. Yet red-tagged children in this same experimental school still were distinguishable from non-red-tagged children as described in the previous paragraphs. How can we account for the improved adjustment found in the experimental school if the poorly adjusted red-tagged children still scored significantly lower on adjustment measures?

One possibility is that the more positive scores of experimental children were contributed by positive changes in the least-maladjusted children. In other words, those who benefited most from the school-wide intervention program may have been the non-red-tagged normal children. This is a possible outcome that any community-wide intervention program must face. If special benefit is provided to all members of a group (to not single out any individuals as needing special attention), those initially most able and adjusted may be in the best position to take advantage of the special benefits being provided.

A second possibility, and the one favored by Cowen and his colleagues, is that all children in the experimental school benefited from the mental health program, including the red-tagged children, but that the latter would have become even worse without the intervention. Cowen argues that intervention slowed a worsening adjustment for the red-tagged children. The evidence in favor of this position is that children who received special individual tutoring by nonprofessional teacher-aides were rated by their parents (Cowen, Dorr, Trost, & Izzo, 1972) and by their teachers (Cowen, 1968) as showing improved adjustment. Those who knew the children receiving special attention thought that the program was helping them. Teachers increased their referrals to the nonprofessional aides to such a point that waiting lists became necessary and the school system, in which the program had originated, decided to hire additional teacher-aides with its own funds (Zax & Specter, 1974).

The Rochester Primary Mental Health Project is perhaps the best example of secondary prevention available in the literature (the project results are summarized in Cowen, Trost, Lorion, Dorr, Izzo, & Isaacson, 1975; and in Weissberg, Cowen, Lotyczewski, & Gesten, 1983). The project has been evolving over time and its most recent research efforts have focused on primary prevention through training in interpersonal problem-solving skills (Gesten et al., 1979). However, as a secondary prevention project, the evidence for the effectiveness of this highly sophisticated research effort is not clear-cut. The ambiguity is not in the success of early case finding (Lorion, Cowen, & Caldwell, 1975) but in the potential of preventive intervention to reverse already identified adjustive disability.

Secondary Prevention and the Problem of Overprediction

Secondary prevention programs often are based upon early case identification, in which individuals with incipient problem behaviors are predicted to develop later psychopathology. How accurate are such predictions? Will those predicted to develop a problem in fact develop one if intervention is not undertaken?

Consider the case of preventing violence in the community. Community psychologists and psychiatrists are frequently called upon to predict when a person is "dangerous" to others as the result of mental disorder, and many thousands of persons are involuntarily committed each year on the basis of those predictions. Yet, if one examines the available data on the validity of psychological and psychiatric predictions of violence, a significant overprediction bias can be detected. Generally, it has been found that the percentage of "false positives," people predicted to be violent who are actually nonviolent when released into the community, exceeds the percentage of "true positives," people accurately predicted to be violent. This finding remains, regardless of who is doing the predicting (psychologists, psychiatrists, computers) or of what variables are used in making the predictions (tests, diagnoses, interviews, case histories). There are many reasons for this great amount of overprediction. The primary one may be simply that it is exceedingly difficult to accurately predict an event with a low base rate. As Livermore, Malmquist, and Meehl (1968) put it:

> Assume also that an exceptionally accurate test is created which differentiates with 95 percent effectiveness those who will kill from those who will not. If 100,000 people were tested, out of the 100 who would kill, 95 would be isolated. Unfortunately, out of the 99,000 who would not kill, 4,995 people would also be isolated as potential killers. In these circumstances, it is clear that we could not justify incarcerating all 5,090 people. If, in the criminal law, it is better that 10 guilty men go free than that one innocent man suffer, how can we say in the civil commitment area that it is better that 54 harmless people be incarcerated lest one dangerous man be free? (p. 84)

Unfortunately, this situation with regard to the poor ability of mental health professionals to predict behavior is not restricted to violence to others. The literature on the prediction of suicide (Beck, Resnik, & Lettieri, 1974), delinquency (Glueck & Glueck, 1972), alcoholism (Plaut, 1972), and child abuse (Steinmetz & Strauss, 1974) is not much better than that for violence. In the Cowen et al. (1973) research just described, the red-tagged children were followed up 13 years later to determine how many of them appeared in a psychiatric case register as adolescents and young adults. The register was a compilation of the individuals who had been hospitalized or who received psychological treatment and who still lived in the area. The results indicated that, of those in the register from the appropriate target schools (the clinical cases), 68 percent had been red-tagged in the primary grades. Thus, individuals who later received psychiatric treatment could be identified in the primary grades at a better-than-chance rate. However, of all the children red-tagged at an early age, "only 19 percent of early identified red-tagged children developed sufficiently serious problems to have shown up in the Register" (Cowen et al., 1973, p. 443). While there are many reasons why vulnerable children do not seek treatment, in this study the overprediction rate that would have occurred if only clinical cases had been studied would have been considerable. While the majority of individuals in treatment showed risk markers as children, *the majority of children with risk markers did not seek treatment as adults.*

Two empirical conclusions emerge from research in this area.

1.   Mental health professionals using psychological and demographic data *can* predict a wide range of behavior at a level of accuracy higher than the base rates for the phenomenon.

2.   Current methods result in more people being incorrectly predicted as a future case of problem behavior than are accurately predicted to be such.

For the prevention program built on the assumption that problem cases can be identified before the problems are manifested, the data we have reviewed have sobering effects. The issue raised by the data concerns the psychological and legal implications for the individual incorrectly predicted to be in need of intervention. Let us take an extreme example. Numerous studies have found alcoholism to be substantially more prevalent among Irish-Americans than among other ethnic minorities (Plaut, 1972). If one took admission of Irish ancestry as a predictor of alcoholism, and then began alcoholism prevention programs with this population, one *would* be isolating a higher-than-base rate proportion of future alcoholics, and to the extent the program was effective, the prevalence of alcoholism would be reduced at least marginally. The problem with such a strategy, of course, is that the vast majority of Irish-Americans would not become alcoholics but would nevertheless be identified in the sample, and the psychological effects of being identified and treated as "pre-alcoholic" could be severe.

Consider a different example. It is standard operating procedure to place drops of silver nitrate into the eyes of newborn infants. This is to avoid a condition (congenital syphilis) which can cause blindness. This condition, however, affects only one in several thousand babies. Statistically, therefore, the case here is similar to that for alcoholism and Irish-Americans: for each correctly predicted case of disorder, there are vast numbers of incorrect predictions. Why, then, would we support the overprediction of blindness in infants and oppose the overprediction of alcoholism in Irish-Americans?

The answer is that overprediction per se is not necessarily bad, but becomes so only to the extent that it has negative effects on those who are overpredicted. In the alcoholism example, the negative effects are extreme (labeling, self-fulfilling prophecy, and so on), while, in the blindness example, the effects of overprediction are negligible since the silver nitrate does not injure the overpredicted infants. The precise nature of the negative effects of overprediction, of course, is sometimes controversial.

Several years ago, there were a series of unprovoked attacks in San Francisco by a man who came to be known as the "Zebra Killer" after his police code name. All that was known of the individual was that he was a black male between 5 feet 8 inches and 6 feet tall. The major of San Francisco, seeking to prevent future attacks by identifying the assailant, ordered police to stop and question any young black male within the given height range. This, of course, resulted in thousands of "false positives"—law-abiding citizens being stopped and questioned. The mayor, who was not a black male in this height range, did not consider the stop-and-question procedure to be an undue imposition. The overpredicted black males, however, took great offense at what they considered a gross violation of their rights. The courts quickly agreed with them and ordered the practice stopped. In this example, both groups—the mayor's office and the black male population—were in agreement that violence was being overpredicted, but each group placed a different weight on the effects of that overprediction.

Crisis Intervention: A Therapeutic Technique with Potential for Secondary Prevention

Crisis intervention developed as a set of procedures to aid individuals recover from the effects of temporary but extreme stress. Initially, the approach was used by clinicians for patients with established symptomatology (Langsley, Pittman, Machotka, & Flomenhaft, 1968; Lindemann, 1944). It has since grown into a popular method for dealing with a variety of clinical problems (Bellak & Small, 1965; Ewing, 1978). One reason for the increased popularity of crisis intervention was its inclusion in the Community Mental Health Centers Act of 1963. To receive federal funds under the act and its subsequent revisions, mental health centers were required to provide five essential services, which included 24-hour emergency care. Interest in crisis intervention increased dramatically as mental health professionals began looking for a therapeutic model that would help them develop emergency services.

If crisis intervention is a clinical procedure to help deal with already distressed individuals, why discuss it in a chapter on prevention? Even though much of the work on crisis intervention was done with individuals already suffering from the deleterious effects of stress, the same procedures, with very little modification, could be used earlier—either in anticipation of stressful events or after their initial impact. Thus, there is a potential for the prevention or reduction of later disability. As is true for competency training more generally, the focus in crisis intervention is on helping individuals adapt to and master the stresses associated with negative life events.

The work on crisis intervention generally can be traced to Eric Lindemann's study of grief reactions among patients who had lost close friends or relatives, and who some time later showed clinical signs of anxiety and depression. Among his patients were a significant number of persons who had lost close relatives in the 1941 Coconut Grove Dance Hall fire in Boston, or who were themselves survivors of that fire. Lindemann came to the conclusion that many of these persons were suffering from inadequate grieving, and coined the term "grief work" to describe what was needed to help his patients become symptom-free (Lindemann, 1944).

Lindemann described grief work as having three significant components:

1.   Acceptance of the painful emotions involved in the loss. The therapist may be required to review the events associated with the traumatic event in evocative detail in order to help the patient express these emotions.

2.   The active review of experiences and events, both positive and negative, which were shared with the deceased. The purpose of this second step is to help the individual appreciate the richness of his relationship with the deceased without idealizing that relationship in an unrealistic manner.

3.   "The gradual rehearsal and testing of new patterns of interaction and role relationships which can replace some of the functions which the deceased fulfilled in the survivor's life" (Lindemann, 1962, p. 73). The purpose of this last step is to help the patient develop new patterns of adaptation and coping.

A careful scrutiny of the three steps in grief work listed above should reveal that they include the major elements of most forms of psychotherapy: emotional catharsis, cognitive reappraisal, and the development of new forms of behavior. Note the sequence in which the elements of grief work were posited to occur. As a psychoanalyst, Lindemann believed that emotional catharsis was the necessary first element and that both catharsis and cognitive reappraisal were antecedent to behavior change.

Lindemann's views of grief were expanded by Gerald Caplan, his junior colleague at the Harvard School of Public Health. Caplan believed that life crises generally, not just loss events, were capable of producing acute symptomatology. Caplan defined a crisis as follows:

> In my terminology, a crisis is a time-limited period of psychological disequilibrium in an individual, precipitated by a sudden and significant change in the person's life situation. This change results in demands for internal adjustment or external adaptation which are temporarily beyond the individual's capacity to achieve.

Notice that Caplan's view of adjustment implies a psychological homeostasis. A crisis disturbs that equilibrium because it presents the individual with demands for a new adjustment that are unanticipated and for which the individual is unprepared to cope. Caplan's definition also stresses the time-limited nature of a crisis and that crises are precipitated by specific life events. Thus, the adverse effects of a crisis could occur in any individual, including those whose adjustment was otherwise normal.

Elements of a crisis intervention approach have been used to help individuals recover from the traumatic effects of natural disasters, such as floods, tornados, and hurricanes, (V. B. Brown, 1980; Cohen & Ahearn, 1980; also see the review by Bloom, 1977), and unpredictable and potentially dangerous aggressive acts, such as hostage-taking, skyjacking, and witnessing an unprovoked murder (Dallas, 1978; Miron & Goldstein, 1978). Crisis intervention procedures also have been used in the training of volunteers to serve on telephone hot-lines and to deal with potentially suicidal individuals (Shneidman, 1973). In each of these instances, the approach utilized is a variation or elaboration of the basic therapeutic ingredients originally proposed by Lindemann—emotional catharsis, cognitive appraisal, and the development of alternative behaviors. There has been a significant addition to crisis intervention practice. This can be seen in the more recent emphasis on rebuilding disrupted social ties and generally increasing the availability of environmental supports.

The major difference between crisis intervention and more traditional forms of psychotherapy is in its ahistorical focus. Crisis workers focus on the conflicts generated by current stressful events. Attempts at personality "reconstruction" are avoided, as are historical interpretations. One does not deal with the question "How did you become the person you are today?" but rather with the issue "How can you deal with and resolve your current predicament?"

Are there any data to indicate whether crisis intervention procedures prevent the occurrence of later disability, or at least reduce the intensity or duration of incapacitating symptoms? Unfortunately, these important prevention questions have not yet been answered. Evaluation research intended to document the effectiveness of crisis intervention is sparse and still is of poor quality (Auerbach & Kilmann, 1977). While a few outcome studies have reported apparent short-term symptom relief, there are few long-term controlled follow-up studies demonstrating enduring effects or reductions in rates of future disability. We again have an example of a promising tool that could be used for prevention but for which programmatic empirical research is sorely needed.

SOME UNANSWERED QUESTIONS ABOUT PREVENTION

How Specific Is the Link between Environmental Stress and Disorder?

In some cases, the role of risk factors in the environment is fairly clear-cut. For example, the role of nutritional deficiencies on cognitive functioning and the manner in which hospital recovery rooms can contribute to increased patient agitation were cited earlier in this chapter. Often, however, the exact role environmental events play in the development of disorder remains obscure and controversial. To illustrate, in the case of schizophrenic disorders, some investigators believe that the role of life events is relatively trivial, compared with genetic and constitutional factors. From this point of view, life events simply "trigger" psychotic episodes in already predisposed individuals. Others believe that major life events, particularly unusual events outside of the subject's control, have a more substantive role in the development of schizophrenic symptomatology (Dohrenwend & Egri, 1981).

Would reducing the impact of negative life events lower the incidence of schizophrenia? We know of no research that can make such a claim. A major reason is that the specific risk factors associated with the etiology of the various schizophrenic disorders for the most part still are unknown. The most popular model for schizophrenia—the diathesis-stress model—describes the factors involved in general terms (e.g., constitutional and genetic predispositions and unspecified environmental stress). Information about specific risks, particularly those associated with environmental stressors, has remained elusive.

In the case of other disorders, knowledge of contributing environmental risks is beginning to accumulate. For example, loss of support has been implicated in depression (G. W. Brown & Harris, 1978; Lowenthal & Haven, 1968). Excessive vigilance and uncontrollable stress have been linked to essential hypertension (Davison & Neale, 1982); and family conflict, peer pressure, and poor academic achievement have long been thought of as precipitants to delinquency. Thus, it is possible that, with increased knowledge, a set of risk factors might be specified for each major psychological problem or disorder. Prevention then would mean decreasing the likelihood of symptomatology by reducing the level of any of the contributing factors.

Another view has been emerging, which suggests that it may not be possible to link specific risks to specific disorders. Stress may not be disorder specific but may produce a generalized vulnerability (Bloom, 1979). Stress may be reacted to differently, depending upon other predisposing factors. Thus, given a specific event, one person might become depressed, another might drink too much, while still another might move closer to psychosis. The implication for prevention is that mastery over stressful life events might improve coping capacity, generally, but would be difficult to detect by looking at incidence rates for specific disorders. According to this view, the effectiveness of prevention should be determined by measuring variables that reflect stress mastery—competence, achievement, and satisfaction.

At this point, there is insufficient information available to choose between these alternative hypotheses. Some researchers may choose to focus on disorders to be prevented (e.g., delinquency, alcoholism, schizophrenia); others will devote their efforts to stress reduction and life crisis mastery. Both types of research should be encouraged until more definitive knowledge is obtained.

In focusing on environmental stressors as risk factors, we will probably discover that certain stressors in society are more easily preventable than others, requiring only changes in environmental design. Other stressors may require a change in social, political, and economic conditions that are beyond the direct influence and control of community interventionists. Whichever the situation, the prevention-oriented researcher and practitioner attempts what is feasible—reducing the deleterious consequences of those stressors that are modifiable, educating the public about those not under his or her control, and helping affected populations cope better with those that are truly unavoidable.

Is the Goal of Prevention a Stress-Free Environment?

Over the years there have been many attempts to find utopian communities that could be described as "Heavens on Earth" (Holloway, 1966) where the stresses and strains of modern society have not developed. If such communities could be found, the expectation was that surely they would be devoid of psychic disturbance.

Dohrenwend and Dohrenwend (1974) review a number of studies of ethnic enclaves that have successfully preserved their traditions while the world was changing about them. None of these studies provide evidence that a simple and relatively uncomplicated way of life provides immunity from mental disorders. The Hutterites can serve as an illustrative example. They are a religiously oriented, self-sufficient communal society, with a stable agrarian economy, who care for and support their own members. The Dohrenwends report that Hutterites were not allowed to become public charges as long as they remained members of the community. Only one divorce and four separations are reported in the history of the group. Yet the rates of psychosis among the Hutterites are relatively high and cannot be differentiated from the rates reported in more urban societies.

What is different about the Hutterites is the type of disorder reported. Whereas most communities report higher rates of schizophrenia than manic-depressive psychosis, the reverse is true for the Hutterites. In their society, cases of manic-depression far outnumber cases of schizophrenic reactions. In addition, persistent and severe antisocial behavior and personality disorders are nearly absent among the Hutterites. This last outcome, which implies a relatively crime-free society, would be the envy of the most "advanced" urban communities.

Symptomatology expressive of social withdrawal or antisocial behavior are infrequent and may be discouraged by the Hutterite way of life. However, the Hutterite society does not provide immunity from mental disorders for its members. It is highly possible that what may appear to be a simple society from the viewpoint of an outsider may not be stress-free. The society may be economically stable, but other stresses and strains may exist. For example, the strain may not be cultural or economic, but religious or existential. We doubt that a truly stress-free society can be found. What does seem clear from the evidence provided by the Dohrenwends is that the form, intensity, and duration of symptomatology differ among contrasting cultural settings. Thus, we return once again to the position that, if stressors can be removed, or their effects reduced, such action would be the preferred prevention strategy. When the environment cannot be changed, valid preventive interventions can be tried that provide improved "immunization" against the anticipated stress.

Is Increasing Social Support a Useful Prevention Strategy?

For some time there has been a growing recognition that socially connected people are in better mental and physical health than are isolates. Data to support this assertion come from a number of sources, the most impressive of which are epidemiological studies relating social ties to morbidity and mortality rates. For example, there are data to indicate that the unmarried are at greater health risk, compared with married individuals (Berkman & Syme, 1979; Kraus & Lilienfeld, 1959). In this research, the greatest risk was experienced by widowed individuals (i.e., losing a spouse creates greater risk than never having had one). Young males who become widowers were at greater risk than were older widowers or widows of any age group. Similarly, individuals who visited often with friends or relatives or who belonged to community organizations had lower mortality rates than did chronic nonparticipants. The evidence from the Berkman and Syme study is extremely compelling because of the care with which the research was done. Other hypotheses that could have accounted for the results, such as health and socioeconomic status of the participants, were systematically controlled. There were no viable alternatives that could explain the findings, other than the health protective effects of social ties.

This research was seen as an example of what became called "the buffering hypothesis," which stated that individuals experiencing significant life stress but with good social support would be protected from developing symptomatology. In other words, social support operated as a "stress-buffer" reducing the psychological impact of stressful life events. Increasing social support then could be seen as a potential preventive strategy for those experiencing significant life crises.

Unfortunately, many of the studies of the buffering hypothesis did not produce results that were as clear as those of the studies just described (see Heller & Swindle, 1983, and Thoits, 1982, for a detailed explication of the problems involved). There is considerable methodological confusion in the research. Furthermore, even in well-done studies, it often is not clear what factors are producing the effects that are noted. Consider a recent study by Blazer (1982), which is one of the most methodologically sophisticated studies on this topic. In this study, elderly persons who perceived themselves to have minimal support from others had a mortality rate that was 3½ times higher at a 30-month follow-up period than did elderly who reported good support from others. This is an impressive finding because, as in the

Berkman and Syme study just reported, other possibly confounding health and social variables were systematically controlled.

The problem is that the factors producing the effects still are unknown. Why did the subjects in the Blazer study believe that they were well supported? What factors contributed to the perception of support? Is it most important for an elderly person to have a confidante, someone with whom to share intimate worries (G. W. Brown, 1979; Lowenthal & Haven, 1968), or will any friend or associate produce similar results? How does a close friend improve an individual's health status? Is the primary ingredient self-disclosure, being able to share worries rather than keeping them unexpressed? Or is it possible that having a friend is more important than being able to talk about worries? Perhaps it is the knowledge that one is not alone that produces feelings of well-being. Still another possibility is that the positive effects of support are produced by a more prosaic process. When we complain about our health to a friend, we are more likely to be told to see a doctor. Thus, the positive effects for support may simply mean that the affiliated receive better health care because of earlier diagnosis and treatment.

The point is that there is still much about social support and its key ingredients that are still poorly understood. This is an extremely promising area of research because of the intriguing possibility that the characteristics of social relationships may have important health outcomes. We should, however, avoid premature adoption of social support as the latest mental health fad before we have a clearer idea of the important characteristics of supportive relationships and under what conditions positive effects are likely to be demonstrated.

A REMAINING ETHICAL CONCERN: CIVIL LIBERTIES AND THE RIGHT TO PRIVACY

Perhaps the most serious problem facing prevention programs is that planned intervention in the lives of others, *before* they are clearly in need of help, violates a cultural norm of privacy: "the right and privilege of each person, and family, in a free society to mind his own business and have others mind theirs" (Bower, 1969, p. 233). Intervention is allowed when individuals are in danger of threatening the health and safety of others or when they may endanger their own lives. But, in these instances, one can "become one's brother's keeper only when 'brother' is in pretty sad shape" (Bower, 1969, p. 233). Yet, if preventive intervention is to be meaningful, it must occur before an individual becomes so clearly in need of special help.

The fear is that the community approach will be co-opted by the forces of social control to make people "uncomplainingly submissive to the will of the elites" (Szasz, 1970, p. 224), and that mental health technology will be used for political repression—not for psychological growth and enhancement. For Szasz (1970), community mental health was spawned by the Roosevelt and Kennedy policies of "modern interventionist liberalism" (p.

32). Its purpose "seems to be the dissemination of a collectivistic mental health ethic as a kind of secular religion" (p. 33). The values of community psychiatry are clear to Szasz: "collectivism and social tranquility" (p. 224).

These charges are strong; and they are disturbing to those who see their community work as *enhancing* rather than *destroying* human autonomy. However, since the potential dangers are real, safeguards for the protection of individual liberties can and must be established. We further believe that the prevention of disability and misery is so serious a concern that the long-run benefits of prevention research must be explored. Only with well-conducted and widely disseminated research will society be in a position to know the potential benefits, and to know how the costs to individual liberty can be minimized.

The following example has been chosen to dramatically draw out the issues involved in the potential conflict between prevention and individual liberties. Consider the following: would we ever be in the position to require a license from the state before we allow couples to have children?

Anyone who observes conferences in the juvenile court soon becomes aware of the danger to children that can be perpetrated by rejecting and neglectful parents. The children who are labeled "delinquent" because of some antisocial act on their part are often the product of problem parents who claim the children as victims. After following case after case of parental neglect, drunkenness, abuse, rejection, or incest, it would not be surprising if the court observer would fantasize how much simpler the life of children would be if "bad parents" were prohibited from having children.

How could such a fantasy be implemented? Suppose we were able to identify the skills necessary for good parenting. We might then be able to develop a test to measure these skills. The test might include some basic knowledge of child development, the role of emotional expression in daily life, and basic principles of human communication. Such a test might include a performance task, in which the ability to relate to children was tested in a standardized role-play situation. The model is similar to the way a state now licenses its automobile drivers. The purpose of the test is not to pass only those with "super" ability but to screen out those who cannot reach some minimal level of acceptable understanding and skill. Through its licensing powers, the state now restricts the civil liberties of individual drivers in the name of the common good. As a group, we are convinced that the harm to the potential victims of dangerous drivers who will not conform to society's standards is so great that we willingly accept this restriction of our freedom. Should we apply similar standards in the home? If we require minimal standards to ensure physical safety on the road, should we not require similar standards for psychological safety in the home?

The possibility of restricting individual freedom in the manner described should raise the hackles of any civil libertarian. Who is to decide what is acceptable parenting behavior? Will the test discriminate against minority groups, whose norms for parenting behavior might be different from those of the major culture? Will the test be used by those in power to prevent citizens with unpopular ideas from multiplying? How will the test be enforced: will couples who defy the order and have children without a license have their children taken from them or be put in jail, or both? Will mandatory sterilization be required of chronic offenders?

We have purposely chosen a "hot" example for discussion. Milder examples of how prevention might threaten individual freedom might lull us into believing that solutions are easy. The solution of complex social problems is never easy. In the example presented above, we might start by asking whether the knowledge exists to identify good parenting skills. If not, this is where the research must begin. If parenting skills can be identified, we must be sure that the knowledge and skills involved can be adequately taught. There would be little point to identifying a standard of behavior to which we should strive if we cannot help all citizens achieve this goal. If community-wide education programs that are available and acceptable to all could not be mounted, the prevention program would be discriminatory from its inception. Once developed, the program could be offered in the public schools before parent status is achieved, thus minimizing the threat to later freedom of choice. For those with special difficulty in mastering the content, extra work or special tutors might be provided. Implemented in this way, society must decide whether such an educational program is of value for its children and whether it should be supported—an easier decision than whether to prevent parents from having children.

A community-wide education program in the high schools reduces the intensity of the moral dilemma but does not remove it entirely. The possibility exists that some small minority might refuse to allow its children to participate in the program, or that even with participation and repeating the program they might achieve such low scores that it is clear that they cannot master its content. If properly pursued, the solution to this problem should involve a balance between the rights of individuals against the rights of society as a collective to develop laws for the common good that will govern the behavior of its citizens. In the example cited, perhaps no further action need be taken. A substantial majority is participating and the minority not in compliance represents so small a portion of the population that efforts to punish noncompliance may be more costly and damaging than the good that might ensue from forced compliance.

We introduced this example by posing the question: would we ever require a license from the state before allowing couples to have children? Our answer to that question by now should be clear. We are *not* advocating the mandatory licensing of parents. Not only would such a law be impossible to enforce, but by comparison with early intervention in the schools, it would accomplish little and at great cost. Prevention programs can be designed with community input to minimize the element of coercion.

There are some who have advocated a retreat from the community, on the grounds that community intervention is too susceptible to abuse by powerful mental health professional groups. The course of action they advocate is for professionals who are working on community problems to return to their offices and wait for the voluntary patient to knock. Though such a plan would resolve the civil libertarian dilemmas, that may be its only virtue. We would be back in the traditional service delivery model, seeing only intelligent middle-class patients and ignoring the social forces precipitating psychological disorder. In our haste to flee from the moral evil of "totalitarianism," we would be returning to a laissez-faire capitalistic system of distributing mental health service. To us, this is an equally obnoxious moral position. The alternative to community intervention "of having private practitioners see one voluntary client at a time is even more dismal and even less responsible" (Denner & Price, 1973, p. 13).

This example and its discussion should alert the reader to the issues involved, in that it highlights the tenuous *balance* between social pressures and individual rights that is constantly tested in a free society. With the development of our specialized and highly technical way of life, the balance must also include the professional as an independent force. All three forces push for dominance, but we doubt that, as a community, we would be happy if any one force was in permanent control. A society in which individual predelictions are given free reign could soon result in anarchy. The opposite, in which individual wishes were always suppressed in favor of a communal goal, would develop excesses of control and conformity. A society exclusively controlled by professional technocrats, with no feedback from citizens, also would be an unhappy place. In other words, the balance which we should seek is one of dynamic equilibrium, with mechanisms developed to prevent the exclusive domination of any one group. With regard to the prevention of psychological disorders, the same dynamic balance should be involved. Professionals should be encouraged to do the research that will result in a prevention technology. They should be encouraged to field test their work in small demonstration projects. Once the data are in, citizen boards should decide if and when particular projects will be implemented. Those who are the recipients of prevention programs should have the right of periodic review and, if appropriate, should be encouraged to develop alternative programs that might better suit their needs. The abuses that occur, and which Szasz so eloquently highlights, are abuses of exclusive power that occur in a passive and unthinking society. As prevention programs are implemented, the mental health professional can take the lead in suggesting how safeguards against abuse can be developed simultaneously. The implementation of safeguards can itself provide a vehicle for activating a passive community. This, too, should be a task to which the community specialist contributes.

CONCLUSION

Prevention is a relatively new word in our psychological vocabulary; thus, it should not be too surprising that it still appears foreign to many psychological practitioners. As used in public health medicine, primary prevention refers to activities aimed at reducing the incidence of new cases of disease.

Transferring the concept to the psychological sphere forces a confrontation with some difficult definitional and methodological problems. Can psychological dysfunction be prevented? Is enough known about etiology to mount effective prevention programs? How can the effects of preventive intervention be assessed when there is still controversy about how cases of disorder are to be defined and counted? These and other conceptual issues have been discussed in this chapter.

Generally, we have concluded that the best approach to the etiology of mental disorders is to adopt a multiple risk-factor orientation. Research and practice should not become too preoccupied with single causal factors. From this perspective, intervention programs can be mounted to reduce the effects of environmental stress at community, institutional, or familial levels; or they may be aimed at strengthening the capacity of vulnerable populations. Strengthening coping skills fits the current interest in competency building, and need not be restricted to populations at risk. Greater attention should be placed on *community-wide* programs for enhancing coping skills and environmental mastery—particularly since the identification of high-risk groups is subject to an overprediction bias.

Good research studies evaluating prevention attempts are beginning to emerge. While research on prevention still is in a rudimentary stage, several significant developments are apparent. The most promising of these are projects aimed at ameliorating the effects of specific life stressors (e.g., school transitions, surgery, widowhood) and those aimed at improving psychosocial competence through instruction in problem-solving techniques. Other interesting work is being done using the media to promote health related behaviors, and in extending crisis intervention procedures to help individuals cope with unavoidable disasters. It is our impression that prevention researchers are beginning to ask more specific questions. We applaud the move to greater specificity because it is our impression that the yield from prevention studies will be greater if: greater precision is used in defining an intervention, there is increased specification of target behaviors to be changed, and interventions are linked to target populations for whom the interventions were designed. The key to obtaining useful knowledge in intervention research is the adoption of more modest and specific questions, coupled with crisper experimental designs.

Are there gaps in the prevention literature? The most glaring is the neglect of environmental-level intervention programs. Too many of the studies reviewed in this chapter are aimed at helping individuals respond to specific life stressors or to improve their general level of coping. There is a subtle assumption in this work that problems of health and adjustment are best solved by individual initiative alone. As other chapters in this book will illustrate, we know quite a bit about the effects of environments on behavior (Chapter Five) and have begun to acquire the tools to help organizations and communities change in various ways (Chapters Eight, Nine, and Ten). To the extent that this work enhances the quality of life and reduces adjustment problems among citizens, it, too, should be considered as having prevention and health promotion effects.

Even after valid prevention technologies have been developed and empirical effects demonstrated, ethical and value issues should be decided before programs are implemented on a massive scale. Questions will arise about who determines the goals of prevention programs, and about what provisions will be made for those who choose not to participate. How much authority over the lives of others should be given to any one group—even the seemingly benign "helping professions?" Our own bias leads us to favor a system of checks and balances similar to that found at the federal level of government. This would imply that, while professionals should be encouraged to do prevention research, the decision to implement findings in the community does not rest with professionals alone. Citizen groups should be empaneled for periodic review of program goals and accomplishments. Similarly, legal safeguards to protect individual rights must be built into all prevention programs. The tenuous balance between individual rights, communal regulation, and professional responsibility is capable of achievement—but requires constant awareness, attention, and vigilance. It is our position that, while community intervention could be used in a repressive fashion, there is no necessity that this be the case. We believe that psychological intervention in the community, free of professional obfuscation, with community input in shaping and evaluating programs, and coexisting with a strong catalogue of individual safeguards, is more than morally acceptable: it is a moral imperative.

References

Adler, P. T. Mental health promotion and the CMHC: Opportunities and obstacles. In F. D. Perlmutter (Ed.), *Mental health promotion and primary prevention.* San Francisco: Jossey-Bass, New Directions for Mental Health Services, March 1982.

Albee, G. W. The uncertain future of clinical psychology. *American Psychologist,* 1970, *25,* 1071–1080.

Albee, G. W. Politics, power, prevention and social change. In J. M. Joffe & G. W. Albee (Eds.), *Prevention through political action and social change.* Hanover, N.H.: University Press of New England, 1981.

Albee, G. W., & Joffe, J. M. (Eds.). *Primary prevention of psychopathology* (Vol. I: *The Issues*). Hanover, N.H.: University Press of New England, 1977.

Allen, G. J., Chinsky, J. M., Larcen, S. W., Lochman, J. E., & Selinger, H. V. *Community psychology and the schools: A behaviorally oriented multilevel preventive approach.* Hillsdale, N.J.: Lawrence Erlbaum Associates, 1976.

Andrew, J. M. Recovery from surgery, with and without preparatory instruction, for three coping styles. *Journal of Personality and Social Psychology,* 1970, *15,* 223–226.

Auerbach, S. M., Kendall, P. C., Cuttler, H. F., & Levitt, N. R. Anxiety, locus of control, type of preparatory information and adjustment to dental surgery. *Journal of Consulting and Clinical Psychology,* 1976, *44,* 809–818.

Auerbach, S. M., & Kilmann, P. R. Crisis intervention: A review of outcome research. *Psychological Bulletin,* 1977, *84,* 1189–1217.

Averill, J. R. Personal control over aversive stimuli and its relationship to stress. *Psychological Bulletin,* 1973, *80,* 286–303.

Barrett, C. J. Effectiveness of widows' groups in facilitating change. *Journal of Consulting and Clinical Psychology,* 1978, *46,* 20–31.

Beck, A., Resnick, R., & Lettieri, T. *The prediction of suicide.* Bowie, Md.: Charles, 1974.

Bellak, L., & Small, L. *Emergency psychotherapy and brief psychotherapy.* New York: Grune & Stratton, 1965.

Berkman, L. F., & Syme, S. L. Social networks, host resistance and mortality: A nine year follow-up study of Alameda County residents. *American Journal of Epidemiology,* 1979, *109,* 186–204.

Blazer, D. G. Social support and mortality in an elderly community population. *American Journal of Epidemiology,* 1982, *115,* 684–694.

Bloom, B. L. The "medical model," miasma theory, and community mental health. *Community Mental Health Journal,* 1965, *7,* 333–338.

Bloom, B. L. The evaluation of primary prevention programs. In L. M. Roberts, N. S. Greenfield, & M. H. Miller (Eds.), *Comprehensive mental health: The challenge of evaluation* (pp. 117–135). Madison: University of Wisconsin Press, 1968.

Bloom, B. L. A university freshman preventive intervention program: Report of a pilot project. *Journal of Consulting and Clinical Psychology,* 1971, *37,* 235–242.

Bloom, B. L. *Community mental health: A general introduction.* Monterey, Calif.: Brooks/Cole Publishing, 1977.

Bloom, B. L. Prevention of mental disorders: Recent advances in theory and practice. *Community Mental Health Journal,* 1979, *16,* 179–191.

Bloom, B. L. Social and community interventions. *Annual Review of Psychology,* 1980, *31,* 111–142.

Bloom, B. L., Asher, S. J., & White, S. W. Marital disruption as a stressor: A review and analysis. *Psychological Bulletin,* 1978, *85,* 867–894.

Bloom, B. L., Hodges, W. F., & Caldwell, R. A. A preventive intervention program for the newly separated: Initial evaluation. *American Journal of Community Psychology,* 1982, *10,* 251–264.

Bogat, G. A., Jones, J. W., & Jason, L. A. School transitions: Preventive intervention following an elementary school closing. *Journal of Community Psychology,* 1980, *8,* 343–392.

Bolman, W. M. Toward realizing the prevention of mental illness. In L. Bellak & H. H. Barten (Eds.), *Progress in community mental health* (Vol. 1, pp. 203–231). New York: Grune & Stratton, 1969.

Bond, L. A. From prevention to promotion: Optimizing infant development. In L. A. Bond & J. M. Joffe (Eds.), *Facilitating infant and early childhood development* (pp. 5–39). Hanover, N.H.: University Press of New England, 1982.

Bower, E. M. Primary prevention of mental and emotional disorders: A conceptual framework and action possibilities. In A. J. Bindman & A. D. Spiegel (Eds.), *Perspectives in community mental health* (pp. 231–249). Chicago: Aldine, 1969.

Brown, B. S. Philosophy and scope of extended clinic activities. In A. J. Bindman & A. D. Spiegel (Eds.), *Perspectives in community mental health* (pp. 41–53). Chicago: Aldine, 1969.

Brown, G. W. The social etiology of depression—London studies. In R. A. Depue (Ed.), *The psychobiology of the depressive disorders: Implications for the effects of stress* (pp. 263–289). New York: Academic Press, 1979.

Brown, G. W., & Harris, T. *Social origins of depression: A study of psychiatric disorders in women.* New York: Free Press, 1978.

Brown, V. B. The community in crisis. In G. F. Jacobson (Ed.), *Crisis intervention in the 1980s.* San Francisco: Jossey-Bass, New Directions for Mental Health Services, 1980.

Bry, B. H. Reducing the incidence of adolescent problems through preventive intervention: One and five year follow up. *American Journal of Community Psychology,* 1982, *10,* 265–276.

Bry, B. H., & George, F. E. Evaluating and improving prevention programs: A strategy from drug abuse. *Evaluation and Program Planning,* 1979, *2,* 127–136.

Caplan, G. *Principles of preventive psychiatry.* New York: Basic Books, 1964.

Caplan, R. B. *Psychiatry and the community in nineteenth century America: The recurring concern with the environment in the prevention and treatment of mental illness.* New York: Basic Books, 1969.

Cassell, S. Effect of brief puppet therapy upon the emotional responses of children undergoing cardiac catheterization. *Journal of Consulting Psychology,* 1965, *29,* 1–8.

Catalano, R., & Dooley, D. Economic change in primary prevention. In R. H. Price, R. F. Ketterer, B. C. Bader, & J. Monahan (Eds.), *Prevention in mental health: Research, policy and practice.* Beverly Hills, Calif.: Sage Publications, 1980.

Cohen, R. E., & Ahearn, F. L., Jr. *Handbook for mental health care of disaster victims.* Baltimore, Md.: John Hopkins University Press, 1980.

Cook, T., Appleton, H., Connor, R., Shaffer, A., Tamkin, G., & Weber, S. *Sesame Street revisited.* New York: Russell Sage Foundation, 1975.

Cowen, E. L. Emergent approaches to mental health problems: An overview and directions for future work. In E. L. Cowen, E. A. Gardner, & M. Zax (Eds.), *Emergent approaches to mental health problems.* New York: Appleton-Century-Crofts, 1967.

Cowen, E. L. The effectiveness of secondary prevention programs using nonprofessionals in the school setting. *Proceedings of the 76th Annual Convention of the American Psychological Association,* 1968, *2,* 705–706.

Cowen, E. L. Social and community interventions. *Annual Review of Psychology,* 1973, *24,* 423–472.

Cowen, E. L., Dorr, D. A., Trost, M. A., & Izzo, L. D. Follow-up study of maladapting school children seen by nonprofessionals. *Journal of Consulting and Clinical Psychology,* 1972, *39,* 235–238.

Cowen, E. L., Gesten, E. L., & Weissberg, R. P. An integrated network of preventively oriented school-based mental health approaches. In R. H. Price & P. E. Politser (Eds.), *Evaluation and action in the social environment* (pp. 173–210). New York: Academic Press, 1980.

Cowen, E. L., Izzo, L. D., Miles H., Telschow, E. F., Trost, M. A., & Zax, M. A preventive mental health program in the school setting: Description and evaluation. *Journal of Psychology,* 1963, *56,* 307–356.

Cowen, E. L., Pederson, A., Babigian, H., Izzo, L. D., & Trost, M. A. Long-term follow-up of early detected vulnerable children. *Journal of Consulting and Clinical Psychology,* 1973, *41,* 438–446.

Cowen, E. L., Trost, M. A., Lorion, R. P., Dorr, D., Izzo, L. D., & Isaacson, R. V. *New ways in school mental health: Early detection and prevention of school maladaptation.* New York: Human Sciences Press, 1975.

Cowen, E. L., Zax, M., Izzo, L. D., & Trost, M. A. Prevention of emotional disorders in the school setting: A further investigation. *Journal of Consulting Psychology,* 1966, *30,* 381–387.

Cumming, E., & Cumming, J. *Closed ranks: An experiment in mental health education.* Cambridge, Mass.: Harvard University Press, 1957.

Dallas, D. Savagery, show and tell. *American Psychologist,* 1978, *33,* 388–390.

Danish, S. J., & D'Augelli, A. R. Promoting competence and enhancing development through life development intervention. In L. A. Bond & J. C. Rosen (Eds.), *Competence and coping during adulthood.* Hanover, N.H.: University Press of New England, 1980.

Davis, J. A. *Education for positive mental health.* Chicago, Aldine, 1965.

Davison, G. C., & Neale, J. M. *Abnormal psychology: An experimental clinical approach* (3d ed.). New York: John Wiley & Sons, 1982.

Denner, B., & Price, R. H. (Eds.). *Community mental health: Social action and reaction.* New York: Holt, Rinehart & Winston, 1973.

Dohrenwend, B. P., & Dohrenwend, B. S. Social and cultural influences on psychopathology. *Annual Review of Psychology,* 1974, *25,* 417–452.

Dohrenwend, B. P., & Egri, G. Recent stressful life events and episodes of schizophrenia. *Schizophrenia Bulletin,* 1981, *7,* 12–23.

Dohrenwend, B. S. Social stress and community psychology. *American Journal of Community Psychology,* 1978, *6,* 1–14.

D'Zurilla, T. J., & Goldfried, M. R. Problem solving and behavior modification. *Journal of Abnormal Psychology,* 1971, *78,* 107–126.

Egbert, L. D., Battit, G. E., Welch, C. E., & Bartlett, M. K. Reduction of postoperative pain by encouragement and instruction of patients. *New England Journal of Medicine,* 1964, *270,* 825–827.

Eisenberg, L. *A research framework for evaluating health promotion and disease prevention.* Paper presented at the First Annual Alcohol, Drug Abuse and Mental Health Administration Conference on Prevention. Silver Springs, Md., September 12–14, 1979.

Evans, R. I. Behavioral medicine: A new applied challenge to social psychologists. In L. Bickman (Ed.), *Applied social psychology annual* (Vol. I). Beverly Hills, Calif.: Sage Publications, 1980.

Ewing, C. P. *Crisis intervention as psychotherapy.* New York: Oxford University Press, 1978.

Eysenck, H. J. The effects of psychotherapy: An evaluation. *Journal of Consulting Psychology,* 1952, *16,* 319–324.

Eysenck, H. J. The effects of psychotherapy. In H. J. Eysenck (Ed.), *Handbook of abnormal psychology.* New York: Basic Books, 1961.

Felner, R. D., Ginter, M., & Primavera, J. Primary prevention during school transitions: Social support and environmental structure. *American Journal of Community Psychology,* 1982, *10,* 277–290.

Felner, R. D., Primavera, J., & Cauce, A. M. The impact of school transitions: A focus for preventive efforts. *American Journal of Community Psychology,* 1981, *9,* 449–459.

Freeman, H. E., Klein, R. E., Kagan, J., & Yarbrough, C. Relations between nutrition and cognition in rural Guatemala. *American Journal of Public Health,* 1977, *67,* 233–239.

Gesten, E. L., Flores de Apodaca, R., Rains, M., Weissberg, R. P., & Cowen, E. L. Promoting peer-related social competence in schools. In M. W. Kent & J. E. Rolf (Eds.), *Primary prevention of psychopathology* (Vol. III: *Social competence in children,* (pp. 220–247). Hanover, N.H.: University Press of New England, 1979.

Glueck, S., & Glueck, E. *Identifying predelinquents.* New York: Intercontinental Medical Book Corporation, 1972.

Goldfried, M. R., & D'Zurilla, T. J. A behavioral-analytic model for assessing competence. In C. D. Spielberger (Ed.), *Current topics in clinical and community psychology* (Vol. I). New York: Academic Press, 1969.

Grantham-McGregor, S., Stewart, M., Powel, C., & Schofield, W. M. Effect of stimulation on mental development of malnourished child (pp. 200–201). *Lancet,* 1979, ii.

Greenberg, B. S., & Heeter, C. Television and social stereotypes. *Prevention in Human Services,* 1982, *2,* 37–51.

Heller, K., & Swindle, R. W. Social networks, perceived social support and coping with stress. In R. D. Felner, L. A. Jason, J. Moritsugu, & S. S. Farber (Eds.), *Preventive psychology: Theory, research and practice in community intervention.* New York: Pergamon Press, 1983.

Herbert, W. The politics of prevention. *APA Monitor,* 1979, *10,* 5, 7–9.

Holloway, M. *Heavens on earth: Utopian communities in America, 1680–1880* (2d ed.). New York: Dover Publications, 1966.

Hughes, E. Z. Angry in retirement. In R. H. Moos (Ed.), *Human adaptation: Coping with life crises.* Lexington, Mass.: D. C. Heath, 1976.

Jason, L. A., & Burrows, B. Transition training for high school seniors. *Cognitive therapy and research,* 1983, 7, 79–91.

Johnston, J. Using television to change stereotypes. *Prevention in Human Services,* 1982, *2,* 67–81.

Keegan, C. A. V. Using television to reach older people with prevention messages: The *Over Easy* experiment. *Prevention in Human Services,* 1982, *2,* 83–91.

Kennedy, J. F. Message from the President of the United States relative to mental illness and mental retardation. Washington, D.C.: The White House, February 5, 1963.

Kent, M. W., & Rolf, J. E. (Eds.). *Primary prevention of psychopathology* (Vol. III. *Social competence in children*). Hanover, N.H.: University Press of New England, 1979.

Kornfield, D. S., & Politser, P. E. The hospital environment: Understanding and modifying its impact on the patient. In R. H. Price & P. E. Politzer (Eds.), *Evaluation and action in the social environment* (pp. 155–172). N.Y.: Academic Press, 1980.

Kornfeld, D. S., Zimber, S., & Malm, J. R. Psychiatric complications of open-heart surgery. *New England Journal of Medicine,* 1965, *273,* 287–292.

Kraus, A. S., & Lilienfeld, A. M. Some epidemiologic aspects of the high mortality rate in the young widowed group. *Journal of Chronic Disease,* 1959, *20,* 207–217.

Lamb, H. R., & Zusman, J. Primary prevention in perspective. *American Journal of Psychiatry,* 1979, *136,* 12–17.

Langsley, D. G., Pittman, F. S., Machotka, P., & Flomenhaft, K. Family crisis therapy: Results and implications. *Family Process,* 1968, *7,* 145–158.

Lazarus, H. R., & Hagens, J. H. Prevention of psychosis following open-heart surgery. *American Journal of Psychiatry,* 1968, *124,* 1190–1195.

Lemkau, P. V. Prevention of psychiatric illnesses. In A. J. Bindman & A. D. Spiegel (Eds.), *Perspectives in Community Mental Health.* Chicago: Aldine, 1969.

Leventhal, H., Safer, M. A., Cleary, P. D., & Gutmann, M. Cardiovascular risk modification by community-based programs for life-style change: Comments on the Stanford study. *Journal of Consulting and Clinical Psychology,* 1980, *48,* 150–158.

Lindeman, B. Widower, heal thyself. In R. H. Moos (Ed.), *Human adaptation: Coping with life crises.* Lexington, Mass.: D. C. Heath, 1976.

Lindemann, E. Symptomatology and management of acute grief. *American Journal of Psychiatry,* 1944, *101,* 141–148.

Lindemann, E. Preventive intervention in situational crises. Proceedings of the XIV International Congress of Applied Psychology, 1962, Vol. 4, Clinical Psychology.

Livermore, J., Malmquist, C., & Meehl, P. On the jurisdiction for civil commitment. *University of Pennsylvania Law Review,* 1968, *117,* 75–96.

Lorion, R. P., Cowen, E. L., & Caldwell, R. A. Normative and parametric analyses of school maladjustment. *American Journal of Community Psychology,* 1975, *3,* 291–301.

Lowenthal, M. F., & Haven, C. Interaction and adaptation: Intimacy as a critical variable. *American Sociological Review,* 1968, *33,* 20–30.

Maccoby, N., & Alexander, J. Reducing heart disease risk using the mass media: Comparing the effects of three communities. In R. F. Munoz, L. R. Snowden, & J. G. Kelly (Eds.), *Social and psychological research in community settings.* San Francisco: Jossey-Bass, 1979.

Mahoney, M. J., & Arnkoff, D. B. Cognitive and self-control therapies. In S. L. Garfield & A. E. Bergin (Eds.), *Handbook of psychotherapy and behavior change: An empirical analysis* (2d ed.). New York: John Wiley & Sons, 1978.

McGuire, J. C., & Gottlieb, B. H. Social support groups among new parents: An experimental study in primary prevention. *Journal of Clinical Child Psychology,* 1979, *8,* 111–116.

Meichenbaum, D. A self-instructional approach to stress management: A proposal for stress inoculation training. In C. D. Spielberger & I. G. Sarason (Eds.), *Stress and anxiety* (Vol. 1). New York: John Wiley & Sons, 1975.

Meichenbaum, D., & Novaco, R. Stress inoculation: A preventive approach. In C. D. Spielberger & I. G. Sarason (Eds.), *Stress and anxiety* (Vol. 5). Washington, D.C.: Hemisphere Publishing, 1978.

Melamed, B. G., & Siegel, L. J. Reduction of anxiety in children facing hospitalization and surgery by use of filmed modeling. *Journal of Consulting and Clinical Psychology,* 1975, *43,* 511–521.

Meyer, A. J., Nash, J. D., McAlister, A. L., Maccoby, N., & Farquhar, J. W. Skill training in a cardiovascular health education campaign. *Journal of Consulting and Clinical Psychology,* 1980, *48,* 129–142.

Minde, K. K., Shosenberg, N. E., & Marton, P. L. The effects of self-help groups in a premature nursery on maternal autonomy and caretaking style one year later. In L. A. Bond & J. M. Jaffee (Eds.), *Facilitating infant and early childhood development* (pp. 240–258). Hanover, N.H.: University Press of New England, 1982.

Minde, K., Shosenberg, N., Marton, P., Thompson, J., Ripley, J., & Burns, S. Self-help groups in a premature nursery: A controlled evaluation. *Journal of Pediatrics,* 1980, *96,* 933–940.

Miron, M. S., & Goldstein, A. P. *Hostage.* Kalamazoo, Mich.: Behaviordelia, 1978.

Novaco, R. W. *Anger control: The development and evaluation of an experimental treatment.* Lexington, Mass.: D. C. Heath, 1975.

Novaco, R. W. A stress inoculation approach to anger management in the training of law enforcement officers. *American Journal of Community Psychology,* 1977, *5,* 327–346.

Osborn, A. F. *Applied imagination: Principles and procedures of creative problem solving* (3d ed.). New York: Charles Scribner's Sons, 1963.

Platt, J. J., Siegel, J. M., & Spivack, G. Do psychiatric patients and normals see the same solutions as effective in solving interpersonal problems? *Journal of Consulting and Clinical Psychology,* 1975, *43,* 279.

Platt, J. J., & Spivack, G. Problem-solving thinking of psychiatric patients. *Journal of Consulting and Clinical Psychology,* 1972, *39,* 148–151.

Platt, J. J., Spivack, G., Altman, N., & Altman, D. Adolescent problem-solving thinking. *Journal of Consulting and Clinical Psychology,* 1974, *42,* 787–793.

Plaut, T. The prevention of alcoholism. In S. Golann & C. Eisdorfer (Eds.), *Handbook of community mental health* (pp. 421–438). New York: Appleton-Century-Crofts, 1972.

Price, R. H. Etiology, the social environment, and the prevention of psychological dysfunction. In P. Insel and R. H. Moos (Eds.), *Health and the social environment* (pp. 287–300). Lexington, Mass.: D. C. Heath, 1974.

Price, R. H. The social ecology of treatment gain. In A. P. Goldstein & F. H. Kanfer (Eds.), *Maximizing treatment gains: Transfer enhancement in psychotherapy* (pp. 383–426). New York: Academic Press, 1979.

Price, R. H. Risky situations. In D. Magnusson (Ed.), *The situation: An interactional perspective.* Hillsdale, N.J.: Lawrence Erlbaum Associates, 1980.

Price, R. H., Bader, B. C., & Ketterer, R. F. Prevention in community mental health: The state of the art. In R. H. Price, R. F. Ketterer, B. C. Bader & J. Monahan (Eds.), *Prevention in mental health: Research, Policy, and Practice.* Beverly Hills, Calif.: Sage Publications, 1980.

Rachman, S. J., & Wilson, G. T. *The effects of psychological therapy.* Oxford: Pergamon Press, 1980.

Reiff, R. Mental health manpower and institutional change. *American Psychologist,* 1966, *21,* 540–548.

Rowland, K. F. Environmental events predicting death for the elderly. *Psychological Bulletin,* 1977, *84,* 349–372.

Sarason, S. B., Levine, M., Goldenberg, I. I., Cherlin, D. L., & Bennett, E. M. *Psychology in community settings: Clinical, educational, vocational, social aspects.* New York: John Wiley & Sons, 1966.

Shneidman, E. Crisis intervention: Some thoughts and perspectives. In G. A. Specter & W. L. Claiborn (Eds.), *Crisis Intervention*. New York: Behavioral Publications, 1973.

Shure, M. B., & Spivack, G. Means-ends thinking, adjustment and social class among elementary-school-aged children. *Journal of Consulting and Clinical Psychology*, 1972, *38*, 348–353.

Shure, M. B., & Spivack, G. Interpersonal problem-solving thinking and adjustment in the mother-child dyad. In M. W. Kent & J. E. Rolf (Eds.), *Primary prevention of psychopathology* Vol. III: *Social competence in children*, pp. 201–219. Hanover, N.H.: University Press of New England, 1979.

Signell, K. A. Kindergarten entry: A preventive approach to community mental health. *Community Mental Health Journal*, 1972, *8*, 60–70.

Silverman, P. R. The widow as a caregiver in a program of preventive intervention with other widows. *Mental Hygiene*, 1970, *54*, 540–547.

Solomon, D. S. Mass media campaigns for health promotion. *Prevention in Human Services*, 1982, *2*, 115–123.

Spivack, G., & Shure, M. B. *Social adjustment of young children: A cognitive approach to solving real life problems*. San Francisco: Jossey-Bass, 1974.

Steinmetz, S., & Strauss, M. (Eds.). *Violence in the family*. New York: Dodd, Mead, 1974.

Szasz, T. *The manufacture of madness*. New York: Harper & Row, 1970.

Task Panel Report on Prevention submitted to the President's Commission on Mental Health, 1978 (Vol. 4).

Thoits, P. A. Conceptual, methodological and theoretical problems in studying social support as a buffer against life stress. *Journal of Health and Social Behavior*, 1982, *23*, 145–159.

Wandersman, L. P., Wandersman, A., & Kahn, S. Social support in the transition to parenthood. *Journal of Community Psychology*, 1980, *8*, 332–342.

Weissberg, R. P., Cowen, E. L., Lotyczewski, B. S., & Gesten, E. L. The Primary Mental Health Project: Seven consecutive years of program outcome research. *Journal of Consulting and Clinical Psychology*, 1983, *51*, 100–107.

Weissberg, R. P., Gesten, E. L., Rapkin, B. D., Cowen, E. L., Davidson, E., Flores de Apodaca, R., & McKim, B. J. Evaluation of a social problem-solving training program for suburban and inner-city third-grade children. *Journal of Consulting and Clinical Psychology*, 1981, *49*, 251–261.

Zax, M., & Specter, G. A. *An introduction to community psychology*. New York: John Wiley & Sons, 1974.

Zax, M., Cowen, E. L., Rappaport, J., Beach, D. R., & Laird, J. D. Follow-up study of children identified early as emotionally disturbed. *Journal of Consulting and Clinical Psychology*, 1968, *32*, 369–374.

PART FOUR

Perspectives on Social and Community Change

CHAPTER EIGHT

Consultation:
Psychodynamic, Behavioral, and Organization Development Perspectives*

---

* This chapter was written by Kenneth Heller.

INTRODUCTION

The director of special education in a large urban school district requested consultation for the home tutors of emotionally disturbed children. The tutors were regular classroom teachers who worked on this program in the late after-noon when their regular classroom duties were over. The tutors spent about 1½ hours each day working with individual children in their homes on a one-to-one basis. The reason consultation was requested was because the teachers had no special training for work with the emotionally disturbed and a number of them were encountering difficulties. Some children were not doing their lessons while others refused to pay attention during their daily session. There were over 100 tutors in this program. The consultant's schedule and the tight financial situation in the school system allowed work on this project for only two hours each week. The consultant wondered how to proceed. After learning about the program, additional questions arose. Most of the teachers were receptive to receiving help with their work, but a few of those who were having difficulties were not. Should the consultant make an extra effort to win over these reluctant teachers, or should a relationship be established only with those who volunteered? If, in the process of consultation, teachers bring up their own personal problems, should these problems be addressed? If the consultant finds that some teachers are completely unsuited for this work, should a recommendation be made to the program director that these teachers be replaced?

Further investigation by the consultant revealed additional problems. The students in this program did not receive regular classroom instruction because they either would not go to school or, at one time, were found to be too disruptive for a normal classroom. The afternoon tutoring was the only formal instruction they received. Further, even if some of the children could be returned to regular classrooms, school principals were extremely reluctant to readmit students who had been labeled as "emotionally disturbed." Some of the parents of these children also did not want them to return to school for various reasons. Some children had unpleasant school experiences in the past, others were in neighbor-hoods that were changing in their racial makeup and parents were afraid to send their children to school, while still others believed that the 1½ hours of individual tutoring was sufficient. The questions these issues raised for the consultant concern the level at which the consultation should take place. Should the work be restricted to helping the teachers do a better job with their students, or should the consultation be approached on a more "systems" level, perhaps working with principals and parents so that the children could be reintegrated more easily into regular classrooms? Still another possibility would be to work with the classroom teachers who referred these children initially to increase their skills in dealing with disturbing children, so that they would be less likely to exclude these children from the classroom in the future.

While all of these alternatives were possible, the dilemma was that the consultant had only been asked to work with the home tutors. How does a consultant change the level of consultation, particularly when the others who may be involved (principals, parents, and regular classroom teachers) have not asked for help?

Consultation refers to an approach to social change through improvement of existing community organizations and institutions. The goals of consultation are modification, renewal, and improvement. Consultants assume that organizations and the personnel within them will be responsive to change. Working to improve organizations also means that a consultant can be considered as an "agent" of an organization—working to perpetuate and not overthrow it. Consultants, at times, may be uncomfortable in this role, because personnel in organizations sometimes espouse values that consultants find abhorrent. Yet in agreeing to offer consultation, consultants are affirming a faith in organizational renewal. They assume that workers can function more optimally, and that, when they do, morale will improve and better services will be offered to the public at large. In this way, the effects of organizational improvement are expected to radiate to the community through more responsive programs and services (Kelly, 1970).[1]

In the example just cited, the consultant accepted the request to help the after-school tutors because of the belief that the children served by the program would benefit if their teachers were better trained to respond to their needs. Although consultation was requested for the tutors only, the consultant hoped that this entry would enable later discussions with teachers and principals in schools that were having difficulties with emotionally disturbed children. The long-range goal was to improve the programs this school system had developed for emotionally disturbed children.

The work began with weekly group meetings with tutors to help them learn how to deal with the distruptive behavior of the children. Once this task was accomplished, the tutors were encouraged to develop plans by which other teachers and principals would allow the children to return to regular classrooms. In effect, the tutors themselves became consultants to

---

[1] At the end of this chapter, we will critique the assumption just described.

their colleagues, using what they had learned to ease the reintegration of the children back into regular classrooms. Although many consultants would share the goal of modifying this school system's programs for emotionally disturbed children, they would differ considerably in how this goal was accomplished. This is because there is no one consultation theory or technique. Consultants vary considerably in their training and experience, and in the assumptions that guide their work (O'Neill & Trickett, 1982). For example, some consultants focus their work on organizational personnel (the consultees), attempting to improve their attitudes or skills, while others focus on organizational climate and improving the linkages between different parts of an organization. However, despite these differences, there are a few clearly recognized perspectives or "models" of consultation.

Among psychological consultants, the major conceptual perspectives can be described as mental health, behavioral, and organization development. Each of these orientations arose from a different historical mission, and each developed goals and methods tied to that mission. For example, the mental health perspective grew among clinicians with traditional psychodynamic and psychoanalytic training who worked in rural or underdeveloped areas with few mental health professionals to share the burden of large case loads. The mandate given to the available mental health personnel was clear—the treatment and prevention of mental disorder. Yet, how could that mandate be carried out with insufficient personnel? There needed to be a way to utilize existing community resources and personnel, even though indigenous community caregivers did not have mental health training. Consultation to community caregivers became the method utilized.

Behavioral consultation arose as a natural extension of behavioral experimentation in laboratories and clinics. Behavior modification generated impressive results, but in many cases gains achieved did not carry over into real-life settings. Clinicians found that they did not control the reinforcement contingencies to which their clients were exposed in real life, and significant progress could be undone by others whose dispensement of reinforcement was maintaining inappropriate behavior. For some behaviorists, the focus of their work changed from modifying deviant individuals to modifying the dispensers of reinforcement (e.g., parents, teachers, peers, and the like) who were maintaining deviant behavior in the natural environment (Patterson, 1971).

Organization development specialists originated as consultants to industry. Over the years, it had become clear that, in the name of production efficiency, manpower practices had neglected to provide for worker morale and satisfaction. Although production gains could be realized by streamlined assembly lines, one could not ignore the attitudes, feelings, and desires of workers without efficiency suffering. Absenteeism, slipshod work, industrial sabotage, alcoholism on the job, and so on became real threats that could negate previous gains in efficiency. Basic human factors related to work could no longer be ignored.

In helping industrial organizations improve efficiency, the early organization development consultants focused on management practices and the *processes* by which decisions were made and carried out. The overarching value was that of optimizing human potential in work settings. This value can be seen in the goals for organization development—creating an open, problem-solving climate throughout an organization; maximizing collaboration; and encouraging a climate that fosters personal development and growth (Bennis, 1969). It was expected that organizations that attended to the psychological needs of their employees would become more productive and profitable.

In practice, the three consultation perspectives provided different emphases. Psychodynamic consultants, such as Gerald Caplan, focused on personal problems or on attributes of staff members that interfered with their work. Behavioral consultants were interested in controlling and modifying behavior through the establishment of incentives. They taught behavioral principles to staff members of an organization to increase their level of skills in behavior management. Historically, consultants following organization development principles primarily were interested in helping an organization achieve a facilitative organizational climate.

What has happened is that over the years these initially distinct orientations began to fuse. However, for purposes of exposition we will treat these views separately. In this way, we will be able to highlight the values, assumptions, and limitations of each perspective. We then will describe an example of how these emphases can be combined, and will conclude with a description and critique of the assumptions and techniques that the consultation perspectives share in common.

MENTAL HEALTH CONSULTATION

Mental health consultation originated in a context of scarce mental health resources—most often in isolated, rural, or undeveloped areas with few mental health professionals. In these settings, it was impossible to recommend costly professional treatment, such as psychotherapy, as long as there was a chronically insufficient supply of personnel to administer such programs. On the other hand, regardless of how rural, almost all communities provide for the health, welfare, and socialization of their citizens through networks of primary caregivers and agents of social control (teachers, ministers, welfare workers, police, physicians, and so on). Since there are very few problems in real life that are exclusively psychological in nature, why not encourage existing personnel to continue to deal with these problems and provide extra help with the psychological component as needed?

Gerald Caplan, perhaps the one individual most influential in the field of mental health consultation, defines the process of consultation in the following way:

> consultation is used in a quite restricted sense to denote a process of interaction between two professional persons—the consultant, who is a specialist, and the

consultee, who invokes the consultant's help in regard to a current work problem with which he is having some difficulty and which he has decided is within the other's area of competence. The work problem involves the management or treatment of one or more clients of the consultee, or the planning or implementation of a program to cater to such clients. (Caplan, 1970, p. 19)

Typical consultees have included teachers, police officers, ministers, and lawyers (Doane & Cowen, 1981; Felner, Primavera, Farber, & Bishop, 1982; Plog & Ahmed, 1977). All of the above are human service professionals who are used by the public in dealing with problem behavior. Other community caregivers who often find themselves responding to distressed individuals include hairdressers (Cowen, Gesten, Boike, Norton, Wilson, & DeStefano, 1979), bartenders (Cowen, McKim, & Weissberg, 1981), and librarians (Haas & Weatherley, 1981). In each of these latter instances the care provided is more informal, but nonetheless can be quite substantial. For example, in the Cowen et al. (1979) survey of 90 hairdressers it was found that approximately one third of the talking time between hairdressers and their clients concerned the latter's moderate to severe personal problems. Furthermore, 55 percent of the hairdressers reported having had one or more telephone calls for help outside of business hours, and 88 percent reported having received letters about such problems.

While some natural caregivers might be interested in consultation to increase their interpersonal skill, others, such as bartenders, often find themselves too busy to respond to patron problems with any level of depth. For example, Cowen (1982) reports that, while hairdressers and lawyers are most likely to respond to personal problems with sympathy and support, bartenders say that their most frequent response to problems is to "just listen." Thus it is not being suggested that *all* natural caregivers should become mental health consultees. However, it would seem appropriate to support natural caregiving systems in the community whenever possible. Since the majority of citizens do not seek out mental health professionals in times of distress (Gurin, Veroff, & Feld, 1960), why not establish working relationships with natural helpers who are contacted by the public and who want to improve their functioning?

Kiesler (1973) provides an example of a mental health consultation program established in a rural area with scarce mental health resources. When Kiesler came to northern Minnesota, he began working in a three-county area the size of the state of Massachusetts, but with only 68,000 residents. The population was relatively isolated and thinly dispersed. There were no mental health specialists in the entire area; yet the three counties had a professional manpower pool of over 300 persons who were in the business of helping troubled individuals. These helping professionals included doctors, lawyers, clergymen, court personnel, school administrators and counselors, welfare workers, and public health and school nurses.

Budget limitations made it clear that the area could only support three mental health professionals. What could one psychiatrist, one psychologist, and one psychiatric social worker do to meet the mental health needs of the area?

Each of the indigenous professional groups wanted to use the mental health specialists in the only way that was really familiar to them—by making referrals to a traditional psychiatric clinic. The family doctors wanted to turn over their most troublesome patients to the psychiatrist. The school administrators wanted the psychologist to do IQ testing. The juvenile court hoped that treatment by the social worker would somehow "turn around" their youthful offenders. The sheriffs wanted to know whether prisoners in jail were "mentally ill" or just "acting up." In general there was a tendency to want to label immature, misbehaving, and troublesome people as "mentally ill" so the responsibility for their care could be turned over to someone else—the mental health specialist.

The three mental health professionals began their work with the decision that none of the existing community caregivers should be allowed to abdicate responsibility for mental health related problems in their existing case load. The method of operation to implement this goal was as follows. Whenever a referral was made, it was accepted; but rather than scheduling an appointment to see the client, the mental health specialists scheduled an appointment with the referring agent instead—even if distance mandated that the contact be by telephone and not in person. During this contact, the case would be discussed and the referring agent would describe what was being done already. Sometimes, little more could be accomplished by mental health intervention, and when appropriate this was pointed out. The caregiving professionals were supported and given confidence to do what they already were doing. There were times when suggestions for alternative strategies were discussed, but only infrequently was the client seen directly. Direct clinical contact and service to clients was provided to only about 20 percent of the families about whom consultations were made. This approach provided a considerable saving, as Kiesler was able to determine that per unit of mental health time, his team was able to influence nine times as many families through consultation as would have been the case for direct clinical service.

Kiesler notes further that consultation does not mean that natural caregivers are trained to function as mental health "experts":

> The fact that more than 8 of every 10 families about whom we consult are never seen by us does not mean that we have set up family doctors, clergymen, sheriffs, social workers, and a host of others in an imitation of psychiatric practice. These people are not interested in stepping into other professional roles than those they already have. Our experience shows that most troubled people in our area obtain no better results with our help than they do with local professional help. One of our working hypotheses is that the earlier the problems of adaptation can be defined by firing-line professionals, the better the results that can be obtained from relatively simple straightforward corrective approaches. (Kiesler, 1973, pp. 105–106)

Types of Mental Health Consultation

Mental health consultants typically distinguish between client-centered, consultee-centered, and program-centered consultation (Mannino & Shore,

1972). In other words, consultation can focus on an agency's clients, staff, or program. Throughout, the emphasis is on work problems—improving on-the-job performance so the agency can deliver more responsive service. It is expected that, as the work problems of staff become resolved, their ability to relate to problem clients in a psychologically meaningful way also will increase. The assumption is that primary caregivers can develop more effective and psychologically sound programs and can learn to understand and deal with the social and emotional components of the problems with which their clients confront them.

A Significant Caution: Consultation Is not Psychotherapy

Note that the content focus of consultation is on work problems, not personal problems (Altrocchi, 1972). This hallmark of mental health consultation was developed for several important reasons. Most basically, mental health consultants respect the professional and personal competencies of their consultees. They assume that consultees are motivated and interested in serving their clients better, and that they usually possess an adequate level of professional skill to utilize the new insights gained from consultation. Furthermore, consultation contracts rarely sanction psychotherapy for agency staff. Attempts to impose a therapeutic relationship once consultation has commenced would be an invasion of the consultee's privacy and would be a breech of professional ethics.

Problems can arise when clinically experienced mental health professionals practice consultation without training in its principles. Without recognition of the dangers involved, it is easy to unwittingly slide into therapeutic or quasi-therapeutic relationships. For the experienced clinician without consultation training, it may be the only professional role with which he or she is familiar. To complicate the problem even further, some consultees seem to be asking for a therapeutic relationship. These individuals may be quick to see personal inadequacies in themselves; and it is sometimes easier to retreat to the relative safety of a therapeutic relationship with a kind clinician than to assume personal responsibility for corrective action in the face of difficulty. Thus, an untrained consultant can be pulled into a therapeutic alliance where both parties erroneously assume that what is transpiring between them is a form of mental health consultation.

In the pages that follow, we shall describe the three main types of mental health consultation, giving examples of each. *Client-centered* consultation is most frequently practiced and is most familiar to specialists in all fields. *Consultee-centered* consultation has greater potential for changing attitudes and behavior but can raise ethical issues if not practiced with the full awareness and consent of consultees. *Program-centered* consultation has the greatest potential for affecting community change. Unfortunately it is also the most difficult form of consultation, requiring the greatest understanding of community functioning.

Client-Centered Consultation: A Frequent Entry Point

Client-centered consultation is the most traditional form of consultation. It occurs when a consultee, having difficulty in the management of a particular case, or group of cases, calls for a mental health specialist to make an expert assessment of the client's problem and suggest ways for the case to be handled. The focus is on how the client can best be helped, but in the process it is expected that the consultees will use this opportunity to so improve their knowledge and skill that in the future they will be better able to handle comparable problems in this or in similar clients on their own.

The first request for help from an agency is most often of this type, as client-centered consultation is most clearly understood. While, in general, defensiveness may be high among potential consultees who fear criticism from the consultant, it is least in this form of consultation since the focus is on the agency's clients, not on staff or program. Thus, it represents an entry point that consultants willingly accept.

Spielberger (1967) described a case-seminar method of consultation developed in collaboration with two colleagues (Altrocchi, Spielberger, & Eisdorfer, 1965) that provides a useful example of client-centered consultation. The project took place in a small city along the coast of North Carolina with few mental health professionals. A case seminar with groups of indigenous community caregivers was developed as the principal consultation procedure. Groups were formed for key personnel, such as public health nurses, ministers, welfare workers, elementary school teachers, and high school guidance counselors. The public health nurses, for example, worked in a variety of settings in the community; some in maternity and well-baby clinics, some as school nurses, with still others receiving home visit assignments to check on possible cases of communicable disease. Very often the nurse, in dealing with an apparently clear-cut health problem, would find that there was a psychological component to the problem that was equally important and that prevented the achievement of restored health. The work of the seminar was to develop an understanding of the case so an effective plan of action could be formulated.

One of the present authors (K.H.) provided a similar form of case consultation to public health nurses in a large Eastern city and can draw upon that experience to provide a specific case example. The problem brought before the group was that of a 50-year-old man with tuberculosis. The TB had been brought under control; but the man was a heavy drinker, and this in turn was leading to a deteriorated physical condition. The drinking also had led to family conflicts, his wife and family had left him, he was lonely, he no longer worked, and he seemed unmotivated to change his habits.

The group discussed the problem of a lonely man who no longer felt useful, who felt that no one cared about him, and who was sliding into alcoholism. This discussion proved illuminating to the nurse. Adopting a fresh perspective, the nurse remembered that the client still had one tie to his family. He was visited occasionally by a 19-year-old son whom he greatly admired. The group suggested to the nurse that she contact the son to see if he would be willing to develop a close relationship with his father—who in turn might develop some motivation to deal with his drinking problem if he felt important to someone once again.

Note that the plan developed for this case did not include psychotherapy for the nurse's client. Not only was this option unavailable but it is extremely doubtful that this form of treatment would have been acceptable to the client. We planned an intervention that was within the role prescriptions and duties of a public health nurse. She felt perfectly comfortable talking to a son about spending more time with his sick father. Eventually, if the father's motivation could be increased, Alcoholics Anonymous might be suggested. But at this point, the focus was on how to prevent a lonely man who felt useless and unwanted from sliding further into a debilitated condition.

Consultee-Centered Consultation

In consultee-centered consultation, the presenting problem may involve a particular case, but the focus of consultation is on the consultee's difficulties with the case. The shift in focus may not be noticed by the consultee since the content of the discussion may remain centered about a case; but the consultant is using the medium of the case to improve a deficiency assumed to be present in the consultee. As described by Caplan (1970), the focus of consultation moves to the consultee when the problem is due to a lack of knowledge or skill, a temporary loss in self-confidence, or a lapse in professional objectivity.

When a problem is due to a lack of knowledge or skill, consultants often vary on how they deal with these deficiencies. Some offer direct training themselves in the problem areas; other refrain from direct intervention, believing that deficiencies in knowledge and skill are more appropriately dealt with through the normal channels of agency supervision. The consultant may possess specialized knowledge not available to other professions (e.g., knowledge of behavior modification principles of benefit to classroom teachers; skill in developing and motivating self-help groups for welfare mothers) and may decide that the simplest route would be to provide the missing knowledge and skill directly. In organizations where supervision is diffuse or nonexistent (e.g., as may occur in many school situations where teachers are expected to function relatively independently in the classroom) there should be little conflict between consultation and supervision. However, in agencies where line workers are closely and actively supervised (e.g., as in a welfare department), the danger exists that direct training would be resented by agency supervisors who would see the consultant's work as infringing on their duties and undermining their authority.

Caplan (1970) advises that, in agencies with good supervisory networks, deficiencies in knowledge or skill among workers should not be dealt with directly by the consultant. Instead, consideration should be given to moving the point of intervention to the supervisors. Training the supervisors can increase their competence and importance in the agency, it does not disturb the traditional lines of authority within the agency, and it has the added advantage of potentially making the consultant's knowledge more relevant to the organization. If accomplished effectively, the supervisory group can translate the consultant's ideas into procedures that would be accepted more readily in the organization. Consultants might be tempted to bypass the supervisors, believing themselves to be more effective teachers who could present their own ideas more clearly. In addition, middle-line supervisors might be found to be most resistant to innovation, a frequent occurrence in bureaucratic organizations. Still, attempting to bypass a powerful supervisory group could easily doom the intervention program—if not immediately, then by slow erosion as the supervisors, uncommitted to the program, slowly drift back to previous procedures.

Work problems due to lapses in professional objectivity can be difficult to handle. If the consultee is aware of personal involvement with the case, this topic can be approached directly in consultation. Personal feelings of anger, frustration, or disappointment can be discussed and viewed as natural responses to difficult work circumstances. A frequently occurring myth in human service organizations is that "true" professionals must not allow themselves to develop personal feelings toward their clients. Thus, when natural feelings of frustration and anger arise, there is no organizational vehicle established to help work through these feelings (Cherniss, 1980). They are suppressed, to avoid the label of being "foolish," "soft," or "unprofessional." The consultant can perform an important service by helping consultees accept and constructively use their personal feelings that develop in the normal course of their work. If these feelings can be dealt with in a group setting, so much the better, for the consultees then could build their own support group that could function independently after the consultant terminates his or her services.

Knoblock and Goldstein (1971) discuss workshops with teachers in which the participants are encouraged to talk about the personal satisfactions and frustrations in their particular work settings. They describe one such group as follows:

> Our teachers wanted to communicate that they could represent themselves as complex individuals. To be sure, they also felt they had good ideas about what could happen in schools with children and teachers. Even more importantly, they believed they had many skills and talents other than teaching skills. Many are talented and creative people who outside of the school pursue many avocations but within the school are asked to turn those off and run the ship as usual.
>
> In a summer workshop dealing with interpersonal competence, a group of teachers began to discuss poetry. One of the participants began to bring her poems to class, some of them inspired by the workshop and its participants. Two things were startling about this experience. One was the very fact that such creative people and behavior were neither acknowledged nor provided for in

their school jobs. The other was that their degree of animation over such "avocational interests" was far more intense and involving than their teaching activities in the classroom.

It would seem from what our group and other teachers report that it is not sufficient to develop a personal and professional life which focuses exclusively on children. Teachers are equally concerned with responding to other adults and in turn being responded to by their colleagues.

In short, teachers would like very much to function as resources within the schools. How paradoxical it is that so many teachers do not see themselves as resources within their own classrooms, but rather as keepers of the peace, curriculum and school tradition. (Knoblock & Goldstein, 1971, pp. 13–14)

The function of the workshops in the Knoblock and Goldstein example was to provide a vehicle for teachers to share their feelings about their personal involvement in their work as one way of combating professional loneliness. As long as no one is talking about job frustrations it is very easy to erroneously assume that "everyone is satisfied so I must be the oddball." The realization that dissatisfaction is shared can be a spark for corrective action to improve the work climate. But even if improvement is not likely, recognizing that satisfaction may have to come from "avocational interests" would still be a valuable lesson that would probably improve morale.

How open should the consultant be in confronting consultee feelings and conflict? When consultees are not aware of personal involvement in their work, the dilemma for the consultant is whether to bring these feelings into awareness or to deal with them more indirectly by discussing the relevant conflict-arousing issues through the medium of the case; that is, by focusing on the behavior of the consultee's client. This indirect approach is recommended by Caplan, who has developed techniques of dealing with personal conflicts in consultees through displacement (see Caplan, 1970, pp. 125–222). As Caplan sees it, in his method the personality defenses of the consultee are not disturbed, since he or she is never required to confront or examine personal feelings or the reasons for overinvolvement with the case. Only the client's personality and reactions are discussed. The problem may be the consultee's, but it is discussed as if it is the client's problem exclusively.

Caplan describes the displacement technique in his description of consultation with an elementary school teacher (Caplan, 1970, pp. 140–42). The student in question—Jean—had become a disciplinary problem, although her behavior had been trouble-free during the first half of the semester. A description of the onset of the problem by the teacher revealed that the change had occurred about the time of the first parent conference, when the teacher had discovered that Jean was the younger sister of a girl she had taught three years earlier. After the vacation following the parent conference, Jean's behavior began to deteriorate rapidly. The consultant remembered that this teacher had consulted him earlier in the year about another girl in the class who was said to be suffering from a learning disorder and who also was described as someone else's younger sister.

The consultant did not know anything about the teacher's personal life, but he hazarded a guess to himself that she probably had a younger sister with whom she had been involved in unresolved conflicts similar in pattern to those she was now imposing on the case of Jean. In this regard it appeared particularly significant that Jean became a problem to the teacher only after she discovered that she was "a younger sister." It also seemed that Jean's poor behavior occurred only in class with that teacher and was apparently a reaction to the teacher's method of handling her. (Caplan, 1970, p. 141)

The consultant did not begin a discussion of the teacher's personal life to find the suspected unresolved conflict. Instead, he discussed the problem as if it were Jean's—that Jean was worried about being a younger sister and was afraid that the teacher would constantly compare her with her successful older sister.

He pointed out that her behavior had regressed following the teacher's interview with her mother before Christmas, during which they had discussed her older sister. He put forward the hypothesis that after this interview the mother had told Jean that the teacher had been very fond of the older sister and remembered her quite vividly, and had possibly told her that the teacher hoped Jean would be as successful a student. The consultant then involved the teacher in a discussion of what this might have meant to Jean, and the nature of the conflict that might have been set up in her mind, so that she now might imagine that the teacher was continually comparing her with her older sister. The teacher, in this discussion, began to identify with the consultant, reversing roles and emphatically imagining how Jean felt as a younger sister. . . . The consultant then posed the management problem as being for the teacher to work out ways of convincing Jean that her teacher was not a representative of her family constellation, and that Jean was a person in her own right and not just a "younger sister."

During the second consultation session, the teacher quite suddenly made a switch in her patterned perceptions of Jean and began to talk about her as a child struggling to overcome in the classroom her misperceptions of her teacher. She then began to plan various alternative ways to dealing with her. . . .

During the remainder of the school year this teacher asked for consultation about two other cases, neither one of which was a "younger sister." She gave follow-up reports on Jean, whose behavior disorder had apparently completely resolved within three to four weeks following the second consultation discussion about her problems. (Caplan, 1970, p. 142)

Caplan's displacement approach has the advantage of reducing defensiveness, in that consultees may become suspicious and anxious and may avoid future contacts if the consultant approaches emotional issues directly. The fear that mental health professionals are "out to psychoanalyze you" becomes confirmed if consultees are led into emotional confrontation without warning. Even forewarned, discussions that move into personal reactions can be seen by potential consultees as a violation of the consultation contract. On the other hand, direct discussion of personal involvement can be supported by the argument that bringing feelings into awareness can be an aid to learning and that learning without awareness is not very effective. In this sense, indirect methods may be too subtle. The main point of the consultant's message may never be received if it is made by analogy, conveyed in a parable, or presented by other similar indirect means.

The problem can be summarized as follows. Dealing with the consultee's inappropriate personal involvement in a work problem, by helping to encourage its conscious recognition, should lead to a more effective resolution as the consultee learns to accept and deal with the emotions engendered by the work situation. However, not all consultees are ready for emotional learning experiences, and they may become anxious or attempt to flee consultation if it becomes apparent that this is the consultant's goal. Indirect methods of consultation that deal with personal involvement but never bring it to awareness would seem better suited to these instances. However, here, too, there are drawbacks. The effectiveness of learning without awareness can be questioned. An ethical question also can be raised concerning indirect methods, in that consultants are forced to work under false pretenses. The focus is on change in the consultee; but great pains must be taken to keep this intent secret, steadfastly maintaining that they are only talking about the consultee's cases.

There is no completely satisfactory resolution to the difficulties raised above. It is our own personal belief that direct methods of consultation for consultee-centered problems are to be preferred when they can be utilized. However, in organizations marked by a lack of openness and a high degree of defensiveness among line staff, the consultant might consider other options. One possibility is to deal with problems involving a lapse in professional objectivity, but only with those who are open to change and willing to examine their own contribution to their work problems. It could be argued that consultation should be offered only when receptivity is high. The problem is that it is difficult to ignore lapses in professional objectivity if they occur in defensive caregivers who occupy important positions in the socialization and caregiving network of a community. For example, one could not expect to have a major impact on the lives of children if their teachers were ignored as being too resistant to change. It is for these special instances, when the need for intervention is particularly acute, that we believe that indirect methods of consultee-centered consultation may have some value.

Program-Centered Consultation

Program-centered consultation offers the greatest potential for significant and enduring changes in an organization. Changes in programs and policies have a far-reaching, radiating effect throughout an entire organization and potentially can have a greater effect than could be obtained from consultation at the case level or by efforts to improve the work performance of individual staff members. Ultimately, the goal of program-centered consultation is to insure that the psychological component of an agency's mission is being handled in the most competent manner. Whether the system is a school, welfare department, or police precinct, consultants align themselves with those policies that allow the agency involved to perform its primary mission (e.g., education, aid to indigents, peace-keeping, and so on) in a manner that best reflects current psychological knowledge. The assumption is that, since primary caregivers constantly deal with human behavior and its problems, they should be aided in developing programs that will reflect psychologically sound and humane policies.

Mann (1971) provides an interesting example of consultation with a police department that became more program-centered over time. During the period of consultation, the consultant was thrust into a police department crisis—how to handle an illegal, massive antiwar demonstration (Mann & Iscoe, 1971). That the planned demonstration was prevented from becoming a riot was to some degree a reflection of the success of the consultant in providing anticipatory guidance and crisis management skills to police officers. In this example, the consultant had access to both sides in the conflict—the police and antiwar groups. As tension mounted, he discussed potential provocations with individuals from both groups, counseling restraint and suggesting ways to avoid overreaction. Most of the participants on both sides wanted to prevent violence but had felt powerless to do so. The consultant was impressed with how easy it was for reasonable persons to become caught up in an escalating situation and noted: "It is a chilling experience to observe both parties to a confrontation preparing for combat, each hoping and wishing that its preparations will prove unnecessary" (Mann & Iscoe, 1971, p. 111).

In the late 1960s, when Mann and Iscoe did this work, not many police departments had procedures for dealing with confrontation with citizens' groups. This is no longer the case. Police academies now include training in handling demonstrations, riots, and hostage-taking as part of their regular training programs, and police departments in some cities have specialized crisis units trained in negotiation skills (Goldstein, Monti, Sardino, & Green, 1977). These programmatic changes occurred because police officers were required to respond to new social pressures. Ordinary citizens were becoming more vocal in protesting government actions than they had been in the past. At the same time, the availability of psychological consultants enabled police departments to respond more appropriately to these volatile situations. Police departments were able to maintain social order, their primary mandate, with other alternatives available than resorting to excessive force.

Despite its potential for helping organizations change, it is surprising how little literature exists describing program-centered mental health consultation. Mannino and Shore (1972) reviewed 16 studies of consultation outcome published between 1958 and 1969. Half of the studies had control groups, and of these eight, five reported positive outcomes. Of special significance to the discussion at this point is that only 1 of the 16 studies was concerned with program-centered consultation. The remainder of the studies dealt exclusively with consultee-centered or client-centered consultation. An update of the consultation literature by Mannino and Shore (1975) found a few additional program consultation studies but the results of these were not impressive.

A recent, still unpublished study of program-centered consultation (Larsen, 1982) is important because it describes the conditions under which program-centered consultation is most likely to succeed. Eighty community mental health centers requesting program-centered consultation were randomly assigned to treatment or control groups so that half of the centers received consultation and half did not. An experienced consultant provided two days of consultation to centers in the treatment group. Results indicated that treatment and control groups did not differ at four-months follow-up, but at eight-months follow-up the centers in the treatment group reported significantly higher levels of problem solution than did centers that did not receive consultation. What this means is that it takes time for the effects of program-centered consultation to be felt in an organization. Consultation was more likely to be effective if the consultant was knowledgeable about the problem area in question, and if the problem was clarified before help was offered. This finding reminds us that a consultant cannot assume that everyone is in agreement about the nature of the problem. "If an organization requests consultation on Topic X . . . [that] may not be the real problem at all; Topic W may be the troublemaker" (Larsen, 1982, p. 14). Also, consultation was more likely to be effective if alternative solutions were offered and discussed, not just one. (Recall the discussion in Chapter Seven about the importance of generating alternatives for competent problem resolution.) Finally, program-centered consultation was more likely to succeed if the organization's leaders and staff were receptive to consultation and if there was support from the community for program changes. This last point emphasizes that consultation does not occur in a vacuum. It is facilitated by a receptive organization and a facilitative climate in the community.

Problems Associated with Program-Centered Consultation

There are a number of difficulties involved in implementing program-centered consultation. To begin, it is not easy to obtain entree into an organization. Agencies rarely call for outside consultation when contemplating program changes, and probably would be reluctant to trust an outsider who volunteered his or her services. Program changes most often are made internally, without the benefit of an outside point of view in the formulation of new policies. A more frequent occurrence is for outside pressures to force an organization to review its practices (e.g., as might occur when dissatisfied parents demand change in school programs, or blue ribbon commissions are set up to investigate prison abuses). In these instances, an organization under stress may seek an outside consultant, not because it wishes a true examination and eventual reform of its policies and procedures but because it hopes to create the appearance of flexibility and cooperation—at least until the pressure is off. Program-centered consultation to organizations experiencing such pressure can be successful if the consultant does not try to reduce outside pressure for reform before those organizational practices which contributed to the problem are thoroughly examined. To illustrate, an elementary school in a low-income area might be experiencing considerable pressure from parents concerned about the chronic low levels of reading skills demonstrated by their children. The school principal may have contemplated adding a part-time remedial reading teacher to the staff, and in initiating consultation hopes that the consultant will endorse the proposal, which in turn will lead to greater parental acceptance. Instead, the consultant might do well to call for a review of the reading curriculum at all levels. The consultant may propose that a more lasting solution will occur if the teachers become involved in curriculum improvement themselves, perhaps through a series of reading workshops with a reading specialist. While more time-consuming, this latter course attacks the problems where they originate—in the classroom. It also demonstrates a problem-solving approach that the school can adopt when curriculum modifications are needed in the future.

A second difficulty in implementing program-centered consultation is the resistance to and fear of innovation, even among seemingly cooperative administrators. It is not unusual to find administrators who are quite willing to give the consultant a free hand to work with their subordinates. It may become clear only after some time that this freedom of operation applies to subordinates but not to the administrator. Administrators sometimes show the all-too-human quality of being in favor of change in others, but fearing that self-examination will reveal "weakness" in themselves. The consultant must know how to deal with fear of exposure and censure once it becomes manifest, by demonstrating to the administrator that consultation does not involve evaluative "blame-casting." However, there are also realistic reasons for administrators to fear change. In most agencies, it is the administrator, not the staff or the consultant, who bears the total responsibility for the actions of the agency, including its mistakes. An administrator has more to lose by an idea gone wrong than anybody else. Administrators know this and are necessarily cautious. Those who are honest may tell the consultant that they do not lack for good ideas, and that they know how their organization should change to make it a model agency. The constraints in carrying out their ideas involve the limitations imposed by community sentiments, budget, and staff competencies. These are realistic constraints, but they are not as insurmountable as administrators usually believe. Often there is room for change and for administrators to show leadership in revitalizing their organizations and in bringing new ideas to the community. There are risks, but administrators of human service organizations are in positions where they are expected to show leadership in solving human problems. To avoid these issues is to subject themselves and their communities to greater pressure in the future as unmet minor issues fester and become major problems.

A final difficulty in carrying out program-centered consultation is that many consultants lack skills in this area. Most consultants who come to community work through clinical training are experts in personality dynamics and interpersonal behavior, skills that are well suited to work at case and consultee levels. Program-centered consultation requires some knowledge of organizational theory and practice, planning, and fiscal and personnel management (Caplan, 1970). In addition, the consultant must be fully aware of community sentiments that impinge upon organizations, and must be experienced in the practical politics of agency survival. Programs cannot change in one agency without affecting the entire community network of caregiving responsibilities. Mental health consultants not having the necessary training and experience will be exposed to considerable frustration and may withdraw to safer case-centered and consultee-centered work.

In summary, we feel that program-centered consultation has the greatest potential for effecting enduring organizational change. However, it is the most difficult form of consultation, because it thrusts the consultant into the vortex of competing organizational and community forces.

BEHAVIORAL CONSULTATION

The behavioral perspective comes to community psychology by way of clinical psychology, where it has come to assume a position of prominence. Sparked by a growing dissatisfaction with dynamically oriented approaches to psychotherapy and a reemphasis on environmental concerns, clinical psychologists in the 1960s became concerned with helping people improve their everyday functioning. The traditional goals of psychotherapy—understanding, inner contentment and acceptance of self—were no longer considered sufficient if they were not accompanied by changes that helped people become more effective in their daily lives (Ford & Urban, 1967). The behaviorists met a receptive audience among clinical psychologists who were grasping for procedures that would allow them to be helpful in dealing with the kinds of changes for which their clients seemed to be asking—symptom removal and increased interpersonal effectiveness.

Behavior modification can be understood best as a special form of behavior influence. It is based upon the general principle that people are influenced by the consequences of their behavior (Stolz, Wienckowski, & Brown, 1975). Much of the early work of behaviorally oriented psychologists was in restricted therapy settings. However, it did not take long for behaviorists to recognize that they did not control the major sources of reinforcement in their patients' lives. Regardless of how much practice in correct responding that patients received in therapy, a punishing environment could undo much of this work. The patient could be well prepared in new ways of coping; but, without environmental reinforcement for these new behaviors, they would soon extinguish. There was a need for methods to achieve better stimulus control of behavior in natural environments. The basic behavior modification techniques were known; the problem was how to transfer them to real-life reinforcement contingencies. Since teachers and parents are key reinforcers in the lives of most individuals during their formative years, behavioral psychologists became consultants to these important reinforcement dispensers.

There are a number of examples of the successful application of behavior modification programs in natural environments (Glenwick & Jason, 1980; Krasner, 1980; Nietzel, Winett, MacDonald, & Davidson, 1977; Tharp & Wetzel, 1969). Much of this literature is case-centered: helping environmental agents deal with individual instances of problem behavior. However, a more recent form of behavioral community psychology involves attempts at so designing cultures and shaping environments that desired behaviors are reinforced in open community settings. The focus is on increasing the baserates of low-frequency but desirable community behaviors. For example, Greene, Bailey, and Barber (1981) demonstrated that noisy disruptive behavior on school buses could be reduced by allowing the children to listen to highly appealing taped music while riding the bus, contingent upon keeping noisy outbursts below a specified level on the previous day. Noise on the bus was monitored by an automated sound-recording device (Noise Guard), which gave feedback to students by means of a light whenever noise outbursts became too intense. Behavioral procedures also have been used: to increase bus ridership (Everett, Hayward, & Meyers, 1974) and to reduce personal driving (Foxx & Schaeffer, 1981); to reduce unwanted litter generally (Geller, 1980) and dog droppings in particular (Jason, Zolik, & Matese, 1979; Jason & Zolik, 1980); to increase the quality of discussion in social studies classes (Smith, Schumaker, Schaeffer, & Sherman, 1982); and to train low-income community board members in problem-solving skills (Briscoe, Hoffman, & Bailey, 1975).

We have purposely chosen to describe work in behavioral community psychology under the consultation rubric to emphasize the crucial role of community agents in maintaining behavioral programs. Behavioral community psychologists may not think of themselves as consultants, since often they take the initiative in establishing research projects to demonstrate the control of behavior in open community settings. Projects are conducted with the researcher's own resources and personnel, so the ties to existing community organizations needed to maintain project accomplishments are not readily apparent. Unfortunately, the result is a plethora of "demonstration projects" that disappear after initial results have been published (Nietzel et al., 1977). To be successfully maintained, some group must be willing to adopt what has been demonstrated. In most communities, this means that contact with established community organizations will be required.

Steps in Establishing a Behavioral Program in a Natural Setting

The basic behavioral strategy is simple; its most prominent feature involves strengthening desirable behavior through reward, while at the same time making sure not to reward undesirable behavior. O'Leary and Drabman (1971) point out that the idea of rewarding good behavior has been known and practiced for centuries. For example, prizes of nuts, figs, and honey were used in the 12th century to reward academic achievement in Torah reading, while in the 16th century there were advocates of cherries and cakes as rewards for learning Latin and Greek. These practices stand in contrast to use of the cane to punish mistakes. It may seem surprising that a good centuries-old idea has taken so long to achieve widespread social acceptance, but such has been the case. For example, the *systematic* application of reinforcement principles to classroom learning is a relatively recent phenomenon. We shall discuss reasons why the behavioral approach has not achieved more widespread adoption. However, at this point, we will first summarize the basic ingredients of a behavioral program to achieve a common understanding of the procedures involved.

The components in a typical behavior modification program have been described in detail by Tharp and Wetzel (1969, pp. 190–200). Our discussion is based upon their presentation.

1. Establish a clear definition of the problem in behavioral terms.

A clear behavioral description is crucial. The tendency to use evaluative labels ("immoral," "crazy," "incorrigible," and the like) or descriptions that refer to internal states ("unmotivated," "a poor attitude," "defiant," "lazy," and so on) are to be avoided. In order to reduce the frequency of undesirable behaviors, reinforcement contingencies must be established so rewards are paired with specific behaviors.

2. Establish means to assure accurate observation and recording of behavior.

Once the problem behaviors have been conceptualized in observable units, baseline recording of their frequency can begin. At the same time, the recording of alternative behaviors should not be neglected, particularly if they are to be increased. The recorder should be the person who can perform the recording task most reliably and economically; sometimes this may mean that a parent, teacher, or work supervisor becomes involved at this point. The choice depends upon who typically is present when the problem behavior occurs.

3. Select an appropriate reinforcement and find an individual (reinforcement mediator) who can maintain the necessary reinforcement contingencies.

Since consultants often do not control the major reinforcements in other people's lives, they must work through those who do. The mediator selected must possess the necessary reinforcements and must be able and willing to dispense them according to an established contingency contract.

4. Establish and maintain *systematic* contingencies between desirable behavior and reinforcement.

Reward and punishments are constantly used in everyday life. What is being added by the behavioral approach is their consistent use. Note that a reinforcement schedule can be intermittent, varying according to some particular ratio of reinforcement to response; but even here, once the schedule has been established, it must be maintained. Reppucci and Saunders (1974) point out that a consultant who insists on program maintenance may be perceived as a "hard ass." There are a variety of circumstances in natural environments that threaten to compromise a behavior modification program, yet the consultant must champion staying with the contingency. Consider the following examples that Reppucci and Saunders provide from their experience at a state training school:

> Last summer, the academic school department announced that it had received a grant for a special summer program and requested that all residents be allowed to participate. The program involved a weekly trip off campus and four days of study related to the trip. The trips included a Broadway play; an old whaling village at Mystic, Connecticut; and the historic Freedom Trail in Boston. The Yale consultants pointed out that behaviorally these trips were rewarding as well as educational and, as such, should be subject to the token economy rules relating to off-grounds privileges. Moreover, we reminded staff that, according to the rules of the token economy, residents were required to work their way through three levels of achievement and that this progression was associated with increasing access to community-based rewards and eventually led to community placement. We argued that we should continue to deny residents in the bottom level of achievement the off-campus rewards such as the school trips because they could be used to motivate residents to earn their way into the higher levels and eventually back into the community. The school department argued that the trips were not rewarding; that there was no distinction between the four days of classroom study and the trip on the fifth day, as it was all educational. The assistant principal of the school even argued that, since it was all educational, no resident in the bottom level of achievement could participate in the study classes if he did not go on the trip. The whole week was educational and the trips were mandatory. . . . In the end, a major exception was made to the token economy rule that boys in the bottom level of achievement cannot go off campus.
>
> . . . by Christmas time it came to the attention of the Yale consultants that the amendment was being violated . . . two members of the school department were taking a group of residents, many of whom were in the bottom level of achievement, off campus on caroling trips. When confronted on this issue, one of the staff involved said that the caroling was being done under the guidance of a music teacher at the school and, as such, was educational. He had not thought much about it, but he assumed that any educational trip off campus was permissible. At about this same point in time, the recreation department was requesting that staff vote on a further amendment, which would allow residents in the bottom level of achievement to compete off campus in basketball games. Naturally, the rationale here was that it was recreational. The convergence of these new threats to the integrity of the token economy elicited a defensive posture on the part of the Yale consultants. Sensing this, and feeling that he might lose where the school department had won, the head of the recreation department called one of the consultants a "hard ass." Although this was a minority opinion, spoken half in jest, it describes well the inflexible attitude behavior modifiers are often seen as assuming in the natural environment. (Reppucci and Saunders, 1974, pp. 656–657)

Problems in Implementing Behavioral Programs in Natural Environments

The behavioral approach outlined above is fairly straightforward and uncomplicated. However, this simplicity is misleading. Behavior modification techniques are precise, and their implementation often requires the behavior modifier to have substantial resources and control over the environment. It is not the case that a determined behavior modifier "armed with a knowledge of learning theory and a stiff upper lip" can manipulate contingencies in the natural environment just as is done in the laboratory (Reppucci & Saunders, 1974).

Tharp and Wetzel (1969) and Reppucci and Saunders (1974) present excellent discussions of the constraints encountered in attempts to implement behavior modification programs in natural settings. The problems encountered can be summarized as follows:

1. Mediator problems. Behavior modification programs require the active cooperation of others who control the reinforcement contingencies to which target subjects are exposed. There are a number of reasons why obtaining the cooperation of these program mediators may be difficult. To begin, the mediator may be disorganized and may be incapable of following a systematic schedule. For example, a mother who is hallucinating may be unable to distinguish the reality of her child's behavior from responses that she thinks she sees. While one does not need a superior level of mental health to follow simple behavioral instructions (there are many examples in the behavioral literature of successful contingencies administered by psychologically disturbed mediators), a minimal level of reality awareness is required.

The mediator's motivation and willingness to participate is a second crucial variable. There are times when mediators are so angry at the target subject that they simply refuse to follow instructions, or sabotage the intervention plan in other ways. Tharp and Wetzel present two dramatic examples of attempts to undermine behavioral programs that succeeded in doing so. The first example illustrates an uncooperative mediator in the home:

> *Case 63.* A very seriously predelinquent adolescent boy had repeatedly engaged in fist-fights with his stepfather. The stepfather had hated the child for years. After four weeks of a closely proctored intervention plan, the boy's misbehavior was rapidly decreasing. The father, fearful that the boy might stay in the home if he reformed, disobeyed every instruction which our staff gave him. The case disintegrated; the boy ran away. It was very clear that the boy's continued presence in the home was so punishing to the father that the rewards our staff offered him—praise, encouragement, attention—were swamped. (Tharp & Wetzel, 1969, pp. 131–132)

In a similar manner, teachers motivated by frustration and anger can also undermine an effective program, ultimately to the detriment of the target child.

> *Case 30.* Benny was a low achieving ninth-grader who felt he was getting an unfair deal from his home environment as well as his school environment. He had struggled through two very inconsistent stepfathers and a number of non-

motivating teachers. The only thing that kept him in school and out of the grasp of the police was his devotion to his mother.

After overcoming a number of crises at the school, and establishing a concrete reinforcer at home, we intervened into Benny's intermittent work habits in the classroom. He began to work quite diligently in all his classes except math, where he had the greatest teacher friction. The math teacher had been opposed to Benny and to the intervention all along. Two weeks after the intervention plan was started, Benny was suspended from math, on the slim pretext that on that day he didn't bring his book to class. The teacher accused him of stealing the book he had, and told him the homework he had been turning in was not up to par. He was called a "no-good bum" and told he would be better off out of school, and certainly out of math class. For Benny this was the last straw. He feared that the same thing would eventually happen in all his classes. He stopped coming to school. His mother, whom we had almost convinced that the school was finally giving her son a new opportunity, sympathized with Benny and did not demand that he return. She allowed Benny to get a job. Benny was a drop-out (or "push-out"); the case was terminated. (Tharp & Wetzel, 1969, pp. 132–133).

As stated previously, the behavioral consultant does not control the reinforcement contingencies for target subjects, but must work through mediators. A major problem in gaining the cooperation of mediators is that the consultant also does not control the major sources of reinforcement to mediators, either. The contingencies that influence the behavior of staff in most settings involve salaries, promotions, and job security. Even if he or she wanted to control these rewards for the sake of increased program efficiency, it is doubtful that society would or should allow the consultant to have such power. From a practical point of view, it is unlikely that the consultant could circumvent civil service merit systems, tenure policies, or union practices that control the potent rewards to mediators in the real world. Instead, the behavior modifier must use more indirect and voluntary methods, such as persuasion and in-service training, to gain the cooperation of mediators.

The need to persuade or to "sell" one's program to mediators takes on a special meaning for behavioral consultants because some people have negative attitudes toward behavior modification principles. For example, some people reject the determinism that is implicit in the behavioral perspective. Others consider reinforcement akin to bribery. In the words of one school principal, "I will not reward a child for doing his moral duty" (Tharp & Wetzel, 1969, p. 128). Others prefer aversive control in the belief that "the rod will prevent spoiling the child" (Tharp & Wetzel, 1969, p. 129). Another attitudinal resistance to behavior modification can be seen in the belief that "all children should be treated alike." From this point of view, altering environmental contingencies for one child is considered "favoritism." While each of these arguments can be countered (e.g., children are rarely treated alike despite the intent), the fact remains that mediators are the key persons who determine the success of behavioral programs. The consultant's conviction about the merits of behavioral programs is not sufficient if the mediator is not equally convinced and cooperative.

Of course, the problem of gaining the cooperation of mediators is not unique to the behavioral perspective. All forms of consultation require the active participation of consultees for program effectiveness. Consultation is a voluntary, not a coercive method. At this point, the issue under discussion is whether the behavioral perspective imposes special conditions that may be impediments to cooperation. Our estimate is that the number of such limiting conditions is not greater than would apply to other forms of consultation. However, their nature is different. Behavioral techniques require more careful and systematic application. They also require a willingness to adopt the values that undergird the techniques.

2. Institutional and agency problems. At times, institutional practices can conflict with the procedures needed to properly execute behavioral programs. Originally set up for the convenience of administration and staff, these procedures can be extremely resistant to change because they regulate what can be complex organizational patterns. Consider the problem of staff communication patterns. Behavioral programs often require follow-through and cooperation by all members of an institution. Staff may be interested and well-meaning, but may not possess the communication channels necessary to carry through on agreed-upon procedures. The problem is well illustrated in the following example:

Case 11. An intervention plan was proposed to a school in which Case 11 would be allowed to participate in the after-school football program as a daily reinforcer for his good behavior in the morning section of his elementary school. The school administration objected to this on two grounds. First, they did not believe they could make after-school football contingent for this one child, when it was a noncontingent opportunity for all the other children. Second, and undoubtedly most important, the school had no way of forwarding information from the morning teacher to the coach of the afternoon activity. Since no communication channel existed, the school pronounced the plan impossible. Nowhere in the school was there an individual whose normal role included carrying such a message. Both the teacher and the coach would have considered it a violation of their job descriptions to seek out the other. It was necessary in this instance, as in many others, to have the BA (behavior analyst) fill in the interstices in the organization and become the communication channel himself. The BA either called or came by in the morning to verify criterion performance with the teacher and delivered the report to the coach.

It should be reported that the administration of Case 11's school was not at all opposed to continuation of behavior modification programming for the child once they had some concrete demonstration of its efficacy. The behavior engineer cannot ask for more openmindedness or opportunity than that; but even with the philosophical support of the principal, still the organizational structure did not allow for these two positions—teacher and coach—to regularly and directly communicate over an individual child. This difficulty was entirely independent of the personalities or values of these two mediators; both were reliable, cooperative, and interested professionals. There was simply no time, no moment of spatial proximity, and no habit which would allow for the transmission of information. (Tharp & Wetzel, 1969, pp. 141–142)

Note that, in the problem just described, the behavioral consultant provided the resources (in the person of an assistant—the BA) to overcome the communication impediment. The BA carried the message from the teacher to the coach. In the real world, resources to carry out behavioral programs can be in short supply. Limited personnel and finances are more likely to be the norm (Reppucci & Saunders, 1974). For example, measuring behavior to establish a baseline may seem like a simple step. Yet many staff consider recording an unnecessary and even overwhelming burden if they are already taxed by their regular duties.

How should behavior consultants deal with the problem of limited resources? On the one hand, as in the previous example from Tharp and Wetzel, they can provide the necessary resources themselves. This is a reasonable alternative if there is an external source of funds (e.g., a research grant) or an available supply of personnel (e.g., students eager to participate in return for academic credit or relevant work experience). However, if the program ultimately is to be adopted by the community, it cannot depend upon external support indefinitely. Ultimately, the institution receiving consultation will have to decide whether it has sufficient funds and whether it is willing to divert some of its resources to support the program.

There are two special situations in which it may be advisable for the consultants to provide their own program resources. (1) Initially, an agency may be unconvinced of the value of the program and may need to be shown definite accomplishment before it will invest its own resources. (2) Another special circumstance occurs when dealing with severe behavioral deficiencies. In this situation, mediators may be unable or unwilling to do all of the complex shaping necessary to establish initial behavioral control, but may be quite willing to *maintain* appropriate behavior once it has been established by special training. Complex or long-standing behavioral deficiencies may require much more intensive effort than can be obtained in a typical community agency. For example, Wolf, Phillips, and Fixsen (1972) described a program for the community treatment of delinquent behavior. The main ingredient in their program was a group home for 6 to 10 youngsters supervised by an adult couple who serve as "teaching-parents." The home was designed according to behavior modification principles. Each day, the boys earned tokens that were cashed in for privileges and rewards. Wolf et al. found that the behavior of the boys often was so disruptive in their usual environments that parents and teachers had great difficulty in gaining behavioral control. Teachers were unwilling to "apply positive social reinforcements for small approximations to appropriate behavior" (Wolf et al., 1972, p. 55). On the other hand, once behavioral control was established in the group home, teachers could maintain that improvement in class by filling out and signing a special daily report card. The child was required to carry the report card and return it to the group home in order to earn his points and privileges there.

Another example of institutional constraints on effective behavioral programming can be seen in typical school policies concerning grades. On first view, it should seem that grades can be powerful rewards. The problem is that usually they are not administered contingent with behavior. A typical grading period of six weeks is too long a gap between performance and consequences to effectively shape the academic behavior of many children. In addition, grades are summed evaluations of the teacher's total response to the child, both social as well as academic behaviors, and reflect the attitude of the teacher as well as the behavior of the child. From the point of view of behavior modification, "because the grade is a reaction to everything, it is not a reaction to anything" (Tharp & Wetzel, 1969, p. 139). To be useful in a behavioral program, grades must be provided daily, hourly, or in terms of instantaneous comments.

3. Community problems. Behavioral consultants soon come to recognize that some of the problems that are called to their attention defy intervention at individual or institutional levels. This is because the problems stem from a confused mandate in the community at large. It makes no sense to work for the elimination of behavioral deviance if, at the same time, the community is implicitly reinforcing the very same behaviors. Consider the following two examples:

> In one city in which the BRP staff has consulted, gambling is legal. Virtually the entire economy—jobs, institutions, social services—is dependent upon the prosperity of the gambling and entertainment industry. The city is alight from dusk to dawn with fantastic and effective stimuli; an electric and human circus exists which is impressively engineered to evoke staying-out-late behavior. The most frequent "predelinquent" complaints in this city are curfew violations.

> BRP case consultation was performed in a northern coast town whose principal product is canned seafood. After a typical escalating conflict between the school and the target, a 15-year-old girl, she dropped out and began to work part-time at the cannery. The income was valued by the family, but the court was determined that she return to school. In investigating the possibilities of making part-time cannery employment contingent on school attendance, we were confronted with the discovery that several adolescent dropouts, school "withdrawals," and flunk-outs were part of the cannery peak-season work force. The reason given for this pattern was that such "kids like to make the money." Only as we began to explore alternatives for the cannery-school arrangement did it become clear that the community could not, with impunity, change things very much. There was a critical labor shortage during the brief peak season. (Tharp & Wetzel, 1969, pp. 145–146)

Problems such as these are really beyond the scope of behavioral technology. Despite the sometimes grandiose rhetoric, behavior modification was never intended to provide a basis for describing, understanding, or changing natural settings (Reppucci & Saunders, 1974). Most often, behavioral technology is applied at the individual level, producing individual not system change. As the examples just described indicate, many community problems reflect conflicting values. However, behavioral techniques are oriented toward helping accomplish agreed-upon goals. Behaviorists generally are not trained to provide guidance in helping communities resolve confused mandates based upon conflicting goals and values (Fawcett, Mathews, & Fletcher, 1980), and need to expand the scope of their theoretical interests in order to develop a better understanding of the social psychology of complex organizations and communities.

In instances in which there is agreement on goals for desired behavior, programs based upon the systematic use of incentives have produced impressive results. Manpower training programs for the chronically unemployed (Nietzel et al., 1977), increased energy conservation, litter control, and improved transportation systems (Glenwick & Jason, 1980) are some of the possibilities that have appeared successful in demonstration projects. The problem for society in considering whether to adopt the behavioral approach to these problems rests with the degree to which citizens would be willing to have their behavior systematically observed and monitored. As Glenwick and Jason (p. 355) aptly note:

> One may wonder about the willingness of our own society to adopt the behavioral community approach on a large scale. Much of the United States population already resents what they perceive as government intrusion into their lives, and science no longer possesses the almost unqualified support it enjoyed in past decades. If the approach described in this book were placed in operation on a broad scale, one might envision a family in the year 2000 exposed to the following conditions, among others: tax incentives for having only one child, a token economy in their child's classroom, prompts (that is, cues) to ride public transportation, feedback on the family's energy usage, participation in a lottery to encourage recycling, and so on. The social behaviors to be included under such a behavioral community system would be largely decided by the concerns of the day and the extent to which suitable interventions could be created. The acceptability to the populace at large of having such a lengthy list of behaviors monitored (either by self or others) remains to be determined. However, such a system—combined incentives, feedback and information, prompts, and person-environment matches—might in actuality be more humane and offer more freedom than one in which behaviors were mandated and proscribed via legislation (with few choices left to the individual). In implementing behavioral community programs, a balance between the needs of individuals and those of society (perhaps the perennial dilemma faced by civilized societies) will need to be maintained or at least striven for. That is, while a society may consciously attempt to produce "prosocial" behavior (as defined by that society) on the part of its citizens, the erosion of civil liberties will have to be guarded against and a respect for individual differences appreciated.

The Effectiveness of Behavioral Techniques: The Problems of Generalization across Settings and Persistence over Time

It seems to us that there is good evidence to support the effectiveness of behavioral techniques in shaping and controlling individual behavior. Despite these successes, a thorny problem remaining for behaviorists concerns the permanence and extent of generalization of effects. It would not be much help if improved behavior did not persist over time or in new situations different from the one in which the original contingencies were established. This is a difficult problem for behaviorists because their theory should lead them to expect that generalization would *not* occur in situations in which reinforcement contingencies were not maintained. Behaviorally oriented psychologists generally reject notions of personality "traits" that the individual carries with him in different situations. Behavior is thought of as situation-specific—that when the situation changes, so does the behavior. The expectation is that, without reinforcement, extinction should occur.

The empirical findings support this expectation, in that most studies have reported that newly reinforced behaviors often do not persist with the removal of reinforcement contingencies. Generalization tends to be difficult to achieve. Thus, from a practical point of view, if generalization is desired it should be specifically included as part of the behavioral program. This can be accomplished in two ways. First, an attempt can be made to increase the similarity between the setting in which the new responses are initially acquired and other settings in the individual's environment (Goldstein, Heller, & Sechrest, 1966). The second method to maximize generalization involves moving from extrinsic reinforcement (money, tokens, candy, and so on) to intrinsic motivation. Improvement is carried forward because the individual is now motivated to learn techniques for self-regulation and self-control. There is a growing body of literature on cognitive approaches to behavior modification that emphasizes self-control techniques (Goldstein & Kanfer, 1979; Kanfer & Goldstein, 1975; Mahoney & Arnkoff, 1978). Still, we must remember that self-control programs require motivation for improvement and active cooperation by participants. Hence we must stress that behavioral programs are least effective as devices for "automatic conditioning." It is the programs relying exclusively on extrinsic motivation that have the most difficulty in demonstrating generalization and persistence of new behaviors once extrinsic rewards are removed.

Behavioral Consultation: A Technology in Need of Values and Goals

Viewed simply as an effective technology, behavior modification techniques can be used for moral or immoral purposes. As Skinner has noted, the technology "is ethically neutral. It can be used by villain or saint" (Stolz, Wienckowski, & Brown, 1975). However, there is some concern that despite this disclaimer the work of behavior modifiers has not been used in a neutral and value-free manner. Winett and Winkler (1972) claim that behavior modifiers have allowed their work to be used to maintain the status quo by reinforcing conformity and adherence to routine. After all, what behaviors should be deemed as inappropriate and in need of modification? How does one decide? Winett and Winkler charge that, in their review of the literature on the uses of behavior modification in the classroom, "inappropriate" behaviors have included: getting out of seat, walking around, rattling papers, crying, singing, laughing, or simply doing something different from that which the child has been directed to do.

Winett and Winkler believe that behavior modifiers accepted the school's apparent desire for conformity and order. Their primary goal was to demonstrate that their techniques worked and that behavior control in the classroom could be achieved. "The nature of the behavior being controlled was a secondary consideration" (Winett & Winkler, 1972, p. 501), and they did not consider the value impact of their work.

Holland (1978) agrees that too often behaviorist techniques have been used to support the status quo. While behaviorism can mean analyzing the impact of environmental structure in order to change them, Holland charges that too often behavior modifiers focus on "fixing" problem behavior rather than working to change societal contingencies that continue to produce problem behavior.

It would seem that, in the final analysis, values must be considered. Reducing disruptiveness can be important if classroom learning is to move forward. The disruptive child impedes his own academic performance and has a similar effect on the progress of other class members. Still, when does reducing classroom disruption become fostering docility? The danger is greatest in those settings in which obedience and order are valued much more highly than learning and creativity. If there already exists a preoccupation with order and control, there is a high likelihood that behavior modification techniques will be abused. These concerns cannot be avoided by the behavioral consultant and should become part of the initial assessment before accepting the consultation assignment.

Behavior modification programs in prisons and mental hospitals present some special ethical problems (Davison & Stuart, 1975; Stolz, Wienckowski, & Brown, 1975). In both types of institutions, residents are incarcerated against their will. The usual caveat applicable to outpatient programs—that participation is voluntary—is a less-meaningful protection of individual rights. Prisoners and mental patients may be told that nonparticipation will not be held against them; but such a statement may be hard to believe, given the ambiguity of what constitutes "rehabilitation" in many inpatient settings, particularly if tenure is indeterminant and a function of staff judgment of "readiness." It would be reasonable for an inmate to expect that participation might lead to early release. If the cost of nonparticipation cannot be assessed (e.g., will the officials really hold it against me if I don't cooperate with a "treatment" that they all insist is good for me?), why jeopardize the possibility of early release. Under these circumstances, "volunteering" does not mean a lack of coercion, however subtle the coercive pressure may be.

Some critics have suggested that behaviorists are naive to think that their programs can remain immune to subversion by punitive institutions. It is not difficult to find evidence to substantiate this charge—instances in which prisons and mental hospitals used behavior modification programs for punishment and control, not for rehabilitation. Either alternative—attempting to improve punitive institutions or deciding they are beyond redemp-

tion—involves some human cost. For example, eliminating behavioral programs from prisons could deny the opportunity for improvement for those
inmates who genuinely want to participate and who might benefit from the
programs (Stolz et al., 1975). There are no easy answers to issues such as
these. Our own personal values and priorities lead us to believe that, when
clearly punitive institutions have been identified, more is to be gained by
designing alternatives than by attempting to support such institutions (see
Chapter Nine). However, we cannot fault psychologists who think otherwise, and who devote their professional energies to improving archaic
prisons and mental hospitals. In these instances, our main concern is that of
safeguards. Procedures must be developed to monitor treatment programs to
insure that participation is not coercive, that consent is truly informed, and
that the programs are rehabilitative and humane. Such procedures as review committees with staff, inmate, and general citizen participation can be
implemented to perform this function. While the potential for abuse is recognized more clearly for behavioral programs, a system of review to protect
individual liberties is crucial for all community programs.

We would conclude that the extreme fear of behavioral technology that
exists in some quarters is unwarranted. Research using behavioral techniques should continue, since they have already demonstrated a potential for
relieving some types of distress and maladaptive behavior resistant to
change by other methods of intervention. Still, once we leave the confines of
the outpatient clinic in which participation is voluntary and under the control
of the patient, potential for abuse becomes a real danger and safeguards are
needed. Behavioral consultants should be at the forefront of those concerned with developing safeguards, and should actively seek opportunities
to explain their work to the public. Ultimately, without public acceptance
there will be no sanction to use this technology to solve real community
problems.

ORGANIZATION DEVELOPMENT

Organization development (OD) has functioned as a change strategy since
the late 1940s, deriving largely from Kurt Lewin's conviction that human
behavior could be fully understood only as an interaction between people
and their natural environments. Some of Lewin's students organized the
National Training laboratories at Bethel, Maine, in 1947, which became the
primary training center for organization development specialists (Benne,
Bradford, & Lippett, 1964).

OD prospered primarily within business organizations where a reaffir-
mation of human values served as a welcome antidote to the depersonalized,
mechanistic values that often grew unchecked in bureaucratic organizations.
At one time corporation executives believed that all that was necessary was
to ''set the work before the men and they will do it'' (Bennis, 1969, p. 45).
Now many business organizations are taking more seriously the problem of
how to integrate human needs and organizational goals.

Today OD is one of the major behavioral science strategies for inducing change at the organizational or agency level. The fact that many mental health personnel are not acquainted with OD approaches reflects the inattention that has traditionally been paid to the "work environment" by psychologists and psychiatrists. With the exception of a relatively small group of "industrial" psychologists, many of whom are engaged in human factors research, such as the location of gauges in airplane cockpits, extraordinarily little attention has been devoted to the area in which most people devote the majority of their adult walking life—their jobs.

Organization development is defined by Friedlander and Brown (1974) as "a method for facilitating change and development in people (e.g., styles, values, skills), in technology (e.g., greater simplicity, complexity), and in organizational processes and structures (e.g., relationships, roles). It is at once a set of personal values, a set of change technologies, and a set of processes or structures, through which the change agent relates to the organizational system" (pp. 314–316). Only by intervening at *both* the technical/structural level *and* at the personal level can meaningful change be accomplished, according to many OD proponents. The joint objectives of OD are optimizing human fulfillment and increasing organizational efficiency.

It is important to recognize that, while there are specific techniques associated with OD (e.g., team-building, job design, survey feedback, sensitivity training, and the like), the field is also marked by an explicit set of values. These are related to the existential view of people, as reflected in concerns for openness and freedom in individual life and the manner in which these values are suppressed by environmental pressures. The values are humanistic and democratic in nature, in that they reflect: a positive view of people; encouraging the effective expression of feelings; authenticity; risk; confrontation; and collaboration (Friedlander & Brown, 1974).

> The objectives of OD are obviously colored by these values. They include creating an open problem-solving climate, supplementing the authority of role and status with the authority of knowledge and competence, locating decision-making and problem-solving as close to information sources as possible, building trust and collaboration, developing a reward system which recognizes the organizational mission and the growth of people, helping managers to manage according to relevant objectives rather than past practices, and increasing self-control and self-direction for people within the organization. (Friedlander & Brown, 1974, p. 316)

Organization development, then, is not just a method that can be used to improve a work setting. It involves theory, techniques, *and* values. It is a systematic approach to managing change in organizations that stresses both rational planning and the recognition of the "human" side of work. These themes can be seen in a second definition of OD offered by Margulies and Raia. They state:

> We would define organization development as a value based process of self-assessment and planned change, involving specific strategies and technology

aimed at improving the overall effectiveness of an organization system. (Margulies & Raia, 1978, p. 24)

The values referred to in this definition are humanistic and democratic. But, OD also is a process based on collecting data, identifying problems, and providing feedback to develop alternative solutions. OD consultants hope to teach this problem-solving approach to organizational personnel so the management of future problems in the work setting can be handled in this same way.

A work setting can be improved by changing its structure (e.g., methods of production, how the job is carried out, and so on) or by improving relationships between job participants. Each of these—structural changes and interaction or process changes—has been a focus of OD consultation. In the next section, each will be discussed in turn.

Technical and Structural Approaches

Structural approaches are of several varieties. In one that Friedlander and Brown (1974) call "sociotechnical systems intervention," the overall system of production is modified. For example, in an early study, Trist and Bamforth (1951) found that different production systems in the British coal mining industry were associated with different levels of absenteeism, productivity, and accidents. Traditional coal mining utilized small, cohesive, and autonomous work teams, in which each worker performed a variety of roles and the work group was paid as a team. "Advances" in technology led to larger work groups that were more impersonal, that divided the labor more narrowly, and that paid on an individual rather than a team basis. The result was lower performance, higher absenteeism and accidents, and a general worker indifference. When the sociotechnical structure was modified to reintroduce group identification and cohesion, noted improvement on the given measures was achieved (Trist, Higgin, Murray, & Pollack, 1963). Similar increases in production quality have been obtained in Scandanavian experiments in "industrial democracy" or "worker control" of production (Hunnius, Garson, & Case, 1973), Japanese "quality control circles" (Cole, 1979) and "quality of work life" efforts at General Motors (Guest, 1979). In each of these examples, workers have been given increased responsibility and incentives for monitoring product quality and upgrading production technology.

Another example of an OD structural intervention can be seen in the study of "Flexi-Time" reported by Golembiewski, Hilles, and Kagno (1974). Flexi-Time simply means flexible work hours. In the version adopted in this research, employees could start work any time between 7:00 and 9:15 A.M. and could stop between 3:00 and 6:00 P.M.; all employees were required to be on duty every day during the core period between 9:15 A.M. and 3:00 P.M. The effects of the intervention were positive for groups on Flexi-Time compared with units of the company on fixed-work time schedules. Flexi-Time increased worker morale and job satisfaction and increased productivity on some key measures. Absenteeism was reduced, as well as the need for overtime to make up for lost manhours. It is interesting to note that, while workers were given freedom to choose arrival and departure times, little change actually occurred—except for extended weekends and changes during the summer months. The freedom to choose flexible work hours may have been more important than a flexible work schedule itself.

Job enlargement is another structural OD strategy. Here, several duties are combined in one job rather than having different persons work on each. Marks (1954), for example, combined several tasks into one job in an industrial shop and noted improvements in output, quality, and worker attitude. When assembly line jobs were changed into independent bench work, production time decreased and quality increased (Conant & Kilbridge, 1965).

Several reviews of job enlargement programs indicate general increases in worker satisfaction and often increases in productivity. Davis (1966) hypothesizes that such improvements are the result of increased variety of tasks, self-determination and self-pacing, increased discretion and responsibility, and a sense of work completion. Job *enrichment* differs from job *enlargement* in that the combination of tasks is vertical, in the case of enrichment, and horizontal, in the case of enlargement. When a job is enlarged, different tasks at the same level in the organization are added. When a job is enriched, more actual responsibility from higher organizational levels are added.

The studies of R. N. Ford (1969) at American Telephone & Telegraph indicate that, when jobs are enriched by adding higher-level responsibilities, both turnover and absenteeism are reduced, quality of service is increased, and employee attitudes are improved. Other studies show similar patterns of results. The notion of "increased motivation" is frequently cited as a causal factor in the observed change.

Friedlander and Brown (1974) conclude that, in general, structural improvements in the work setting do tend to increase performance and productivity, often as a result of increases in the quality of the work, lowered absenteeism, and lowered turnover. Kahn (1974) agrees that structural modifications seem to have positive and persisting effects, and he suggests that this may be so because the trend in industry toward job fragmentation has gone too far; and that "gains in performance and satisfaction are obtainable by reducing the fragmentation and increasing the variety of content" (Kahn, 1974, p. 495). Still, improvements from structural changes are not always forthcoming. For example, job enlargement tends to result in a more socially isolated worker, which must be compensated for by social restructuring of the work group (i.e., building in opportunities for increased interaction). Job enrichment is not always successful because some workers respond negatively to complex jobs. For example, some people may prefer jobs that are not demanding and that allow them time to socialize or daydream (Nystrom, 1981). The evidence seems to be that the degree of satisfaction is a function of the cognitive complexity of the employee. Some workers respond well to challenge, variety, and complexity; others do not. To achieve maximal benefit, technostructural modification must also pay attention to individual difference and human process variables.

Human Process Interventions

Process interventions focus on the relations among people in a work setting. However, the distinction between structural and process techniques is clearly arbitrary and can be misleading. Organizational structures and processes are not independent, in that both represent *interdependent* patterns, which can recur over time (Kahn, 1974). Increasingly, current OD practice is a combination of structural and process approaches (Burke, 1975, 1977). For example, Seashore and Bowers (1970) present impressive data on the durability of change in one organization (the Weldon Company) measured five years after OD activity terminated. The authors believe that their success may have been due to the interdependence of structural changes in the work system, combined with an early legitimization of concern about organizational process. Still, the distinction between process and structure is useful, if for no other reason than to describe more accurately the different activities of OD consultants.

Types of OD Process Intervention

One problem that has slowed the large-scale adoption of OD human process technology has been the lack of clearly delineated operational descriptions of the methods of intervention (Schmuck & Miles, 1971). There is no generally agreed-upon set of procedures, and, in addition, many OD consultants do not describe their techniques explicitly. However, there have been several attempts at synthesis.

Friedlander and Brown (1974, p. 325) describe human process intervention as focusing on "human participants and the organization processes (e.g., communication, problem solving, decision making) through which they accomplish their own and the organization's goals." The goals of human process intervention usually are the strengthening of relationships among members of a group (group development) or between persons in different groups that must relate to one another (intergroup development). There are numerous methods used by OD practitioners to reach these goals, most of which have been summarized by Schmuck and Miles (1971, p. 9) as follows:

1. Training or education: Procedures involving direct teaching or experience-based learning. Such technologies as lectures, exercises, simulations, and T-groups are examples.
2. Process consultation: Watching and aiding on-going processes and coaching to improve them.
3. Confrontation: Bringing together units of the organization (persons, roles, or groups) which have previously been in poor communication; usually accompanied by supporting data.

4. Data feedback: Systematic collection of information, which is then reported back to appropriate organizational units as a base for diagnosis, problem-solving, and planning.
5. Problem-solving: Meetings essentially focusing on problem identification, diagnosis, and solution invention and implementation.
6. Plan-making: Activity focused primarily on planning and goal setting to replot the organization's future.
7. OD task force establishment: Setting up ad hoc problem-solving groups or internal teams of specialists to ensure that the organization solves problems and carries out plans continuously.

An example of process intervention. Schmuck and Runkel (1972) present an interesting demonstration of the use of organizational training by a school system. The purpose of the demonstration was to communicate *experientially* the nature of OD training to those with little experience in it. The demonstration was a prelude to a two-year program of OD within the entire school district. Attending the demonstration were the superintendent, his cabinet, elementary and secondary school principals, and selected teachers who were key officers in the local educational association. Other teachers were added to this group so there would be at least one teacher from every school building.

The event lasted four days, but only the superintendent's cabinet was present all of the time. On the evening of the first day, before others arrived, the superintendent and his cabinet discussed ways in which communication had broken down among them, the lack of clarity in their role definitions, the ambiguous norms that existed in the cabinet, and, finally, their strengths as a group. The trainers gave structure to the discussion and kept it centered on organizational topics.

On the second day, the principals joined the cabinet in a specially designed confrontation that brought into the open organizational problems seen by each group as involving the other. First, the entire group divided into three units: cabinet, elementary principals, and secondary principals. Next, each of these units met separately to consider helpful and unhelpful work-related behaviors of the other two groups toward their own group. At the end of two hours, all perceived actions of the other groups were written in large letters on sheets of newsprint. Problems between groups brought to the surface were earmarked for future problem-solving procedures. The session ended with a brief period of training in the communicative skills of paraphrasing and behavior description.

Next, one group sat in a circle, surrounded by members of the other two groups. Participants sitting in the outer ring read aloud the descriptions they had written of the inside group. A member of the inner circle then paraphrased the description to make sure that his colleagues understood it. During this step, group members in the inner circle who were receiving descriptions of their own group were *not* allowed to defend their group against the allegations made by the others. After all items describing the inside group were read, the remaining two groups took their turns in the center circle.

After this step, the three groups again met separately to find evidence that would support the descriptions they had received; they were instructed to recall examples of their own behavior that could have given the other group its impressions. The three groups then came together once again with one group forming an inner circle. Each inner group told the others of the evidence it had recalled to verify the perceptions of the others. Once again, the inner group was discouraged from defending itself; members were asked simply to describe the behavioral events they thought supported the others' perceptions.

On the evening of the second day, teachers arrived to join the principals and cabinet, and for four hours all of the key line personnel in the Kent district were together. A modified confrontation design was continued, culminating in a meeting in which the three groups indicated the organizational problems they thought existed in the Kent district. Discussion was lively, penetrating, and constructive; most personnel had never before confronted persons in other positions so openly with their perceptions of district problems. The principals went back to their buildings the next day, leaving time for teachers and cabinet to interact with one another. On the fourth day, the cabinet met alone to schedule some dates for future problem-solving. (Schmuck & Runkel, 1972, pp. 27–28)

Survey Feedback as an OD Strategy

In survey feedback intervention, data are systematically collected from members of an organization or agency (usually by questionnaires), summarized, and given back to the members. The assumption is that discrepancies between organizational ideals and actual responses will generate motivation for change. This process is strikingly similar to that employed by Moos (1975), who administered two forms of his social environment scales to the staff of an adolescent treatment center. On one form, the staff and residents were told to describe the program as it really was, and on the other form as it ideally should be. Data about discrepancies between the two assessments were given to the center's members and actions were taken toward their reduction. Six months later, movement of the real toward the ideal perceived environment was recorded when the scales were readministered.

There is some evidence that survey feedback is one of the more potent OD techniques, particularly in terms of attitudinal changes in participants (Bowers, 1973). Participation in feedback can affect a group's perceptions and expectations; which, in turn, can lead to changes in group interaction and subsequent increases in job satisfaction. The effectiveness of survey feedback is increased even further when workers participate fully in designing the questions to be asked and collecting the relevant data. However, improved satisfaction does not always mean that substantive organizational changes will take place. The active participation of supervisory personnel also is important because a resistant or antagonistic superior can undermine the process. Furthermore, without planning for follow-up, little change may occur after the initial glow of involvement wears off. Friedlander and Brown conclude that the primary effects seem to be on attitudes and perceptions, and that "there is little evidence that survey feedback *alone* [emphasis added] leads to changes in individual behavior or organizational performance" (Friedlander & Brown, 1974, p. 327).

Feedback also has been a key ingredient in activities that are oriented toward group and intergroup development. For example, in attempting to reduce intergroup conflict, the goal generally has been to foster a "problem-solving" approach to intergroup relations. The interventions are based on the sharing of information, confrontation of differences, and "working through" problems to develop mutually acceptable solutions (Friedlander & Brown, 1974, p. 330). The prototypical design of Blake, Mouton, and Sloma (1965) involves each group listing perceptions of itself, the other group and its views of the other's perceptions of itself (e.g., "how do you think they perceive you?"), and then sharing these lists as a basis for improved understanding and future cooperation.

One of the authors of this text (KH) had an opportunity to use survey feedback to improve access to recreational facilities among youth in a midwestern community.

The survey was conducted when the planning and research arm of a local United Fund organization commissioned a study of countywide youth-oriented programs. The funding group wanted to know about overlap and duplication of services and also wanted information to confirm or deny their suspicions that certain segments of the youth population were underserved by existing programs. . . .

It was decided to conduct a survey of area youngsters in grades 3 through 12 in which questions were asked concerning leisure time activities and participation in organized groups. Five hundred and fifteen youngsters were individually interviewed in schools throughout the county. The main findings of the survey were that unmet needs were greatest for children from the lowest socioeconomic groups and for those living in rural sections of the county. Girls also tended to be underserved. On the other hand, the clientele of the various youth-serving agencies was quite similar—middle- and upper-class boys predominated as members, across a wide variety of activities.

The main concern of the consultant was how to provide data feedback to youth-serving agencies in a way that would maximize consideration and use of the findings. To accomplish these goals and increase receptivity to the survey, the following steps were taken.

1. Agencies were informed of the project from the start. For example, while the project was still in the planning stages, a meeting was held with agency personnel to describe the survey, solicit reactions, display the tentative questionnaire, and request suggestions for its modification. . . .

2. The consultant operated on the assumption that responsive agencies did not need to be coerced into self-improvement and that program modification could be encouraged through presentation of objective data and open discussion. . . .

3. Once the data had been tabulated, regular meetings were held with agency representatives to consider data interpretation and to work through implications for action. This proved to be a crucial step since agency defensiveness was never completely eliminated. For example, as public agencies, membership was nominally open to any youth in the community. It was difficult for staff to believe that specific groups of young persons (e.g., poor youngsters) felt unwelcome. Once the finding was accepted as valid, the initial reaction to it was to "blame the kids." Statements were made such as: "These kids are unmotivated; they don't participate constructively when they are here"; "when they do participate, they are so dirty and smell so bad that other kids complain"; "their own

parents don't help out and we can't get our regular volunteer staff to work with them,'' and so on.

It took several meetings building intergroup cohesion to reach the point where other alternatives could be considered. Without directly contesting previously stated views, the consultant steadfastly emphasized that reaching underserved groups was a challenge to all. While no one agency was solely responsible for the complex social problems involved, each could find ways to improve access and design more interesting programs to better provide for the needs of underserved groups. With this constant but gentle prodding and faced with the objective data of underutilization by underprivileged groups, agencies began to consider programmatic alternatives. For example, some developed plans for outreach sites throughout the county, while others worked on plans for improved staff and volunteer training. (Heller, 1978, pp. 422–423)

Sensitivity Training as an OD Strategy

Feedback is also a focal ingredient in group development via sensitivity training (T-groups). Participants in this type of activity honestly inform each other about how the other's behavior is interpreted by them, and the feelings that follow from the interpretation. In such a fashion, information is obtained that is otherwise unavailable to the individual due to the social constraints of everyday interaction. Individuals become more aware of the effects of their behavior on others, and of the cues to which others are responding. Some persons, for example, may think that their frequent suggestions to others are motivated by their concern and helpfulness. In the T-group they may find out that others, in fact, perceive these acts as critical and hostile. Thus, having been made aware of the effects of their behavior on others, they then are in a position to either (1) modify their behavior to change the way others view it, or (2) introspectively examine the actual meaning of their behavior (e.g., were they really being hostile?). Whatever the outcome, the assumption is that these individuals are better off with this information than without it.

It is interesting to note the differences between the organization development approach using T-groups and mental health consultation as practiced by Caplan. Sensitivity training, with emphasis on the cathartic venting of feelings and resentments, and the freedom of group members to offer interpretations of each others' behavior, is clearly more similar to traditional group psychotherapy than is Caplanian consultation. Caplan would probably hold that the confrontation fostered in T-groups would tread on unconscious themes of some members, and they would be unable to cope with the results. In addition, once "word got around" of the self-disclosing nature of the groups, other members of the organization would feel too threatened to approach the consultant with work problems, lest they open themselves to being candidates for a group.

There is some controversy concerning the commitment to sensitivity training as a method of promoting change by OD practitioners. Burke argues that "the T-group as such is simply not a major OD device" (Burke, 1973, p. 198). On the other hand, Bennis (1969) and Kahn (1974) point out that the major OD intervention discussed in the literature tends to be some form of T-group experience. Bennis feels that OD is not "simply sensitivity training"; but confusion exists in people's minds because many OD cases that finally reach print focus almost exclusively on the T-group as the basic strategy of intervention.

While the popularity of sensitivity training can be documented in the early OD literature, the T-group has become less popular over the years for a number of reasons. For example, sensitivity sessions can serve the useful purpose of exposing participants to individuals they would normally avoid in daily contact, and provide an opportunity to learn something of the point of view and experience of the avoided and stereotyped other. But what of those organizational situations where the problems are not ones of interpersonal misunderstandings, but rather concern substantive issues of organizational policy? Here the members of the organization may understand *exactly* what the underlying difficulties are, any may strenuously disagree on their resolution. A T-group involving the oppressed employees of a feudal sweatshop and the management would more likely lead to a revolt than to the amiable resolve of "misunderstandings." In this instance, the workers need power and organization, not sensitivity training.

There are still other organizations that have managed to maintain a tenuous cohesion among their members despite basic differences on policy issues. Differences may be real and irreconcilable. In these instances, one may wonder whether sensitivity training should be attempted if there is a strong likelihood that the resultant effort will not resolve differences but simply help the participants see their differences more clearly. Bringing true dissension to the fore, and treating it as if it were simply a problem in communication, may serve to destroy the delicate balance that allowed for organizational continuity.

OD Research

There are not many empirical studies to support the claims of OD theorists. The field is long on theory and very short on empirical confirmation (Alderfer, 1977; Faucheux, Amado, & Laurent, 1982; Friedlander & Brown, 1974). In part, the paucity of research reflects the difficulty of doing controlled studies of change in complex organizations. In part, it also reflects the lack of interest in research and empirical confirmation among many OD practitioners. The research that is available demonstrates mixed results. Much of it consists of case studies, with the better controlled studies generally demonstrating more pessimistic conclusions (Porras, 1979).

The most informative case studies are those that honestly describe mistakes and the limits of what can be accomplished (see Mirvis & Berg, 1977, for examples of OD failures). For example, Walton (1977) studied eight firms that had undertaken comprehensive changes in work restructuring at specific localized work sites. These experiments initially were judged to be successful, but only some of them were adopted by the firm in its other locations. Walton concluded that diffusion of an innovative program was least likely to occur under the following conditions:

1. Inconsistencies in the initial design that lead to confusion about the key elements of the project.
2. Loss of support from levels of management above the experimental unit.
3. Premature turnover of leaders or consultants directly associated with the project.
4. Stress and crisis in the firm that leads to more authoritarian management.
5. Tension in the innovative unit's relations with other groups in the firm (e.g., staff in other units, supervisors, labor unions).
6. Excessive publicity about the innovative unit which leads to jealously on the part of staff in other units and disappointment as the unit's accomplishments turn out to be more modest than the initial claims indicated.
7. Inadequate diffusion of the results to other parts of the organization which isolates the original experiment and its leaders.

There are a small number of well-controlled OD studies demonstrating positive results. For example, one well-designed study can be seen in the work of Keys and Bartunek (1979), who conducted a complex OD training program with teachers in seven elementary schools in a Catholic archdiocese. Compared to a control group of teachers in nonparticipating schools, teachers who received the program reported more participation in school decisions and greater ability to deal with interpersonal conflicts. However, there tended to be a specificity of effects, in that the ability to deal with political factions in the schools was not affected by the program. This is not a surprising finding since this last topic was not covered in the program.

If an OD intervention is aimed at improving interpersonal functioning, how much generalization should there be to other behaviors in the work setting? Kimberly and Nielsen (1975) found that, as a result of an OD intervention in an automobile plant, changes occurred in group attitudes and perceptions, and in *quality* of product output but not in the level of production. The authors speculate that the reason production levels were not affected by OD was because, in this case, production levels were determined by corporate policy and market conditions and not by the efficiency of a single plant operation.

What these studies demonstrate is the need for specificity in behavior change research. Outcome measures need to be clearly delineated and linked to the intervention attempted. OD practice has been criticized because the interventions are not clearly described. The same criticism applies to the need to specify outcome measures and the relationship between outcome and intervention. For example, intervention aimed at improving interpersonal relations may or may not improve production. Kaplan (1979) believes that process-centered OD will increase production only in those instances in which there are interpersonal problems among employees who must work cooperatively. Process-centered OD should have less of an effect on already adequately functioning groups. Similarly OD may be inappropriate in organizations in which independent performance, not cooperation, is valued and rewarded.

OD Values: A Humanistic Orientation versus Power and Profit Motives

It is to their credit that the proponents of OD are explicit about the value context in which their activities take place. OD attempts to look at men and women as "whole persons," as people "in process." It encourages the expression of feelings and resentments, risk, "authenticity," and confrontation. The specific objectives of OD are heavily colored by its existential and humanistic underpinnings. OD operates on an "attitude change strategy" (Walton, 1965), a "truth-love" model (Bennis, 1969) based on humanistic values, rather than a "power strategy" (Gamson, 1968) based on conflict and coercion. Power considerations are more relevant to such approaches as social advocacy.

While OD is to be lauded for articulating a coherent set of social values, articulation is not the same as implementation. The joint goals of OD are to increase *both* organizational efficiency and human fulfillment. The assumption is that these values will go hand in hand: more actualized people should be more efficient workers. Everybody wins.

Given that OD consultants typically are paid by management, there may be a more than trivial bias that when productivity and fulfillment are at odds—as they often can be—OD should favor the former. As Friedlander and Brown (1974, p. 335) put it: "OD as a field runs the risk of encouraging and implementing subtle but persuasive forms of exploitation, curtailment of freedom, control of personality, violation of dignity, intrusion of privacy—all in the name of science and of economic and technological efficiency." OD, they state, "may well be another organizational palliative," engaged in "making some people happier at the job of making other people richer" (Ross, 1971, p. 583).

OD initially developed as part of the social change movement of the 1960s and early 1970s (Tichy, 1978). Its roots were as a social reform movement whose goals were to instill humanistic values in organizations by using specific group techniques. Krell (1981) charges that, over time, as the country turned in a more conservative direction, the unique values of OD became lost but the social technology remained.

> While the original practitioners made use of the technology to convert organizations to a "better" form of social sytem, today's practitioners, in the interest of making a living, are using the technology to perpetuate the original social system. The original practitioners were attempting social change; today's practitioners are building careers. (Krell, 1981, p. 322)

McLean, Sims, Mangham, and Tuffield (1982) agree that OD is in a period of transition but believe that some of the current criticism represents an overreaction against OD's original strongly humanistic stance. They state: "The cycle of fashion is such that not only has OD ceased to be fashionable, but the current fashion seems to require increasingly emphatic and colorful assertions of its demise" (McLean et al., 1982, p. 121). They believe that OD is maturing and is being modified in the following ways.

1.   Practitioners are becoming more comfortable with their own views and there is less emphasis on acquiring someone else's theories or techniques.

2.   Aspirations are becoming more modest. OD is slow and painstaking, requiring great patience. Small projects are being undertaken, with less rhetoric about "system-wide" change.

3.   OD's strongly humanistic stance about how people in organizations ought to act has been persistently criticized as unrealistic. In reality, people are motivated by much more self-interest. OD practitioners now rarely "preach" the gospel of trust, openness, and authenticity.

4.   The practice of some OD consultants has become more political. OD practitioners operate less as neutral facilitators, being more active in influencing events in the organizations in which they work.

Thus we see a major dilemma for OD as a social change strategy applied to business organizations. The early OD practitioners were able to convince business managers that humanizing work conditions and giving workers greater opportunities for participation and decision making would lead to increases in productivity. These predictions were borne out in many cases, otherwise OD would surely have had an early death. But change has been difficult to obtain because profit motives and humanism do not mix well. The members of corporate board rooms have not suddenly become "born-again" humanists. It is still the case that, in most instances, the psychological needs of workers are likely to be fulfilled only if doing so enhances profit margins.

Can OD Be Applied to Public and Professional Organizations?

OD values are appealing to some of those who work in the public sector, and there have been attempts to apply OD to schools, universities, governmental units, and human service agencies. Some of these have produced positive results (e.g., Sikes, Schlesinger, Kraus, Appley, & Carew, 1977; Schmuck & Runkel, 1975) but cautions also have been noted. Weisbord (1978) believes that OD is not likely to be successful in organizations in which independence is rewarded and there are no incentives for collaboration. He cites universities and medical centers as examples of organizations in which professionals are not rewarded for working together on a specific product. In these organizations, the major sources of reward and self-esteem are external to the organization. Being a team player does not provide much prestige. Furthermore, being a brilliant lecturer, a productive researcher, a superb diagnostician or therapist usually depend upon individual, not group effort. Prestige for these activities often comes from sources outside the organization (professional organizations, research granting institutions, and the like) and these external evaluations are used by the organization to reward performance. Activities which require high levels of participation (e.g., committee work) often are seen as wasting time and as activities that detract from "real" problems. Weisbord (1978, p. 23) concludes:

> If you want to humanize the performance of work, do not look to social-work agencies, mental health centers, or university departments of the humanities; instead, think "cardboard-box factories"; think "chemical businesses"; think "pet-food plants." These are the settings in which people have maximum incentive to engage in participative problem solving, to confront each other face-to-face, to stand or fail together in the daily performance of their tasks.

Goodstein (1978) is in basic agreement, and argues that focusing on interrelationships among members is not likely to be productive in organizations in which individuals are not required to work closely together. In organizations with high member independence, the OD consultant is advised to focus on clarifying organization goals and procedures around those issues in which cooperation might be important (e.g., agency mission, standards of practice, client scheduling, grading standards, student morale, and the like) and to avoid "process" discussions and exercises.

Given the nuances among different types of organizations, the wise OD consultant does not try to "sell" a particular method of operation simply because that happens to be a favorite procedure—one that the consultant knows best. OD work begins by assessing the organization's major needs and designing interventions to meet those needs. A decision to be made is whether to concentrate on structural and program changes or whether to focus on improvements in interpersonal processes. Both are important, as is the sequence in which these activities should occur. On the one hand, one could argue that, if people overcome their misunderstandings, they will work constructively on program changes. Conversely, it is likely that reducing job stresses by redesigning programs and the structure of work tasks also can provide the needed motivation for later focus on improvements in interpersonal relations. Equally possible is that focusing on interpersonal processes may not be needed if goals and task structure improve and motivation increases. The OD approach can provide useful tools for organizational self-improvement, but the specific procedures for organizational change must be carefully considered.

SUMMARY OF CONSULTATION ASSUMPTIONS

Regardless of specialized content or techniques, the essential similarity among consultants of the various perspectives is that they all are oriented toward a similar goal—that is, to improve human service and socialization institutions either through modifying their programs or by increasing the psychological sophistication and work capacity of the primary caregivers within these institutions. Consultants assume that communities have well-developed systems for providing human services, and that the greatest benefit can be obtained if their expertise is used to insure that these services are administered in such a way that stressful environmental conditions are minimized.

The consultant's long-term goal is to obtain some permanent change in the consultee or the consultee's institution. There would be little economic gain if all problems with a psychological component were called to a consultant's attention. Neither would there be any particular advantage if consultants were sought out for some particular difficulties; but over time, the nature of the problems referred to them remained the same. Consultants hope that their efforts will go beyond the specific case material brought to their attention. It is in this sense that consultation can be thought of as a radiating process (Kelly, 1970). Improved functioning by consultees or better programs developed by consultee institutions affect the client populations who are the beneficiaries of the improved service. Thus, the impact of consultation is most appropriately measured not just by changes in consultees but by changes in those who are served by the consultees.

It should be clear from the above that consultation does not denote a new profession independent of others. A consultant must have a background in some substantive content area that relates to understanding the human condition. The area of specialization need not be the traditional mental health professions—some would argue that the mental health fields represent too narrow a view of community life. But whatever the area, it must have a body of knowledge and skills that consultants can use in orienting the direction of their work. Nothing is sadder to see in the field than consultants who have nothing to offer the host organization, and who seem to assume that their mere presence alone will "make things happen."

The substantive areas from which a mental health consultant might draw are quite varied, including the range from urban planning, sociology, and public health nursing to the more traditional mental health "team"—psychiatry, psychology, and psychiatric social work. Caplan (1970) suggests that the consultant's particular expertise is in the mental health area. However, there are consultants who would prefer to describe their work as "psychological" or as "behavioral" rather than accept the language of health and illness. Other consultants would point out that their expertise is in "problem solving," so the help they provide is not circumscribed by a particular type of problem. Instead, they teach problem solving skills that should be applicable to work difficulties of almost any content.

Consultation to a Public Library:[2] An Example of Combining Perspectives

One usually thinks of a library as an archive or as an information center not as a place where psychological information or skills might be useful. Yet, as

---

[2] Material for this example was provided by Dr. John L. Werner, executive director, South Central Mental Health Center, Bloomington, Indiana.

is true for any open facility in which the public is encouraged to congregate, the library gets its share of marginally adjusted individuals whose behavior can be disruptive to others (Haas & Weatherley, 1981). In this example, a psychological consultant was approached by a staff member of a local community library for help in managing "difficult" patrons. The problem behaviors noted by the librarians included individuals who talked to themselves too loudly; patrons who seemed intoxicated; parents who left their children in the library for a good part of the day or evening while they went shopping, with subsequent acting-out behaviors by these unsupervised children; and angry, demanding patrons who expected librarians to bend rules for them or whose behavior toward the librarians was demeaning. The librarians were becoming increasingly frustrated by the demands being placed upon them to respond to situations that were beyond their traditional roles and the previous training they had received for these roles.

A consultant's response to a request of this sort depends on how the problem is conceptualized. A behavioral consultant would see the problem as involving skill deficits among the librarians and would probably initiate workshops in behavior management. For example, the workshops might provide practice in assertion, so the librarians would learn how to firmly insist that angry and demanding patrons obey library rules. Or, the consultant might teach the librarians how to help borderline individuals monitor their behavior, so they do not disturb others.

A Caplanian consultant would recognize that some skill training might be necessary, but would expect that the supervisory staff at the library would be in the best position to teach whatever specific skills were needed by librarians in their day-to-day contacts with patrons. Consultation with the supervisors might be initiated to increase their competence in behavioral management, so they then could translate the consultant's ideas into procedures that would more readily fit the library's mission and the typical operating style of librarians. A Caplanian consultant would be interested in difficulties of individual librarians if it seemed that these were due to lapses in professional objectivity. This might occur if the problems in the library were not common to all staff members but were unique to specific persons. For example, perhaps only one or two staff members had trouble with angry patrons, and some other staff members were upset by patrons who talked to themselves too loudly. The consultant then would concentrate on these individuals to help them overcome their specific work difficulties perhaps caused by personal problems.

The consultant with an organization development perspective initially would wonder why an organization that must contain some very talented people was not able to solve these problems on its own. Suspecting that there might not be adequate problem-solving mechanisms within the organization, the consultant would approach the request as an opportunity to develop appropriate organizational structures that could be used, not only for the immediate problem but for any that might arise subsequently.

In this example, the consultant began with just such a perspective. Contact was made first with the director of the library to assess his view of the problem and to obtain permission to embark on consultation. The director agreed, and initial interviews were conducted with key library personnel.

Interviews revealed widespread agreement among staff members that finding better methods for dealing with disruptive clients were needed; but, surprisingly, there had been no previous attempts to articulate policy on these matters. The consultant discovered that the director of the library had been reluctant to develop policies which, if implemented universally, might be offensive to some influential patrons. As a public institution, the library was dependent on citizen good will for its financial security. The director wanted to maintain good relations with citizens and feared that a crackdown on problem patrons might inadvertently include some of the library's strongest supporters. The staff sensed the director's concern; but since the matter was not discussed openly, it was never resolved. Staff members interpreted the lack of policy and procedures toward patrons as a reflection of the director's unwillingness to delegate responsibility and also a lack of trust in *them*.

This example demonstrates some of the complexities a consultant is likely to face in assessing the problems that are the focus of consultation. The librarians did lack knowledge and skill in dealing with disruptive patrons. However, behavioral skill training by itself would not be sufficient as long as the library administration had doubts about the wisdom of giving staff members the authority to deal with problem patrons. There needed to be a way for the librarians at all levels in the organization to begin working together on these problems, so trust between staff and administration could develop. The consultant came to the conclusion that there was an organizational problem imbedded in the call for help about problem patrons.

Since the library had no mechanisms to deal with librarian/patron relationships, a major goal of the consultation was to develop work groups to deal with articulating policies and procedures. The consultant decided that the best way to approach this task would be for the library staff to develop their own operating procedures which staff librarians could administer, with backup from supervisory personnel in those instances when special handling might be necessary.

The consultant initiated the process of work group formation by first meeting with the entire library staff in an open discussion of problem patrons. In this meeting, he provided an opportunity for staff members to voice their frustration and concern, and he increased staff involvement from the start by forming small discussion groups ("buzz" groups) to describe and rank patron problems that were of greatest concern. After the major problems were clarified, committees were formed for each problem area to develop appropriate policies and procedures. The job of the committees was not only to describe how each problem should be handled but to discuss contingency plans (e.g., what could go wrong and what alternative procedures might be necessary). It was this latter step that gave the library director the confidence that problem patrons could be handled by the staff. Competent procedures were developed and were codified into a librarian's handbook.

In this example, the consultant was guided primarily by an organizational perspective, but also provided knowledge of disordered behavior, and helped the librarians develop skills that could be used to develop procedures of their own. For example, the librarians had the same fears of persons who talked to themselves as did ordinary citizens. Fearing that such persons were "mentally ill" and would become "out of control" if asked to moderate their behavior, the librarians retreated and did nothing. They needed knowledge about mental disturbance and its behavioral effects to recognize that most disturbed persons are not dangerous. They also needed to acquire some interpersonal skills that would help them approach such persons calmly but firmly. The consultant was able to enlist colleagues from the mental health center who demonstrated skills that the librarians could then model and practice in role-play exercises. However, skill training by itself would not have been sufficient without the development of librarian-run task groups that gave the director confidence in his staff, and allowed the development of consistent policies toward problem patrons which the library administration then was willing to support.

CRITICAL COMMENTS

Not All Human Service Workers Can Benefit from Consultation

There are several problems confronting those attempting to develop a program of intervention based upon the above assumptions—problems that are not typically addressed by consultation theorists. To begin, one may ask whether it is reasonable to expect non-mental health personnel to perform psychological functions. The consultant *does* ask human service workers to concern themselves with the psychological components of their work. To those who respond that their training does not equip them to "dabble in the psyche of others," the consultant replies that their normal work functions are made more difficult when attempts are not made to understand and deal with behavior patterns of clients. There is accumulating evidence to support the consultant's claim that non-mental health personnel can be trained to respond in psychologically helpful ways (Durlak, 1979; Guerney, 1969). However, a problem is that not all can be so trained. Some individuals who have gravitated to community caregiving and socialization roles may be so deficient in interpersonal sensitivity and skill that no amount of training will improve their functioning. We are not referring to consultees who simply differ in values or interpersonal style from their consultants. Most consultants already know that they must guard themselves against the tendency to assume that all who disagree with their mission are of dubious mental health. We are referring to those individuals whose entry into a human service field was clearly in error and who are unamenable to change by a consultant despite his or her best effort.

All human service professions (including the mental health professions) contain a small minority of members whose adjustment is tenuous, and who should not be in work that requires sensitivity and responsiveness to others. Undoubtedly, the professions themselves could do a better screening of those who apply to their training programs. The consultant who finds these individuals in working with agencies has very few options. The point we are making here is simply that consultation should not be expected to be effective under all circumstances. There are primary caregivers who are not amenable to change. However, in working for institutional change from within organizational structures, the consultant hopes and expects that the majority will be basically competent and psychologically healthy and will be responsive to improving their work performance.

Consultation Is Impeded by Conflicting Goals between Agency and Consultant

A greater constraint on the work of consultants occurs when their goals and the primary goals of consultee institutions are so antithetical that consultees are prevented from acting in a psychologically helpful manner, although they have the skill and capacity to do so. It is here that the consultant encounters the greatest difficulties. Many community agencies have multifaceted missions, among which the psychological well-being of their clients may not be primary. These competing goals may be unstated, but nonetheless may be important motivators of behavior supported by powerful community sanctions. For example, agencies assigned formal caregiving, socialization, or rehabilitation functions might also be responding to community sentiments, such as the need to control those who disrupt the social order, economic motives (e.g., saving the taxpayer's dollar) or upholding social customs (e.g., the maintenance of racially segregated living patterns). Faced with agency goals that conflict with a psychological mission, the consultant may attempt to demonstrate that some divergent goals are not irreconcilable. For example, it may be possible to show that social control in a classroom need not be sacrificed by attending to the psychological needs of students, or that motivating welfare clients toward self-care may be more economical in the long run than demoralizing investigations followed by impersonally administered aid. However, if differences in goals are indeed irreconcilable, the consultant might find the time better spent outside the agency; for example, by working toward a change in community sentiments impinging on agency policy. The consultant and institution need not share all goals, but must be willing to work toward some meaningful common goals that are congruent with the values of both parties.

Gains from Consultation Can Be Used for Oppressive Purposes

An ethical issue raised by consultation concerns the ultimate use of the new knowledge and skills provided by the consultant. Consultants assume that its use will be benevolent and that primary caregivers are sincerely interested in the welfare of their clients. However, we also know that, in varying degrees, institution members are interested in the maintenance of their institution and their roles within it. What happens when values surrounding institutional maintenance and the welfare of clients conflict? How will skills, newly learned through consultation, be used? A case in point involves consultants who teach behavior modification skills that can be used oppressively in the service of social control or used benevolently to insure more effective learning. For example, a teacher who learns new techniques of behavioral management is likely to have a less-disruptive classroom, which in turn increases the possibility of decreased tension and acting-out behaviors and more effective learning. But increased control in the classroom *by itself* is a poor goal and one that can lead to stultifying oppression. The point is that consultants cannot simply assume that intervention automatically will improve a situation. The effects of their work can be good or bad and, without appropriate evaluation, they will never know.

Institutional Rigidity Limits Gains from Consultation

A final problem concerns the general responsiveness of institutions to the needs of clients served. Some community institutions charged with a helping mission may be resistant to change and yet may also so aggravate the conditions they are supposed to correct that no amount of internal repair initiated by a consultant can salvage effective functioning. Community agitation for more responsive institutions may be necessary. What complicates a clear assessment of the situation is that, from the point of view of the casual observer, institutions almost always appear more rigid than they are, and the danger of impatience with slow progress is ever present. Still, consultants are not magicians, and questions about feasibility of operation in unresponsive institutions must be faced, and methods for assessing the responsivity of institutions must be developed. In the words of one consultation theorist: "Resources are too limited to be dissipated in futile efforts to achieve currently unattainable ends" (Caplan, 1970, p. 41).

CONCLUSION: A COMPARISON AMONG CONSULTATION PERSPECTIVES

Three approaches to consultation were highlighted in this chapter. Since each was developed from a different conceptual tradition, the assumptions and procedures of each naturally reflect these differences.

The most widely cited point of view describing mental health consultation was developed by Gerald Caplan. Hence we selected Caplan's psychodynamic views as the starting point for our discussion. Mental health consultation, as initially developed by Caplan, was focused on the consultee, or primary caregiver. Case-centered consultation was seen as the entry point— as the way to reach the consultee to effect enduring changes in attitudes and behavior. The problems of the consultee could be deficiencies in knowledge or skill, but the problems of greatest interest to Caplan were those described as "lapses in professional objectivity." These were hypothesized to be caused by unresolved personal problems of which the consultee was probably unaware, or at least was resistant to explore. With such a clearly clinical intrapsychic orientation, there was a need to sharply distinguish consultation from formal psychotherapy. Compared to psychotherapy, consultation had a more restricted scope. The consultant was interested in the consultee's conflicts only as they might affect on-the-job performance; aspects of the consultee's personal life were off-limits to investigation. Furthermore, the content of personal conflicts was never explored directly, and was dealt with only if they could be displaced onto case material. It was expected that clarifying the case and achieving an improved case outcome would help dissipate the consultee's problem also, to the extent that it was projected onto the case material.

A number of mental health consultants believe that the intrapsychic orientation outlined above is much too narrow. By concentrating on the personality of the consultee, roles within the organization as well as organizational characteristics that impinge upon individual behavior are too easily overlooked. Generally, mental health consultation has become more eclectic, borrowing from organizational theory and social and environmental psychology. Depending upon background and training, the consultant offers help at a number of organizational levels (line staff, supervisors, or administrators) and for a variety of problems (low morale, lacks of knowledge or skill, deficiencies in interagency linking patterns, and the like). Mental health consultation has become so diverse that it can be misleading to speak of a unitary consultation perspective.

Still, there is some agreement that, by focusing primarily on work problems rather than on agency personnel, the consultant is allowed a less-defensive entry. Slowly, over time, as the consultant gains the confidence of organization members, the focus of consultation may change. The greatest benefit to the organization is expected to accrue through program-centered consultation; and the consultant is more likely to be asked to work on programmatic concerns after demonstrating competence in handling other agency requests. This slow process of trust-building can be contrasted with the organization development approach that requires an initial commitment to self-examination as a *prerequisite* for consultation.

Organization development (OD) developed from an orientation quite different from the intrapsychic formulation of Caplan. OD practitioners, heavily influenced by Kurt Lewin and gestalt psychology, focused on the interaction of environmental pressures and individual characteristics. An organization's "environment" consisted of both structural and psychosocial elements, the latter referring to the processes by which individuals within the setting interact. These processes proved to be the primary interest of OD specialists.

Organization development seems best suited to problems of distrust, alienation, and poor morale in organizations that are engendered by faulty interpersonal communication and interaction. Poor communication leads to a downward spiral of misunderstanding, inaccurate perception, and further misunderstanding. Getting people together in open communication in which honest feedback can be transmitted is one of the primary goals of the OD specialist. It is expected that aware and interpersonally honest personnel will lead to more humane and effective institutions and organizations. But these characteristics need to exist to a moderate degree as a prior condition, before organization development can be initiated. Basic to OD work is member motivation and commitment, and minimal organizational defensiveness. Because OD activity is more direct and confrontive, more can be accomplished in a brief time period. But in order to tolerate confrontation, consultee motivation and receptivity must be high. Honest feedback falls on deaf ears if those for whom it is intended are unwilling to receive the message.

Behavioral consultation has its roots in clinical theory and practice. Initially, behavioral consultants worked as clinicians applying a learning-based technology to difficult management problems. This work was moved from the clinic to more real-life settings for two main reasons: The clinician did not control the important reinforcers in the patient's life, and behavior change was more likely to be maintained if reinforcing stimuli could be developed in the patient's natural environment.

The initial efforts of behavioral consultation were case-centered, aimed at demonstrating that stimulus control over difficult behavior could be maintained by reinforcement "mediators" in the patient's environment. The mediator is the consultee in Caplan's typology, so translating across consultation perspectives, what was accomplished was "consultee-centered case consultation" with an emphasis on providing the consultee with new knowledge and skills. In this work, personal characteristics of consultees are not considered, except as they may interfere with the successful implementation of behavioral programming. Communication patterns and relationships between members of the organization or setting also are not given primary attention. Unfortunately, these member characteristics and organizational problems can be the very issues that torpedo the successful execution of behavioral programs.

More recently, behavioral psychologists have become interested in fostering change at community levels. To the extent that total control of the environment will be required by these efforts, opportunities for behavioral management in the community probably will remain limited. There is a literature on the successful application of "token economies," but these programs have been undertaken primarily in closed institutions (mental hospitals, prisons, and the like) that already exert nearly complete control over their members. It is unlikely that society would allow the behavioral consultant to dictate the rules that govern behavior in other natural settings.

There is still unexplored potential in the behavioral approach, which we can see if we shift the focus of discussion slightly. Rather than continuing the preoccupation with behavioral "control" and its attendant problems, we should remember that the behaviorist also is providing us with a message about *incentives*. If desired community behaviors are reinforced, their frequency of occurrence is likely to increase. We need only be clear about the desirable behaviors to be encouraged, and be willing to provide incentives for their performance. Are we willing to meaningfully and consistently reward pro-social behaviors, like citizen participation and responsibility? Coercion would not be required; much could be accomplished through voluntary incentives as described in the experiments aimed at reducing littering and increasing bus ridership. However, we should remember that given the present structure of society, there are realistic limits to a plan based solely on incentives. In a society in which rewards are distributed unevenly, unrelated to performance, and in which there is often no relationship between wealth and desirable behavior (e.g., is the TV entertainer really more socially useful than the garbage collector?), a meaningful behavioristic society based on voluntary incentives is a long way off.

We close this chapter by returning to the basic similarity among the consultation perspectives with regard to community change. All focus on the improvement of existing social institutions. All hope to expand the programmatic scope of agencies and organizations. Community life is expected to improve as service delivery becomes more responsive and psychologically sophisticated. But what if agencies, and personnel within them, are unwilling or unable to change? These more pessimistic outcomes lead to the considerations described in the next two chapters.

References

Alderfer, C. P. Organization development. *Annual Review of Psychology*, 1977, *28*, 197–223.

Altrocchi, J. Mental health consultation. In S. E. Golann & C. Eisdorfer (Eds.), *Handbook of community mental health* (pp. 477–508). New York: Appleton-Century-Crofts, 1972.

Altrocchi, J., Spielberger, C. D., & Eisdorfer, C. Mental health consultation with groups. *Community Mental Health Journal*, 1965, *1*, 127–134.

Benne, K. D., Bradford, L. P., & Lippett, R. The laboratory method. In L. P. Bradford, J. R. Gibb, & K. D. Benne (Eds.), *T-Group theory and laboratory method* (pp. 15–44). New York: John Wiley & Sons, 1964.

Bennis, W. G. *Organization development: Its nature, origins and perspectives.* Reading, Mass.: Addison-Wesley Publishing, 1969.

Bowers, D. OD techniques and their results in 23 organizations: The Michigan ICL study. *Journal of Applied Behavioral Science*, 1973, *9*, 21–43.

Blake, R. R., Mouton, J. S., & Sloma, R. L. The union-management intergroup laboratory: Strategy for resolving intergroup conflict. *Journal of Applied Behavioral Science*, 1965, *1*, 25–57.

Briscoe, R. V., Hoffman, D. B., & Bailey, J. S. Behavioral community psychology: Training a community board to problem solve. *Journal of Applied Behavior Analysis*, 1975, *8*, 157–168.

Burke, W. W. Organization development. *Professional Psychology*, May 1973, 194–200.

Burke, W. W. (Ed.). *New technologies in organization development*. La Jolla, Calif.: University Associates, 1975.

Burke, W. W. Changing trends in organization development. In W. W. Burke (Ed.), *Current issues and strategies in organization development*. New York: Human Sciences Press, 1977.

Caplan, G. *The theory and practices of mental health consultation*. New York: Basic Books, 1970.

Cherniss, C. *Professional burnout in human service organizations*. New York: Praeger Publishers, 1980.

Cole, R. E. *Work, mobility and participation: A comparative study of American and Japanese Industry*. Berkeley: University of California Press, 1979.

Conant, E. H., & Kilbridge, M. D. An interdisciplinary analysis of job enlargement: Technology, costs and behavioral implications. *Indiana Labor Relations Review*, 1965, *18*, 377–395.

Cowen, E. L. Help is where you find it: Four informal helping groups. *American Psychologist*, 1982, *37*, 385–395.

Cowen, E. L., Gesten, E. L., Boike, M., Norton, P., Wilson, A. B., & DeStefano, M. A. Hairdressers as caregivers. I. Descriptive profile of interpersonal help-giving involvements. *American Journal of Community Psychology*, 1979, *7*, 633–648.

Cowen, E. L., McKim, B. J., & Weissberg, R. P. Bartenders as informal, interpersonal help-agents. *American Journal of Community Psychology*, 1981, *9*, 715–729.

Davis, L. E. The design of jobs. *Industrial Relations*, 1966, *6*, 21–45.

Davison, G. C., & Stuart, R. B. Behavior therapy and civil liberties. *American Psychologist*, 1975, *30*, 755–763.

Doane, J. A., & Cowen, E. L. Interpersonal help-giving of family practice lawyers. *American Journal of Community Psychology*, 1981, *9*, 547–558.

Durlak, J. A. Comparative effectiveness of paraprofessional and professional helpers. *Psychological Bulletin*, 1979, *86*, 80–92.

Everett, P. B., Hayward, S. C., & Meyers, A. W. The effects of a token reinforcement on bus ridership. *Journal of Applied Behavior Analysis*, 1974, *7*, 1–9.

Faucheux, C., Amado, G., & Laurent, A. Organizational development and change. *Annual Review of Psychology*, 1982, *33*, 343–370.

Fawcett, S. B., Mathews, R. M., & Fletcher, R. K. Some promising dimensions for behavioral community technology. *Journal of Applied Behavior Analysis*, 1980, *13*, 505–518.

Felner, R. D., Primavera, J., Farber, S. S., & Bishop, T. A. Attorneys as caregivers during divorce. *American Journal of Orthopsychiatry*, 1982, *52*, 323–336.

Ford, D. H., & Urban, H. B. Psychotherapy. *Annual Review of Psychology*, 1967, *18*, 333–372.

Ford, R. N. *Motivation through work itself.* New York: Amenaan Management Association, 1969.

Foxx, R. M., & Schaeffer, M. H. A company-based lottery to reduce the personal driving of employees. *Journal of Applied Behavior Analysis,* 1981, *14,* 273–285.

Friedlander, F., & Brown, L. D. Organization development. *Annual Review of Psychology,* 1974, *25,* 313–341.

Gamson, W. A. *Power and discontent.* Homewood, Ill.: Dorsey Press, 1968.

Geller, E. S. Applications of behavior analysis to litter control. In D. Glenwick & L. Jason (Eds.), *Behavioral community psychology: Progress and prospects.* New York: Praeger Publishers, 1980.

Glenwick, D., & Jason, L. *Behavioral community psychology: Progress and prospects.* New York: Praeger Publishers, 1980.

Goldstein, A. P., Heller, K., & Sechrest, L. B. *Psychotherapy and the psychology of behavior change.* New York: John Wiley & Sons, 1966.

Goldstein, A. P., & Kanfer, F. H. (Eds.). *Maximizing treatment gains: Transfer enhancement in psychotherapy.* New York: Academic Press, 1979.

Goldstein, A. P., Monti, P. J., Sardino, T. J., & Green, D. J. *Police crisis intervention.* Kalamazoo, Mich.: Behaviordelia, 1977.

Golembiewski, R. T., Hilles, R., & Kagno, M. S. A longitudinal study of flexi-time effects: Some consequences of an OD structural intervention. *Journal of Applied Behavioral Science,* 1974, *10,* 503–532.

Goodstein, L. D. Organization development in bureaucracies: Some caveats and cautions. In W. W. Burke (Ed.), *The cutting edge: Current theory and practice in organization development.* La Jolla, Calif.: University Associates, 1978.

Greene, B. F., Bailey, J. S., & Barber, F. An analysis and reduction of disruptive behavior on school buses. *Journal of Applied Behavior Analysis,* 1981, *14,* 177–192.

Guerney, B. G., Jr. (Ed.). *Psychotherapeutic agents: New roles for nonprofessionals, parents and teachers.* New York: Holt, Rinehart & Winston, 1969.

Guest, R. H. Quality of work life—Learning from Tarrytown. *Harvard Business Review,* July–August 1979, 76–87.

Gurin, G., Veroff, J., & Feld, S. *Americans view their mental health: A nationwide survey.* New York: Basic Books, 1960.

Haas, L. J., & Weatherley, D. Community psychology in the library: Potentials for consultation. *American Journal of Community Psychology,* 1981, *9,* 109–122.

Heller, K. Facilitative conditions for consultation with community agencies. *The Personnel and Guidance Journal,* 1978, *56,* 419–423.

Holland, J. G. Behaviorism: Part of the problem or part of the solution? *Journal of Applied Behavior Analysis,* 1978, *11,* 163–174.

Hunnius, G., Garson, G., & Case, J. *Workers' control.* New York: Random House, 1973.

Jason, L. A., Zolik, E. S., & Matese, F. Prompting dog owners to pick up dog droppings. *American Journal of Community Psychology,* 1979, *7,* 339–351.

Jason, L. A., & Zolik, E. S. Follow-up data on two dog-litter reduction interventions. *American Journal of Community Psychology,* 1980, *8,* 737–741.

Kahn, R. L. Organization development: Some problems and proposals. *Journal of Applied Behavioral Science,* 1974, *10,* 485–502.

Kanfer, F. H., & Goldstein, A. P. *Helping people change: A textbook of methods.* New York: Pergamon Press, 1975.

Kaplan, R. E. The utility of maintaining work relationships openly: An experimental study. *Journal of Applied Behavioral Science, 1979, 15,* 41–59.

Kelly, J. G. The quest for valid preventive interventions. In C. D. Spielberger (Ed.), *Current topics in clinical and community psychology* (Vol. 2, pp. 183–207). New York: Academic Press, 1970.

Keys, C. B., & Bartunek, J. M. Organization development in schools: Goal agreement, process skills, and diffusion of change. *Journal of Applied Behavioral Science, 1979, 15,* 61–78.

Kiesler, F. Programming for prevention. In B. Denner & R. H. Price (Eds.), *Community mental health: Social action and reaction* (pp. 101–111). New York: Holt, Rinehart & Winston, 1973.

Kimberly, J. R., & Nielsen, W. R. Organization development and change in organizational performance. *Administrative Science Quarterly, 1975, 20,* 191–206.

Knoblock, P., & Goldstein, A. P. *The lonely teacher.* Boston: Allyn & Bacon, 1971.

Krasner, L. (Ed.). *Environmental design and human behavior: A psychology of the individual in society.* New York: Pergamon Press, 1980.

Krell, T. C. The marketing of organization development: Past, present and future. *Journal of Applied Behavioral Science, 1981, 17,* 309–323.

Larsen, J. K. *The impact of consultation: Executive Summary.* Paper presented at the annual meeting of the American Psychological Association, August 1982.

Mahoney, M. J., & Arnkoff, D. Cognitive and self-control therapies. In S. L. Garfield & A. E. Bergin (Eds.), *Handbook of psychotherapy and behavior change: An empirical analysis.* New York: John Wiley & Sons, 1978.

Mann, P. A. Establishing a mental health consultation program with a police department. *Community Mental Health Journal, 1971, 7,* 118–126.

Mann, P. A., & Iscoe, I. Mass behavior and community organization: Reflections on a peaceful demonstration. *American Psychologist, 1971, 26,* 108–113.

Mannino, F. V., & Shore, M. F. Research in mental health consultation. In S. E. Golann & C. Eisdorfer (Eds.), *Handbook of community mental health* (pp. 755–777). New York: Appleton-Century-Crofts, 1972.

Mannino, F. V., & Shore, M. F. Effecting change through consultation. In F. V. Mannino, B. W. MacLennan, & M. F. Shore (Eds.), *The practice of mental health consultation* (pp. 25–46). New York: Gardner Press, 1975.

Margulies, N., & Raia, A. P. *Conceptual foundations of organizational development.* New York: McGraw-Hill, 1978.

Marks, A. R. N. *An investigation of modifications of job design in an industrial situation and their effects on some measures of economic productivity.* Unpublished doctoral dissertation, University of California, Berkeley, 1954.

McLean, A. J., Sims, D. B. P., Mangham, I. L., & Tuffield, D. *Organization development in transition: Evidence of an evolving profession.* Chichester, England: John Wiley & Sons, 1982.

Mirvis, P. H., & Berg, D. N. *Failures in organization development and change: Cases and essays for learning.* New York: John Wiley & Sons, 1977.

Moos, R. H. *Evaluating correctional and community settings.* New York: John Wiley & Sons, 1975.

Nietzel, M. T., Winett, R. A., MacDonald, M. L., & Davidson, W. S. *Behavioral approaches to community psychology*. New York: Pergamon Press, 1977.

Nystrom, P. Designing jobs and assigning employees. In P. C. Nystrom & W. H. Starbuck (Eds.), *Handbook of organizational design* (Vol. 2), Remodeling organizations and their environments (pp. 272–301). New York: Oxford University Press, 1981.

O'Leary, K. D., & Drabman, R. Token reinforcement programs in the classroom: A review. *Psychological Bulletin,* 1971, *75,* 379–398.

O'Neil, P., & Trickett, E. J. *Community consultation*. San Francisco: Jossey-Bass, 1982.

Patterson, G. R. Behavioral intervention procedures in the classroom and in the home. In A. E. Bergin & S. L. Garfield (Eds.), *Handbook of psychotherapy and behavior change: An empirical analysis* (pp. 751–775). New York: John Wiley & Sons, 1971.

Plog, S. C., & Ahmed, P. I. *Principles and techniques of mental health consultation*. New York: Plenum, 1977.

Porras, J. I. The comparative impact of different OD techniques and intervention intensities. *Journal of Applied Behavioral Science,* 1979, *15,* 156–178.

Reppucci, N. D., & Saunders, J. T. Social psychology of behavior modification: Problems of implementation in natural settings. *American Psychologist,* 1974, *29,* 649–660.

Ross, R. OD for whom? *Journal of Applied Behavioral Science,* 1971, *7,* 58–85.

Schmuck, R. A., & Miles, M. B. (Eds.). *Organization development in schools*. Palo Alto, Calif.: National Press Books, 1971.

Schmuck, R. A., & Runkel, P. J. *Handbook of organization development in schools*. Palo Alto, Calif.: National Press Books, 1972.

Schmuck, R. A., & Runkel, P. J. Integrating organizational specialists into school districts. In W. W. Burke (Ed.), *New technologies in organization development: I* (pp. 168–200). La Jolla, Calif.: University Associates, 1975.

Seashore, S. E., & Bowers, D. G. Durability of organizational change. *American Psychologist,* 1970, *25,* 227–233.

Sikes, W., Schlesinger, L., Kraus, W., Appley, D., & Carew, D. Two approaches to collaboration and change in higher education. In W. W. Burke (Ed.), *Current issues and strategies in organization development* (pp. 264–304). New York: Human Sciences Press, 1977.

Smith, B. M., Schumaker, J. B., Schaeffer, J., & Sherman, J. A. Increasing participation and improving the quality of discussions in seventh-grade social studies classes. *Journal of Applied Behavior Analysis,* 1982, *15,* 97–110.

Spielberger, C. D. A mental health consultation program in a small community with limited professional mental health resources. In E. L. Cowen, E. A. Gardner, & M. Zax (Eds.), *Emergent approaches to mental health problems* (pp. 214–236). New York: Appleton-Century-Crofts, 1967.

Stolz, S., Wienckowski, L. A., & Brown, B. S. Behavior modification: A perspective on critical issues. *American Psychologist,* 1975, *30,* 1027–1048.

Tharp, R. G., & Wetzel, R. J. *Behavior modification in the natural environment*. New York: Academic Press, 1969.

Tichy, N. M. Demise, absorption or renewal for the future of organization development. In W. W. Burke (Ed.), *The cutting edge: Current theory and practice in organization development.* La Jolla, Calif.: University Associates, 1978.

Trist, E. L., & Bamforth, R. Some social and psychological consequences of the long wall method of coal-getting. *Human Relations,* 1951, *4,* 3–38.

Trist, E. L., Higgin, G. W., Murray, H., & Pollack, A. B. *Organizational choice.* London: Tavistock, 1963.

Walton, R. E. Two strategies of social change and their dilemmas. *Journal of Applied Behavioral Science,* 1965, *1,* 167–179.

Walton, R. E. The diffusion of new work structures: Explaining why success didn't take. In P. H. Mirvis and D. N. Berg (Eds.), *Failures in organization development and change: Cases and essays for learning.* New York: John Wiley & Sons, 1977.

Weisbord, M. R. Input- versus output-focused organizations: Notes on a contingency theory of practice. In W. W. Burke (Ed.), *The cutting edge: Current theory and practice in organization development.* La Jolla, Calif.: University Associates, 1978.

Winett, R. A., & Winkler, R. C. Current behavior modification in the classroom: Be still, be quiet, be docile. *Journal of Applied Behavior Analysis,* 1972, *5,* 499–504.

Wolf, M. M., Phillips, E. L., & Fixsen, D. L. The teaching family: A new model for the treatment of deviant child behavior in the community. In S. W. Bijou & L. Ribies-Inesta (Eds.), *First symposium on behavior modification in Mexico.* New York: Academic Press, 1972.

Alternative Settings and Social Change*

* This chapter was written by Shulamit Reinharz.

THE ALTERNATIVE AS AN ANTIBUREAUCRATIC COLLECTIVE

CONSULTING TO THE ALTERNATIVE SETTING

Three Alternative Settings: A High School, A Mental Health Service, and A Women's Health Center

In Cambridge, Massachusetts, there is a high school designed specifically for working-class youth. Established in 1971, this school has several unconventional features. Students, who pay no tuition, constitute the majority of the members of all the school committees, including teacher-hiring and policy-making. Students are thus decision-makers in their school. In addition, school staff divide their income equally and make do with lower salaries than those available in the public schools. The school's curriculum combines basic skill education, job preparation, and consciousness-raising courses, such as the history of the working class (Graubard, 1979). The school's philosophy is centered on the concept of a "just community" (Kohlberg & Candee, 1981) which includes property sharing and participation in decision-making. According to test results, students who attend this alternative school have shown a greater than expected increase in their level of moral reasoning (see Snarey, Reimer, and Kohlberg, 1982).

* * * * *

Since 1972, the Southwest Denver Community Mental Health Services, Inc., (serving an area of 105,000) has relied on families in the community instead of mental hospitals to help people who are undergoing acute suicidal, homicidal, or psychotic crises. Such people are brought to the family's home and then heavily medicated for two or three days in order to "sleep out the psychosis." After the crisis, family members care for the patient who in turn responds to pressures to act normally in a stranger's home. After an average of 10 days, during which time one other patient may be in residence, the patient returns home or is helped to find another suitable environment. While living with the foster family, the patient is visited by social workers and psychiatrists, but most of the patient's interaction takes place with the "home sponsor."

Families and single persons with different lifestyles have been selected as "home sponsors." The heterogeneity of "home sponsors" enables mental health personnel to match patients with the most appropriate environment. "Home sponsors" are on retainer ($100–200/month) with the mental health agency, and are paid generously on a daily basis when they actually care for a patient. At any time there are 3 to 5 homes in the system and to date 15 homes have taken part. One of these families has housed 175 acutely distressed persons. This innovative mental health service system also has a community board composed of local legislators and citizens. The function of the board is to encourage community acceptance, raise funds, supply housing and employment opportunities for patients after their home stay, and recruit volunteers to serve patients as advocates and companions.

Between 1972 and 1979, 600 people or 85 percent of all the acute cases in the Southwest Denver catchment area were placed in family homes rather than in an acute psychiatric hospital ward (Brook, 1980). This drastic decline in hospital use for acute psychotic episodes has produced a 40 percent financial saving. In addition, six-month follow-up research comparing the effects of community homes and state hospitalization, using a randomized controlled design, showed that the home group patients achieved better psychological status and were more satisfied with services than were their counterparts (Polak and Kirby, 1976).

*   *   *   *   *

The Feminist Women's Health Center founded in Los Angeles in 1971 is one of 1,200 small health-oriented groups run by women throughout the country (Gottlieb, 1980) to provide well-woman gynecological care and public education, and to create changes in the health care establishment. Women who work and volunteer in these centers criticize conventional medicine which, in their view, keeps women ignorant of how their bodies function, focuses on disease rather than health and prevention, and treats normal processes such as childbirth and menopause as if they were diseases (Women's Self Help Clinics, 1976). Women who establish these centers are angry that modern medical treatment, such as carcinogenic estrogen therapy (DES), has produced devastating iatrogenic problems for women. They believe that abortion is unnecessarily difficult to obtain, and that its control is too much in the hands of physicians rather than the women themselves (Schlesinger and Bart, 1983).

By contrast, the Feminist Women's Health Center staff arranges for women clients to give each other treatment, learn about their own bodies, and do their own and each other's breast and cervical examinations, diaphragm fittings, pregnancy screenings, blood pressure and anemia tests, pap smears and uterine checks. They also make films about such practices to educate other women and to facilitate the formation of women's health groups around the country. When women visit the health clinic they usually are scheduled to meet with other women who have a similar health concern. Thus, the value placed on privacy and confidentiality in conventional medical practice are replaced by a preference for self-disclosure and mutual education. For the sake of completeness and the fostering of sisterhood and empowerment, case histories are done in groups. Group discussions bring new clinical information to light that the client may have overlooked. This process of exploring a client's case through group dialogue is called "herstory" and contrasts with what its advocates consider the intimidating, routinized, incomplete history-taking characteristic of conventional medical practice.

The clinic stresses participation and egalitarianism so that significant healing relationships can develop between patients (Marieskind and Ehrenreich, 1975). The staff attempt to minimize status differentiation among staff and between staff and clients, and try to reach out to minority women. However, their purpose extends beyond the health needs of individual women to the health needs of all women. This is accomplished by disseminating information, encouraging others to follow their lead, and challenge conventional medical practice (Peugh, 1982). Although critical of mainstream medical practice, the Los Angeles Feminist Women's Health Center cooperates with traditional services by making referrals to physicians. Other women's health centers may be more radical or conservative in their goals, practices, and relation to mainstream services (The Women and Mental Health Project, 1976).

AN OVERVIEW OF ISSUES CONCERNING ALTERNATIVE SETTINGS

The three examples just described were developed by groups greatly dissatisfied with the services available from dominant institutions. There are, of course, other actions dissatisfied people can take. They may engage in protest activities, appeal to elected officials, or become apathetic. In this chapter we will focus on the creation of alternative settings as a strategy for changing service systems that are not responsive to the needs of citizens or clients. We also will discuss ways in which psychologists can and do relate to this strategy of alleviating individual and community problems. Our analytic perspective will be ecological, that is, we will consider the alternative setting within the context of the community of which it is a part.

The Ubiquity of Alternative Settings

The concept of alternative services is popularly thought of as a phenomenon confined to the late 1960s—the period of the counterculture—but this is misleading. Alternative settings and services have *always* existed (Yinger, 1982) and will continue to be created whenever there is tension between dominant and opposing ideologies and groups. Although the development of alternatives has consistently been part of the force for social change in this country, the specific form that alternatives have taken and the problems they have addressed have changed over time (e.g., communes and settlement houses were innovations of the 19th century, whereas child guidance clinics, free schools, and halfway houses were created in the 20th).

Alternatives have developed under wide-ranging socioeconomic conditions. For example, during the Great Depression, producer cooperatives were formed by workers attempting to establish viable employment opportunities (Aldrich & Stern, 1978). In the late 1960s and early 1970s, when the

country experienced a period of economic growth and social reform, telephone hotlines, free medical clinics, and alternative schools were created.
Alternatives can flourish during such periods because resources for organizational experimentation become available. At times of economic retrenchment, alternatives develop because there is a sense of urgency.

It should be noted that those groups which challenge the status quo
actually support dominant American values, such as the desirability of
change, the efficacy of voluntary association, and the social utility of competition among people. Just as alternative settings are not limited to a specific
historical or economic period, they are not confined to people with one
particular type of political ideology, left or right. In sum, because alternatives are consistent with dominant American values, and because our society is imperfect, alternatives have been ubiquitous in American society.

The Rationales for Creating Alternative Settings: Choice, Diversity, and Social Change

Alternative settings represent a service option for people who desire more
choice in meeting their needs. Increased choice is particularly important
when people perceive standard services as inaccessible, ineffective, costly,
restrictive, punitive, or alienating. Such negative evaluations are not an
uncommon assessment of our schools, mental hospitals, prisons, nursing
homes, and other services. Citizen complaints about conventional human
services are commonplace. Nearly every day, local newspapers publish stories of groups or individuals who are so disillusioned with the quality of
services that they create their own alternatives. Child Find, for instance, is
an organization set up by parents dissatisfied with the attitudes and abilities
of police regarding their missing children. Similarly, the nonprofit organization, Golden Cradle, Inc., was established by an automobile spare parts
distributor dissatisfied by professional adoption agencies which had caused
him and his wife years of frustration. His alternative service introduced
many new ideas. First, like the women's clinic which uses groups to empower women, Golden Cradle arranges monthly meetings among families
who want to adopt a child. These families post advertisements offering help
to pregnant women who want to give up their children for adoption. An
interested woman is housed with one of these families until she gives birth.
All of her expenses are paid by another family, in the support system, whom
she never meets. Thus the pregnant woman obtains care for herself and the
child, the adopting families have confidence in the prenatal care of the
mother and child, and the families offer each other assistance. In three
years, the organization has arranged 180 adoptions in this unconventional
way and has provoked professional organizations to reexamine their relatively less-successful approaches (McBride, 1983, p. A17). One source of
the Golden Cradle's success is its redefinition of adoption from a problem of
couples competing against each other for a child into a shared community
problem on which couples and pregnant women can cooperate.

The Golden Cradle illustrates the way individuals create alternatives to obtain more choice in meeting their needs. This choice leads to social change when mainstream services change their procedures or when community norms are altered. Alternative settings can accomplish two major goals with regard to social problems. The first is to address the immediate needs of their members or clients. The second is to challenge and change society more generally by promoting a new set of values or laws.

The Functional Effects of Alternative Settings: For the Individual and the Community

As our examples show, alternative settings may be very functional in meeting the needs of clients. Schlesinger and Bart (1983) have shown that participation in an alternative human service as a staff member also is likely to have an empowering effect (i.e., lead to a greater sense of competence and autonomy) on the staff.

Alternative services also may be functional for the community as a whole. For example, if there are both mainstream and alternative services in a community, their competition for clients can enhance the quality of both. Thus, if parents withdraw their children from public schools and send them to alternative schools, we can expect public schools to attempt to change in order to reattract these children and the public funding they would bring.

If the innovative strategies of alternative services are successful and visible, conventional service workers may be motivated to adopt their practices. Ultimately, the intention of most creators of alternative services is to change society in precisely this way. The most common form of an alternative's impact is its incorporation by a more conventional social institution. Thus, for example, when the first alternative high school in Cambridge, Massachusetts, was launched, "conservative school-board members . . . wanted to close it down" because it was too permissive (Graubard, 1979, p. 53). But now the school board has incorporated several different alternatives and is proud of them.

Theorists of alternative services have mixed assessments of such an incorporation. On the one hand, it is clear in the case of the school that its creators were successful in convincing people in power that the school system should be diversified to meet the needs of a varied population. Similarly, the fact that the alternative school was incorporated into the public school system probably contributed to its survival. On the other hand, by having alternative schools managed by the mainstream school system, it is possible that their special spirit and mission will be eliminated. When alternatives are integrated into the mainstream, their unique characteristic may be distorted.

The Dysfunctional Effects of Alternative Settings: For the Individual and the Community

We also must keep in mind that alternative settings may be dysfunctional, either for the individual or the community. Because alternative settings do not usually have the resources to hire top-level staff (McShane & Oliver,

1978), it is possible that clients of alternative services may get less than optimal care. Another dysfunctional effect is that workers in alternative settings are likely to experience a great deal of stress or burnout (see below). Similarly, the proliferation of alternative settings may deplete the resources of a community or may discourage a community from acting on its problems if the failure of one alternative becomes thought of as a reason not to attempt other solutions.

The creation of an alternative service may have the ironic effect of leading the public to believe that the problem addressed by the alternative has been solved when in fact it has been solved only for a segment of the population. For instance, school administrators sometimes use the existence of one alternative school to argue against the need for additional alternatives. The success of one feminist counseling center in Philadelphia made it difficult for other alternative centers to raise funds because potential funders believed one was enough for the women of the city (Galper & Washburne, 1976). Similarly, the success of rape crisis centers founded and staffed by young white middle-class feminists may indirectly function to lessen the chances that black women will receive proper rape services (Noel, 1980). This is because service-providers with a feminist interpretation of rape may not be attractive to lower-income black women. These women may not use rape crisis center services unless they are located or known in the black community. Yet the larger community is likely to overlook the need for additional services when *some* alternative services for *some* women do exist.

Thus, while alternatives solve some problems, they may create others or have their effectiveness impeded by certain community processes. For these reasons, alternatives require serious study to determine how they can be a significant method for providing needed social change. In the following section, we offer some frameworks in which the study of alternatives has been conducted.

ALTERNATIVES IN THE FRAMEWORK OF THE EVOLUTION OF SOCIAL PROBLEMS

Spector and Kitsuse (1977) have outlined a four-stage process (summarized below) showing how alternative settings develop in response to social problems ignored or minimized by the general public or by personnel in major social institutions. This model clarifies the triangular relation between interest groups, public officials, and the general public.

Stage 1:   Groups coalesce and try to convince the public that there is an "offensive, harmful, or otherwise undesirable" condition which deserves action. If they are successful (particularly if they get media coverage), they stimulate enough controversy that their concern becomes a recognized social problem.

Stage 2:   In response to the controversy they have created and the general public's ensuing demand for accountability, the responsible "official, organization, agency, or institution" acknowledges the legitimacy of the group's complaint. The official body then may establish a committee to study or actually deal with the issue. In some cases, the effect of these actions is to eliminate the problem.

Stage 3:   On the other hand, if the aggrieved group is dissatisfied with the speed or nature of the official action, it may reassert its demands that something be done. Other aroused groups may join the original group in the concerted attack on the officials.

Stage 4:   Finally, the irate group loses interest in appealing to officials and begins to consider the officials themselves as, in part, responsible for their problems. Upon abandoning the official route, the dissatisfied group develops its own response in the form of "alternative, parallel, or counter-institutions." At this point, the complaining groups have reached the conclusion that "it is no longer possible to 'work within the system' " because the system is "hopeless" (Spector & Kitsuse, 1977, p. 153). They abandon their strategy of protesting against the established procedures and create in their place alternative solutions for the perceived problem.

New alternative settings usually address the social problem on the local level. By dealing with the problem on a small scale, it is likely that they initially will be successful. This success increases the setting members' desire to persist and, perhaps, even expand to a broader scale.

We would suggest that there can be an important additional step in the evolution of an alternative. When creators of alternative settings, building on their successes, motivate others to form similar settings, they can be instrumental in the creation of a social movement. The history of the establishment of domestic violence shelters provides a good illustration of this process. The first contemporary shelter, Cheswick's Women's Aid, was begun by Erin Pizzey in London in 1971. She then published a book, *Scream Quietly or the Neighbors Will Hear* (1974), and went on an international speaking tour. These publicity efforts are credited with triggering the formation of 150 shelters in England and with being the catalyst for the American domestic violence shelter movement which began with such shelters as Rainbow Retreat, Phoenix, Arizona, 1973 and Haven House, Pasadena, California, 1974. In response to all of this activity, the British Parliament investigated the issue and in 1976 passed a law to better protect battered women. By 1980, a national organization of women's shelters had been established in England. In the United States the creation of shelters has led to changes in police procedures in quelling domestic fights and to an increased public awareness of the problem. In sum, the women's movement spawned some shelters, which in turn spawned a shelter movement, which has become the backbone of shelters. Kalmuss and Strauss (1983), tested this relation empirically and found that the best predictor of the number of spouse abuse services in a particular state was the level of feminist organization in that state—not its per capita income, political culture, individual feminist sentiment, or domestic violence legislation. Other social problems, such as child abuse or elder abuse, have not triggered grass roots advocacy groups and, thus, have not witnessed the emergence of alternative settings. Although the Spector and Kitsuse model is useful in explaining the context in which some alternative settings are created, it should be noted that other alternative settings are created as soon as a need is identified, without the preliminary steps of creating controversy or pursuing the help of officials.

The Founders of Alternative Services: Socially Conscious Rebels

The sociologist Robert K. Merton proposed a theory which described five responses of individuals to the norms of their environments: conformity, innovation, ritualism, retreatism, and rebellion. The one which is germane to our discussion is "rebellion." People who "rebel" try to introduce new norms because they are alienated from the current way of doing things. Interestingly, Merton wrote that rebellion should be differentiated from resentment. In the latter attitude, there is no interest in changing norms, only a diffuse feeling of hostility, a sense of powerlessness, and the continual reexperiencing of impotent anger. Rebellion, on the other hand, involves not valuing what others value, coupled with feeling competent to implement new values. Rebellion occurs when people give up their allegiance to the status quo and substitute in its place an allegiance to "new groups possessed of a new ideology" about how things should be done (Merton, 1968, p. 210). According to Merton, this new ideology has two functions: "to locate the source of large-scale frustrations in the social structure and to portray an alternative structure which would not, presumably, give rise to [similar] frustration of the deserving. It is a charter for action" (p. 210).

The ideology of a founding group of an alternative setting combines a critique of the mainstream condition and a proposal for change. This ideology need not be complex or even clear. Sometimes it is very simple, such as "free medical care to anyone who needs it," and is more like a slogan than a well-worked out plan. The meaning of the alternative organization's ideology is constantly debated among the founders. If there is a written form it may not correspond exactly to the organization's activities but rather to its ideals. The purpose of the ideology is to give direction to the new setting and to attract support from the wider public. The ideology of the founders is usually more explicit about the problem addressed than the solution being attempted.

Merton explains that the segment of society most likely to rebel is not the one which is economically most depressed, nor the one which is the most well-off. The former has a reduced sense of competence and lacks resources; the latter has a vested interest in the status quo. Rather, it is the middle class. Social innovators also are most likely to be found within a certain age group—young adults who are not yet entrenched psychologically and professionally in dominant social institutions. In her empirical study of alternative settings, Rothschild-Whitt (1979, p. 520) confirmed this theory. She found that members of these settings were young middle-class individuals from privileged homes.

The Process of Founding Alternative Settings: Emergencies, Community Organizing, or Long-Range Planning

Unfortunately, there is almost no large-scale research on the exact conditions under which alternative settings are founded. Therefore, to understand how settings are founded we must rely on case studies. These histories of particular settings reveal that alternative services are sometimes founded in a period of emergency. For instance:

> During riots (in a middle-size city) a group of "street medics"—mostly nonprofessionals, but some with considerable training—took over a vacant school building and started dispensing first aid. At the end of the week of disturbances, a curious coalition had formed behind them. Liberals in the community had been unsuccessfully pressuring the city health department for years to provide an outpatient clinic for an area heavily populated by students and transients. Now they took the initiative. Ministers, nurses, shopkeepers, students, street people, and other citizens banded together and announced that the Gilford free clinic would stay open. (Taylor, 1979, p. 17)

Most alternatives are not created by a group responding to an emergency but rather evolve through a deliberate community organizing effort. For example:

> [A] group of parents of small children gathered together . . . committed to the spirit of educational reform. . . . Graduate students, junior faculty, single mothers launched a campaign for an alternative public school, calling for open education, effective parent control, and serious attention to issues like racism and sexism. Calling themselves the Committee for an Alternative Public School (CAPS), they recruited more parents, printed brochures, organized petition campaigns, lobbied school-committee candidates, gave talks and slide shows, and entered into frustrating negotiations with a generally unsympathetic school bureaucracy. After two years, however, their work paid off. The school committee voted 5 to 2 in favor, and an alternative public school—kindergarten through second grade, scheduled to grow a grade a year—came into being. (Graubard, 1979, pp. 51–52)

Some complex alternative settings have a very long planning period. Hampshire College is a case in point (Kegan, 1981). Its roots go back to a group which was interested in forming an "experimental liberal arts institution." They gathered in the 1950s and by 1958 had published a book outlining their views (Barber, Sheehan, Stoke, & McCune, 1958). In 1965 an Amherst College alumnus gave $6 million to implement the New College Plan, and Hampshire College was granted a charter from the Commonwealth of Massachusetts. Thus, the school planners required 15 years to mobilize sufficient resources and legitimacy to begin their alternative institution.

The creators of alternative settings are interested in building new social models. Some start with action (e.g., dispensing free medical care), others start with forming a planning group, and others first work on their ideological statement. Although ideology is important, creators of alternative settings do not remain ideologists—they soon become implementors. They do not propose new ideas for what people should do someday, but rather make a commitment to act. In some instances, a founding group will coalesce around a charismatic figure, an attractive person who has a vision of what needs to be created. Charismatic figures provide an inspirational model of total personal commitment to a new set of values. While charismatic leaders may facilitate the creation of new settings, other conditions are even more important. Members must recognize that some specific events or a general situation is deeply disturbing, they must feel a sense of responsibility for doing something about it, and they must have a plan of action for providing an alternative to counteract the problem.

TWO MODELS OF ALTERNATIVE SERVICES AND PROFESSIONALS

Conflict and Separation

Grass roots groups create alternative services to fill gaps left by professionals or to provide a substitute for professional services. These gaps may exist even where there is a plethora of professional services. For example, in 1969 in Chapel Hill, North Carolina, a citizen committee established a drug crisis service staffed almost exclusively by nonprofessionals (Baldwin, 1975). This clinic quickly evolved into a general youth counseling center, with later additions of a residential treatment center and a short-term transition facility for pre-delinquent adolescents. Chapel Hill has a well-developed community health center, a medical school with a large psychiatry department, and other professional training programs, but the professionals associated with these programs were excluded by the alternative drug-related services.

The ideology of many alternative settings holds that in numerous ways professionals contribute to social problems. One argument levelled against professionals by developers of grass roots alternatives is that the *licensing of care* makes it difficult, if not illegal, for other types of people to deliver services. According to the alternative ideology, professionals create a monopoly in the service market. Thus when a feminist health center was sued for practicing medicine without a license, a counter-suit was filed stating that the doctors were engaged in monopolistic trade practices.

Second, because of the very nature of professionalism, the alternative ideology argues, there are large groups of *underserved* people, particularly among the poor, powerless, and deviant (Hollingshead & Redlich, 1958; Sanua, 1966; Duff & Hollingshead, 1968; and Lorion, 1973) who cannot afford quality services. Supporters of alternative settings also are critical of professionals for providing services in *impersonal, condescending, mystifying ways*. Instead, they believe that the most appropriate people to deliver services are lay persons or clients themselves. While these people may not have technical knowledge, they do have experiential knowledge, and the help offered is mutual and among equals. Alternative setting members also believe that the most important type of help to offer people addresses the issue of the client's empowerment. By contrast, they argue, professionals reinforce clients' powerlessness and dependence.

When alternative grass roots groups organize, they generally eschew professional involvement, supervision, or control (Baldwin, 1975). If professionals are involved, they are usually limited to the role of consultant, trainer, back-up advisor, or liaison to funders and other agencies. They rarely have the role of providing direct services (Gordon, 1974). When a formerly powerless group creates an alternative setting, it tends to carefully guard its new authority. Thus, Judi Chamberlin, a spokesperson for ex-mental patients, distinguishes between "real" alternatives that truly empower ex-mental patients and "false" alternatives that are "taken over by professionals" and "humiliate" former patients (1978). She considers as "false" halfway houses and other facilities, in which professionals and non-professionals are partners in providing services while retaining basic status differences. In her view, this partnership model perpetuates the abuses found in the traditional mental health system. She rejects as "false" even alternatives in which professionals merely play a supportive role. For Chamberlin, the only "real" alternative is based on a "separatist" approach: "ex-patients provide support for one another and run the service" (1978, p. 87).

Just as alternative setting members are hostile to or ambivalent about working with professionals, so, too, professionals are generally hostile or ambivalent about forming ties with grass roots alternative settings. This hostility can take the form of ridicule or anger. For example, in early 1972 when Bay Area Women Against Rape (BAWAR), the first rape crisis center, was formed:

> its claim to the advocacy role was first laughed at. Its members were looked upon as usurpers by the criminal justice personnel. Doctors at the hospital were outraged that lay women had the nerve to tell them their medical practices were harmful, and they rejected positive suggestions to improve their treatment of rape victims. (Schwendinger and Schwendinger, 1983, p. 9)

There are frequent suggestions by community psychologists among others (e.g., Pollard & Fair, 1982) that professionals become more active in alternative settings, but professionals will not be warmly welcomed (Freudenberger, 1973; Brooke & Heiligman, 1975; Reinharz, 1980/81) unless they alter their attitudes and behaviors. Professionals are ambivalent because they are threatened by another service group providing competing services and because they do not wish to be associated with a service whose performance could be perceived as substandard or even unethical (Lester, 1973). Addressing this latter issue, Genther (1974) posed a standardized problem to 10 crisis hotlines staffed by nonprofessionals and did not identify the research purpose of the call. He found that none "of the telephone counselors was able to offer the caller even the minimal levels of empathy, respect, and specificity" (Baldwin, 1975, p. 740).

Ironically, attributes of the professional model may be incorporated unwittingly into the alternative setting, even if the service is delivered by nonprofessionals. One study found that peer-counselors' rhetoric of reject-ing professional helping strategies did not match their actual behavior (Ago-pian, Dellinger, & Geis, 1975). Instead, peer-counselors adopted the role of "junior psychiatrist" and set up book-lined offices complete with large sofas and attaché cases. When seeing a "client," they posted the sign, "In ses-sion, do not disturb." When talking to "clients," they used psychoanalytic concepts.

The dynamic changes that a grass roots alternative setting usually under-goes have implications for its ties with professionals. In the early stages, extensive involvement with professionals may undermine the setting's au-tonomy and clear definition of purpose and roles. After all, the ability to attract volunteers and clients depends on establishing a reputation as a place which has something different to offer. If the setting attains an attractive and sound reputation, its members may later feel secure enough to incorporate people with other (i.e., professional) helping perspectives. Similarly, at this later stage, professionals may be less wary of the setting since it has proven itself over time. In the case of "separatist" alternatives, however, such rapprochement is unlikely to develop at any stage.

Cooperation and Integration

Much of our discussion has focused on alternative settings created by dissat-isfied grass roots groups, but it should be evident that alternative settings also can be created by dissatisfied professionals. The Southwest Denver Community Mental Health Services, Inc., "home sponsor" program (de-scribed on pages 287–288 of this chapter) is a case in point. In that case, as in many others, professional human service workers and grass roots groups join forces to create an alternative service. In fact, Fairweather (1979) ar-gues that an alternative service can succeed and demonstrate its success to others empirically *only* if grass roots groups, social scientists, and human professionals join forces.

Sometimes these groups do not actually join forces, but rather develop similar ideologies independently. For example, during the 1960s and 1970s grass roots and professional approaches to mental health treatment merged. During this period, small-scale organizations were created by grass roots groups to compensate for what they perceived to be the poor quality of professional services for the mentally ill (Holleb & Abrams, 1975). Govern-mental programs were criticized for being "confusing and wasteful in their multiplicity" and "run by bureaucrats that often seemed self-serving, unre-sponsive, and unaccountable" (Leiby, 1978, p. 298). Conventional therapy was defined as oppressive (Agel, 1971; Chesler, 1972; Glenn & Kunnes, 1973). The grass roots groups offered crisis intervention (Lindemann, 1944), peer and nonprofessional self-help, education, mobilization of supports, so-ciopolitical reinterpretation of individual problems, and the use of telephone counseling. The first setting of this type was the telephone-based Los Angeles Suicide Prevention Center established in 1957 (Baldwin, 1975).

Drug clinics, free medical clinics, hotlines, runaway houses, and crisis centers were established for the young in order to keep them out of the traditional medical, correctional, or psychiatric systems. Ironically, many of these treatment approaches were later adopted by professionals.

As soon as alternative services proved successful, professionals and bureaucrats became sympathetic and provided grants and other funding. At the same time the idea of mental health alternatives received the support of lawmakers and judges. Two legal concepts emerged from cases in which it was found that mental hospital patients were restricted unnecessarily and did not receive proper treatment. The concepts are the constitutional *right to treatment* and the *least restrictive alternative* (LRA) (*Lake* v. *Cameron*, 1966). The former makes it unconstitutional to force a person to be in a setting for his or her therapeutic benefit unless sufficient therapy is actually provided there. The latter means that when a person's rights are diminished because she or he is compelled to receive treatment, it must be offered in a setting which does not overly restrict the person's freedom of movement and choice. In practice this means that service providers must move patients toward "less structured living, smaller facilities, smaller living units, individual residence, places integrated with community living and programming, and independent living" (Levine, 1981, p. 128). These were the same ideas developed separately by grass roots groups.

Moreover, the right to treatment and the LRA concepts have encouraged *professionals* to develop alternative, community-based settings (Miller, 1982). States which did not have such settings or plans for them were forced to create them by court order. Hospitals were required to submit plans for providing individualized treatment for committed persons. In March 1976 such court orders were in effect in 10 states (Levine, 1981, p. 104). Individual law suits, class action suits, and court orders have been the chief legislative approach to the creation of community-based mental health settings. A final strategy used by professionals has been the closing of institutions. In Massachusetts, for example, all training schools for juvenile delinquents have been closed and community alternatives were developed in their place (Bakal, 1973; Lerman, 1975; Ohlin, Miller, & Coates, 1977).

THE CONTRIBUTION OF SOCIAL SCIENTISTS TO ALTERNATIVE SETTINGS

In addition to grass roots groups, human service professionals, and the courts, social scientists also have a role to play in creating and sustaining alternative settings for community change. First, the existence of grass roots alternative settings sometimes spurs social scientists to examine specific social problems, and the resulting publicity may help the alternative setting. Second, scientists may help clarify issues or provide consultation for the innovating group. They may also aid policymakers by collecting data which will suggest directions officials can take in addressing the problem.

Nelson and Caplan (1983) appeal to social scientists to link local alternative settings with needed public policy. They use the domestic violence shelter as an example:

> The evolution of shelters for battered women . . . grew out of grass roots workers' understanding of the gravity of the problem. As domestic violence rapidly gains attention from social scientists and policy makers, it is crucial that the problem definition be relevant and accurate, and that theory, research, policy, and practice be cohesively articulated and linked. (p. 512)

Building on Fairweather's idea of coalitions for change (1979), intervention in a recognized social problem may be most effective when a "bottom-up" strategy of grass roots groups creating alternatives is combined with a "top-down" strategy of experts and officials developing new laws, knowledge, and funding opportunities.

We will now examine two areas in which such collaboration among activists, scientists, and legislators has occurred. In the first area—the deinstitutionalization of mental patients—social scientists are beginning to tackle the difficult problem of understanding the community reaction to alternative settings for ex-mental patients. In the second area discussed here—the development of alternatives for the elderly—social scientists are evaluating the effectiveness of new programs to prevent the unnecessary institutionalization of the elderly.

Alternatives to Mental Hospitals: The Problem of Community Acceptance

For many years social scientists, clinicians, and grass roots groups have been experimenting with the design of alternatives to the institutionalization of mental patients. The focus of these efforts has been to ease people back into the community after being hospitalized or to prevent hospitalization in the first place.

Although these programs vary in numerous respects, they share the common characteristics of using small facilities in which patient autonomy is emphasized and of providing opportunities, such as employment training, to reintegrate patients into mainstream community activity (e.g., Fairweather, Sanders, Maynard, & Cressler, 1969). Many of these programs have been carefully evaluated, and their impact on patients has been compared to the effectiveness of hospitalization on matched patients. Using only studies which employed random assignment of persons to hospitals or "alternative care" conditions, Kiesler (1982a, 1982b) found that, in 10 different programs, alternative care was better than hospital care in several ways. Patients who received traditional mental hospital care were more likely to be rehospitalized and did not improve as much as did those in alternatives. In addition, the alternatives often cost less. Kiesler concluded that "within the limits of minimal scientific methodology there has been no single *unsuccessful* effort to discover alternative treatment" (1982b, p. 1335, emphasis added).

Several questions are then raised. Why are alternatives to institutionalization not the exclusive mode of treatment? Why has social change not been thorough and complete? Why have mental hospitals not been closed? And why is the rate of hospitalization for psychiatric problems actually increasing in this country (Kiesler, 1982b)? Kiesler's answer is that public and private insurance *financing methods* are the primary barrier to the use of community-based alternative care. *Public fear* of mental patients and opposition by traditional *professional groups* are the two other major stumbling blocks. For these reasons, the creation of alternative settings for mental patients requires the fostering of attitudes of community and professional acceptance. In some areas, people have been receptive to the idea for humanistic reasons, or because the development of alternative facilities has brought new jobs through increased state and federal funding (Miller, 1982). But, generally, residents vigorously resist the location of alternative treatment facilities in their neighborhoods (Aviram & Segal, 1973; Cramer, 1978; Chase, 1973; Kirk & Therrien, 1975; Miller, 1982; Talbott, 1979) and continue to oppose such programs after they have been established (Segal & Aviram, 1978). Attitudes toward these facilities may vary among the subgroups within a single community. For example, 70 percent of the general population in a rural North Carolina area felt that mental hospitals should be used to protect the public from mental patients, whereas only 35 percent of the community leaders felt this way. Obviously, the relative openness of the community leaders in this study did not reflect public opinion (Bentz & Edgerton, 1970).

Community residents give many reasons for rejecting such settings. They fear that patients will commit crimes, or that the staff will "dump" the patients on the neighborhood without adequate supervision. They also believe that once a neighborhood accepts one such facility, it will be flooded with others (Arce, 1978). Johnson and Beditz (1981) found that community residents believed patients in alternative settings would make the neighborhood unsafe, would cause their property values to depreciate, and would never be cured. The vehemence of community opposition to alternative psychiatric facilities has been documented in several case studies (Gaylin & Rosenfeld, 1978; Itzkowitz, 1978; Wallach, 1978).

To deal with this problem, research is needed to determine the likelihood that a particular community will accept or reject alternative psychiatric facilities. To this end Davidson (1981) studied all the community-based treatment centers in one Delaware county (n = 25). The previous literature had led him to expect that these facilities would be located in "low-resistance neighborhoods," areas in which residents either tolerate deviant behavior, do not care enough about the neighborhood to "defend" it, or do not have sufficient resources to do so. Davidson expected that low-resistance neighborhoods could be found either in inner-city neighborhoods or in poor, racially heterogeneous "transitional neighborhoods." By contrast, he expected to find that alternative psychiatric facilities would be barred from white middle-class suburbs. Interestingly, Davidson found that this stereotype about where alternative facilities are located can be misleading. (See Table 9–1.)

True, those facilities which serve people perceived as "dangerous" or highly sigmatized in other ways were largely restricted to poor urban neigh-

TABLE 9–1
*Location of Alternative Facilities by Client and Facility Characteristics**

Neighborhood Type	
Low socioeconomic status Low owner occupancy High percentage of black residents	High socioeconomic status High owner occupancy Low percentage of black residents

Client type
  Substance abusers
	Dependent and neglected
	  children

Juvenile offenders Homeless adults Former mental patients	Physically handicapped Mentally retarded
Client Age Adults	Children
Gender composition of clients Single-gender group	Mixed-gender group

Center's name
  Contains explicit reference
    to center function
	Contains no
	  reference to
	  center function

* Adapted from Davidson, 1981, pp. 232–233.

borhoods. On the other hand, centers for low-stigma persons were tolerated in more affluent suburbs. In other words, client type was a crucial factor in determining if an alternative setting would be located in a particular neighborhood. Suburban residents accepted alternative facilities if they were not frightened by the clients. In some cases, because the facilities predated the suburban neighborhood, they were accepted as a *fait accompli*. Davidson found that communities also tolerated facilities that were ecologically isolated by large lots, dense woods, barriers of heavy traffic, or high fences. Thus physical "invisibility" made them disappear from the "cognitive maps" of their suburban neighbors.

We also need to know the conditions for successful outcomes for clients in community-based settings. Segal and Aviram (1978) found that the factor that best predicted whether deinstitutionalized mental patients would be able to live outside institutions on a long-term basis was the way they were treated by their neighbors. Successful incorporation into community life depended on whether or not clients were invited into homes and interacted with neighbors on a casual basis.

But, as Kiesler pointed out, community resistance is not the only barrier to deinstitutionalization programs. An additional important barrier is the attitudes of mental hospital staff. Worcester State Hospital (WSH) in Worcester, Massachusetts, provides a vivid example of staff resistance to the creation of an Adolescent Treatment Complex (a network of community-based, small-scale mental health services to deinstitutionalize adolescents) (Walsh, 1980). The director of nursing did not want to lose control over nurses and attendants who would be redeployed in new, autonomous roles. The ward psychiatrists did not want their power over client management diluted by personnel in a new program. Hospital administrators felt that resources were too scarce to launch new programs. Of all the staff, the older unionized workers with job security were the most resistant to the new program. They claimed it was cruel and absurd to "throw people out" of the hospital since they were certain to be rehospitalized. Others accused the administration of sending people to the alternative facility in order to make money, since patients had to pay to live at the alternative facility. And finally, staffed voiced fear of losing their jobs.

Fairweather (1979), the originator of the first empirically evaluated, professionally developed, alternative community for deinstitutionalized mental patients, has been engaged in an extensive research program to determine the conditions under which psychiatric hospital staff decide to implement or resist such programs. When he approached nearly all the psychiatric hospitals in the United States (n = 255), he found that clear-cut evidence of his program's effectiveness for patients was not enough to guarantee hospital adoption of this innovation. Rather, he found:

1. There must be a group working together for the innovation—an individual is not enough.
2. The initial contact person in the hospital need not be very powerful in terms of rank in the hospital hierarchy.
3. Implementers of the innovation are likely to come from the lower ranks because higher ranked professionals want to preserve their traditional programs.
4. Active demonstration of a program is more persuasive than written descriptions or oral presentations.
5. Outside consultants knowledgeable about the program and able to work with the group are essential.
6. Organizations with good communication are more likely to adopt the alternative facility, especially if the top persons in the hospital are not opposed.

These studies have clarified when and how a community will accept such a facility and when and how a hospital will launch one.

Alternative Programs for the Elderly: Avoiding Unnecessary Institutionalization

"Alternatives" in the domain of services for the elderly consist of *activities* to prevent loneliness and boredom, and of specialized *housing* and service delivery programs in the home to prevent unnecessary institutionalization. The key to effective activities for the elderly is the mitigation of "role loss"

(Rosow, 1973) which underlies the feelings of being useless and devalued. But alternatives for the elderly have varied widely in their ability to mitigate "role loss." Rosow believes that programs that simply fill time by "glamourizing retirement, leisure, and similar diversions are fundamentally bankrupt" (Rosow, 1967, p. 317). Thus, it is not surprising that research evaluating such program alternatives for the elderly have produced inconclusive results (Gurland, Bennett, & Wilder, 1981).

Here we will focus on research concerning housing alternatives which, as a whole, are more promising. Housing alternatives for the elderly are defined as environments which are supportive without being restrictive, and which sustain independence without undermining abilities. They are "ecological niches" that prevent institutionalization and sustain the full potential of the elderly individual as long as possible.

To put the problem of unnecessary institutionalization in perspective, we should note that only a small fraction of all elderly people are institutionalized: less than 1 percent of those in their 60s, about 3 percent of those in their 70s, and more than 14 percent of those in their 80s (Tobin and Kulys, 1981), or a total 5 to 6 percent of all persons over 65. These low rates represent an active avoidance of institutionalization by older people who view institutions as places in which to die (Lawton, 1981; Tobin & Kulys, 1981). Even those elderly who are severely impaired tend to avoid being institutionalized.

Gurland, Bennett, and Wilder (1981) report that, in New York City, there are three seriously disabled elderly living on their own for every one in an institutional facility. Furthermore, it was found that 17 percent of elderly people who live on their own do so despite the fact that they are extremely hampered in carrying out their daily activities (Tobin & Kulys, 1981). The elderly prefer continuity—they want to "age in place" (Felton & Shinn, 1981, p. 169). Older people are more likely to remain out of institutions if their health permits; if they are not yet very old (83 percent of the elderly in institutions are over 75; 35 percent of the elderly in the community are over 75); if they have family support, particularly a spouse; if they are not poor; and if they have more, rather than fewer, children (Lawton, 1981, p. 104).

From the foregoing discussion we can predict that the elderly tend to be institutionalized when there is a change in their family supports (e.g., an adult child dies, or retires and moves, or a spouse dies or becomes severely ill). A second cause of institutionalization is poverty. Stevens-Long argues that 25 percent of the elderly are in institutions primarily because they are poor (1979). Unfortunately, another cause of premature institutionalization of the elderly is involvement by professionals who want to relieve the family of the burden of caring for a dependent elderly relative. Blenkner, Bloom, and Nielsen (1971) compared the propensity of professionally prepared social workers as contrasted with less-trained workers to recommend institutionalizing the elderly who were referred to them. Professional workers institutionalized 34 percent of their elderly clients, compared with 20 percent of the clients of para-professional workers. In the first year of the study, the death rate was higher among those institutionalized by the professional than by the control group (25 percent versus 18 percent). This mortality differential was attributed to the effects of institutionalization (Tobin & Kulys, 1981).

Social scientists and professionals are concerned that, even if the rates of institutionalization of the elderly are low, some people are institutionalized unnecessarily with possible disastrous results. Estimates of the rates of elderly who have been placed inappropriately in long-term care institutions range from 10 to 18 percent at the low end to 60 percent at the high end (Lawton, 1981). According to Lawton, the lower estimate is based on "quantitative functional assessments of institutionalized elderly," while the higher estimates reflect the view of "strident advocates for community-based alternatives to institutions" (1981, p. 103).

The largest group (90 percent) of the elderly live on their own and may use special services in medical centers, community mental health centers, sheltered workshops, luncheon clubs, or senior citizen centers. Younger married elderly people often choose to live in planned retirement villages or mobile home communities for the elderly. There are also a few groups of elderly who have formed cooperatives where residence, resources, and work are shared.

The most common residential alternative for the elderly is senior citizen housing for independent living. This alternative is available only to "competent" older people whose morale and health are both good. To date, 700,000 such units have been built with federal assistance, and a similar number have been constructed with private funds. This form of housing provides private apartments, common social space, and some activities programs. People who live in such projects tend to be single and to have fewer children than do other elderly.

A domiciliary facility (also called adult home, proprietary home for adults, personal care home, group home, or enriched housing) is a shared residence with a high level of physical and psychosocial support for moderately dependent older persons. These facilities cater to elderly persons who are not severely disabled, but who do require some nursing care. A variety of supportive services may be provided, including one hot meal per day, home-health care, housekeeping, counseling, and transportation. Residents in these units are often less "competent" (i.e., they are older, in poorer health, less active, less "happy," and use more services).

There are only a few studies comparing the effects of independent living, alternative facilities, and institutional care for the elderly. Recently, Sherwood and her colleagues (1981) completed a major experimental study, which examined the impact of medically oriented specialized housing on physically impaired and elderly adults as compared with similar people who lived on their own in the community. This five-year field experiment in Fall River, Massachusetts, is an excellent example of action research, in which a preventive project was designed by researchers, practitioners, and citizens to reduce unnecessary institutionalization. The project was designed to evaluate an alternative setting called Highland Heights, a low-income, 14-story apartment building with design specifications for elderly and impaired adults constructed by the Department of Housing and Urban Development on the grounds of a hospital. Available in the building were a range of health and community services. For example, the basement housed an outpatient clinic, which provided physical therapy, occupational therapy, and medical treatment. In addition, there were meeting halls, a congregate dining room, offices, and rooms for social events.

In this study, persons admitted to the facility were matched with controls who had applied but were not admitted. The researchers followed both groups for five years to determine whether the new facility had an impact on hospitalization or death rates. The findings were dramatic. During the five years of the study the residents of Highland Heights were significantly less likely to become institutionalized than were their matched controls. The experimental group was also less likely to die, at least for the first years of the study. The results with regard to acute hospitalization were equivocal: the experimental group did have a greater number of acute hospitalizations than did the controls but spent less total time in the hospital. Also, the alternative setting was more economical than institutional care.

Whereas the Highland Heights study demonstrated the possibility of *preventing* institutionalization by using alternative facilities, another study attempted to determine the conditions for successful deinstitutionalization or *release* from institutional care. In this case, Nielsen, Blenkner, Bloom, Downs, and Beggs (1972) compared home-based care (the alternative) with unsupported community living. One hundred discharged patients from a geriatric hospital were randomly assigned to experimental and control groups of 50 each. Home-aid service was given to the "experimentals" to help these older persons maintain their ordinary activities. The control group received no special assistance. Both the control and experimental groups had a relatively low rate of re-institutionalization. The researchers concluded that the primary factor which prevented re-institutionalization was the presence of relatively undamaged families (Tobin & Kulys, 1981, p. 150). When compared with the controls, the elderly in the experimental group were more content, spent fewer days in long-stay institutions, but showed no difference in survival. Differences also arose *within* the experimental group. For example, severe stroke patients did not benefit from home services. Home service was particularly effective in preventing re-institutionalization if the elderly lived with another person. Thus, unnecessary institutionalization can be reduced by providing home care and supporting the families of the elderly.

A major value of alternatives for any age group is the choice they offer. Choice is meaningful, however, only if it is truly informed and if the costs and benefits of each option are understood. Social scientists have an important role in producing and disseminating this kind of information. They also have a role in determining what types of choices the elderly desire. Clearly, we now know that the elderly desire to participate freely in social settings in which choice and decision-making rights remain theirs. As our population ages, it is not surprising that the elderly have begun to form political and social organizations to protect these rights (see Kautzer's study of L.I.F.E.—an advocacy organization of nursing home residents, 1983). Here, as for other groups, political action is a necessary supplementary activity to the creation of alternative settings.

Having examined two instances in which social scientists have aided the work of service professionals who create alternative settings, we can now look at the contributions they have made to the understanding of alternative settings that have unusual organizational features.

THE ALTERNATIVE AS AN ANTIBUREAUCRATIC COLLECTIVE

In addition to addressing social problems, people who create alternative settings may experiment with formulating organizational designs that are antibureaucratic. This is done when members of the proposed setting believe that bureaucracies embody principles that run counter to the purposes of the setting. The antibureaucratic organization is called a counter-institution, participatory democracy, or collective (Lindenfeld & Rothschild-Whitt, 1983). Rothschild-Whitt (1979), a sociologist, has identified eight ways in which bureaucracies and antibureaucracies differ (see chart below). Those who want to establish a collective try to have their organization adhere to the qualities in the right-hand column of the following chart (Table 9–2). For instance, they would try to eliminate formal rules and rely instead on personal persuasion, or they may have everyone do all the jobs in rotation rather than have people specialize in jobs arranged hierarchically in terms of power and prestige.

THE MAINTENANCE AND TRANSFORMATION OF ALTERNATIVE SETTINGS

A primary purpose of the counter-institution is to enhance the members' skills and freedom by enabling them to share organizational power. At first, it is believed that the way to achieve this is to eliminate all organizational structures. Rules, roles, meeting procedures, agendas, and organizational charts are rejected because they are thought to limit the creative potential of the individual. For this reason, the initial phase of the counter-institution has been called "consensual anarchy" (Holleb & Abrams, 1975, pp. 143–44). Consensual anarchy lasts as long as members are motivated by ideology and are satisfied with intrinsic rewards, such as experiencing personal growth. Soon, however, the structurelessness becomes apparent and produces strife (Joreen, 1973). One crisis center worker put it this way: "'Organizationally, we are so flexible that there is often concern whether or not we even exist—people do what they want and sometimes things don't get done'" (Echterling & Wylie, 1981, p. 344).

TABLE 9–2
*Comparisons of Two Types of Organizations**

Dimensions	Bureaucratic	Collectivist
1. Authority	Possessed by those in office	Possessed by group as a whole
2. Rules	Formal, fixed	Minimally stipulated
3. Social control	Direct supervision, standard rules, and sanctions	Personalistic and moralistic appeals
4. Social relations	Ideal of impersonality, relations are role-based, segmental, and instrumental	Ideal of community; relations are wholistic, personal, valued in themselves
5. Recruitment and advancement	Employment based on specialized training and formal certification	Employment based on friendship, values, personality attributes, and informally assessed knowledge and skills
	Employment is part of a career, with advancement based on seniority or achievement	No career, no hierarchy of positions
6. Incentive structure	Remunerative	Normative, solidarity
7. Social stratification	Differential rewards by office, hierarchy justifies inequality	Egalitarian
8. Differentiation	Maximal division of labor; dichotomy between intellectual and manual work	Minimal division of labor; reduced division between intellectual and manual work
	Specialization of jobs, ideal of specialist-expert	Generalization of jobs, demystification of expertise

* Adapted from Rothschild-Whitt, 1979, p. 519.

If an organization is to survive, it needs to convert chaos into order and define new rewards for members. But, by making these changes, the organization loses its antibureaucratic character. For researchers and activists, the problem is which conditions will permit an alternative setting to survive yet remain a counter-institution.

In her research, Rothschild-Whitt (1976) posed this very question. To answer it she used a sample of four different organizations: a free medical clinic, a free high school, an alternative newspaper, and a food cooperative. Rothschild-Whitt found that when the setting members had the eight characteristics listed below, their counter-institution was *not* likely to transform into a bureaucratic organization:

1. They expect the setting to be *transitory*.
2. They define their service and values in *opposition* to the status quo.
3. They have a group of *supportive professionals* to turn to when needed.
4. They see themselves as part of a *social movement*.
5. The *knowledge* that was essential to achieve the goals of the organization is *diffused* throughout the setting.
6. There is a regular, approved process in which setting members *criticize themselves* and each other.
7. They *limit their growth* and their *affiliations* with other organizations.
8. They lead a *marginal economic* existence.

Kanter (1972) studied larger collectives (i.e., Israeli kibbutzim and American utopian communes) to ascertain the factors that differentiated those which survived from those which quickly disappeared. She found that successful collectives utilize powerful "commitment mechanisms," which induce members to feel committed to the group. These "commitment mechanisms" are a set of activities through which people detach themselves from the outside world by making sacrifices, cutting off ties, and losing their individuality in the group. At the same time, people enhance their identification with the collective through physical and financial investment, sharing, regular contact, and adopting an ideology. Those settings that survived had well-developed "commitment mechanisms."

Alternatives may be ideological and antibureaucratic when founded, but as time passes they frequently move into a second, more bureaucratic stage. When a setting is created, the leader(s) or core group are enthusiastic, have good will toward one another, and naively believe that their relationship will remain free of difficulties. In the initial stage, members believe that individuals working in the setting should be free to work exactly as they please, and that somehow the setting will eventually attract sufficient resources (Sarason, 1972).

The initial assets of a new setting can become its subsequent weaknesses. For example, excessive idealism may lead to group discouragement. Eagerness to experiment with new ideas may engender boredom if "newness" cannot be sustained. The very occurrence of organizational problems may lead to disappointment. The setting also may suffer from too much success (i.e., too great a demand for services), or the wrong kind of success (i.e., being inundated by people the staff cannot help). The original goal of "openness to all" may have to be tempered, and with this comes disillusionment.

Lack of resources, such as physical space, money, equipment, clients, and skilled staff, is not a barrier during the founding phase of a grass roots alternative setting. A survey of all the free medical clinics for youth that existed in 1970, for example, found they all started with no money and an all-volunteer staff (Smith, Bentel, & Schwartz, 1971). Resources become important in the second phase, when the major issue becomes the maintenance rather than the creation of the setting.

Often, attempts are made to mobilize individuals in the surrounding community to provide resources in the form of space, money, and volunteers. With the influx of outside support, however, come new demands on the organization, such as demands for good bookkeeping, compliance with rules not made by the setting members, and other forms of accountability. While the founding members initially may have been admired, now, with the influx of new staff and volunteers, they may become the targets of resentment.

At this phase, the problems of the organization revolve around who has the power within it, and thus, who will chart its course. A new leader may emerge: not a charismatic figure, but a capable administrator. In an attempt to mediate between conflicting views, organization members may create more rules, thus making the organization more bureaucratic and less consistent with the original goals of egalitarianism and freedom. They also may recognize that people working in the organization need to have a regular source of income in order to maintain their commitment to delivering high-quality services. Neither the organization, nor the people in it, can survive on enthusiasm alone. When this point is reached, the alternative setting has reached the turning point in its development—will it return to its original counter-institutional form, will it continue in the direction of increasing bureaucratization, or will it disband completely?

According to organizational theory, all organizations that are begun by charismatic leaders become differentiated bureaucracies when the charismatic leader leaves (Weber, 1947). Roberto Michels's "Iron Law of Oligarchy" holds that it is functionally necessary for power eventually to come into the hands of a small group of people, whether the form of government is democratic, socialist, communist, or any other (Theodorson & Theodorson, 1969). This means that, even if the ideology of the organization is to disperse power widely, power will flow into the hands of a small group. Members of the group will seek to maintain their power by directing their energies to sustaining their organization and their role within it, even if such action means that the organization will be less successful in achieving its ideological goals.

Some alternative settings avoid this "inevitable" process by imposing rules that prevent it. For instance, Ozone House in Ann Arbor, Michigan, a

TABLE 9–3
*Factors Predicting Organizational Outcomes in Feminist Movement Organizations**

Maintenance of a Collective or Antibureaucratic Structure	*Transformation into a Bureaucratic Structure*	*Decay and Disintegration*
Proposition 1	**Proposition 2**	**Proposition 3**
FMOs will maintain a collectivist organizational structure if:	FMOs will develop a hierarchical organizational structure if:	FMOs will decay and disintegrate if:
1. Skills and knowledge are distributed fairly equally throughout the FMO	1. Expertise is distributed inequitably throughout the group	1. Some members value efficiency while others value participation
2. The FMO is small in size	2. The FMO is large (i.e., the woman-power available exceeds that needed for the jobs at hand)	2. The conditions facilitating a hierarchical organizational structure (outlined in Proposition 2) prevail but the FMO uses collectivist practices;
3. The FMO is financially dependent on its members for support	3. An independent source of funding is used (e.g., foundation or government grants)	3. The conditions conducive to collectivity (outlined in Proposition 1) prevail but the FMO uses hierarchical practices
4. Processes of self and mutual criticism are regular and sanctioned occurrences with the FMO	4. Rewards for organizational participation are primarily remunerative, rather than interpersonal in nature	
5. Procedures are developed which permit efficient responses to external demands (e.g., where appropriate, the needs of rape victims)	5. Members value organizational efficiency over participation;	
6. Members expect and value participation over organizational efficiency	6. Networks of friendship, expertise, and support are contiguous, resulting in the centralization of informal power	
7. Members receive interpersonal rewards as incentives for participation;		
8. Networks of friendship, expertise, and support do not overlap, preventing the centralization of informal sources of power		

* Adapted from Riger, forthcoming.

free counseling service for youths and families, which provides emergency food, temporary foster housing, and numerous other services, has been in existence for 15 years and has gained wide community support. One of the reasons for its longevity as a collective is its rule that paid staff members may work there only one year. This rule is imposed, even though it prevents talented people from staying on.

Alternatives that survive beyond their initial founding phase will continuously struggle with the tension between maintaining a collective structure, converting into a conventional bureaucratic organization, or disbanding. In Table 9–3 we have listed the conditions that Riger (forthcoming) suggests are predictive of the structure that alternative settings will adopt as they mature. Her discussion is in the context of feminist movement organizations (FMOs), but can be applied to other alternative organizations as well. Her list of conditions that facilitate an antibureaucratic (collective) structure, a bureaucratic structure, or can lead to the demise of settings can be used to help setting members understand the long-term consequences of daily decisions. For instance, if members are satisfied to have their work rewarded by friendship (proposition 1, point 7), rather than money (proposition 2, point 4), the setting is more likely to remain antibureaucratic.

PROBLEMS THAT THREATEN THE VIABILITY OF ANTIBUREAUCRATIC ALTERNATIVES: INTERNAL ORGANIZATIONAL PROBLEMS

Collectivist characteristics are difficult to maintain because of internal organizational problems and external environmental problems. Internal problems arise from the antibureaucratic organizational structure. Mansbridge identified three such internal organizational problems—"time, emotion, and inequality" (1973)—based on her participant observation in a women's center, a radical workplace, a food co-op, and a small Vermont town governed by participatory democracy. Mansbridge noted that decision making can be extremely time-consuming if every group member participates in making all decisions. In participatory democracy, unlike representative democracy, everyone is involved in decision making. Decisions must represent the consensus rather than the majority opinion of the group, and much time must be invested to reach consensus. In Table 9–4, the differences among various modes of group decision making are presented. Decision by consensus, the type usually adopted by antibureaucratic groups, is characterized by superior and more generally accepted decisions, but requires the most time.

Mansbridge found that emotions are a source of stress because the commitment of members to alternative settings is based on interpersonal ties rather than rules. These ties among friends can conflict with the stand individuals want to take for the good of the organization. When this occurs, interactions become laden with intense emotion.

> The process of making an important decision involving strong feelings on all sides can completely dominate the emotional lives of the people in the group.

TABLE 9–4
Relative Merits of Various Decision-Making Forms*

Type	Autocratic	Consultative	Majority	Consensus
Definition	One person makes final decision	Autocrative but includes advice from others	Voting with results determined numerically	Gradual buildup of group commitment to a decision
Positive features	Decisions can be made quickly Effective in crisis situation	Decisions can be made quickly Expert advice can be integrated Other input also improves quality of decisions and amount of acceptance	Familiar to most people Can be used in any size group	Better decision since it represents a synthesis of many ideas Elicits commitment Empowers people All opinions are aired
Negative features	Least likely to be good decision Least likely to be accepted by others	Takes more time Overall chance of commitment by others to decision is low	Issues become personalized A win/lose mentality develops in the group Losers have a low commitment to the decisions	Takes a long time Group must have shared values Process can be impeded by single individual Limited to small groups Can be emotionally draining Can sometimes produce agreement on lowest common denominator among ideas

* Adapted from Bernstein and Bowers, 1978, p. 9.

Members may have nightmares, talk and think about nothing else, cry uncontrollably during the day, have fits of paranoia, be unable to work, begin to distrust themselves, and often have to leave the group. In a Vermont town, several people do not go to town meetings because the emotional strain is too great. One man says, without exaggerating, that he is afraid of having a heart attack. (Mansbridge, 1973, p. 359)

People who work in alternative settings often are expected to engage in open discussions of feelings. In one alternative therapeutic community, the staff had special terms for sharing their feelings: they had to be ready to "give haircuts (verbal reprimands), probes, to call encounters, to have encounters called on them, to rap, to receive criticism, to be sympathetic, to be firm, to have patience, to ignore their own discomfort and preferences almost without respite" (Freudenberger, 1975, p. 75). By contrast, Kanter (1977) found that, in large bureaucratic corporations, members are expected to get along, keep emotional distance, and have a smooth interpersonal style. The antidote to the blandness of corporate life was the T-group, introduced by organizational consultants to help managers "get in touch with their feelings." The antidote to the stress of working in alternative settings may be to train people to reduce their overcommitment and emotional intensity (Freudenberger, 1975).

When workers in alternative settings are unable to do this, they are said to be "burning out." Freudenberger (1973) coined the term *burn-out syndrome* to describe the stressful impact of the unique characteristics of antibureaucratic alternative settings. He believed that "the very nature of alternative institutions almost guarantees that burn-out will take place" (p. 82). Based on his experience in free clinics and other settings, Freudenberger found that people who burn out (particularly founders) usually do so after working in a setting for at least a year, when they recognize how difficult it is to achieve their dreams. People who burn out develop physical complaints, such as feeling run down, having frequent headaches and gastrointestinal disturbances, or difficulty sleeping. They also may have psychological reactions, such as overcommitting themselves, complaining chronically, being cynical, and finding all activities boring. They begin to criticize the organization and other members harshly and suggest new, energy-consuming, even more idealistic directions for the organization to take. Or they may just hang around, wandering aimlessly, not knowing what to do. In a survey of campus-based women's centers, 75 percent of the groups claimed that the tendency of the staff to overcommit time and energy was a problem for the group (Sorce, 1979).

In describing inequality as a stressor in alternative settings, Mansbridge implied that, even though an organization may claim that everyone is equal, individuals differ with regard to their expertise, personal attractiveness, verbal skill, self-confidence, access to information, and interest in the task at hand. These personal differences lead to differences in the contributions individuals are able to make to the group, which in turn, lead to differential influence on the group. In some cases, the key to a group's success is its acceptance of member inequality. In these instances, there is a recognition that, while people may be differentially endowed, they need not be differentially rewarded. In other instances, the desire to sustain equality is so ideologically important for a group that a norm develops to eliminate any signs of individual differentiation, including the possession of skills. Unfortunately, the adoption of this norm leads the more highly skilled people to feel that they are being dragged down to the lowest common denominator in the group. One woman who had been a member of numerous alternative settings put it this way:

> At the beginning even though the skill levels were hopelessly unequal the fact that you thought there was a commitment to learning things made everything seem possible. . . . It later began to be apparent that there was not this commitment; instead there was . . . "militant amateurism." . . . In the case of the (alternative music band), one woman in the movement seriously advanced the idea that we should not put our names on the record because that would separate us from all our sisters who couldn't be on the record and weren't playing in bands. For a long time we never played on a stage because that would elevate us symbolically above The People. (Wenig, 82/83, p. 18)

The Avoidance of Evaluation

An important contributor to burn-out in alternative organizations is the lack of clear information about how well the organization or particular members are doing. Kanter (1977, p. 59) has noted that this problem of "evaluation uncertainty" also is found in large corporations and leads to anxiety and tension-produced disorders in executives. In large corporations evaluation uncertainty stems from the interdependence of members' work (i.e., everyone's performance is dependent on the performance of everyone else). In alternative settings (as in human service organizations generally), the evaluation problem takes a different form—little meaningful evaluation may occur at all. People simply do not know how efficacious their work is.

The general lack of evaluation research on alternative settings is not an arbitrary state of affairs. Rather, it is related to difficulties in implementing evaluation research in any community program (Cowen & Gesten, 1980) and is compounded by the special difficulties of doing summative evaluation research in alternative settings. Since contemporary alternative settings usually are struggling for funds, even if their staff wanted to conduct their own evaluation studies they would be unlikely to have the resources to do so. Also, they are unlikely either to attract staff with sophisticated research skills or to attract sympathetic outside researchers to volunteer their skills. Without resources for preparing papers for scientific journals and other media, the effective work carried out by grass roots alternative settings may be unknown by professionals or even the general public (Gonnzales, Hayes, Bond, & Kelly, 1983).

Because the goals of alternative settings are ideologically defined, they typically are diffuse and difficult to measure. Without a clear definition of objectives, however, it is not possible to do definitive evaluation research. The following statement of objectives of an alternative counseling center illustrates the difficulty: "Ideally, the service will become an informal collaborative, role-free, and accepting community, in which helping is not sharply differentiated from other activities" (Jaffe & Clark, 1975, p. 29). In her study of Berkeley's alternative schools, Swidler found that, although defining educational goals and evaluating student performance are difficult for all teachers, these problems are compounded in alternative schools because teachers and students strive to equalize their status (1979, p. 124).

An additional barrier to research in alternative settings is related to the specific content of their ideological orientation. Agopian, Dellinger, and Geis (1975) have argued that the absence of sophisticated research is an intrinsic characteristic of alternative settings and is connected with the nonjudgmental ethos. A deliberately nonevaluative stance is developed by workers in alternative settings in order to contrast themselves with traditional professional services (Reinharz, 1980/81). Thus, it is not unusual to find that research is actively resisted (Cherniss, 1972; Pollard & Fair, 1982; Schlesinger & Bart, 1983).

If an antiprofessional outlook pervades the setting, then researchers are likely to be defined as part of the "problem." Setting members object to "cold-blooded and impersonal analysis, work which is defined as self-serving for the researcher and useless for the client" (Agopian et al., 1975, p. 500). Setting members also may believe that they "know" a program is successful but doubt that this success could be picked up by standardized measures. The existence of a substantial discrepancy between insiders' perceptions and outsiders' data-based assessment is very common.

Concern for the physical safety of clients can be an additional barrier to research in such settings as women's shelters. In his evaluation of a free drug clinic, Agopian (1974) found that the workers' concern for client protection interfered with rigorous evaluation. In order to protect clients:

> [a]ll identifying materials were removed from the questionnaires before the tabulation was begun, and the matching of pre- and post-test had to be accomplished by comparing the birth dates on the questionnaires and, if there were duplicates in this category, by a variety of other amateur detective tactics, including handwriting comparisons (p. 84).

In addition, one of the methods used "to gently persuade" a client to fill out the evaluation questionnaire was to tell him or her that participating in the research was vital to the center's continued funding. Although this study did demonstrate changes in client drug use which could be attributed to clinic services, the author himself could not fully accept his findings because of these methodological shortcomings (Agopian, 1974).

Concern only for the here and now, rather than for the past and future, are additional barriers to record keeping and research (Baldwin, 1975, p. 738). Similarly, since alternative settings are service-oriented, they are unlikely to agree to "randomize their intake, on the grounds that to deprive anyone seeking assistance because of research priorities is both inhumane and unethical'' (Agopian et al., 1975, p. 500).

A final psychological barrier to research is that it can be so difficult simply to mount some alternative services that their existence is perceived as an achievement in and of itself, and not requiring further research. However, in the long run, resistance to research may be inimical to the interests of alternative setting participants because evaluation studies may demonstrate their worthiness, and thus make it easier to attract funds and influence mainstream institutions. Evaluators have made some progress in finding ways to modify evaluation research to make it more acceptable to alternative settings. Two major deviations from traditional research designs are the use of qualitative methods and the emphasis on having setting numbers collaborate in designing the evaluation in ways that make it usable in the setting itself. In the Marcy Open School in Minneapolis, for example:

> parents, staff, and children had a right to choose programs, goals, systems of governance, and evaluation methods which were compatible with their values and educational needs. (Patton, 1980, p. 85)

Outside consultants, in coordination with people involved in the school, wrote a document establishing the framework in which the evaluation would take place. The evaluation principles were taken directly from the members' description of their setting. For example, the members wrote: ''Participants in the school believe that experience is the best transmitter of knowledge.'' Thus, in choosing their form of evaluation, they stated ''the evaluation will attempt to provide an opportunity for the reader to experience the school and its children'' (Patton, 1980, p. 86).

We have seen that many internal organizational factors exert pressure on individuals who work in alternative settings: the necessity to commit a great deal of time, the intensity of member interactions, the difficulty of achieving the ideal of equality, and the lack of clear evaluative feedback. Some of these problems, such as burn-out, are shared by all types of work settings. Others are particularly characteristic of alternative settings (e.g., the attempt to achieve equality among members). Thus, although alternative antibureaucratic settings attempt to redress some of the problems created in other institutions, they do so in settings that are themselves stressful.

Forms of Community Resistance to Alternative Settings: External Environmental Problems

Community rejection is yet another source of stress in alternative settings. Opposition can come from mainstream service providers who are being challenged by the alternative, and from the general public. Opposition can take several forms: legal, social, and financial.

Instances of legal resistance are common. For example, free medical clinics have reported harassment by the police, city health authorities, and conservative groups who feared that the clinics were a haven for drug users

(Smith, Bentel, & Schwartz, 1971). In the case of the Los Angeles Feminist Women's Health Center, its founder, Carol Downer, was charged with practicing medicine without a license. She was arrested and charged with a misdemeanor offense after the California Department of Consumer Affairs and the state Board of Medical Examiners sent undercover agents to observe classes at the center. Ms. Downer had a five-day trial which attracted national attention. Her defense, based on a woman's right to examine her own body, was successful. Another undercover investigation occurred four years later and caused physicians who worked with the center to resign. In this case, the charges were dropped even before the case went to trial. "Investigations" have occurred in other feminist health centers throughout the country. Alternative settings build networks, such as the national organization of women's health centers and WATCH (Women Acting Together to Combat Harassment), to protect themselves against this form of resistance (Women's Self Help Clinics, 1976, p. 13).

Social resistance or ostracism, or both, also can occur, and sometimes they are accompanied by violence or threats of violence. One white family, who attempted to create a racially integrated commune, reported this reaction from their relatives and neighbors:

> Maybe it was this sense of "doing the right thing" which gave us the strength to withstand the storm of disapproval which arose from our friends and families . . . . Even today, most members of our families have still not forgiven us for rejecting the value system they hold dear. . . . Our community kids took lots of pressure. They were (and are) commonly called "commune kids" and "nigger lovers." . . . Some of us lived through threats, fires in the night, cars loaded with Ku Klux Klan following us around, mysterious figures hiding in the woods. (Thompson, 1982/83, p. 6)

These same community reactions of ostracism and violence can occur when alternative facilities for former mental patients or other deinstitutionalized individuals are set up in residential neighborhoods. The vehemence of the community reaction reflects the strength of the threat to their values that the alternative represents.

The most common form of community resistance faced by alternative settings is the difficulty in attracting operating funds. Many grand dreams of alternative setting innovators have been shattered on the rocks of insufficient funding. For example, in the late 1960s, professional urban planners and social scientists developed an innovative form of community called the "new town." These "new towns" were supposed to draw people away from urban sprawl and to avoid the social problems of unplanned communities. Between 1968–74 the Department of Housing and Urban Development financed 15 such new towns and planned at least 10 more such projects per year until the year 2000 (Shostack, 1975). New towns had many innovative features, such as being auto-free and providing on-the-job training in special workplaces to combat poverty. These features were threatening to the locales in which the new towns were created, and thus from the beginning the new towns suffered from inadequate local acceptance. Banks and real estate agents undermined the efforts to create these racially and economically integrated communities. Old city mayors "remained aloof, when not hostile; and local area politicians guilefully undermined the projects, fearing that these embryonic cities would soon grow so large as to dominate the entire host region" (Shostack, 1975, p. 132). Most of the new towns that were implemented soon failed financially.

When not overtly resistant, some funding sources express resentment against alternative institutions by using delaying tactics. Graziano (1969) offers a vivid example of the reaction by a local United Agency to a parents' group for autistic children (ASMIC). The group sought funds to challenge what it perceived as the ineffective treatment given these children by the local mental health clinic.

> For three years ASMIC had met all of the United Agency's conditions (for obtaining funds); they had provided a detailed proposal, launched the program, had successfully operated for three years, had expanded, had received high professional evaluations, had resolved duplication-of-service issues, had provided the exemption voucher but could not, they explained, provide confidential information such as names, addresses, and father's places of employment. The United Agency, however, blandly refused support because ASMIC was, after all, uncooperative in refusing to supply the requested information. (Graziano, 1969, p. 12)

Alternative settings are vulnerable to a community's financial resistance because members typically are not wealthy and usually do not like to charge their clients a great deal for services. In their study of 50 alternative services for women, the Women and Mental Health Project (1976) found that 19 offered free services, 5 requested a small donation, 4 used a flexible standard fee, 4 permitted client bargaining about fees, and 13 used a sliding scale and catered to low-income clients. The desire to offer inexpensive services means that staff must volunteer or receive low wages unless there are alternate sources of funds available. In the early phases of an organization it may be possible to offer low wages to workers, but, as time passes, staff begin to want more adequate financial compensation (Holleb & Abrams, 1975).

Women in Transition (WIT), a multiservice mental health center in Philadelphia, illustrates the financial problems that are typically encountered by alternative settings. Originally, WIT staff consisted of two women, who were paid a salary, and many volunteers. All WIT services were free and hundreds of women used its services in its initial stage. At first, WIT was successful in obtaining sizable grants, but later, funding agencies expected their seed money to be replaced by the stable funding the organization would raise on its own. Some funders were interested only in new projects or in research-generating service; others wanted WIT to merge with the local community health center. In the end, the city of Philadelphia agreed to fund two WIT staff members if WIT agreed to "affiliate with a local community mental health center which would have an unspecified degree of control over program and expenditures'' (Galper & Washburne, 1976, p. 255). Under this new arrangement clients would be charged a fee for service. In retrospect, Galper and Washburne (1976), two leaders of WIT, say that their idealistic position was costly to the organization and its workers. A minimal fee-for-service might have brought in some needed income without excluding low-income women. Instead, the organization stuck to its ideals and disbanded.

Keys to Survival: Building Community Ties with Other Alternatives, Incorporation into the Mainstream, and Professional Consultation

Some factors that correlate with the longevity and success of a grass roots alternative setting are beyond the control of setting members. For example, they cannot manipulate sociological factors, such as the health of the economy, yet the economy may directly affect trends in service needs. Other factors, however, can be influenced by local grass roots groups. They include ties with other alternatives and with mainstream groups. There are three groups with which an alternative setting can have organizational ties: other alternative settings, mainstream agencies, and community members (lay persons, neighbors, clients). There has been almost no research on the effect of any of these ties on the survival of alternative settings and yet, case histories point to their significance.

Most alternative settings have ties with other alternative settings. These ties may be formal or informal, supportive or competitive. When ties are supportive, alternative services bolster each other's chances for achieving goals and surviving, and also may assist in creating additional new settings. Alternative settings may join forces to form mutual funding associations (Galper & Hemmendinger, 1977; Bloch, 1977), information exchanges (Rossman, 1978), or lobbying networks (e.g., Leofanti & DeJean, 1977). They may purchase property jointly, produce common publications, or establish mutual consultation programs (e.g., the Community Congress of San Diego). Although she did not use ''survival'' as her dependent variable, O'Sullivan (1977) surveyed all the known rape crisis centers in the United States to determine whether the number of organizational ties an alternative center had with mainstream agencies affected its ability to achieve its goals. She found that centers varied greatly in the number of ties they developed in the community, and that a rape crisis center's number of interorganizational ties did not affect its ability to attract clients. On the other hand, the number of ties did affect the number of volunteers a center was able to recruit. Her data also showed a significant statistical relationship between the extent of an agency's ties and the number of its minority volunteers. This relationship occurred because these ties led to having representatives of minority organizations serve on the rape crisis center's board of directors.

Popular alternatives which become part of a community's organized service delivery system are likely to survive. If the alternative is connected with a social movement that succeeds in making changes in the law, the setting may be supported by the new laws. For example, rape crisis centers' staffs not only provided useful services to rape victims but advocated for new laws. Eventually, rape statutes were changed in many states and rape services were included in the federal Mental Health System Act (PL96-398) passed by Congress on October 7, 1980. Under the provisions of this law, community mental health centers must "assist in rape treatment, prevention and control programs" (Levine, 1981, p. 195). Thus, services for rape victims which started as a critique of mainstream institutions became integrated into and got substantial funding from the mainstream. In the first study of these rape services, however, Forman and Wadsworth (1983) found that many federally funded CMHCs did not provide *any* rape-related services despite the mandate to do so, and those CMHCs which did, provided services which were not comprehensive because the CMHC allocated insufficient funds.

The model of rape crisis centers became the forerunner of domestic violence shelters, and these, too, have now become partially integrated into mainstream procedures. In Montana, for example, the $30 marriage license fee contains a $14 component that finances the Montana Domestic Violence Program, whose services include shelters, 24-hour phone lines, transportation to safer areas, temporary housing, food, clothing, and legal assistance for women and their children. Fifteen other states finance their spouse-abuse programs through a marriage license surcharge. Thus, the success of one type of alternative setting can pave the way for others.

Consultation is a third strategy for survival used by alternative setting staffs. Consultation may be provided by organizations (such as the New School for Democratic Management, San Francisco) or by individuals. There is now enough knowledge about the characteristics of alternative settings that consultants can aid them in reducing the stress produced by their collectivist organizational form—and perhaps can aid them in survival. In the next section we provide a case illustration in which one of the authors provided consultation to an alternative bakery in order to help its members deal with organizational problems that were undermining the setting's chances for survival (see also Reinharz, 1983).

CONSULTING TO THE ALTERNATIVE SETTING[1]

The target of this consultation effort was a small, nonprofit, worker-controlled collective bakery. "Our goal is to promote a new society based on values fundamentally different from those existing today" was a statement frequently heard in this alternative setting. The bakery's strategies for promoting "the new society" were (*a*) to be a model of a successful alternative workplace; (*b*) to develop an interdependent relationship with the surrounding community; (*c*) to teach community groups about new forms of work;

---

[1] In this section, quotation marks indicate language used by setting members.

and (*d*) to raise people's awareness about the politics of food and nutrition (Uprisings Collective, 1983).

The evolution of this particular bakery follows the pattern of the creation of grass roots, antibureaucratic alternative services and businesses (Holleb & Abrams, 1975; Jaffe & Clark, 1975; Lisanevich, 1980, Schactman & Lefkovitz, 1980). In the early 1970s a few friends decided to work together to change the community by baking the best possible products and selling them at the lowest possible price. By 1973 they were baking bread at night in scattered kitchens and selling it at an open-air market and at fresh produce co-ops. After a year, the group decided to establish a bakery which would rely on volunteer labor and be owned by "the community." The whole-grain low-technology bakery would combat "poor nutrition" and "worker alienation" while also being a physical setting available to local "street-people." The bakery was envisaged as a veritable community agency with a drop-in center, outreach food programs, individual counselling, and community organizing components.

In early 1975 the group received a loan from the state's federation of food cooperatives to purchase the equipment of a bankrupt bakery, and a small loan from the intercooperative council of the local university to defray initial rent and purchases. Although successful in mobilizing external resources, the group's internal structure was underdeveloped. The bakers worked long hours and paid themselves very little. Their commitment was ideological and emotional rather than instrumental (Back & Taylor, 1976; Kanter, 1972; Zald & Ash, 1966); that is, it was based on political idealism and friendship rather than financial compensation. Keeping wages down forced other incentives to be important, but also restricted participation to those who could manage on a very low income.

During the subsequent phase, the group grew, the operation expanded, and an organizational structure was developed whereby the bakers ("coordinators") formally constituted a collective. Community meetings, open to anyone, were held for deciding policy questions. The first accomplishment of the friends of the bakery who attended community meetings was to create a workable budgeting and pricing system for bakery products. At the same time, a policy was established whereby volunteers would be paid a one-week discount at any local co-op in exchange for one hour's work.

In September 1977 the founding group (except for one member) left the bakery, citing "burn-out" and a need to move on. These people were motivated to found settings, not sustain them. Turnover was viewed ambivalently: new workers would bring new ideas and energy, and would allow the setting to "educate" more people. But turnover also brought the burden of retraining and the need to develop new interpersonal relationships. It created guilt and doubt (What did we do that made him or her leave?). One baker was left to integrate and train five unskilled coordinators while keeping the business afloat. The hourly wage was still set at the legal minimum; the hard physical work was incessant.

At the time of the consultation the bakery consisted of six paid coordinators and more than 60 volunteers. The physical setting had been designed to "educate" and involve customers in bakery procedures. "We have arranged our space so that anyone walking in the front door cannot help but see everything that is going on" (Marvel, 1980). "Anyone" who wants to learn about baking simply appears and volunteers. The functions of volunteers (e.g., cashier, retailer, baker) had been defined as the same as those of coordinators except for some specialized jobs (e.g., bookkeeper). Volunteers spent fewer hours than coordinators in the bakery, however, and did not earn cash. "Our bakery depends on volunteers. This dependence comes about through our purposefully low level of mechanization. We chop onions and nuts by hand, for example" (Marvel, 1980). The coordinators' major responsibilities were to teach the volunteers, organize the work shifts, and be a model of worker cooperation.

The bakery accepted volunteers who had been assigned by a court to do "volunteer time" in a nonprofit community service organization as a "deferred sentence" for the crimes of theft, drunk-and-disorderly, or prostitution. Court-referred volunteers were not differentiated from other volunteers in terms of earning bread and discounts. Whereas there were few blacks among the other volunteers, half of the "deferred sentencers" were black high school students. Many of them continued to frequent the bakery after completing their legal obligation to do so. The coordinators saw this program as an opportunity to reach an otherwise uninterested segment of the population and to practice nonracist and egalitarian behavior. Their vivid "sense of community" was expressed on their product label: "We are a nonprofit community service relying on volunteers. All are welcome."

Because the bakery had an open-door policy, it became a small drop-in center dispensing informal care, as can be found among natural community helpers, such as beauticians, taxi drivers, and bartenders (Comeau, 1978; Cowen, 1982). The bakers did not define themselves, however, as delivering a mental health service. Instead, they saw the setting itself as a healing or empowering environment. The bakery was both a business and a human service. It provided food but also created an educational imperative, since community involvement was *required* both for production and decision making. The coordinators believed that, by demystifying bread making, decision making, and business, they had partially empowered "the community."

The bakery's community-oriented ideology was operationalized in yet more diverse ways. Products were varied to lure different population segments that could "benefit" from good food. Potlucks were held with other cooperatives. Resources were shared with local alternative businesses and services, and the bakery was part of a network of more distant bakeries and collective workplaces. Rather than oppose competitors, the bakery helped other collectives start new food ventures. In addition, it was involved in many outreach ventures, including a "Rolling-in-Dough" program to introduce the practice of bread-making and "cooperating without bosses" to children in local schools. Finally, the bakery donated to local nonprofit social service organizations or to needy individuals all bread not sold within 48 hours. In sum, the bakery's definition of success was not increased profits but an expanded reach into "the community" through a widening array of services.

The six coordinators were all in their 20s and white, and a majority was female. Although their homogeneity facilitated consensus decision making, it conflicted with their goal of being representative of the local neighborhood. Recently, the coordinator group has expanded and hired one young white woman, one middle-aged white woman, and one older black man. Now that the membership of the collective is less homogeneous, however, difficulties are arising in achieving consensus.

Coordinators work equivalent numbers of hours per week, earn equal pay, and choose shifts by preference. As is characteristic of "oppositional organizations" (Rothschild-Whitt, 1979, p. 510), individual roles are broad and diffuse in order to prevent power differentiation within the collective. As in all voluntary work systems, tension mounts when members are reluctant to take on unpopular jobs, when someone wants to spend a lot of time doing "superfluous" tasks, or when someone does not work well. Informal persuasion is the only recourse, since there is no "boss" or formal set of rules. Coordinators are usually unable to reach consensus that someone's work performance is unacceptable, particularly if that someone is one of the coordinators. Instead of engaging in open criticism, they prod each other with mutual support: they choose the "right" background music, offer each other holistic health remedies, take breaks together, stagger difficult work, and celebrate off the job.

Coordinators hope that the process of negotiating a consensus will induce members to internalize decisions rather than experience them as externally imposed. However, the correlate is that those issues privately perceived as unlikely to yield a consensus are left to smolder or are confined to cathartic gossip. Since consensus is believed to emerge from give-and-take, covert faction-building is deplored. Special friendships also are suspect. Factions do form, however, within the collective. The most enduring and troublesome division is between what the coordinators called "business types" and "social change types."

The concerns of the coordinators are those of any bakery—planning, purchasing, processing, and selling products. Equally important are the concerns of an alternative collective setting—rotating tasks and reaching consensus. Finally there are the tasks of a service setting—educating community groups and giving support to troubled individuals. These three functions are stimulating for the bakery workers but invite conflicts. In response to such conflicts, alternative settings typically develop bureaucratic solutions, such as rules, or disintegrate (Zald & Ash, 1966). When the bakers called in a consultant, they feared they had reached this turning point.

The Consultation Process

Creating a helpful relation with such a group starts with respect for their values (Durman, 1976; Lieberman & Borman, 1976; Rappaport, 1981) in order to avoid being distrusted as an "Establishment Professional" (Brooke & Heiligman, 1975; Chamberlin, 1978; Gordon, 1974; Kleiman, Mantell, & Alexander, 1976; Reinharz, 1980/81). Since I (S.R.) accepted the group's values, an appropriate foundation for consultation was in place. As is typical in consultation, I invited the coordinators to express themselves privately in individual discussions with me. Thus, I could assess the group's readiness for consultation and they could assess me. The following is an excerpt from one such discussion:

> Our relations are not close. "We are incompatible. We're all involved in back-biting and aggressive face-to-face stuff about how everyone works. We're mired in muck and it doesn't feel good to be here." The weekly group business meeting is dreaded by everyone as something to "get over with." Some people are lazy; others are martyrs. Whenever the issue is hinted at, however, people become defensive and close-minded. There are conflicting definitions of what the bakery is all about. Our lack of consensus makes us pessimistic about the bakery and doubtful about our own self-worth. People "feel like we're barely surviving." "Are we going to make it?" (Consultation notes, S.R.)

Although the bakers considered themselves closed off from one another, they seemed to be open about their troubles with a neutral outsider.

My assessment was that the tension about which way the bakery should develop was blocking the implementation of effective organizational procedures and leading to interpersonal strife. I assumed that the coordinators' difficulties stemmed from organizational rather than personality problems. Since there were no institutionalized sanctioning mechanisms, except occasional (nonbinding) community meetings, the coordinators had no tools for solving problems within the collective. Similarly, since collectives were "supposed" to be characterized by openness, no procedures for working out bothersome feelings had been established. Thus, individual bakers experienced a lack of control in their workplace although, ironically, the collective structure is supposed to enhance worker control (see Joreen, 1973).

After our individual meetings, the collective decided to hire me to lead periodic discussions about the bakery after work hours. The general community meeting supported the collective's decision and increased the price of bread enough to pay the consultant $10 an hour plus a loaf of bread for each meeting (see also Goldberg & Kane, 1974). There was no contract. Since our meetings were defined as work, the bakers also paid themselves for their time spent at our meetings. They called our sessions "feelings meetings."

After we had agreed to start, I asked the members to prepare a joint list of their shared hopes. They wrote:

> improve meeting skills, "honesty without rudeness, with each other and with our customers," sharing information about individual goals as bakers and as

people, understanding leadership problems, making decisions better, being a facilitator, handling "complete disagreement," developing clear ideas as to what the bakery is, and particularly "how not to let each other's 'downness' get us 'down'." (Consultation notes, S.R.)

This list reflects two concerns: their desire to communicate openly and effectively and to improve the bakery's structure.

During the ensuing year I was on call whenever the bakers wanted a "feelings meeting." The resulting frequency was 11 monthly meetings rotating among the bakers' homes and lasting between 1½ and 3½ hours each, then a break of 14 months while I was unavailable and replaced by a friend, and 7 subsequent sessions. Meetings were attended exclusively by the collective members, were not interrupted by any distractions, had perfect attendance, had no agenda, did not press for resolution of issues raised, and had little time pressure. In these meetings I challenged and supported individuals in the expression of their feelings, and tried to connect these feelings with their setting's inherent ideological conflicts.

Synopses of Sample Meetings

Meeting 1.   I asked the collective to decide how to spend its first meeting time. (This request served as a model of the overall consultation goal, i.e., to encourage the group to solve its problems; see Schein, 1969.) The group floundered, expressing fear that they would waste their time and not accomplish anything. Gradually, they agreed that they wanted to learn to communicate openly. They suggested numerous procedures, all of which avoided expressing negative feelings.

I created an exercise to overcome this problem. (Members were asked to write negative feelings others probably had about them.) The exercise surprised them, because it altered the habit of dwelling on negative thoughts about others. As individuals began to disclose what they had written, others responded to clarify. It was discovered that some pairs already communicated openly. I tried to underscore this as a resource for the rest of the group.

Meeting 3.   Through persistent questioning we learned that antagonism usually stemmed from miscommunication, which in turn resulted from camouflaging negative feelings. We also learned that people misread each others' emotions—particularly anger. We tried to "legitimize" anger, even in a "joyful work-place." The group applied this idea to the hiring process: they decided to question applicants about how they express anger.

Meeting 5.   The group was beginning to feel enough mutual trust for one member to volunteer to "discuss a heavy." She wanted to know what conditions would make people quit. Group members were gratified to hear that others did not want them to leave.

Meeting 6.   Because of the discussion of quitting, I devised an exercise to help people explore the issue further. (Participants were asked to score themselves and each other on an imaginary "burn-out scale," with ratings from 1 to 10.) We learned that, without exception, people rated themselves as being *less* burned out than other people considered them. After this "evidence" of commitment, the bakers were willing to disclose their actual ambivalence about earning excessively low pay and having to put up with the unpredictable "weirdos" who drop in. The degree of anger felt by some of the bakers against the volunteers surprised them since it had not been expressed previously.

The issue of volunteers prompted me to challenge the collective. Did the bakery have no boundaries? And if not, what were the consequences for those with the greatest commitment? The bakers reached the conclusion that they could not take care of others until they took care of themselves. This could be accomplished by giving greater attention to each other's emotional needs, and also by improving the pay, benefits, vacations, and working hours/conditions. Their decision left them questioning if these remedies represented a weakening of their social movement orientation and an increasing trend of self-concern.

Meeting 7.   Again the problem was a "boundary" issue. In its effort to be open to the community, the baking collective was lending its premises at night to a food processing collective, which was damaging the equipment. The bakers had given the group ample warning about eviction, but there was no improvement. Nevertheless, the bakers were "conflicted" about carrying through the eviction in light of their commitment to alternative food cooperatives. The member who timorously raised this issue was surprised to learn that others shared this previously unexpressed resentment.

This discussion led me to ask the collective members if they could rank their goals. Their lengthy debate concluded with the following ranking: they were responsible for good products, for each other, and for upholding their values. The following day, the baking collective evicted the other collective. The bakers then called a community meeting, which resulted in modest raises, some paid vacation time, and a shortening of the bakery's hours.

Meeting 8.   For the first time a meeting was called for a specific crisis: the sudden resignation of a collective member. The departing baker vented negative feelings he had harbored since being hired. This meeting also was attended by the person who was to replace the resigning baker. Surprisingly, the newcomer expressed her own resentment at being hired in a haphazard way. In the name of informality, the group had overlooked her need for clarity. The group then devised a plan by which they would meet separately to discuss whether or not they "really" wanted to hire the new coordinator. Individuals said they learned that avoiding clear decisions did not enhance collective functioning.

Meeting 10.   A new baker explained how he was experiencing being incorporated into the collective. The old-timers reminisced and laughed about their first days at work and the mistakes they had made. People acknowledged that they still made mistakes: "We're all insecure and should ask each other for help." Comparing the meeting to an energizing "vitamin," the newcomer contrasted it with the communication he had known in other businesses. His description was seen by the other bakers as "evidence" that they had in fact changed.

After the 10th meeting, the group conducted a "feelings meeting" on its own, with the outside consultant acting as silent observer, offering feedback at the end of the session. In the current period, the group conducts "feelings meetings" without an external consultant. A specific time and place is set aside for the regular expression of conflict, which is now legitimized as a collective challenge rather than an interpersonal deficiency. The fact that this intervention has been institutionalized is a strong indicator of its effectiveness (Goodstein, 1978).

When asked to define the consultant's role in retrospect, the bakers say it was to clarify, paraphrase, interpret, confront, and point out contradictions or glossed-over issues. The most important role, in their view, was to "be active in dealing with the group rather than take a back-seat therapeutic stance" and "to give people a sense of security, to make it safe to take risks."

Consultation Outcomes

Several phenomena that occurred spontaneously toward the end of this consultation effort are qualitative indicators (Patton, 1980) of its successful outcome.

1.   New coordinators publicly expressed disbelief that the bakery once had the problems listed by the coordinators.
2.   The bakery has survived into its 10th year and has expanded its "outreach." Members no longer express fears about its imminent demise.
3.   Several "original" collective members are still working; those who have left have not disrupted the setting; the collective has incorporated new members and has grown.
4.   Instead of avoiding problems, members bring prepared issues to "feelings meetings."
5.   Members report relief and satisfaction during the meetings. (On the importance and validity of self-reported satisfaction, see Meyers, 1977.)
6.   Members conduct "feelings meetings" on their own. (On the importance of this indicator, see Schein, 1969.)
7.   The bakers have recommended this form of consultation to other collectives, which in turn have followed through and requested consultation.
8.   The bakers informed community members of the gains they have made as a result of the consultation. Interviews to this effect have been published in local newspapers.

9. The business meetings and workshifts were modified to include open communication techniques, and structural changes have been implemented. The collective evaluates our 2½-year relationship as having prevented the disintegration or bureaucratization of the setting.

CONCLUSIONS

We have examined the multiple meanings of "alternative settings" as critical grass roots or professional responses to the perceived deficiencies of mainstream institutions and practices. We have described numerous problems faced by these settings: community rejection, professional rejection, difficulty in obtaining funding, burn-out of participants, and barriers to definitive evaluation research, among others. Nevertheless, despite the obstacles to survival and the uneven records of success, those who wish to use the creation of alternative settings as a vehicle for changing the status quo should not be disheartened. After all, true change in basic societal processes, values, or structures is difficult to achieve. Rather, we believe that alternative settings are an attractive way of addressing social problems, even if their successes are not always demonstrated empirically. First of all, as mentioned earlier, they are consonant with the American values of being optimistic and action-oriented (i.e., attempting to master the environment and to solve social problems). In addition, founders of alternative settings work for change but do not resort to extreme conflict strategies, such as violence, passive resistance, or boycotts (Fairweather, 1972). The constructive orientation of builders of alternative settings and their desire to meet the needs of underserved segments of society are admirable and make them likely to remain a viable social change option. Since participation is voluntary, only those who are interested need join the efforts of people working in alternative settings. There is neither coercion nor extreme conflict in this strategy.

Alternatives essentially function to introduce diversity into a social system. They provide demonstrations of new social forms that others can adopt if they so choose. People operating in traditional ways can learn from these innovative settings, but only if they are open to them. As we saw in the case of Fairweather's research on the adoption by psychiatric hospitals of empirically tested successful innovations, people do not act only in terms of data. If people were entirely rational, innovations would be adopted in a straightforward manner: "evidence, assessment of results, verification, and adoption" (Back, 1972, p. 16). Instead, people react to alternatives on the basis of many other factors, such as the degree to which the alternative threatens their vested interests.

Community psychologists have a role to play, therefore, not only in helping alternative settings become established and succeed but also in opening lines of communication and developing good working relations between alternative settings' members and members of other groups. Research is needed to understand how alternatives are perceived by the mainstream and what set of conditions would enhance the interchange of ideas. Conversely, people working in alternative settings need information about the best strategy to increase the likelihood that their ideas will infiltrate the mainstream. Specifically, under which condition is a conflict-oriented, separatist, or cooperative strategy effective? Thus, to recapitulate a theme discussed earlier in this chapter, we believe that social scientists have an important role to play vis-à-vis alternative settings. They could contribute greatly to describing and evaluating these innovations, to disseminating their accomplishments, and to helping these innovative models stimulate needed changes in society.

References

Agel, J. *The radical therapist*. New York: Ballantine Books, 1971.

Agopian, M. *The open door: An assessment report, 1974*. Unpublished Report. California Lutheran College, Thousand Oaks, Calif. 91360.

Agopian, M., Dellinger, R., & Geis, G. Therapists or helpers? Notes on a youth-type free clinic. *Journal of Sociology and Social Welfare*, 1975, 2(4), 499–507.

Aldrich, H., & Stern, R. Social structure and the creation of producers' cooperatives. *Working Paper 29*, Ithaca, N.Y.: Cornell University, NYSSILR, 1978.

Arce, A. A. Approaches to establishing community services for the mentally disabled. *Psychiatric Quarterly*, 1978, 50(4), 264–268.

Aviram, U., & Segal, S. P. Exclusion of the mentally ill—Reflection on an old problem in a new context. *Archives of General Psychiatry*, 1973, 29, 126–131.

Back, K. W. *Beyond words*. New York: Russell Sage Foundation, 1972.

Back, K. W., & Taylor, R. S. Self-help groups: Tool or symbol? *Journal of Applied Behavioral Science*, 1976, 12(3):295–309.

Bakal, Y. *Closing correctional institutions*. Lexington, Mass.: Lexington Books, 1973.

Baldwin, B. Alternative services, professional practice and community mental health. *American Journal of Orthopsychiatry*. 1975, 45(5):734–743.

Barber, C. L., Sheehan, D., Stoke, S. M., & McCune, S. *The new college plan: A proposal for a major departure in higher education*. Amherst, Mass.: Office of the Four College Coordinator, Smith College, 1958.

Bentz, W. K., & Edgerton, J. W. Consensus on attitudes toward mental illness between leaders and the public in a rural community. *Archives of General Psychiatry*, 1970, 22, 468–473.

Bernstein, P., & Bowers, L. Democratic organization and management. *Journal of Alternative Human Services*, Winter 1978, 3(4), 7–11.

Blenkner, M., Bloom, M., & Nielsen, M. A research and demonstration project of protective services. *Social Casework*, 1971, 52, 483–499.

Bloch, S. Local Motion. *Journal of Alternative Human Services*, 1977, 3(3), 27–28.

Brook, B. D. Community families: A seven-year program perspective. *Journal of Community Psychology*, 1980, 8, 147–151.

Brooke, B., & Heiligman, A. Can professionals work in the counterculture? *Social Work*, 1975, 400–401.

Chamberlin, J. *On our own: Patient-controlled alternatives to the mental health system.* New York: Hawthorne, 1978.

Chase, J. Where have all the patients gone? *Human Behavior,* 1973, *2,* 10–18.

Cherniss, C. Personality and ideology: A personological study of women's liberation. *Psychiatry,* 1972, *35,* 109–125.

Chesler, P. Women in the psychotherapeutic relationship.'' In V. Gornick & B. K. Moran (Eds.), *Women in sexist society* (pp. 262–292). New York: New American Library, 1972.

Comeau, K. Lay persons as helpers. *Journal of Alternative Human Services,* 1978, *3,* 13–16.

Cowen, E. L. Help is where you find it: Four informal helping groups. *American Psychologist,* 1982, *37*(4), 385–395.

Cowen, E. L., & Gesten, E. L. Evaluating community programs: Tough and tender perspectives. In M. S. Gibbs, J. R. Lachenmeyer, & J. Sigal (Eds.), *Community Psychology* (pp. 363–393). New York: Gardner, 1980.

Cramer, P. K. Report on the current state of deinstitutionalization: Period of retrenchment. *Commentaries on Human Service Issues,* May 1978 (Philadelphia).

Davidson, J. L. Location of community-based treatment centers. *Social Service Review,* June 1981, 221–241.

Duff, R., & Hollingshead, A. *Sickness and society.* New York: Harper & Row, 1968.

Durman, E. G. The role of self-help in service provision. *Journal of Applied Behavioral Science,* 1976, *12*(3), 433–438.

Echterling, L., & Wylie, M. L. Crisis centers: A social movement perspective. *Journal of Community Psychology,* 1981, *9,* 342–346.

Fairweather, G. W. *Social change: The challenge to survival.* Morristown, N.J.: General Learning Press, 1972.

Fairweather, G. W. Experimental development and dissemination of an alternative to psychiatric hospitalization: Scientific methods for social change. In R. Munoz, L. Snowden, & J. Kelly (Eds.), *Social and psychological research in community settings* (pp. 305–342). San Francisco: Jossey-Bass, 1979.

Fairweather, G. W., Sanders, D. H., Maynard, H., & Cressler, D. L. *Community life for the mentally ill: An alternative to institutional care.* Chicago: Aldine, 1969.

Felton, B., & Shinn, M. Ideology and practice of deinstitutionalization. *Journal of Social Issues,* 1981, *37*(3), 158–172.

Forman, B. D., & Wadsworth, J. C. Delivery of rape-related services in CMHCs: An initial study. *Journal of Community Psychology,* 1983, *11*(3), 236–240.

Freudenberger, H. The psychologist in a free clinic setting: An alternative model in health care. *Psychotherapy: Theory, Research, and Practice,* 1973, *10*(1), 52–61.

Freudenberger, H. The staff burn-out syndrome in alternative institutions. *Psychotherapy: Theory, Research and Practice,* 1975, *12*(1), 73–82.

Galper, J., & Hemmendinger, B. The people's fund. *Journal of Alternative Human Services,* 1977, *3*(2), 17–26.

Galper, M., & Washburne, C. K. A women's self-help program in action. *Social Policy,* 1976, *6*(5), 46–52.

Gaylin, S., & Rosenfeld, P. Establishing community services for the mentally ill: A summary of lessons learned. *Psychiatric Quarterly,* 1978, Winter, *50*(4), 295–298.

Genther, R. Evaluating the functioning of community-based hotlines. *Professional Psychology,* 1974, *5:*409–414.

Glenn, M., & Kunnes, R. *Repression or revolution: Therapy in the United States today.* New York, Harper & Row, 1973.

Goldberg, C., & Kane, J. Services-in-kind: A form of compensation for mental health services. *Hospital and Community Psychiatry,* 1974, *25,* 161–164.

Gonnzales, L., Hayes, R., Bond, M., & Kelly, J. Community mental health. In M. Hersen, A. Kazdin, & A. Bellack (Eds.), *The Clinical Psychology Handbook.* New York: Pergamon Press, 1983.

Goodstein, L. D. *Consulting with Human Service Systems.* Reading, Mass.: Addison-Wesley Publishing, 1978.

Gordon, J. Coming together: Consultation with young people. *Social Policy,* July–August 1974, 40–52.

Gottlieb, N. (Ed.) *Alternative social services for women.* New York: Columbia University Press, 1980.

Graubard, A. From free schools to "educational alternatives." In J. Case & R. Taylor (Eds.), *Co-ops, communes and collectives* (pp. 49–65). New York: Pantheon Books, 1979.

Graziano, A. Clinical innovation and the mental health power structure: A social case history. *American Psychologist,* 1969, *24*(1):10–18.

Gurland, B., Bennett, R., & Wilder, D. Reevaluating the place of evaluation in planning for alternatives to institutional care for the elderly. *Journal of Social Issues,* 1981, *37*(3), 51–70.

Holleb, G., & Abrams, W. *Alternatives in community mental health.* Boston: Beacon Press, 1975.

Hollingshead, A., & Redlich, F. *Social class and mental illness: A community study.* New York: John Wiley & Sons, 1958.

Itzkowitz, M. Relocating "The Bridge": A case history of politics in mental health. *Psychiatric Quarterly,* 1978, Winter, 50(4), 282–287.

Jaffe, D., & Clark, T. *Number nine: An autobiography of an alternative counseling service.* New York: Harper & Row, 1975.

Johnson, P. J., & Beditz, J. Community support systems: Scaling community acceptance. *Community Mental Health Journal,* 1981, *17*(2), 153–160.

Joreen. The tyranny of structurelessness. In Anne Koedt, Ellen Levine, & Anita Rapone (Eds.), *Radical Feminism.* New York: Quadrangle Press, 1973.

Kalmuss, D., & Strauss, M. Feminist, political and economic determinants of wife abuse services. In D. Finkelhor, R. J. Gelles, G. T. Hotalin, & M. A. Straus (Eds.), *The dark side of families: Current family violence research* (pp. 363–376). Beverly Hills, Calif.: Sage, 1983.

Kanter, R. M. *Commitment and community.* Cambridge, Mass.: Harvard University Press, 1972.

Kanter, R. M. *Men and women of the corporation.* New York: Basic Books, 1977.

Kautzer, K. *Do not go gentle: A field study of the LIFE organization.* Unpublished manuscript, Brandeis University, 1983.

Kegan, D. Contradictions in the design and practice of an alternative organization: The case of Hampshire College. *Journal of Applied Behavioral Science*, 1981, *17*(1), 79–97.

Kiesler, C. A. Mental hospitals and alternative care: Noninstitutionalization as potential public policy for mental patients. *American Psychologist*, 1982a, *37*(4), 349–360.

Kiesler, C. A. Public and professional myths about mental hospitalization: An empirical reassessment of policy-related beliefs. *American Psychologist*, 1982b, *37*(12), 1323–1339.

Kirk, S. A., & Therrien, M. E. Community mental health myths and the fate of former hospitalized patients. *Psychiatry*, 1975, *38*, 209–217.

Kleiman, J. A., Mantell, J. E., & Alexander, E. S. Collaboration and its discontents: The perils of partnership. *Journal of Applied Behavioral Science*, 1976, *12*(3), 403–410.

Kohlberg, L., & Candee, D. *Relationships between moral judgment and moral action*. Paper presented at the Florida International Conference on Morality and Moral Development, 1981.

Lake v. Cameron 364 F.2d 657 (D.C. Cir. 1966).

Lawton, M. P. Community supports for the aged. *Journal of Social Issues*, 1981, *37*(3), 102–115.

Leiby, J. *A history of social welfare and social work in the United States*. New York: Columbia University Press, 1978.

Leofanti, C., & DeJean, P. Chicago Youth Network Council. *Journal of Alternative Human Services*, 1977, *3*(2), 22–30.

Lerman, P. *Community treatment and social control*. Chicago: University of Chicago Press, 1975.

Lester, D. Role of psychologists in crisis telephone services. *American Psychologist*, 1973, *28*, 448–449.

Levine, M. *The history and politics of community mental health*. New York: Oxford University Press, 1981.

Lieberman, M. A., & Borman, L. D. Self-help and social research. *Journal of Applied Behavioral Science*, 1976, *12*(3), 455–463.

Lindemann, E. Symptomatology and management of acute grief. *American Journal of Psychiatry*, 1944, *101*:141–148.

Lindenfeld, F., & Rothschild-Whitt, J. (Eds.) *Workplace democracy and social change*. Boston: Porter Sargent, 1983.

Lisanevich, X. Bookpeople. *Communities*, 1980, *45*, 17–20.

Lorion, R. Socioeconomic status and traditional treatment approaches reconsidered. *Psychological Bulletin*, 1973, *79*(4):263–270.

Mansbridge, J. J. Time, emotion and inequality: Three problems of participatory groups. *The Journal of Applied Behavioral Science*, 1973, *9*(2/3), 351–368.

Marieskind, H., & Ehrenreich, B. Toward socialist medicine: The women's health movement. *Social Policy*, 1975, *6*(2), 34–53.

Marvel, J. *Wildflour Bakery*. Unpublished manuscript, Ann Arbor, Mich. 1980.

McBride, J. Adoption king who delivers the babies (p. A17). *Boston Globe*, Sunday, January 23, 1983.

McShane, C., & Oliver, J. Women's groups and alternative human service agencies. *Journal of Sociology and Social Welfare*, 1978, *5*(5), 615–626.

Merton, R. K. Social structure and anomie. In *Social theory and social structure* (pp. 185–214). New York: Free Press, 1968.

Meyers, W. R. *Evaluation of consultation to social change programs: Some issues.* Paper presented at the American Psychological Association meeting, San Francisco, August 1977.

Miller, R. The least restrictive alternative: Hidden meanings and agendas. *Community Mental Health Journal,* 1982, *18*(1), 46–55.

Nelson, S., & Caplan, N. Social problem solving and social change. In D. Perlman & P. Cozby, *Social Psychology* (pp. 503–532). New York: Holt, Rinehart & Winston, 1983.

Nielsen, M., Blenkner, M., Bloom, M., Downs, T., & Beggs, H. Older people after hospitalization: A controlled study of home aid service. *American Journal of Public Health,* 1972, *62,* 1094–1101.

Noel, J. The lower-income black woman rape victim: The case for hospital-based services. *Journal of Alternative Human Services,* 1980, *6*(3), 17–20.

Ohlin, L., Miller, A., & Coates, R. *Juvenile correctional reform in Massachusetts.* Washington, D.C.: U.S. Government Printing Office, 1977.

O'Sullivan, E. Interorganizational cooperation: How effective for grassroots organizations? *Group and Organization Studies,* 1977, *2*(3), 347–358.

Patton, M. G. *Qualitative evaluation modes.* Beverly Hills, Calif.: Sage Publications, 1980.

Peugh, J. The Santa Cruz Women's Health Collective. *Communities, 52,* 1982, 19–27.

Pizzey, E. *Scream quietly or the neighbors will hear.* Short Hills, N.J.: Ridley Enslow Publishers, 1974.

Polak, P., & Kirby, M. A model to replace psychiatric hospitals. *Journal of Nervous and Mental Disease,* 1976, *162,* 13–21.

Pollard, C., & Fair, S. Community psychology and the alternative counseling center: Indications for future rapprochement. *Journal of Community Psychology,* 1982, *10,* 48–53.

Rappaport, J. In praise of paradox: A social policy of empowerment over prevention. *American Journal of Community Psychology,* 1981, *9*(1), 1–26.

Reinharz, S. The paradox of professional involvement in alternative settings. *Journal of Alternative Human Services,* 1980/81, *6*(4), 20–22.

Reinharz, S. Consulting to the collectivist workplace: A model for community psychology. *Journal of Community Psychology,* 1983, *11*(3), 199–212.

Riger, S. Vehicles for empowerment: The case of feminist movement organizations. *Prevention in Human Services,* forthcoming.

Rossman, M. Open collective memory systems. *Journal of Alternative Human Services,* 1978, *4*(3), 22–26.

Rosow, I. *Social interaction of the aged.* New York: Free Press, 1967.

Rosow, I. The social context of the aging self. *The Gerontologist,* 1973, *13,* 82–87.

Rothschild-Whitt, J. The collectivist organization: An alternative to rational-bureaucratic models. *American Sociological Review,* 1979, *44,* 509–527.

Rothschild-Whitt, J. Conditions facilitating participatory-democratic organizations. *Sociological Inquiry,* 1976, *46*(2), 75–86.

Sanua, V. D. Sociocultural aspects of psychotherapy and treatment: A review of the literature. In L. E. Abt & L. Bellak (Eds.), *Progress in clinical psychology* (Vol. VII, pp. 151–190). New York: Grune & Stratton, 1966.

Sarason, S. *The creation of settings and the future societies*. San Francisco: Jossey-Bass, 1972.

Schactman, B., & Lefkovitz, M. Art collectively. *Communities,* 1980, *45,* 3–16.

Schein, E. *Process consultation: Its role in organization development:* Reading, Mass.: Addison-Wesley Publishing, 1969.

Schlesinger, M. G., & Bart, P. Collective work and self-identity: Working in a feminist illegal abortion collective. In F. Lindenfeld & J. Rothschild-Whitt (Eds.), *Workplace democracy and social change* (pp. 139–153). Boston: Porter Sargent, 1983.

Schwendinger, J., & Schwendinger, H. *Rape and inequality.* Beverly Hills, Calif.: Sage Publications, 1983.

Segal, S. P., & Aviram, U. *The mentally ill in community-based sheltered care.* New York: John Wiley & Sons, 1978.

Sherwood, S., Greer, D. S., Morris, J. N., Mor, V., & associates. *An alternative to institutionalization: The Highland Heights experiment.* Cambridge, Mass.: Ballinger, 1981.

Shostack, A. New towns and social welfare prospects: 1975–2000 A.D. *Journal of Sociology and Social Welfare,* 1975, *3*(2), 131–135.

Smith, D. E., Bentel, D., & Schwartz, J. L. (Eds.) *The free clinic: Community approach to health care and drug abuse.* Beloit, Wis.: STASH Press, 1971.

Snarey, J. R. Reimer, J., & Kohlberg, L. *The social-moral development of kibbutz adolescents: A longitudinal comparison of kibbutz-born, city-born, and city-born but kibbutz-educated youth.* Paper presented at the 1982 Conference of the Academic Council of Kibbutz Studies, Kellogg Conference Center, Columbia University, 1982.

Sorce, P. *Identified needs of women's centers as feminist organizations.* Paper presented at the meeting of the Association for Women in Psychology Conference, Dallas, March 1979.

Spector, M., & Kitsuse, J. *Constructing social problems.* Menlo Park, Calif.: Benjamin Cummings (Addison-Wesley), 1977.

Stevens-Long, J. *Adult Life: Developmental Processes.* Palo Alto, Calif.: Mayfield Publishing, 1979.

Swidler, Ann. *Organization without authority: Dilemmas of social control in free schools.* Cambridge, Mass.: Harvard University Press, 1979.

Talbott, J. A. Deinstitutionalization: Avoiding the disasters of the past. *Hospital and Community Psychiatry,* 1979, *30,* 621–624.

Taylor, R. Free medicine. In J. Case & R. Taylor (Eds.), *Co-ops, communes and collectives* (pp. 17–48). New York: Pantheon Books, 1979.

Theodorson, G. A., & Theodorson, A. G. *A modern dictionary of sociology.* New York: Crowell, 1969.

Thompson, P. How it feels to give it all away. *Communities,* 1982/1983, *56,* 4–7.

Tobin, S. S., & Kulys, R. The family in the institutionalization of the elderly. *Journal of Social Issues,* 1981, *37*(3), 145–157.

Uprisings collective. *Uprisings, the whole grain bakers book.* Ann Arbor, Mich.: Uprisings Publishing Co. (P.O. Box 2755), 1983.

Wallach, M. B. The Flatbush episode. *Psychiatric Quarterly,* 1978, *50*(4), 278–281.

Walsh, B. Transcending organizational boundaries: The adolescent treatment complex. In J. Morrisey, H. H. Goldman, & L. Klerman (Eds.), *The Enduring Asylum* (pp. 179–198). New York: Grune & Stratton, 1980.

Weber, M. *The theory of social and economic organization.* New York: 1947.

Wenig, M. Still serving that dream: An interview with Virginia Blaisdell. *Communities,* 1982/1983, *56,* 15–22.

The Women and Mental Health Project. Women-to-women services. *Social Policy,* 1976, *7*(2), 21–27.

Women's Self Help Clinics. *Journal of Alternative Human Service, 1976, 2*(3), 11–13.

Yinger, J. M. *Countercultures: The promise and peril of a world turned upside down.* New York: Free Press, 1982.

Zald, M. N., & Ash, R. Social movement organization: Growth, decay and change. *Social Forces,* 1966, *44,* 327–41.

Citizen Participation*

---

* This chapter was written by Abraham Wandersman.

> In our modern urban civilization, multitudes of our people have been con-
> demned to urban anonymity—to living the kind of life where many of them
> neither know nor care about their own neighbors. They find themselves isolated
> from the life of their community and their nation, driven by social forces beyond
> their control into little individual worlds in which their own individual objectives
> have become paramount to the collective good. Social objectives, social wel-
> fare, the good of the nation, the democratic way of life—all these have become
> nebulous, meaningless, sterile phrases. (Alinsky, 1946, p. 68)

As early as 1830, Alexis de Tocqueville (1945) argued that citizens could
overcome the sense of isolation and powerlessness of a large society only by
active involvement in common concerns. Tocqueville suggested that civic
associations and decentralized local government could operate as mediating
structures between the individual and the central state. The concept of mediating structures has been given great importance in more recent work as
well. Nisbet (1953) suggested that people need to participate in intermediate
structures, such as a neighborhood, which would allow them to feel meaningfully related to the larger society. According to Berger and Neuhaus
(1977, p. 7):

> One of the most debilitating results of modernization is a feeling of powerless-
> ness in the face of institutions controlled by those whom we do not know and
> whose beliefs we too often do not share. Lest there be any doubt, our belief is
> that human beings, whoever they are, understand their own needs better than
> anyone else—in say 99 percent of all cases. The mediating structures of [neigh-
> borhood, family, church, and voluntary association] are the principal expres-
> sions of the real values and the real needs of the people in our society.

In this chapter, we examine the relationship between the individual and
the community from the perspective of citizen participation in agency and
community settings. The first two sections, "What Is Citizen Participation?" and "Clarifying the Process of Citizen Participation," provide basic
concepts for understanding the social and psychological dynamics associated with participation. Then, we examine citizen participation in community mental health centers and in community (e.g., neighborhood) settings.
Our goals are to clarify what participation is and to help us understand why
there is so much controversy surrounding it. In line with the central themes
of this book, we will discuss the role of participation in the development of
community, and will illustrate how psychology can play a role in understanding participation. Finally, we will demonstrate the use of psychological
research in developing strategies for improving participation experiences.

WHAT IS CITIZEN PARTICIPATION?

A Definition

"I participated in the Governor's Cup six-mile run."
"I participated in a PTA bake sale."

"I participated in the meeting where our neighborhood association decided to work to get a park built on that empty lot."

"I participated in the meeting where our work shift decided who would be the new foreman."

The term *participation* is commonly used to suggest taking part in an activity, usually in association with other people. In our discussion of participation, we narrow the definition of participation to having a role in decision making. Therefore, the first two uses of the term above (running in a race, baking cakes for the bake sale) probably do not involve participation in decision making while the third and fourth uses (influencing the decisions of the neighborhood organization and the industry) do. Power and influence are important elements in our use of the term participation. We define citizen participation in the following way: *Citizen participation is a process in which individuals take part in decision making in the institutions, programs, and environments that affect them.*

The Scope of Participation

The idea that people should be able to influence their environments and institutions can be heard in many domains of our everyday lives. Citizen participation is a process that has been used by groups in different settings (e.g., health, work, education, and government) for both liberal and conservative goals. For example, while Saul Alinsky started his community organizing activities with the poor, his later activities generalized to helping other groups oppose the centers of power. By 1971, much of his work was aimed at middle-class citizens whom he felt were oppressed by corporations. He called the middle-class the "have some, want more's" and helped them battle utility-caused pollution (Alinsky, 1971). An example of conservative middle-class citizen participation was the movement to pass Proposition 13 in California in 1978, which greatly reduced property taxes and threatened the delivery of many public services.

Citizen participation occurs in many settings, for example:

1. Work settings—workers are playing a role in making decisions about production strategies (e.g., Zwerdling, 1980), and in some cases, workers are becoming participatory owners as well as employees (e.g., Klein, 1982).
2. Health care programs and environments—citizens are board members of Health Systems Agencies that make regional health planning decisions, such as whether a hospital can expand its capacity (e.g., Checkoway, 1981); and, legislation requires that there be citizen advisory or governing boards in community mental health centers receiving federal funds (e.g., Ciarlo & Diamond, 1981; Dorwart & Meyers, 1981).
3. Planning and use of architectural environments—neighborhood residents have been involved in designing and building neighborhood parks (e.g., Francis, 1982); and tenants in some city housing projects have

become project managers (e.g., Manpower Demonstration Research Corporation, 1981).
4. Community organizations—citizens have developed block and neighborhood organizations to obtain traffic lights, keep schools from closing down, and so on (e.g., Perlman, 1978); and citizens have formed thousands of block and neighborhood crime watch programs to reduce crime (e.g., Washnis, 1976).
5. Public policy decision making—citizen advisory committees are common in many government agencies, such as the Army Corps of Engineers and the National Park Service (e.g., Rosenbaum, 1978; Rich & Rosenbaum, 1981); and several cities have developed neighborhood councils for citizen participation in the development and implementation of local government policy (e.g., Rich, 1980a). Citizen movements, such as the nuclear freeze movement, have influenced policy formation and debate (e.g., Langton & Markey, 1982).
6. Education—children play an important role in deciding what to study and for how long in open classroom education (e.g., Gump, 1978); many public schools have Parent Advisory Councils, which review budgets and make suggestions about hiring (e.g., McClure & Depiano, 1983).
7. Science and technology—citizens have become involved in performing social science research (e.g., Wandersman, Chavis, & Stucky, 1983); and citizens are members of research ethics panels, which rule on whether a particular research project may be conducted.

The goals of citizen participation, in these and many other areas, are to improve programs, to increase their responsiveness to people's needs, and to gain community acceptance. While citizen participation has enormous potential in a broad range of areas, it often conflicts with other social values and frequently raises practical problems.

A Conflict between Participation and Professional Expertise

Citizen participation is an ideal in our society. Langton (1981) draws several basic rationales in favor of citizen participation, including:

1. Citizen participation is the essence of a democratic system. People should have a significant role in their governance. "Unless citizens are capable and willing to act on this belief there can be no democracy" (p. 8).
2. It is a check against elitism and provides a constructive force for "creating a community of shared experiences and reciprocal relationships" (p. 8).

Essentially, advocates of citizen participation (e.g., Coates, 1971; Peattie, 1967; Tilley & Carr, 1975) argue that people need to participate in planning the environments or programs that affect them because participation gives individuals a feeling of control and is a major way that individual needs and values can be taken into account.

Although participation is as American as apple pie, there have been debates about its costs and benefits. The "expert" position argues that the expert or professional, by virtue of education, training, and experience, can do a better job in designing environments or planning programs. This approach argues that citizen participation is not necessary, and is often undesirable, since citizens (consumers, clients, or residents) get in the way, do not have the necessary expertise, and make planning much more expensive and time-consuming. The expert position implies that the *quality* of the program or environment determines satisfaction, and that participation is of little importance (cf. Bazan et al., 1973; Goldblatt, 1968; Skinner, 1953; Wandersman, 1979a).

Citizen participation advocates cite many examples of problems with the expert approach. For example, in designing the New Town of Columbia, Maryland, the planners wanted to promote interaction, neighboring, and sense of community. Each house was part of a defined neighborhood, and each neighborhood was to have a neighborhood center, swimming pool, and convenience (grocery) store. The convenience store could safely be reached in only five minutes on walkways or bike paths. Therefore, it was expected that automobile usage would be reduced and interaction between neighbors increased. Children were expected to play a useful role by picking up groceries. However, when people moved in, many preferred a five-minute car ride to the village center, which had a large shopping center and supermarket, rather than a five-minute walk to the convenience store. Many of the convenience stores went broke. In addition, the planners decided that all of the mailboxes should be centrally located on a block in order to increase social interaction when people collected their mail. However, many residents hated the "gang" mailboxes because they preferred privacy and could not go outside in their robes. They protested bitterly, but the planners thought it was a good idea and kept the gang mailboxes. The "expert" design had not taken into account some of the lifestyle preferences of residents. These examples suggest that well-intentioned plans developed by experts may not always work and that the participation of citizens may have avoided major problems.

Citizen participation, however, is complex and offers potential complications as well as benefits. For example, Corbett (1973) evaluated the reactions of students who volunteered to participate in a project to design and build individual dome dormitories. The students chose the dome they wanted, its exterior color, and location. Then they designed and constructed the interiors. The most common reason students gave for their involvement was that it gave them a chance to express their individuality by designing and creating a unique room. The students tended to be very satisfied with the dorms. They rated the physical amenities of their dorms higher than students who lived in other housing rated their own dorms. The students also felt that participation in design had been a good experience and that they had acquired new skills. In contrast, various architects and architectural students (i.e., experts) criticized the dorms for being unesthetic and crude in design; and the county planning commission called them "unsightly igloos" which should not be encouraged. There is a methodological problem in interpreting the results of this study. We do not know if the students' ideas produced an environment well suited for student life, or if they liked their environment because they had a role in planning it, or both. The effects of participation in decision making and the actual quality of the environment need to be analyzed separately. There is also a practical problem. If a resident must participate in the design of his or her own room or environment to be satisfied with it (as implied by some advocates of participation), the building would have to be torn down when the resident moves out. On the other hand, if residents can be satisfied with a good environment (whether it is planned with the residents or for them), the building may be reused with equal levels of satisfaction when the original residents leave.

Many arguments concerning the merits of participation have been confused because the debaters use different conceptions of participation. In the area of resident participation in planning environments, for example, some have argued that user participation "feels good" and "is better" (Lamb, 1975). Others have argued that participation is time-consuming and often leads to poor designs (Bazan et al., 1973). Still others have argued that it leads to better designs and greater user satisfaction with the environment (e.g., Alexander, 1975). The two concepts underlying the arguments view participation as either: (1) a *value* that is rewarding in and of itself, because participation is integral to democracy; or (2) a *technique* to design better environments or programs. Many advocates of citizen participation believe in the *value* of participation regardless of its efficacy, but argue for its worth as a technique for planning better environments or improving administrative decision making. Whether or not participation has the proposed beneficial effects on participants can be tested. The efficacy of citizen participation in planning better environments or improving decision making also can be tested. Clarifying the specific benefits and costs of participation can facilitate empirical evaluation of its efficacy.

CLARIFYING THE PROCESS OF PARTICIPATION

Forms of Participation: Grass Roots and Government-Mandated

In the 1980 presidential election, only 53.9 percent of the eligible voters actually voted, the lowest percentage in a presidential race in 32 years. In the 1978 congressional election, an all-time low of 35.2 percent voted (Langton, 1981). In 1982, a slightly higher percentage (35.7 percent) voted in the congressional election (*Congressional Quarterly Weekly,* 1982). On the other hand, there has been a dramatic increase in the number of citizen organizations and public interest groups. The women's movement, civil rights and environmental protection groups, public interest groups, such as Common Cause and Ralph Nader's Public Citizen, and grass roots groups that have formed thousands of block and neighborhood organizations throughout the country are evidence of active citizen involvement.

Three different forms of participation can be distinguished: electoral participation, grass roots participation, and government-mandated participation. *Electoral participation* (often called political participation) involves voting, working for a political candidate or party, and supporting or opposing a political issue. Electoral participation is a major form of citizen participation and is studied continuously by political scientists. Electoral participation primarily involves voting for a person to *represent* a constituency. The elected official then has the power to make decisions on many different issues. In this chapter we will focus on grass roots and government-mandated participation, which tend to involve citizens more directly in decision making.

Grass roots participation refers to organizations and social movements initiated by citizens (Langton, 1978). The citizens start the group and generally define its goals and methods (sometimes referred to as bottom-up participation). Grass roots groups include neighborhood groups, consumer groups, environmental protection groups, and advocacy groups. There are estimates of 6 million voluntary associations and 8,000 neighborhood organizations nationwide, and 10,000 block organizations in New York City alone (Perlman, 1978). The estimate includes 350 environmental action groups and 15,000 consumer and citizen groups (Langton, 1978). Grass roots participation has been credited with such reforms as consumer legislation, the revitalization of neighborhoods, and bringing to a halt the construction of highways and nuclear power plants. The women's movement and grass roots groups are responsible for numerous changes in the opportunities and safety of women in the United States (Reinharz, 1983).

In *government-mandated citizen participation,* the government requires that there be citizen input in the operation of a public agency. Citizen input is elicited through citizen surveys, public hearings, and advisory committees (Rich & Rosenbaum, 1981). There are citizen involvement rules in many federal agencies, including the Army Corps of Engineers, the Food and Drug Administration, the Federal Trade Commission, and the Consumer Protection Agency, and at the state and local level (Advisory Commission on Intergovernment Relations, 1979). Community mental health centers that receive federal funds are required to have citizens on their governing boards and advisory committees. Langton (1978) cites two different reasons for the involvement of citizens in governmental programs. The first, a "watchdog function," is to regulate and watch government officials who may overstep their legislated authority. Legislators often are too busy to fulfill this responsibility. Second, government officials do not like to make unpopular decisions. Citizen involvement can help improve decisions and generate public support for those decisions.

A Framework of Participation

Participation is much more complex than many of its advocates or critics have acknowledged. While there are thousands of empirical studies in the area of participation, they have not left us with a clear formulation of what is known about participation. Several basic issues and questions about participation have emerged.

1. What are the characteristics of people who participate? Why do they participate? Who are the people who do not participate and why do they not participate?
2. What are the effects of different forms of participation? What are the benefits and costs to the individual who participates? How does participation affect the program or community in which it occurs?
3. What are the characteristics of organizations or environments that facilitate or inhibit effective participation?

The questions are straightforward; the answers are complex. For example, if we are interested in who participates in citizen groups, we can look at the demographic characteristics of participants (e.g., race, sex, approximate age, length of community residence, education, occupation, and so on), or we might be interested in the personality characteristics of the participants. For example, do they have high self-esteem and feelings of internal control (i.e., perception that what happens to them is due to their own actions)? The demographic and personality information can give us a lengthy description of the participants, but this information does not explain why many others with similar demographic characteristics and personality scores do not participate. To understand why someone participates requires an approach that looks at how a person perceives and values a situation.

A framework to help clarify the important concepts in participation was developed by Wandersman and his colleagues (Wandersman, 1979b; 1981; Wandersman, Kimbrell, Wadsworth, Myers, Livingston, & Braithwaite, 1982; Wandersman, Chavis, & Stucky, 1983). The framework describes the antecedents of participation, the process of participation, and the effects of participation, and focuses on the concepts and variables important to understanding participation (see Figure 10–1).

FIGURE 10–1
A General Framework of Participation

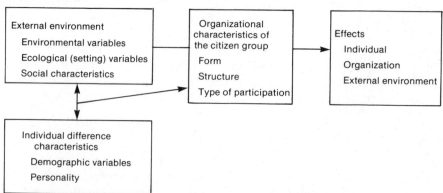

The *external environment* shown in Figure 10–1 is the community or institution within which a citizen group operates. The external environment can be described in terms of environmental characteristics (e.g., noise, density), ecological characteristics (e.g., number and/or quality of settings), and social characteristics (e.g., social networks, norms, and service delivery). Information about the external environment describes the opportunities and resources available for participation, the pressures and politics that will make it easier or more difficult for a citizen group to operate, and whether or not citizens think there are important issues or problems in which to become involved. The *organizational characteristics of the citizen group* include the form (government-mandated or grass roots), size, and structure of the group. Organizational characteristics specify the type of participation (power) available. These variables often are involved in determining the characteristics of successful versus unsuccessful organizations (e.g., those that last versus those that quickly die out). *Individual difference characteristics* (e.g., demographics, personality) influence which people participate and has implications for increasing participation. Finally, in a reciprocal manner, participation has *effects* on the individual, the organization, and the external environment. At the individual level, participation may affect level of satisfaction, feelings toward those in authority, feelings of control and alienation, and degree of social interaction. At the organizational level, the legitimacy and growth of the organization may be affected by participation levels. At the external environment level, participation may affect the environment and the social settings.

In the next section, the framework will be used to organize an exploration of citizen participation in mental health centers.

CITIZEN PARTICIPATION IN COMMUNITY MENTAL HEALTH: AN EXAMPLE OF GOVERNMENT-MANDATED PARTICIPATION

Federal and state laws mandate citizen participation in a variety of educational, health, and community service agencies. Government-mandated citizen participation became widespread in the 1960s as a means of increasing the responsiveness of government agencies to their constituencies. While citizens have traditionally been involved in mental health services as volunteers and as members of mental health associations, the Community Mental Health Centers legislation gave citizens a more crucial role in a decentralized and citizen-responsive mental health system. The Community Mental Health Centers Amendment of 1975 mandated the establishment of citizen advisory or governing boards for community mental health centers and required that these boards be involved in the operation of the centers. The boards also were required to be representative of the populations served by the centers.

In an extensive review of citizen participation groups in community mental health, Livingston (1981) found instances in which citizens groups recommended or aided in creating services, solicited financial and political support, helped identify community needs, and coordinated community services. Morrison and Cometa (1979) found that, when clients of a mental health center participated in a citizen advisory group, their feelings of independence and their awareness of center staff and programs increased, and the services of the center became more congruent with client needs.

Citizen participation, however, often meets with difficulties. For example, the director of a multidisciplinary diagnostic evaluation and rehabilitation clinic for the mentally retarded listed a number of such difficulties encountered in working with a consumer advisory board:

> Foremost is the basic ambivalence of both consumers and professionals. Both feel that those in authority possess skill and expertise and that the public is not equipped to evaluate or regulate. This "medical model" views the consumer as a patient to whom help is given and who cannot "prescribe" for himself. This reasoning is often applied to both service and administrative judgements. The professional is often threatened by parents projected into decision-making positions on policy-making boards, while the parent or client often prefers to be placed in a passive role of being given treatment. (Cohen 1975, p. 408)

Cohen noted the difficulties involved in recruiting parents who were representative of all segments of the geographic service delivery area. For example, most of the parents who came to the meetings were middle-class. He noted additional problems:

> Old timers discouraged newcomers with tales of past failures and lack of progress when they lobbied to help the developmentally disabled. The consumers who showed up at all community meetings to express their own views were often not representative and tended to dominate the meetings. . . . (p. 408)
>
> As the process of forming the consumer advisory board continued, senior professional staff began to show anxiety about its creation and possible powers. One particularly difficult problem was the anger expressed by certain parents aimed at individual professionals who provided specific programs. Examples of such conflicts were: (1) when short-term residential or intensive treatment was offered by staff, but long-term residential programming was the primary goal of the specific parent or family, (2) when the staff felt that a child was no longer appropriate for a program and the parents were approached about a referral to another program, the child's parents vocalized their hostility, (3) some parents disliked parent group counseling, while other parents lobbied for more group counseling. . . . (p. 409)
>
> Despite the effort to encourage consumer participation in planning and program development and the efforts we made in community education, there are basic unresolved questions which cause concern and reservations among community service planners. The concerns include whether consumer participation, or even control, is as helpful in creating better programs as it appears to be in lobbying for needed services. Is joint decision making too cumbersome? Too time-consuming? How much will conflicts of interest interfere with consumers' participation in deciding global issues? How productive are community education efforts? Since there are few data to answer any of these questions, creative thinking and extensive research will be needed to attempt to resolve these issues. (p. 410)

Cohen's discussion illustrates some of the problems with citizen participation from the point of view of an administrator (expert). In addition, lack of support from the treatment staff for the involvement of citizens in community mental health center operations seems to be a pervasive reaction (Robins & Blackburn, 1974; Kane, 1975; Tischler, 1971). There are a number of reasons for staff reluctance, including skepticism that laymen do not have the necessary knowledge to be involved in mental health services, an unwillingness to give up control over services, and anxiety and insecurity about citizen evaluation of their work.

The problems of citizen involvement in an agency from the citizen's point of view are the lack of staff support, lack of a clearly defined role, lack of responsibility for decision making, and lack of orientation and training of both staff and citizens (Morrison, Holdridge-Crane, & Smith, 1978). The absence of clearly defined goals is a major problem that often leads to confusion. Some would restrict citizen involvement to tasks such as fund-raising, while others would insist on citizen empowerment goals in which citizens have partial or total control over major decisions. The legislation requiring citizen participation and the bylaws for citizen groups often do little to clarify the goals of participation. For example, the "purpose" section of the bylaws of one citizen advisory committee consisted of one sentence, "The purpose of this committee shall be to advise the Board of Directors of the [name of the mental health center] with respect to the operation of the Center."

From the point of view of administration and staff, citizen participation can be seen as a time-consuming struggle which threatens their control of services and has questionable benefits. From the point of view of citizens, participation can sometimes be seen as a time-consuming strain with vague purposes, unclear strategies, and undefined powers.

A Study of Citizen Participation in a Community Mental Health Center

The framework for conceptualizing citizen participation (previously described) has been applied to participation in mental health center operations (see Figure 10–2) by Wandersman, Kimbrell, Wadsworth, Myers, Livingston, & Braithwaite (1982). Wandersman et al. obtained information from three groups in a large community mental health center with a staff of 100: members of the citizen advisory committee (the citizen participation group), the board of directors, and the staff of the center. The board of directors had 15 members, appointed by the governor, and had policymaking and operational authority for the center. Although the board was made up of citizens from the catchment area, it was not demographically representative of the community. The board created the citizen group to develop a link between the center and the community and to increase the responsiveness and visibility of the center in the community. The researchers were asked by the citizen group leader to assess the citizen group in order to provide information about the structure and functioning of the group. Some of the

FIGURE 10–2
A Framework of Citizen Participation in Community Mental Health Centers

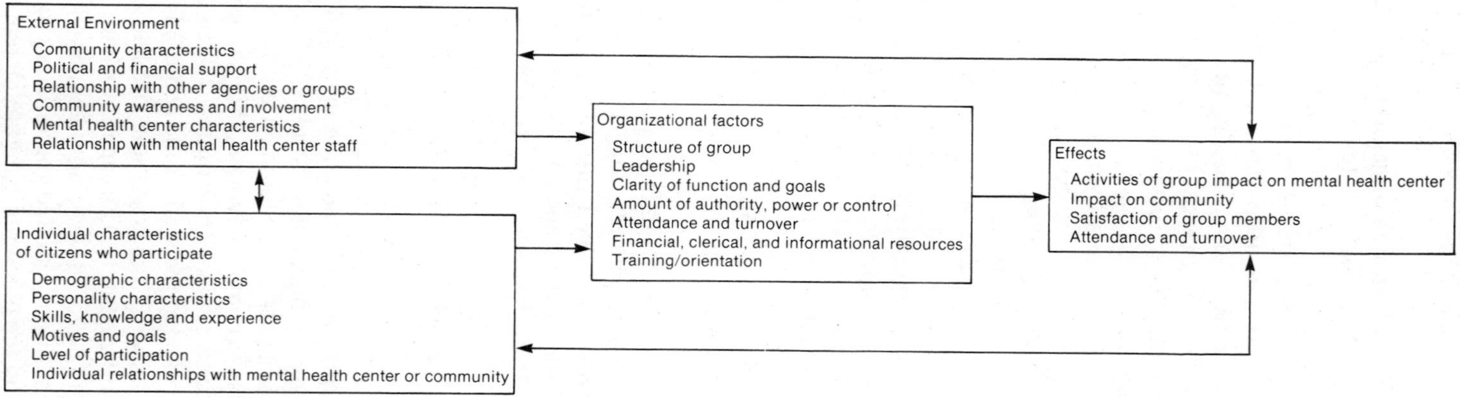

External Environment

Community characteristics
Political and financial support
Relationship with other agencies or groups
Community awareness and involvement
Mental health center characteristics
Relationship with mental health center staff

Individual characteristics
of citizens who participate

Demographic characteristics
Personality characteristics
Skills, knowledge and experience
Motives and goals
Level of participation
Individual relationships with mental health center or community

Organizational factors

Structure of group
Leadership
Clarity of function and goals
Amount of authority, power or control
Attendance and turnover
Financial, clerical, and informational resources
Training/orientation

Effects

Activities of group impact on mental health center
Impact on community
Satisfaction of group members
Attendance and turnover

results are described according to the components of the framework in Figure 10–2.

1. *External environment and relationships* involve factors outside the citizen group and the relationship of the citizen group with the center and with the community. The external environment includes the services needed by the community, the financial resources available to the center, and the resources provided by the center's staff to the citizen group. In this study, the citizen group felt that the community was largely unaware of its role, and that it was important to make the community more aware. They felt they had little impact on policies and service delivery. The citizen group was reasonably satisfied with the amount of material and clerical support it received from the center, but was critical of deficiencies in its access to information about budgets and programs, lack of early involvement in policy development, and difficulties in communicating openly with the staff and the board.

2. *Individual characteristics* of the citizens who participate involve the characteristics of the citizens (e.g., demographic, personality) and the reasons why they participate. The individual characteristics influence the resources and connections the group has and the extent to which it represents the community. In this study, members of the citizen group were not demographically representative of the community; they were predominantly white middle-class professionals and managers (97 percent had attended at least some college and 43 percent had graduate degrees). The most common reason given for joining the citizen group was an interest in mental health. Other reasons included a sense of obligation to offer skills and a desire to make a contribution to the community.

3. *Organizational characteristics* of the citizen group involve the goals, structure, and process characteristics of the group. Organizational characteristics influence the functioning and efficacy of the group, and the costs and benefits members receive from participation. The results of the study showed that the three groups disagreed concerning the functions and purposes of the citizen group: the citizen group felt that seeing that community mental health needs were met was its most important function; the board of directors felt that the citizen advisory committee should advise the board regarding policies and programs, while the staff felt the citizen advisory committee should help increase public awareness and support for the center. Citizens, then, thought that their role should involve more power in decision making than did the staff. In addition, 53 percent of the citizen advisory committee members reported no training or inadequate training for their participatory role. This limited the role the citizen group could play in decision making.

4. *Effects of the citizen group* involve several levels of effects, including effects of the citizen group on the functioning and programs of the center, on the community's relationship with the center, and on the participants themselves. In this case study, the citizen group reported that its major accomplishments were giving a banquet honoring outstanding staff members and volunteers, and reviewing the center's plan of operation.

When asked about the personal costs of participation, the amount of time it took to participate and frustration from lack of progress were cited most often. The personal benefits included an increased knowledge of mental health and a sense of contribution and helpfulness.

In summary, the results showed there was some disagreement about the functions and purposes of the citizen group. The citizens were dissatisfied with the amount of information they received, access to staff, and with their impact on the operation of the center. Many felt that they needed more training. Since the external environment exerted little pressure on an individual to participate, individual motivation was paramount in the decision to participate. Structure and decision-making power were low and ambiguous. The low pressure, low structure, low power, and high individual motivation of the citizen group contributed to their sense of frustration. The effects of participation on center functioning or community attitudes were minimal. The results suggest that increasing the structure and power of the citizen group and increasing communication between citizens, staff, and board might lead to more effective citizen influence on the functioning of the center.

Training for Citizen Participation

Some community psychologists have become involved in reducing the problems that are common in advisory and governing boards. In an early effort in behavioral community psychology, applied behavior analysis techniques were used to train a community board in formal group decision-making procedures (Briscoe, Hoffman, & Bailey, 1975). Board members were trained in problem-solving skills: stating the problem, finding solutions to the problem, and implementing the action required for a solution. Silverman (1981) and Zinobar and Dinkel (1981) have taken a more comprehensive approach to training. Silverman worked with a planning group composed of advisory board presidents and members to develop a training program for board members. The planning group generated the topics for training (e.g., fund-raising, clinical service, grantsmanship, and accountability) and provided advice on the curriculum and techniques. The training involved 12 monthly sessions of five hours each. The educational techniques included short lectures, panel discussions, and problem solving. A pre/post evaluation of advisory board members who were trained with the curriculum showed that trainees were very satisfied with the training and gained knowledge about the centers. The trainees also reported that training influenced their own functioning and the functioning of their boards, and to some extent affected the center's operations. The training program primarily served as a source of information and motivation.

Zinobar and Dinkel (1981) and their colleagues developed both a manual and a training workshop for involving citizens in community mental health programs. The manual provided information and tips on such issues as: how to decide what type of citizen to recruit, how to recruit group members, how to establish a cohesive group in a short time period, how to encourage attendance at meetings, and how to get citizen ideas put into action. For example, they suggest that efforts in three areas will increase the likelihood of implementing citizen recommendations.

1.   Maintain a working relationship between the center staff, the board of directors, and the citizen group. This can be accomplished by having citizen participation training for all the groups, by involving board and staff in the citizen group from the beginning, by reporting to top board and staff on a regular basis, and by having the citizen group chairperson attend board meetings. There should be a follow-up meeting of the citizen group with center staff six months after the recommendations are made to discuss progress and discuss any possible problems.

2.   Make sure that citizen recommendations are specific and are accompanied by statements that clarify the need for change, the specific changes being requested, and the feasibility of the changes. The recommendations should be appropriate to the mandate of the center or the citizen group can lose credibility.

3.   Help the community become aware of the activities of the citizen group and the problems that need correction. The citizen group can publicize its activities by getting local newspaper coverage, inviting a reporter to citizen group meetings, providing reporters with press packets containing background about the group, and sharing recommendations with groups or agencies outside the mental health center who can serve as program advocates.

In summary, government mandated citizen participation offers potentials and pitfalls to an agency.

> On the one hand, citizen participation is a control mechanism when citizens perform a monitoring or "watchdog" function. On the other hand, citizen participation provides an assistance function regarding agency decisions. Ironically, citizen participation may represent either a threat or a way of reducing threats to an agency. (Langton, 1978, p. 7)

Langton (1978) concludes that it is not surprising that many agency administrators are ambivalent about citizen participation. We would add that it is not surprising that many citizens who participate in citizen advisory committees are ambivalent about their participation and are confused about their purpose on committees and boards.

Government-mandated participation offers citizens an opportunity to make services more responsive to citizen needs and values. However, simply mandating participation does not provide the strategies, training, or motivation to develop effective participators. The research and consultation skills of community psychologists can and should be used to bridge the gap between citizen and expert and, thereby, increase the effectiveness of citizen participation in government and service agencies. Even at its most effective levels, however, government-mandated participation in social agencies has limited power to influence the daily lives of citizens. In the next section we examine government-mandated and grass roots participation in communities.

CITIZEN PARTICIPATION AND THE DEVELOPMENT OF COMMUNITY

> Part of the reason I got involved in organizing the block association was for safety, tenants' rights, and so on. But when you get right down to it, what it really was, was that I was craving more real, human contact with my neighbors. For years and years, I let myself get accustomed to the no-eye-contact, live in your own world ways we'd come to regard each other. I decided that even at my age, it was worth struggling out of that to something better, something more like community. (A 73-year-old woman cited in Yankelovich, 1981, p. 253)

This quotation suggests that the development of community involves both improving the living conditions of the community and increasing the sense of community. Citizen participation in community organizations has been proposed as a major method for improving the quality of the physical environment, enhancing services, preventing crime, and so on (e.g., Altshuler, 1970; Hallman, 1974; Morris & Hess, 1975; Perlman, 1976; Yates, 1973; Yin, 1977. In addition, citizen participation has been proposed as a means for creating sense of community and fighting alienation. Community organization is an area of theory and practice whose purpose is the development of community. In this section, we compare two citizen participation strategies of community organization: community development and social action. Then we discuss government-mandated community organization with examples of the community development approach and the social action approach. This is followed by a discussion of the neighborhood movement, an example of grass roots community organization.

Community Organization

Community organization entails interventions at the community level that aim to influence community institutions and to solve community problems (Cox, Erlich, Rothman, & Tropman, 1970). Community organization can take three forms: *community* (locality) *development, social action,* and *social planning.* Community development is concerned with the creation of improved social and economic conditions through emphasis on voluntary cooperation and self-help efforts of the residents. Social action occurs when a disadvantaged segment of the population becomes organized to make demands on the dominant institutions. Social planning is the technical process of problem solving largely concerned with the delivery of goods and services to people who need them. Because our focus is on citizen efforts, we will discuss only community development and social action in which citizen participation plays a major role. It is important to note, however, that an expert often is used in the community development and social action approaches as well—namely, a community organizer. The organizer's role is to attempt to bring citizens together to solve problems, and to provide citizens with technical assistance (specific knowledge and enhancement of citizen skills). The organizer can be the one who initiates citizen participation efforts, or can be called into the community by a group of citizens who have started an organization and want help.

Community development and social action represent two different strategies in the use of citizen participation. Each has different assumptions about how participation activities should be implemented. The two strategies are contrasted in the following sections.

Community development as a consensus-building strategy. The term *community development* came into use after World War II in the efforts to improve village life in newly independent developing countries. The model has been used to address the problems of America's cities. Clinard (1970), lists the components in urban community development as follows:

1. Creation of a sense of social cohesion on a neighborhood basis and strengthening of group interrelationships.
2. Encouragement and stimulation of self-help, through the initiative of the individuals in the community.
3. Stimulation by outside agencies when initiative for self-help is lacking.
4. Reliance upon persuasion rather than upon compulsion to produce change through the efforts of the people.
5. Identification and development of local leadership.
6. Development of civic consciousness and acceptance of civic responsibility.
7. Use of professional and technical assistance to support the efforts of the people involved.
8. Coordination of city services to meet neighborhood needs and problems.
9. Provision of training in democratic procedures that may result in decentralization of some government functions. (Clinard, 1970, p. 126)

Eugster (1974), a community organizer, provides an example of community development that follows the steps described by Clinard. Working in a black neighborhood called West Heights, Eugster initially found an area of 400 citizens isolated from the rest of the city, with a poor standard of living, few city services, and dilapidated and overcrowded homes. Until 1955, the children of West Heights were educated in an all-black two-room schoolhouse. When school integration became mandatory, the children of the area were bused to previously all-white schools. Both before and after school desegregation, West Heights children performed at levels up to five years behind their white peers. Eugster's community development effort began with a series of educational lectures at one of the local churches. Eugster's goal was to help the community come together to develop a plan of action to alleviate *one* specific problem. In West Heights, the specific problem was not difficult to choose; everyone was concerned about the poor school performance and disruptive school behavior of the area's children. Yet, since the adults in the community were poorly educated themselves, they felt powerless to deal with this problem. Eugster suggested a tutoring program, hosted and supervised by parents but using the services of educated volunteers from the larger community. Additional tutors and neighborhood homes in which they could work were recruited, and the program was on its way.

The larger community, which in the past had tended to isolate and neglect the West Heights citizens, now began to offer help. School principals, who did not volunteer their help initially and who believed that West Heights parents were not seriously interested in the schooling of their children, were taken aback when the plan actually materialized. They quickly agreed to participate once the plan was successfully under way. Other civic organizations also became interested, and soon West Heights children were invited to plays, concerts, trips to the zoo and circus, and tours of some local laboratories. After two and a half years of the program, the school board agreed to incorporate the program into its educational system and hired two full-time field educators to work toward its continuation and expansion.

Eugster reported that, over time, the original education committee was expanded into the West Heights Citizen Association, with members from every clique and faction within the community. The association obtained garbage collection services and successfully fought an effort by a group of businessmen to have part of the West Heights land zoned for commercial use. The school reported improved school attitudes and performance, the probation department reported a decrease in delinquency, and the public health nurse reported improved upkeep of homes and higher family morale.

In recent years, community development corporations (CDCs), which are nonprofit corporations operated by neighborhood residents, have been formed in many cities. They vary in size from large multimillion-dollar corporations, such as Bedford Stuyvesant Restoration Corporation, to small corporations located in rural areas. The goals of community development corporations are to build the community economically and physically. The income generated by its activities is used to pay staff, provide new projects, and generate jobs. Their activities range from developing food co-ops, to developing and managing housing, to producing solar heating products. For example, the Greater Southwest Development Corporation was created in southwest Chicago when neighborhood residents formed a coalition with local financial institutions and businesses to help restore neighborhood confidence in a working-class neighborhood. A major building in the neighborhood's business district was being vacated, and the prospective tenants included adult bookstores and betting parlors. The development corporation was instrumental in renovating the building and attracting such reputable businesses as a jewelry store and a delicatessen. The building tripled in value. The corporation also renovated a 48-unit apartment building that had been a reputed haven for drug addicts and was scheduled for demolition (Capraro, 1979).

A problem for community development: Limits of consensus and cooperation. Community development is based on an optimistic view of people and community change. But in most communities there are constraints which can prevent cooperation and consensus alone from achieving constructive change. Interference can come from the constraints of inadequate time, money, energy, and ability, and from organized opposition.

Another limitation of cooperation strategies, when practiced exclusively, can be summarized best by the "squeaky wheel" principle. Squeaky wheels get greased; those that are silent are left alone. A strategy of talking to local officials without "squeaking" (i.e., by keeping everything "nice" and cooperative), allows for the interpretation that one's group may not be hurting enough to require official action. Alinsky quotes Franklin D. Roosevelt as having told a reform delegation who visited him to plead for a specific change: "Okay, you've convinced me. Now go out and bring pressure on me!" (Alinsky, 1971, p. xxiii).

Social action and conflict strategies. Basically, conflict strategies function to stir passive communities by spotlighting the problems of a group of citizens and by raising basic questions about commonly accepted community roles and procedures. Conflict strategies are designed to make people uncomfortable. There are communities in which the major social institutions do not reflect the values of large segments of the community, and there is a rigidity in accommodating to community needs. In such communities, confrontation and conflict seem unavoidable.

Social action is part of the democratic system. Social action groups focus on making the official system work for them, too. Conflict strategies often depend on using the official system of government (e.g., laws, elections). By swaying public opinion, localities can be forced to confront difficult problems and to develop better procedures to solve them. If it appeals successfully to national sentiment, social action can be the stimulus for new laws or significant national programs. For example, much of the progress in such areas as civil rights, housing, and urban development was stimulated by conflict tactics employed by disadvantaged minority groups.

The principal goal of social action is to achieve a shift in power relationships to insure a more equitable distribution of resources. Alinsky (1971) states this goal in simple terms by pointing out that the battle is between the Haves and the Have-Nots.

> The purpose of the Haves is to keep what they have. Therefore, the Haves want to maintain the status quo and the Have-Nots to change it. . . . The Haves want to keep; the Have-Nots to get. (Alinsky, 1971, pp. 19 and 42)

Alinsky is convinced that the only way to get power is to seize it and use strength to convince the Haves that it is in their best interest to negotiate. Ultimately, gains come through negotiation, but "no one can negotiate without the power to compel negotiation" (Alinsky, 1971, p. 119).

Alinsky provides an example of how power, or in this case the threat of power, forced negotiation. Commitments made by Chicago civil authorities to the Woodlawn community organization were not being honored. The Woodlawn group felt it needed a new plan to maintain the pressure necessary for its goals to be achieved. A plan was devised, targeting the bathroom needs of jet travelers at Chicago's busy O'Hare airport:

> [The] "tactic becomes obvious—we tie up the lavatories." An intelligence study was launched to learn how many sit-down toilets for both men and women, as well as stand-up urinals, there were in O'Hare Airport complex and how many men and women would be necessary for the nation's first "shit-in."
>
> The consequences of this kind of action would be catastrophic in many ways. People would be desperate for a place to relieve themselves. One can see children yelling at their parents, "Mommy, I've got to go," and desperate mothers surrendering, "All right—well, do it. Do it right here." O'Hare would soon become a shambles. The whole scene would become unbelievable and the laughter and ridicule would be nationwide. It would probably get a front page story in the London Times. It would be a source of great mortification and embarrassment to city administration. It might even create the kind of emergency in which planes would have to be held up while passengers got back aboard to use the plane's toilet facilities.
>
> The threat of this tactic was leaked (again there may be a Freudian slip here, and again, so what?) back to the administration, and within 48 hours the Woodlawn Organization found itself in conference with the authorities who said that they were certainly going to live up to their commitments and they could never understand where anyone got the idea that a promise made by Chicago's City Hall would not be observed. At no point, then or since, has there ever been any open mention of the threat of the O'Hare tactic. Very few of the members of the Woodlawn Organization knew how close they were to writing history. (Alinsky, 1971, pp. 142–144)

Why is conflict a necessary ingredient in the Alinsky approach? Could more progress be made by conciliation and cooperation? Alinsky would answer that one cannot negotiate and compromise from a weak position. Conciliation only occurs among equals who see that it is in their self-interest to cooperate. Alinsky sees people as essentially selfish; not sharing unless forced to do so.

Social action strategies have become widespread, and they have taken many creative forms. For example, many poor and lower working-class families have little hope of ever owning a home, while many houses in cities have been abandoned. Milton Street, a community activist, helped over 200 families become homeowners through a program called walk-in homesteading. Armed with steel snippers, Street and neighborhood volunteers clipped the locks on abandoned houses and made them livable by fixing the roofs, getting the electricity and water running, and so on. After promising to finish renovating a house and to remain living there, a family in need of housing moved in. Many of the homesteaders have become homeowners through a purchasing agreement arranged by Street. The program has drawn praise from the federal Department of Housing and Urban Development and from the mayor because vacant houses are turned into community assets. "The irony is that the first step in the process is to break the law—although it is a trespass that is nearly always soon forgiven" (Cassidy, 1981, p. 86)

Problems for social action strategies. There are potential problems in the use of social action strategies:

1. The possibility of unleashing an attitudinal backlash in the majority community.

Despite Alinsky's admonition to "keep the pressure on," a point can be reached where the larger community, pushed to the limits of its ability to accommodate, will find itself frustrated and angry rather than defeated and conciliatory. If constructive solutions are unavailable or are rejected by majority community sentiment, more destructive and repressive solutions may be adopted. Therefore, social action may work best when there are also those within the system working for change along more traditional routes.

2. The assumption of static resources.

The conflict strategist assumes that communities cannot increase scarce resources to give all citizens a better life. This means that an advantage for one group can be expected to occur only at the expense of another. The poor can get more only if the rich get less; and since the rich will not reduce their consumption voluntarily, conflict is necessary.

This view neglects the possibility that, with proper planning, an organized community can expand its resources. For example, with increased motivation, workers may be more productive; increased educational opportunities may widen the base of available technical skills; more productive use of people can mean less money being spent for supervision and control (e.g., police, prisons, and the like); and more constructive use of leisure time can increase the job opportunities in such occupations as recreation, park maintenance, and the arts.

3. Power without program is not enough.

An additional problem involves the neglect of substantive programmatic concerns on the part of those agitating for change from a conflict perspective. Quite naturally, disenfranchised groups will spend a significant amount of time preparing for the assumption of political power. But when the battle has been won, the same complex problems of housing, education, health care, and employment, which the powerholders found so difficult to solve, still remain. After the community organization stage has been passed, what then? Power without program will lead to little improvement in people's lives (Miller & Riessman, 1968) and may simply substitute a new bureaucracy and new injustices for the old. Without innovative programs and resources with which to implement programs, the lives of the many will remain untouched. The community organizer who believes that infinite wisdom resides in the oppressed may find to his or her dismay (Pearl, 1971) that programs depend upon the knowledge of experts (e.g., in economics, law, social relations), and that, without this knowledge, the poor are impotent to generate constructive change. Changing the group which has control does not mean that better decisions will be made.

Choosing a consensus or conflict strategy. We have discussed community development and social action as separate strategies in order to clarify their different assumptions. *In practice, however, many professionals and practitioners involved in community organization believe that both consensus and conflict strategies must be used in community organization,* and that total reliance on only one of the strategies will be unsuccessful in most cases. One might start with a power-building strategy to compel negotiation, but a point may be reached in which more can be accomplished by negotiation and compromise than by continued disruption. Many community organizations use a combination of strategies. For example, after the Woodlawn Organization used social action strategies (e.g., in the airport example described earlier), it gained recognition and legitimacy in the community. Then it developed a community development corporation to operate profit-making businesses and put the profits into community services. The Woodlawn Organization (T.W.O.) operates businesses, such as T.W.O./Hillman's Supermarket and T.W.O./Maryland Theatre, real estate developments, including several residential complexes, and such community services as budget counseling, manpower training programs, a day-care center, and a Head Start program (Lewis & Lewis, 1978, 1979). Community organizers also combine strategies. For example, Milton Street, who organized the walk-in homesteading program discussed earlier, went on to become a state senator.

Government-Mandated Community Organization

> This requirement [of citizen participation] grows out of the conviction that improving the quality of life of the residents of the model neighborhood can be accomplished only by the affirmative action of the people themselves. This requires a means of building self-esteem, competence, and a desire to participate effectively in solving the social and physical problems of the community. (From the Department of Housing and Urban Development policy statement requiring citizen participation in the Model Cities Program, quoted in Spiegel, 1968, p. 29)

In the 1960s, the federal government developed a major urban policy initiative through its social programs and the creation of a new cabinet-level department, Housing and Urban Development (HUD). The War on Poverty and the Great Society programs were developed to tackle the problems of the poor and urban decay. The War on Poverty was largely a top-down approach. Unlike other social reforms, the War on Poverty did not arise from the pressure of overwhelming public demand, but from presidential mandate (Sundquist, 1969). President Kennedy asked his advisors for a broad new program to tackle the bedrock problems of poverty. After President Kennedy's death, President Johnson (spurred partly by the urban riots of the 1960s) pushed through many of the War on Poverty programs. Several major programs relevant to community organization were passed, including the Model Cities Program and the Community Action Program (CAP). The Model Cities Program provided funds for renewal and renovation of urban core areas. CAP was an antipoverty effort to empower low-income people by involving them in the design and administration of their own social and economic programs. Direct relationships were established between the federal government and the neighborhood itself, bypassing the local government.

Both the Model Cities and CAP programs called for widespread citizen participation. The problems that the programs encountered have important implications for understanding citizen participation and its implementation. For example, a major problem with CAP legislation was its lack of specifity. How was the original mandate of the presidential planners to be put into operation? Did the poor need greater opportunity, more income, increased services, or more political power? The legislation tried to provide all of these possibilities within the same agency. Well-intentioned planners were unaware of the full range of problems they would encounter.

The hallmark concept of the legislation was the *maximum feasible participation* of the poor. Even among the original planners, the concept was never clearly understood or agreed upon. For some, the phrase meant a "process of encouraging the residents of poverty areas to take part in the work of community-action programs and to perform a number of jobs that might otherwise be performed by professional social workers" (Yarmolinsky, 1969, p. 49). That is, the poor were to participate in the administration of programs and services. For others, the local community action program was like a "three-legged stool" (Wofford, 1969) in which representatives of the poor would enter all phases of planning and administration. The poor would be equal partners with the local public officials and representatives of traditional social service agencies (a community development approach). For still others, the representatives of the poor were not expected to "necessarily be poor themselves" (Moynihan, 1969, p. 180)! What is clear is that the original planners did not expect that many of the poor would adopt a conflict strategy and attempt to topple local governmental units.

Regardless of original intent, CAP programs in many communities soon found themselves caught up in a political struggle over who "owned" the poverty program. Without clearly prescribed guidelines and procedures, federal administrators found themselves powerless as some local CAP groups adopted the assumption that the enemy was "the establishment"—the very groups with whom cooperation was to be encouraged. As this attitude became pervasive, local CAP groups encountered resistance and a backlash in attitudes even before programs were established. Political groups hoping to emasculate CAP programs were led by the very people needed to keep the three-legged stool on an even keel—the mayors and the traditional social service professionals.

By 1968, funds were shut off to the most radical CAP units, and their directors were replaced. Those CAP units that survived were the ones that had developed either from a social service model, or from a community development model in which local political units were included in a cooperative fashion. In the social service model, the emphasis was on service programs whose impact on institutional change was minimal. In the community development model, innovative, cooperative self-help projects took some faltering but significant steps toward maturity. Consumer cooperatives, credit unions, planned parenthood programs, health maintenance organizations, and parent effectiveness classes became available in some poor neighborhoods for the first time.

There is still disagreement today on the overall evaluation of the effectiveness of the Model Cities and CAP programs. However, there is general agreement that:

> Model Cities and the CAP agencies proved to be a great training ground for thousands of poor people in public administration and politics not to speak of public relations, communication, organization, construction, social welfare, health services, and manpower training. It proved . . . that citizens learn primarily by "doing" and only secondarily by formal education. (Erber, 1976, p. 9)

In 1974, the federal government developed a new approach to community development. As part of the "New Federalism" introduced by the Nixon administration, the Housing and Community Development Act of 1974 consolidated a number of Great Society categorical programs (e.g., urban renewal, Model Cities) and gave the money and the responsibilities to the cities in the form of block grants. Communities were to develop their own programs, primarily for the benefit of low- and moderate-income groups. This is known as the Community Development Block Grant program (CDBG), and it has included the development of hundreds of local projects, such as housing rehabilitation, downtown development, and capital improvements (e.g., new sewer lines). While the law and regulations required that the applicant provide citizens with "an adequate opportunity to participate in an advisory role in planning, implementing, and assessing" the CDBG program, the HUD regulations clearly stated that the city had the ultimate authority to develop and execute the programs (presumably as a lesson learned from programs such as CAP). Citizen participation guidelines were established which called for widespread citizen representation (e.g., minority, elderly, the business community) throughout all stages of the program. There was a written requirement for having at least two public hearings; one for soliciting proposals and a second for citizen feedback on the final proposals. A study by Nathan, Donnel, Liebschutz, and Morris (1977) and case examples suggest that there has been a fairly high level of citizen participation in the CDBG program. In 1982, however, the Reagan administration sharply relaxed the citizen participation requirements of the CDBG program, and the role and extent of citizen participation then depended on local politics.

The Neighborhood Movement: An Example of Grass Roots Community Organization

> In Southeast Baltimore, a curious coalition of housewives, social workers, and preservationists took on City Hall and the federal government in a fight against

an eight-lane expressway scheduled to slice through their neighborhood. They stopped the highway and formed a community "congress"—now staffed by more than 40 full-time employees and in charge of $16 million in neighborhood programs. (McBride, 1978, p. 38)

While many of the government-mandated community organization programs were targeted for low socioeconomic neighborhoods, a large part of the neighborhood movement of the 1970s and 80s has taken place in blue-collar and lower-middle-class white ethnic neighborhoods and in inner-city neighborhoods into which middle-class residents have been moving. While many in the 1960s thought the plight of cities was hopeless, there has been a resurgence of hope in cities—partly due to a neighborhood renewal and neighborhood revitalization movement in which neighborhood organizations have played a major role. The National Commission on Neighborhoods compiled a list of 8,000 neighborhood organizations nationwide. According to a national Gallup poll conducted in 1977 in communities over 50,000 (*Christian Science Monitor,* December 12, 1977), 12 percent of the adult population belonged to a neighborhood group, and an additional 29 percent said they would like to belong if one existed in their neighborhood. In addition, 89 percent of the people surveyed said they would be willing to perform a neighborhood activity (e.g., sign a petition, testify at a public hearing, volunteer time, or serve on a neighborhood committee), and a majority of the sample (52 percent) actually had engaged in some type of neighborhood activity in the previous five years. According to Gallup (in McBride, 1978), the neighborhood movement represents a low-cost approach to strengthening neighborhoods.

Neighborhood revitalization

America's older neighborhoods need to be saved. In cities across the country, older neighborhoods are in various stages of decline, and the homeowners are worried about increasing crime rates, poor schools, a physical shoddiness that is becoming obvious, and the future value of their homes. These neighborhoods are not slums, but they will become slums unless preventive action is taken. (Ahlbrandt & Brophy, 1975, p. 1)

Neighborhood renewal, revitalization, or conservation (the terms often are used interchangably) is not a major federal program directed at severely deteriorated neighborhoods populated with the poor. Rather, it is more often a local effort with individual citizens, neighborhood organizations, banks, and, to some extent, local government playing key roles in moderate- and middle-income neighborhoods. Clay (1979) has distinguished two types of renewal: gentrification and incumbent upgrading. Gentrification involves the movement of middle-class and upper-class residents into a low-income neighborhood. The "gentry" creates a middle-class climate and style that can lead to higher prices and to displacement of the lower-income residents who had been living there. Incumbent upgrading, which is more common, involves the physical improvement of a neighborhood by its residents. This generally occurs in moderate-income neighborhoods, and there is little change in the demographic characteristics of the residents.

Most of the attention in neighborhood development has been paid to economic and physical characteristics. However, an important study by Ahlbrandt and Cunningham (1979) suggests that the *social fabric* (e.g., personal relationships within the neighborhood, interactions among clubs and organizations, use of goods and services in the neighborhood) and *sense of community* play major roles in neighborhood stability and preservation. They found that sense of community and social fabric were more highly related to a commitment to stay in the neighborhood than were resident satisfaction with public services, housing, and neighborhood conditions. They also found that plans to make home repairs were directly related to the homeowner's attachment to the neighborhood. In addition, citizen participation in neighborhood organizations was related to commitment to the neighborhood.

Neighborhood revitalization is complex and requires public investment in services as well as private investment (bank loans and resident investment in maintenance and improvement). Also, there are forces outside the city itself that affect metropolitan areas, including general demographic trends, industrial migration to the suburbs or other regions of the country, suburban housing development, and general economic cycles (Ahlbrandt & Cunningham, 1979; Downs, 1981; Schoenberg & Rosenbaum, 1980). Advocates of neighborhood revitalization and preservation argue that it is precisely because cities cannot control many of these large-scale forces that they should work where they can hope to have an impact—for example, by developing strategies that will keep middle-class and working-class populations in city neighborhoods (thus retaining their tax base). Ahlbrandt and Cunningham (1979) conclude that city government must develop policies for neighborhood preservation that encourage maintaining the social fabric of neighborhoods and the sense of community and commitment of citizens. These goals can be achieved by supporting neighborhood organizations.

Summary. The community organization literature tends to be case study oriented, and often uses detailed interviews with organizers or community organization leaders as the primary source of information. This approach tends to provide important details about the process of community organization, but it may be selective by concentrating on positive effects or by providing the point of view of only a few of the people involved. Eugster's West Heights example suggests some factors that may facilitate community development: a persistent leader, choosing a specific problem shared by many, developing a concrete strategy, and seeking broad-based support. These conditions create an opportunity for individuals to participate and a structure for decision making. The example suggests some of the potential benefits that can be obtained by individuals and communities. However, not all community organization efforts are as well-organized or successful.

Some fizzle and others backfire. Often community organization efforts have difficulty getting or maintaining participation. The case study approach makes it difficult to know why one case is successful and another is not. A systematic approach that investigates key questions about citizen participation and that enables us to compare results from different settings can foster the development of our understanding of citizen participation. In the next section, we discuss a research project that was guided by a framework of participation to explore how neighborhood organizations develop and what influences their continual functioning.

THE NEIGHBORHOOD PARTICIPATION PROJECT: THE USE OF PSYCHOLOGICAL APPROACHES TO INVESTIGATE CITIZEN PARTICIPATION IN NEIGHBORHOOD (BLOCK) ORGANIZATIONS

There are many gaps in our knowledge of citizen participation and its role in the development of community. For example, why don't more people want to participate in neighborhood organizations? In the Gallup poll mentioned previously, when residents were asked if they would like to belong to a neighborhood organization, 42 percent said no and 16 percent said don't know. Why do some community organizations survive and others quickly die out? Much of the literature we discussed on citizen participation, community organization, and neighborhoods comes from political science, sociology, and social work. We believe that psychological perspectives, concepts, and methods also can be helpful, and that a major role of community psychology is to investigate the interface between the individual and society. As a way of illustrating the role that community psychology can contribute to understanding citizen participation, we will describe some of the results of the Neighborhood Participation Project (NPP). The research described here will focus on two of the major issues in neighborhood organizations—how organizations are formed and how they are maintained.

The Setting

The Neighborhood Participation Project was conducted by Wandersman and his colleagues in Nashville, Tennessee, to increase understanding of factors leading to citizen participation in block organizations. The project was a longitudinal study that collected data on 39 blocks and over 1,200 individuals.

The Waverly-Belmont neighborhood in Nashville is typical of many American transitional urban neighborhoods. Following a post-World War II exodus to the suburbs by middle-class residents, the neighborhood experienced urban decay—decreasing property values, an increasing crime rate, and a deteriorating physical environment. Recently, however, there has been a reverse migration to urban areas, such as this one, which offers spacious older homes with the conveniences and amenities of an urban location. Although the neighborhood is racially integrated, individual blocks tend to be more homogeneous, having primarily either white residents or black residents of varying socioeconomic status. For the most part, houses are primarily one-family and two-family dwellings with a few multiple (3-to-4-family) units interspersed.

In 1975, Neighborhood Housing Services (NHS) began offering services to residents of the neighborhood. NHS is a nonprofit, cooperative organization of neighborhood residents, city government, and local lending institutions. It uses a community development approach to assist neighborhood residents in revitalizing their neighborhood. NHS programs are developed in neighborhoods in which the housing shows evidence of deterioration and lack of maintenance, and which already have some neighborhood participation. NHS services provide citizens with assistance in financing and rehabilitating homes and in obtaining government services. The NHS approach ties the neighborhood movement to community organization by bringing neighborhood residents into a partnership with lending institutions and with local government. It is the single most widely employed model for neighborhood upgrading (Ahlbrandt & Brophy, 1975). In 1983, there were over 160 NHS programs operating in 140 cities across the United States. While there is a nonprofit organization that provides technical assistance to NHS organizations throughout the country, each NHS is a local, independent organization.

One of the ways NHS stimulates citizen action is to assist in the development of block organizations. The organizing procedure employed by NHS organizers in Nashville involved door-to-door contact with residents on each block. Organizers attempted to assess each household's concerns, needs, and interests on the block through discussion of a list of common problems usually associated with urban neighborhoods. When a profile of block concerns emerged, organizers used this information to illustrate to residents that they shared similar concerns which could be addressed through collective action. During the initial organizing effort, the organizer would try to find one person or family to host the first block meeting in their home. The organizer then assisted the host in contacting all the people on the block, and helped arrange the date and time of the first meeting. The organizer also assisted in follow-up meetings that were held.

The Formation and Maintenance of Block Organizations

Wandersman (1981) proposed a framework of participation in community organizations (similar to Figure 10–1) that guided the major issues studied in the Neighborhood Participation Project. In this section we discuss some of the research in the context of the formation and the maintenance of block organizations.

Formation of block organizations. The formation of block organizations was studied from several viewpoints: (1) Who participates, who does not participate, and why? (2) How does the interaction of the person and the situation influence participation? (3) How do the social and environmental characteristics of the block influence participation?

1. Who participates, who does not participate, and why? (The individual level.)

Background. Supporters of participation, such as advocacy planners (Halprin, 1974; Sanoff, 1975) or neighborhood advocates (Kotler, 1969; Hallman, 1974) believe that the benefits of participation are so clear and powerful that it is assumed there is a general need to participate, and everyone will participate if given the opportunity. However, the community organization experience and research literature (e.g., Peattie, 1967; Warren, 1974) suggests that, in many cases, relatively few people actually participate in community organizations when given the opportunity. If citizen participation is so good for people and has so many benefits, why don't more people participate? Many sociological and political science studies have investigated participation by relating background demographic characteristics— including sex, age, race, marital status, education, and occupational status—to voluntary action participation (Smith, 1975). A number of investigators (e.g., Alford & Scoble, 1968; Hyman & Wright, 1971; Milbrath, 1965) suggest that middle-class people, in general, are more likely to participate than lower-class people. Orum (1966) and Williams, Babchuk, and Johnson (1973) found that blacks are more likely to participate in voluntary associations than whites of the same class.

While race and socioeconomic class have been related to participation, they may have limited explanatory and predictive power. Recent research indicates that social background loses much of its direct explanatory power in predicting participation when intervening attitudes, personality, and situational variables are controlled statistically (Smith, 1975). It is possible, for instance, that those groups who avoid participation in the larger society because of their own perceived inefficacy, will respond with enthusiasm to concrete, visible activities which could affect their own block. For example, low-income neighborhoods can be mobilized when facing a common fate at the intrusive hands of realtors, city planners, industry, or politicians (Suttles, 1972).

The NPP. By relating many characteristics to participation simultaneously in the NPP, Wandersman, Jakubs, and Giamartino (1981) were able to rank the importance of variables which differentiated members and nonmembers in a specific block organization. The results suggested that, at least at the block level, participation in voluntary organizations is related to demographic indicators of being "rooted" to a place (e.g., older, married, homeowner, female, lived on the block longer). Race, occupation, and education were not related to participation. The psychological variables indicated that compared with nonmembers, members were more active in other community activities, had a higher sense of civic duty and political efficacy, perceived more problems on the block, engaged in more neighboring activities, felt a greater sense of community, and had higher self-esteem. Conversely, nonmembers were more likely to be renters, to have lived on the block less time, and did not plan to stay as long. Nonmembers felt less sense of community and rated the block as less important.

Members of block organizations were asked to name their most important reason for joining the organization. Improvement of the residential environment was the most frequent reason given, followed by the influence of others, and a sense of duty. Nonmembers were asked to name their most important reason for *not* joining the organization. Lack of time, scheduling difficulties, or the respondent's poor physical condition were cited by a majority of the respondents. A small percentage endorsed a "free-rider" effect—others would do the work.

2.   How does the interaction of the person and the situation influence participation?

Background. The personality literature in psychology may help us understand what types of people participate. There have been a few attempts to relate some personality (e.g., trait) variables to participation. For example, it has been suggested that individuals who have higher self-esteem and who feel they are able to influence what happens to them (internal locus of control) are more likely to participate. On the other hand, the personality trait approach has been criticized because people do not act consistently in all situations (e.g., people do not participate in every organization available). Many psychologists now agree that an interaction position makes the most sense—there is a complex interaction between the characteristics of the person and the environment that produces and sustains behavior. For this reason, an individual is likely to participate in only a few of the many organizations available. The organization(s) chosen are selected on the basis of the individual's own characteristics (e.g., needs, values, and personality) and of the characteristics of the organization (e.g., purposes, efficacy, location).

Despite the consensus on the need for an interactional psychology, few approaches have been developed to investigate the interaction between the person and the situation. Mischel (1973, 1976) suggested five cognitive social learning variables which are useful in conceptualizing how the qualities of the person influence the impact of situations and how each person generates distinct patterns of behavior in interaction with the conditions of his or her life.

The NPP. In the Neighborhood Participation Project, Wandersman and Florin (1981), and Florin and Wandersman (1982) operationalized the five cognitive social learning variables in relation to the block and neighborhood environment and participation in neighborhood-type organizations:

Construction competencies—the ability to construct particular cognitions and behaviors. Examples of construction competencies in participation include the ability to lead a group and the ability to organize people for action.

Encoding strategies—the way the environment or situation is perceived, coded, and categorized by each person. Relevant encoding strategies include perceptions of the environment and attributions of responsibility for problems in the environment.

Expectancies—expectancies about the consequences of different behavioral possibilities in that situation, such as expectancies of the effectiveness of individual action.

Subjective stimulus values—the values which the person assigns to expected outcomes. Relevant subjective stimulus values include the importance of the environment and various possible outcomes of participation.

Self-regulatory systems—the plans by which the person regulates his or her behavior. Relevant self-regulatory systems include a person's standards and sense of duty with regard to participation in the public sphere.

The results showed that the variables are promising for their use in both predicting and understanding participation. The set of cognitive social learning variables was compared with a larger set of traditional demographic and personality trait variables for ability to discriminate members from nonmembers. They accounted for more of the variance in participation. In other words, the cognitive social learning variables were able to predict membership better than a combination of demographic and personality variables. The cognitive social learning variables are more likely to contribute to the practice of citizen participation because demographic and personality variables offer few practical suggestions for interventions to increase participation. A community organizer has little hope of changing age, locus of control, or renter status to home ownership, while expectancies and competencies are more amenable to change.

3. How do the environmental characteristics of the block influence participation? (The group level.)

Background. Population characteristics (e.g., race, class, homogeneity), which often are referred to as characteristics of the human aggregate, can serve as a press or ecological force that inhibits or facilitates participation. This hypothesis received support in a study of participation in the initial stages of block organization (Wandersman & Giamartino, 1980). The NPP results suggested that the average characteristics of the residents of a block, such as participation in volunteer organizations, feelings of civic duty, willingness to work to improve the block, were related to whether or not block organizations formed. Since these characteristics did not differentiate members from nonmembers at the individual level, the researchers suggested that these characteristics, when averaged for a block, form a "block climate" that influences block organization development.

An aggregate concept that helps explain citizen participation in block organizations is degree of neighboring. There are some general findings which indicate that people with more informal contacts tend to participate more in voluntary organizations (Axelrod, 1956), and that people rely on contacts with friends and acquaintances in making their decision to join

(Booth & Babchuk, 1969). Ahlbrandt and Cunningham (1979) showed that neighboring was related to levels of satisfaction and commitment to the neighborhood which, in turn, might lead to increased participation. Hunter (1974) found that people who had most of their friends living in their locale were more likely to be members of a block or neighborhood organization than those who had most of their friends outside of the area. Thus, several studies suggested that neighboring can influence participation. There are several ways that neighboring might do this. A neighbor may inform another of the existence of the organization, drop reminders about meeting times, and encourage participation directly by expressing enthusiasm or indirectly by providing a familiar face at meetings.

The NPP. In an exploratory analysis, Unger and Wandersman (1983) assessed the degree of neighboring on seven blocks and then examined which blocks later became successfully organized. They found that residents on the four blocks which successfully developed active organizations had significantly greater neighboring activity *prior* to any attempt at organization than did residents of the three blocks which were not successfully organized. Thus, neighbors on blocks that successfully organized were interacting more with each other even before a community organizer arrived. The degree of neighboring on a block may thus be an important factor in identifying blocks which have the potential to be successfully organized.

Interestingly, what was true at the aggregate level of the block was not true individually. Contrary to expectations, members of the organizations interacted *less* with their neighbors prior to the organization's development than did residents who did not become members. Unger and Wandersman speculated that members may have used the organization as a vehicle to become part of the existing neighboring network on their block, whereas those residents who were already neighboring may have felt less necessity to join. Crensen (1978) has suggested that individuals who are part of a close-knit neighborhood are not likely to join an organization; instead, they find alternative informal ways to work toward solving neighborhood problems and meeting mutual needs. However, there are alternative explanations (e.g., more activity outside of the block may mean less time for neighboring on the block).

Members' participation in other community organizations like the PTA was assessed to determine if they were more involved than nonmembers in the larger community beyond the block. Members belonged to significantly more community organizations than nonmembers. The results suggested that members, especially block organization leaders, neighbored less than nonmembers prior to organizing. However, members had more ties to other community organizations than nonmembers. This enabled them to rely on a greater array of skills and experiences, and provided linkages to resources of other organizations, which in turn may have encouraged their block organization's success.

Whatever brought members to the organizations, their neighboring increased as a result of membership. While members did initially neighbor less than nonmembers, members' neighboring activities (especially leaders) increased after participation in a block organization. The neighboring of nonmembers after the same period remained relatively stable, as did the neighboring of residents of blocks which were not successfully organized.

The results show interesting and sometimes divergent patterns, depending on the level of analysis used—block (successfully organized versus unsuccessfully organized), organizational (members versus nonmembers) and individual (members prior to and after the formation of the block organizations). These distinctions support the discussion of the importance of level of analysis in the methodology chapter (Chapter Three). The results also support the importance of longitudinal research because, if the researchers would have looked at neighboring *only after the block organizations had been formed,* they would have found no significant differences in neighboring between members and nonmembers and would have missed some of the most interesting results.

Maintaining Viable Organizations

Background. Maintaining an active block organization is more difficult than initiating one, and several studies have described the nature of the difficulties (Helper, 1965; Lipsky & Levi, 1972; Yates, 1973). For example, in a study of some 500 block associations that applied for small grants from an experimental program in New York called Operation Better Block, Yates (1973) reported that more than 50 percent of the associations failed to move beyond the simple clean-up level of activity and subsequently declined. He suggested several reasons for the decline of these organizations. Following the initial burst of activity, many block organizations turned into heavily bureaucratic organizations, burdening participants with committee work. They no longer were able to provide members with the spontaneous collective action that increased group cohesiveness and sense of community. There was a constant need to monitor activities like garbage pickup, and these became monotonous chores. Finally, many block organizations were unable to deal with the disillusionment following an encounter with an unsolvable problem. Many block leaders lost confidence in themselves and in the organization's ability to achieve its goals. Other studies (e.g., Goering, Robison, & Hoover, 1977; Lipsky & Levi, 1972; Rich, 1980b) have noted similar difficulties in initiating or maintaining viable organizations. As with other voluntary organizations, neighborhood organizations need to stimulate and maintain the interest, participation, and satisfaction of their members.

The organizational psychology literature, which is based largely on formal industrial organizations, may be helpful in understanding the functioning of neighborhood organizations. For example, the concept of social or organizational climate has received considerable attention for its utility in assessing participants' perceptions of the organization (Schneider, 1975). Climate has been described as a set of descriptive, nonevaluative perceptions of an organization's characteristics. Climate characteristics have been found to be associated with organizational members' satisfaction and performance in a variety of organizations, including banks, mental hospitals, prisons, and schools (Jones & James, 1979; Moos, 1976).

The NPP. Giamartino and Wandersman (1983) assessed the social climate of 17 block organizations as well as member satisfaction and involvement with the organizations. Moos and Humphrey's (1973) Group Environment Scale was used to assess social climate.

Block organizations in which members reported being satisfied with the progress of the organization, and in which members reported that they enjoyed their membership, had a social climate which was more cohesive, had greater clarity of group rules, norms and sanctions, and had leaders who helped direct the group, make decisions, and enforce the rules of the group. Perceptions of the strength of the organization were associated with the above dimensions as well as with feelings that the leaders displayed concern, friendship, and help to the members, and that the group was practical or "down to earth" in its orientation. These results suggest that structure and strong, supportive leadership are important to the functioning of block organizations. With regard to involvement in the activities of the group, the same general pattern of relationships with climate emerged, but to a lesser extent. Here, too, structure and strong leadership were demonstrated to be important aspects of groups which maintained the involvement of their members. Thus, the picture of the block organization in which members are satisfied and involved is one in which there is a balance of positive interpersonal relations and a concern for the orderly management of group relations and tasks. In addition, the social climate accurately predicted which block organizations would be "active" (still meeting) versus "inactive" (not meeting) *one year later*. The social climate results were strong and offered implications for interventions to maintain organizations. (For information on the use of social climate scales to facilitate change, see Moos, 1979.)

Potential Uses of the Research

In the Neighborhood Participation Project, a concept called "participation potential" was developed. Participation potential involves the identification of community and individual characteristics that indicate a high or low probability for successful block or neighborhood organization. For example, if a primary weakness was a perceived lack of residents' skills relevant to participation, then workshops could be given to develop such skills. If skills were high but neighboring and sense of community were low, an organizer might promote social interaction through block parties or other vehicles. Or, if expectations of success were low, modeling from other areas and testimonials from residents of successfully organized blocks could be arranged. Thus, interventions could be fine-tuned to the specific strengths and weaknesses of the block, making the successful initiation and maintenance of an organization more likely. Characteristics of block organizations relevant to their maintenance include:

1. Group cohesiveness.
2. Task orientation.
3. Leadership patterns.
4. Satisfaction with organizational processes.
5. Satisfaction with the outcomes of the organization.
6. Organizational structure.
7. Members' work patterns.
8. Level and type of participation by residents.

To maximize maintenance, or "staying power" of an organization, leaders could be informed how their styles and the orientation and structure of the group are perceived. If needed, activities could be planned to engage residents in meaningful action. Goals could be planned to maximize the reinforcement of participation through small successes. The specificity of this type of assessment should make maintenance more likely.

The potential for using the research to help the residents help themselves is illustrated in a case study of the NPP (Chavis, Stucky, & Wandersman, 1983). After sending out interviewers each summer to administer a 60-minute interview, the researchers found that the hospitality of the host community was being taxed by the research. Now that they had the data, the researchers asked themselves, "How can this data be used to benefit the community where it was obtained?"

The researchers believed that passing out a fact sheet, research summary, or final report would be inadequate, and that the best vehicle for using the information to its greatest potential was through the existing neighborhood organizations. A planning committee for the feedback process was constituted, consisting of three members of the neighborhood organization (the president and two other officers) and three members of the research project. It was decided that the best method for explaining the research findings would be a workshop format.

At the workshop for representatives of 12 block organizations, the researchers explained the project in "everyday language" and presented highlights of relevant research results to the participants. The neighborhood leaders then broke into small discussion groups to discuss issues important to them, such as participation in block clubs and the social and physical environment of their neighborhoods. By introducing and comparing the research information and the actual experiences of the participants, the researchers learned what was relevant about their data, while the residents were able to substantiate some of their intuitive thoughts about neighborhood participation. As a result of the workshops, some of the groups developed action plans, which included assisting in the formation of new block clubs, devising an odd-job listing for teenagers, and investigating the possibility of an alley clean-up program.

Both direct and indirect benefits resulted from the workshop. The action plans were followed to varying degrees. A committee, formed to organize block clubs, requested information from the researchers on each of the blocks to aid in their organizing efforts. In response, NPP staff developed written profiles on all 39 blocks, which were used in promoting and organizing block clubs. Youth and crime prevention programs were developed, based on needs determined in the workshop. The research supported a claim by some residents concerning the displacement of poor black residents. This gave birth to organizational efforts to minimize this process. After the workshop, residents stopped by the research office to ask about articles, books, and other materials related to neighborhood revitalization, crime prevention, participation, and skill development. Therefore, *citizen participation* in planning and implementing the workshop led to the effective use of the research information by citizens, to the development of citizen skills for obtaining and using research, and to the researchers having better knowledge about the meaning and usefulness of the research.

CONCLUDING COMMENTS

Citizen participation is a process which allows citizens to provide input into the programs and policies which affect them. It has the potential of increasing participants' feelings of control, and allows them the opportunity to develop or select programs which match their needs and values (Wandersman, 1979b). As such, it represents a process for empowering people. The aim of empowerment is to increase the possibilities for people to control their own lives (Berger & Neuhaus, 1977; Kieffer, in press; Rappaport, 1981). Rappaport suggests that even seemingly desirable programs and policies, such as prevention, reduce people's power if the programs are planned by experts and the citizens are treated as clients. Empowerment is increased when experts treat citizens as collaborators. As one community organizer put it, "We've got ordinary people who come from public housing projects, retirement centers, and churches, who've never spoken before a crowd who are now sitting down and talking to the governor, to legislators, to the heads of utility companies and who are learning the skills of active citizenship" (Martha Ballou in Boyte, 1980, p. 38).

What have we learned about citizen participation? Due to the complexity of participation, we have approached this chapter from a perspective of how we can find out what citizen participation is and why it works, rather than as a summary of knowledge about citizen participation. That is why we have paid considerable attention to frameworks and categories. By looking at specific issues within the general framework of citizen participation, we can provide a brief summary of the research which has implications for increasing participation and its effectiveness.

1. How does the external environment of the citizen group affect the opportunities and resources for participation? The external environment provides a setting that either facilitates or inhibits participation. For example, in the community mental health center study, the lack of support or structure provided by the staff and the board increased the difficulties experienced by the citizen group and contributed to its lack of accomplishment. In the CAP example, local government officials often were in conflict with citizen members of the CAP board. The result was political pressures that eventually reduced the funding of the CAP program. In the Eugster example, when school and city goals coincided with the community development goals, the schools provided resources to the community development effort.

2. Who participates in citizen groups and what are their reasons for participation? Studies have shown moderate relationships between demographic variables (e.g., race, sex, education) and participation. For example, people who are better educated are more likely to be members of a citizen group at a mental health center. Also, people who are more invested (e.g., "rooted" in their blocks) are more likely to be members of an organization. Members join to help others, and to improve the program or environment. We also saw that understanding how individuals value a situation, their expectancies for success, and their skills in that situation influence whether or not they participate. Also, the group level (e.g., the block environment) had an influence on participation that was independent of the characteristics of the individual.

3. What are the characteristics of organizations that facilitate or inhibit effective participation? A lack of clarity in the purposes of the group was shown to be strongly related to ineffectiveness and the eventual demise of citizen groups. Strong leadership, task orientation, and the ability to accomplish tasks played important roles in maintaining viable organizations. The potential use of psychological knowledge and skills to maintain organizational effectiveness were illustrated in the manual developed by Zinobar and Dinkel for community mental health centers and in the social climate assessment and implications for intervention in block organizations.

4. What are the effects of participation on the individual and on the program or community? The effects of participation are influenced by the appropriateness and meaningfulness of the participation experiences (e.g., the form and type of participation). In the citizen group in the community mental health center, the effects were very limited. The citizens felt they had little impact on the programs of the center, although they did perform some services for the center (e.g., holding a banquet). The personal benefits included a sense of contribution and helpfulness. The individual costs were the amount of time it took up and frustration about lack of progress. In a study of client involvement in a mental health center (Morrison & Cometa, 1979), client satisfaction increased, and the services became more responsive to client needs. In the community organization literature, a number of accomplishments were discussed, including improving the education of children,

revitalizing neighborhoods, and providing training for people to learn how to participate in the decisions which affect them.

Citizen participation and the development of community through neighborhood organizations represent important strategies for confronting many societal problems. Citizen participation gives people an opportunity to affect the environments which impinge upon them. Large institutions and professional workers are not necessarily eliminated by allowing for citizen input. Experts always will be needed in complex societies; but citizens have expertise of their own, which if tapped appropriately can help move institutions toward becoming more in touch with citizen needs and values.

Citizen participation has its problems and limitations as well. Citizen participation can be time-consuming, costly, cumbersome, and ineffective. It also can be nonrepresentative since not everybody participates. While programs have been developed to reduce these problems, for example through the training of administrators and citizens, participation, by itself, will not cure all of the ills of complex technological societies. However, with greater understanding of the process and effects of citizen participation, more effective strategies for citizen participation can be developed.

There are multiple causes for contemporary social problems and we will need multiple problem-solving strategies, some of which involve networks, formal organizations, government-mandated participation, and grass roots participation. We should be an experimenting society in which professionals and citizens work together in developing, implementing, evaluating, and refining problem-solving strategies.

References

Advisory Commission on Intergovernmental Relations. *Citizen participation in the American Federal System.* Washington, D.C.: U.S. Government Printing Office, 1979.

Ahlbrandt, R. S., Jr., & Brophy, P. *Neighborhood revitalization: Theory and practice.* Lexington, Mass.: Lexington Books (D. C. Heath), 1975.

Ahlbrandt, R. S., Jr., & Cunningham, J. V. *A new public policy for neighborhood preservation.* New York: Praeger Publishers, 1979.

Alexander, C. The Oregon experiment. New York: Praeger Publishers, 1975.

Alford, R. R., & Scoble, H. M. Community leadership: Education & political behavior. *American Sociological Review,* 1968, *33,* 259–272.

Alinsky, S. D. *Reveille for radicals.* Chicago: University of Chicago Press, 1946.

Alinsky, S. D. *Rules for radicals.* New York: Random House, 1971.

Altshuler, A. A. *Community control: The black demand for participation in large American cities.* New York: Pegasus, 1970.

Axelrod, M. Urban structure and social participation. *American Sociological Review,* 1956, *21*(1), 13–18.

Bazan, G., et al. *Wesleytown report.* Unpublished paper, Pennsylvania State University, 1973.

Berger, P. L., & Neuhaus, R. J. *To empower people.* Washington, D.C.: American Enterprise Institute, 1977.

Booth, A., & Babchuck, N. Personal influence networks and voluntary association affiliations. *Sociological Inquiry,* 1969, *39,* 179–188.

Boyte, H. C. *The backyard revolution: Understanding the new citizen movement.* Philadelphia: Temple University Press, 1980.

Briscoe, R. V., Hoffman, D. B., & Bailey, J. S. Behavioral community psychology: Training a community board to problem solve. *Journal of Applied Behavior Analysis,* 1975, *8,* 157–168.

Cassidy, R. Grassroots urban renewal. *Quest/81,* March, 51–86.

Congressional Quarterly. November 13, 1982, *40*(46), p. 2850.

Capraro, J. F. The revitalization of Chicago Lawn: A private sector response to local decline. *Commentary* (publication of the National Council for Urban Economic Development), October 1979, *3*(3), 11–14.

Chavis, D. M., Stucky, P. E., & Wandersman, A. Returning basic research to the community: A relationship between scientist and citizen. *American Psychologist, 1983, 38*(4), 424–434.

Checkoway, B. *Citizens and health care: Participation and planning for social change.* Elmsford, N.Y.: Pergamon Press, 1981.

Ciarlo, J. A., & Diamond, H. (Eds.) Special issue on "Citizen participation in community mental health services." *Community Mental Health Journal,* 1981, *17,* (1).

Clay, P. L. *Neighborhood renewal.* Lexington, Mass.: Lexington Books, 1979.

Clinard, M. B. *Slums and community development: Experiments in self-help.* New York: Free Press, 1970.

Coates, G. *Action research and community power: A prospectus for environmental change.* Unpublished paper, Cornell University, 1971.

Cohen, H. J. Obstacles to developing community services for the mentally retarded. In M. J. Begab & S. A. Richardson (Eds.), *The mentally retarded and society: A social science perspective.* Baltimore, Md.: University Park Press, 1975.

Corbett, J. Student-built housing as an alternative to dormitories. *Environment and Behavior,* 1973, *5,* 491–504.

Cox, F. M., Erlich, J. R., Rothman, J., & Tropman, J. E. *Strategies of community organization: A book of readings.* Itasca, Ill.: F. E. Peacock Publishers, 1970.

Crensen, M. A. Social networks and political processes in urban neighborhoods. *American Journal of Political Science,* 1978, *22*(3), 578–594.

Downs, A. *Neighborhoods and urban development.* Washington, D.C.: Brookings Institution, 1981.

Dorwart, R. A., & Meyers, W. R. *Citizen participation in mental health: Research and social policy.* Springfield, Ill.: Charles C Thomas, 1981.

Erber, E. Why citizen participation? *HUD Challenge,* January, 1976.

Eugster, C. Field education in West Heights: Equipping a deprived community to help itself. In F. M. Cox, J. L. Erlich, J. Rothman, & J. E. Tropman (Eds.), *Strategies of community organization: A book of readings* (2d ed.). Itasca, Ill.: F. E. Peacock Publishers, 1974.

Florin, P., & Wandersman, A. *Cognitive social learning constructs and community development.* Paper presented at American Psychological Association, 1982.

Francis, M. Designing landscapes with community participation and behavioral research. *Landscape Architectural Forum,* Spring 1982, 15–39.

Giamartino, G., & Wandersman, A. Organizational climate correlates of viable block organizations. *American Journal of Community Psychology,* 1983, *11*(5), 529–541.

Goering, J. M., Robison, M., & Hoover, K. *The best eight blocks in Harlem: The decade of urban reform.* Washington, D.C.: University Press of America, 1977.

Goldblatt, H. Arguments for and against citizen participation in urban renewal. In H. Spiegel (Ed.), *Citizen participation in urban development* (Vol. 1). Washington, D.C.: NTL Institute, 1968.

Gump, P. V. School environments. In I. Altman & J. F. Wohlwill (Eds.), *Children and the environment.* New York: Plenum, 1978.

Hallman, H. W. *Neighborhood government in a metropolitan setting.* Beverly Hills, Calif.: Sage Publications, 1974.

Halprin, L., et al. *Taking part.* Cambridge, Mass.: MIT Press, 1974.

Helper, R. Neighborhood association diary. *Journal of Housing,* 1965, *22,* 136–140.

Hunter, A. *Symbolic communities.* Chicago: University of Chicago Press, 1974.

Hyman, H., & Wright, C. Trends in voluntary association memberships of American adults: Replication based on secondary analysis of national sample surveys. *American Sociological Review,* 1971, *36,* 191–206.

Jones, A. P., & James, L. R. Psychological climate: Dimensions and relationships of individuals and aggregated work environment perceptions. *Organizational Behavior and Human Performance,* 1979, *23,* 201–250.

Kane, T. J. Citizen participation in decision-making: Myth or strategy. *Administration in Mental Health,* 1975, *2,* 29–34.

Kieffer, C. H. Citizen empowerment: A developmental perspective. *Prevention in Human Services,* in press.

Klein, K. J. *Community psychology and workplace research: Studying employee ownership.* Paper presented at American Psychological Association meeting, Washington, D.C., August 1982.

Kotler, M. *Neighborhood government: The local foundations of political life.* Indianapolis and New York: Bobbs-Merrill, 1969.

Lamb, C. *User design.* Paper presented at the EDRA 6 Conference in Lawrence, Kansas, 1975.

Langton, S. *Citizen participation in America.* Lexington, Mass.: D. C. Heath, 1978.

Langton, S. What's right and what's wrong with citizen participation. *Citizen Participation,* May/June 1981, *3*(5), 8–9, 19–20.

Langton, S., & Markey, E. Enough is enough: The rise of the nuclear disarmament movement. *Citizen Participation,* May/June 1982, *3*(5), 3–4, 22.

Lewis, M., & Lewis, J. The Woodlawn experience. *Journal of Alternative Human Services,* 1978, *4*(4), 12–16.

Lewis, M., & Lewis, J. The Woodlawn experience: Part two. *Journal of Alternative Human Services,* 1979, *5*(1), 23–26.

Lipsky, M., & Levi, M. Community organizations as a political resource. In H. Hanh (Ed.), *People and politics in urban society.* Beverly Hills, Calif.: Sage Publications, 1972.

Livingston, G. *Citizen participation groups in community mental health: A review of the empirical literature.* Unpublished manuscript, University of South Carolina, 1981.

Manpower Demonstration Research Corporation, *Tenant management: Findings from a three-year experiment in public housing.* Cambridge, Mass.: Ballinger, 1981.

McBride, S. Gallup urban poll: Residents view their cities. *Nation's Cities,* 1978, *16*(11), 316–348.

McClure, L., & Depiano, L. School advisory council participation and effectiveness. *American Journal of Community Psychology,* 1983, *11,* 687–704.

Milbrath, L. W. *Political participation: How and why do people get involved in politics?* Skokie, Ill.: Rand McNally, 1965.

Miller, S. M., & Riessman, F. *Social class and social policy.* New York: Basic Books, 1968.

Mischel, W. Toward a cognitive social learning reconceptualization of personality. *Psychological Review,* 1973, 252–283.

Mischel, W. The self as the person: A cognitive social learning view. In A. Wandersman, P. Poppen, & D. Ricks (Eds.), *Humanism and behaviorism: Dialogue and growth.* Elmsford, N.Y.: Pergamon Press, 1976.

Moos, R. *The human context: Environmental determinants of behavior.* New York: John Wiley & Sons, 1976.

Moos, R. *Evaluating educational environments.* San Francisco: Jossey-Bass, 1979.

Moos, R., & Humphrey, B. *Group environment scale: Technical report.* Social Ecology Laboratory, Department of Psychiatry, Stanford University, 1973.

Morris, D. E., & Hess, K. *Neighborhood power: The new localism.* Boston: Beacon Press, 1975.

Morrison, J. K., & Cometa, M. S. The impact of a client advisory board on a community mental health clinic. In J. K. Morrison (Ed.), *A consumer approach to community psychology.* Chicago: Nelson-Hall, 1979.

Morrison, J. K., Holdridge-Crane, S., & Smith, J. E. Citizen participation in community mental health. *Community Mental Health Review,* 1978, *3,* 2–9.

Moynihan, D. P. *Maximum feasible misunderstanding: Community action in the war on poverty.* New York: Free Press, 1969.

Nathan, R. P., Donnel, P. R., Liebschutz, S. F., Morris, M. D., et al. *Block grants for community development.* Washington, D.C.: Department of Housing and Urban Development, U.S. Government Printing Office, 1977.

Nisbet, R. A. *The quest for community.* New York: Oxford University Press, 1953.

Orum, A. M. A reappraisal of the social and political participation of Negroes. *American Journal of Sociology,* 1966, *72,* 32–46.

Pearl, A. *The psychological consultant as change agent, or change: Real and unreal, sufficient and insufficient, backwards and forwards.* Paper presented at the meetings of the American Psychological Association, Washington, D.C., 1971.

Peattie, L. Reflections on advocacy planning. *Journal of American Institute of Planners,* March 1967, 80–88.

Perlman, J. E. Grassrooting the system. *Social Policy,* 1976, September/October.

Perlman, J. E. Grassroots participation from neighborhood to nation. In S. Langton (Ed.), *Citizen participation in America.* Lexington, Mass.: D. C. Heath, 1978.

Rappaport, J. In praise of paradox: A social policy of empowerment over prevention. *American Journal of Community Psychology,* 1981, *9,* 1–26.

Reinharz, S. The other side of the coin: Women as competent community builders.

In A. Rickel, I. Iscoe, & M. Gerrard (Eds.), *Social and psychological problems of women*. Washington, D.C.: Hemisphere Publishing, 1983.

Rich, R. C. A role for neighborhoods in urban governance? In T. K. Barnekov & M. H. Callahan (Eds.), *Neighborhoods*. Newark: University of Delaware, 1980a.

Rich, R. C. The dynamics of leadership in neighborhood organizations. *Social Science Quarterly,* 1980b, *60,* 570–587.

Rich, R. C., & Rosenbaum, W. A. (Eds.) Citizen participation in public policy. *Journal of Applied Behavioral Science,* 1981, *17*(4).

Robins, A. J., & Blackburn, C. Governing boards in mental health: Roles and training needs. *Administration in Mental Health,* 1974, *3,* 37–45.

Rosenbaum, W. A. Public involvement as reform and ritual: The development of federal participation programs. In S. Langton (Ed.), *Citizen participation in America,* Lexington, Mass.: D. C. Heath, 1978.

Rothman, J. Three models of community organization practice. In F. Cox et al. (Eds.), *Strategies of community organization.* Itasca, Ill.: F. E. Peacock Publishers, 1970.

Sanoff, H. Son of rationality. In B. Honikman (Ed.), *Responding to social change,* Strousberg, Pa.: Dowden, Hutchinson, & Ross, 1975.

Schneider, B. Organizational climates: An essay. *Personnel Psychology,* 1975, *28,* 447–479.

Schoenberg, S. P., & Rosenbaum, P. L. *Neighborhoods that work: Sources for viability in the inner city.* New Brunswick, N.J.: Rutgers University Press, 1980.

Silverman, W. H. Self-designed training for mental health advisory governing boards. *American Journal of Community Psychology,* 1981, *9,* 67–82.

Skinner, B. F. *Science and human behavior.* New York: Macmillan, 1953.

Smith, D. H. Voluntary action and voluntary groups. In A. Inkeles, J. Coleman, & W. Smelser (Eds.), *Annual Review of Sociology* (Vol. 1). Palo Alto, Calif.: Annual Reviews, 1975.

Spiegel, H. B. (Ed.). *Citizen participation in urban development* (Vol. 1). Washington, D.C.: Center for Community Affairs, NTL Institute for Applied Behavioral Science, 1968.

Sundquist, J. L. *On fighting poverty: Perspectives from experience.* New York: Basic Books, 1969.

Suttles, G. D. *The social construction of communities.* Chicago: University of Chicago Press, 1972.

Tilley, S., & Carr, S. *Downtown Washington streets for people: User consultancy.* Paper presented at EDRA 6 Conference in Lawrence, Kansas, 1975.

Tischler, G. I. The effects of consumer control on the delivery of services. *American Journal of Orthopsychiatry,* 1971, *41,* 501–505.

de Tocqueville, A. C. *Democracy in America.* New York: Alfred A. Knopf, 1945.

Unger, D. G., Wandersman, A. Neighboring and its role in block organizations: An exploratory report. *American Journal of Community Psychology,* 1983, *11,* 291–300.

Wandersman, A. User participation in planning environments: A conceptual framework. *Environment and Behavior,* 1979a, *11,* 465–482.

Wandersman, A. User participation: A study of types of participation, effects, mediators, and individual differences. *Environment and Behavior,* 1979b, *11,* 185–208.

Wandersman, A. A framework of participation in community organizations. *Journal of Applied Behavioral Science,* 1981, *17,* 27–58.

Wandersman, A., Chavis, D., & Stucky, P. Involving citizens in research. In R. Kidd & M. Saks (Eds.), *Advances in applied social psychology* (Volume 2). Hillsdale, N.J.: Lawrence Erlbaum Associates, 1983.

Wandersman, A., & Florin, P. A cognitive social learning approach to cognition, social behavior and the environment. In J. Harvey (Ed.), *Cognition, social behavior and the environment.* Hillsdale, N.J.: Lawrence Erlbaum Associates, 1981.

Wandersman, A., & Giamartino, G. Community and individual difference characteristics as influences on initial participation. *American Journal of Community Psychology,* 1980, *8,* 217–228.

Wandersman, A., Jakubs, J. F., & Giamartino, G. Participation in block organizations. *Journal of Community Action,* 1981, *1,* 40–48.

Wandersman, A., Kimbrell, D., Wadsworth, J. C., Myers, D., Livingston, G., & Braithwaite, H. Assessing citizen participation in a community mental health center. In A. M. Jeger & R. S. Slotnick (Eds.), *Community mental health and behavioral-ecology: A handbook of theory, research and practice.* New York: Plenum, 1982.

Warren, R. L. The model cities program: An assessment. In H. B. Spiegel (Ed.), *Citizen participation in urban development* (Vol. III: *Decentralization*). Fairfax, Va.: Learning Resources Corporation/NTL, 1974.

Washnis, G. J. *Citizen involvement in crime prevention.* Lexington, Mass.: Lexington Books (D. C. Heath), 1976.

Williams, J. A., Babchuk, N., & Johnson, D. R. Voluntary associations and minority status: A comparative analysis of anglo, black, and Mexican-Americans. *American Sociological Review,* 1973, *38,* 637–646.

Wofford, J. G. The politics of local responsibility: Administration of the Community Action Program—1964–1966. In J. L. Sundquist (Ed.), *On fighting poverty: Perspectives from experience* (pp. 70–102). New York: Basic Books, 1969.

Yankelovich, D. *New rules: Searching for self-fulfillment in a world turned upside down.* New York: Random House, 1981.

Yarmolinsky, A. The beginnings of OEO. In J. L. Sundquist (Ed.), *On fighting poverty: Perspectives from experience.* New York: Basic Books, 1969.

Yates, D. T. *Neighborhood democracy: The politics and impact of decentralization.* Lexington, Mass.: Lexington Books (D. C. Heath), 1973.

Yin, R. K. Goals for citizen involvement: Some possibilities and some evidence. In P. Marshall (Ed.), *Citizen participation certification for community development.* Washington, D.C.: NAHRO, 1977.

Zinobar, J. W., & Dinkel, N. R. (Eds.). *A trust of evaluation: A guide for involving citizens in community mental health program evaluation.* Tampa, Flor.: The Florida Consortium for Research and Evaluation, 1981.

Zwerdling, D. *Workplace democracy: A guide to workplace ownership, participation, and self-management experiments in the United States and Europe.* New York: Harper & Row, 1980.

Integration and Future Directions

"The Tragedy of the Commons" described by Hardin (1968) refers to the use of common grazing land typical in New England villages in colonial times. These public grasslands existed in villages where anyone could graze their cows. Such an arrangement worked reasonably well until individual farmers realized that they could profit more by increasing the number of cattle grazing on the public land. But as each individual farmer increased his herd, the grass became scarcer until the commons was destroyed entirely. Thus, individual owners seeking individual gains ultimately experienced a collective loss rather than a gain. The problem is not the result of any single person doing anything that is unethical or bad, nor can it be solved by one or two heroes volunteering not to graze their cows on the commons.

. . . the Tragedy of the Commons is essentially a problem of the allocation of scarce resources. And a half-hour's thought will turn up a dozen mechanisms that we use every day for dealing with such problems. In various societies, scarce resources of various kinds may be allocated by force, by tradition, by inheritance, or by election. When they are to be distributed to many people, they may be distributed by lot, or to the loudest voices, or by first-come-first-served, or by auction, or by selling tickets, as to a World Series baseball game. Fish and game commissions are set up, often with the support of the fishermen and hunters themselves, to sell licenses, set bag limits, and limit the hunting season so as to maintain the ongoing resource undiminished. (Platt, 1973; Price, 1983)

One of the central messages of community psychology is that social and community problems require concerted action for their solution. In our society, the emphasis is on freedom of action for the individual. Citizens expect that their individual voices as voters and taxpayers should count; unfortunately, they often do not. "Getting things done" in a community usually requires more than individual interest and motivation.

The first step toward resolution involves recognizing and properly defining the problem. The groups most affected usually cooperate and abide by the decisions reached because they recognize that it is in their interest to do so. The awareness of the problem by single individuals alone is not enough. There must be sufficient consensus concerning the problem and its solution so that the rules established will be followed by the majority.

Problem recognition and agreement on the need for group action can be difficult to attain. For example, energy conservation in this country has not met with great success. Most people still are not convinced of the dangers of continued reliance on fossil fuels. Like the colonial farmers at the New England commons, they seem unwilling to give up immediate gain to avert a disaster that appears too far in the future to worry about. Ultimately though, group consensus will be required for any solution, whether it be the use of small, energy-efficient autos as is currently the case, greater use of mass transportation (buses, trains, carpools), or funding the development of alternative energy sources.

Finding solutions becomes more complicated when the stakeholders in the problem have competing interests. In the Love Canal example with which we opened this book, both industry and government officials were frightened by the enormous financial liability they might be required to assume if they recognized the validity of citizen complaints. They delayed development of a plan of action until forced to do so by continued citizen pressure and the adverse publicity that citizens were able to mobilize. Officials finally acted when it appeared to them that most people wanted the problem resolved and that taking no action would reflect negatively upon them. Again we see the importance of group action and consensus building as necessary ingredients in constructive social change.

FACTORS IN COMMUNITY STABILITY AND CHANGE

Activity to solve social problems begins with collective attempts to remedy a condition that some group perceives to be offensive or undesirable (Spector & Kitsuse, 1977). Citizen complaints may be acted upon depending on a number of factors: the power of the complaining group and its ability to attract sympathetic others to the legitimacy of its complaint; the existence of an official body to hear the complaint and act upon it; the existence of resources to solve the problem; and a willingness to utilize resources for problem solution. Thus, there may be several reasons for inaction on citizen complaints. For example, the concerned group may have insufficient power to press its claims. As Spector and Kitsuse (1977) note: "other things being equal, groups that have a larger membership, greater constituency, more money and greater discipline and organization will be more effective in pressing their claims" (p. 143). Power also can be achieved by convincing others of the legitimacy of one's claims. The civil rights marchers of the 1960s initially were not a large group, but they succeeded in attracting sympathetic converts because others became convinced of the moral rightness of their cause.

Officials may be reluctant to take action on citizen complaints. However, ignoring complaints will succeed only if the citizens' group is weak and disorganized. Otherwise, the complaints are likely to continue and probably will escalate in intensity. A group that initially complains in private may hold demonstrations or contact the media if it is continuously ignored. Thus, powerful groups usually are taken seriously.

Why do government officials often resist citizen claims and act so slowly in redressing grievances? Part of the answer to this question can be traced to the cumbersome structure of bureaucracies that slows decision making. Rule books usually tell officials how to handle familiar grievances, not how to deal with new ones. But there is another answer as well. Regulatory officials (social regulators[1]) usually represent the will of the majority, and unless they sense that the majority wants change, they will be reluctant to act.

---

[1] We shall use the term *regulators* to describe those community representatives who have a role in preserving the social order. Thus, regulators include government officials but also teachers, ministers, police officers, welfare workers, etc. Gamson (1968, p. 21) uses the term

Community Traditions as Equilibrium Maintaining Factors

Cumming (1968) describes social order as arising from a continual compromise between constraint and freedom, between the interest of the individual and the goals of society. This compromise takes place informally whenever people interact, but informal regulation alone is not sufficient to maintain order. Formal systems of social regulation supplement informal controls and are administered by a network of agents and agencies that perform both supportive and controlling functions. The active agents in this network represent the community's social regulators, whose performance of both supportive and controlling functions often occurs within the same agency. In fact, it is the conflict between support and control functions that often blurs the clarity of mission of some agencies. A prime example of the conflict of functions can be seen in the typical probation department attached to a court. The probation worker wins the confidence of clients and, in the name of rehabilitation, provides helpful suggestions, support, and advice. Yet at the time of a hearing, if further legal action is required, this same worker now must reveal the information collected even if this information is to be used against the client.

Regulators act according to established *traditions,* which can be thought of as the generally accepted rules governing community life. Traditions represent community attitudes, sentiments, norms, and mores that have an action component. Traditions offer a frame of reference that allows regulators to function, confident that they are enforcing an accepted mandate from the community. Regulators perpetuate traditions, and since traditions change slowly, regulators rarely function as innovators in society unless they have specifically come to power with some mandate for change.

Social Strain: The Production of Disequilibrium in Communities

As changes occur in society, new accommodations are required. These may occur in a gradual or in a precipitous manner. Strain develops when changes that occur in the composition and value structure of society are difficult to assimilate into ongoing community life. Smelser (1963), who uses the term *strain* to refer to "the impairment of relations among parts of a system," notes that strain in society can result from several factors. Strain can be produced by the ambiguities associated with unpredictable natural and social forces, or it can result from beliefs which change over time and which, in turn, can lead to changes in operating rules as old role relationships conflict with new values (e.g., the role of fathers in child care). In other words, strain can occur in all but the most static of societies. Population shifts, changes in the balance of available natural resources, economic dislocation, increases

---

authorities to describe those "who for any given social system make binding decisions in that system." Our use of the term *social regulators* includes authorities but also any social control, socialization, and primary-care agents who have the power to enforce control over the fate of other community members.

in automation, and changes in cultural values all have the potential for activating social disequilibrium.

New groups coming into the community and changing conditions within society require new accommodations. Unless dealt with adequately, the new forces produce social strain. The strain may occur first in the new groups, as they find existing arrangements ill-suited to their needs. Or strain may occur in the community at large as new forces continue to disrupt the existing social order.

IMPLICATIONS FOR INTERVENTION

Consultation to Social Regulators

Regulators may become aware of growing strain associated with impinging events and yet resist acting upon citizen complaint. The problem is that regulators cannot improvise freely to reduce strain. Their actions generally conform to existing rules that circumscribe their alternatives—rules developed formally from previous laws and decisions by authorities or informally from the history of policy implementation and standard operating procedures.

Helping regulators change their perceptions of minorities.[2] Regulators are most responsive when they sense a community-wide mandate. That is why community-wide strain is most likely to produce change. However, strain usually is restricted to a minority group, at least initially. If members of such a group are isolated from community life, with restricted access to regulators, it may be difficult for them to make their needs known. Isolation produces distortions in perceptions for both sides, so that without contact and access to others, estrangement is heightened by misunderstanding, distortions, and unchecked stereotypes.

Mental patients are one example of a minority group that tends to be isolated from the community and its social regulators. Cumming and Cumming (1962) report an incident in which the staff of a mental hospital was asked to train police recruits in the proper handling of mental patients. The staff asked a patient group to help conduct the training program. The patients initially refused to participate. Many had painful experiences in their previous encounters with police. It took some time to overcome these initial fears and resistances, but when the patients finally agreed, the police arrived at the hospital for their first training session. The patients were surprised to see that the police were as uncomfortable and frightened about sitting in a room with "crazies" as they were about meeting the police. Isolated from one another and with only limited and formal contact, both groups had relied on distorted and inaccurate perceptions.

---

[2] Note that the term *minority* is used to indicate a small group with relatively few members and does not imply any particular racial or religious group composition.

The example from Cumming and Cumming demonstrates how the perception of the problems of an isolated minority can be changed through constructive exposure. The police had contact with mental patients but always in the same kind of situation—one in which an anxious and upset patient was disturbing the equilibrium in a community. The hospital meeting was a chance to understand patients as persons with "normal" fears and aspirations, as well as a chance to see them in other more normal roles, as hosts and meeting participants. In one sense, exposure of this type does not change the basic values or traditions of the community at large. The police as well as most other community members undoubtedly still believed that disturbances of community tranquility must be stopped. However, the police view may be changed as to why the disturbance was occurring, and this change in perception can be crucial in affecting how they react to the call for help. If the disturbance is caused by a person now seen as upset and not as "crazy therefore dangerous," the police are likely to react in a more humane fashion rather than in a provocative way that might further exacerbate the agitated behavior (Monahan & Geis, 1976).

This example also illustrates another principle: namely, that the action of social regulators can itself cause strain among community groups. The mandate of regulators is to reduce strain and protect members of society at large. Unfortunately, protection of the majority can mean abuse of the minority. In the example cited, community members may want disturbing patients removed from their midst and probably give no thought as to how this is to be accomplished. Closer examination might reveal that the issue of importance to the community is not patient removal at all but the cessation of the disturbing behavior. Options other than removal might be possible if they were available (e.g., support for families in crisis, group homes and halfway houses, follow-up care by outreach workers) and if social regulators could be made aware of them and educated in their use.

Helping regulators increase their options for constructive action. An example of increasing options in dealing with mental patients is provided by Hansell (1967) who described a "screening-linking-planning conference" convened by a mental health center whose goal was to maintain potential patients in the community and return them to effective citizenship as soon as possible. This study was a forerunner of the current interest in maintaining mental patients in the community. A main ingredient of the conference was linking patients and their families to helping resources in the community (e.g., a minister, public health nurse, or homemaker) with follow-up by a mental health "expediter" to make sure that contact was being maintained and help provided. Without this support, the family's tendency was to want their disturbing member hospitalized. With support, the family learned to deal with crisis events to which the patient's behavior was a reaction.

By the time the family reached the mental health center, it was convinced that the only recourse was hospitalization, and it was ready to undertake commitment proceedings. The judges who signed the commitment orders also were unaware of any other way to help the families who came before them. The mental health center explained their goal to the judges and invited them to observe the screening-linking-planning conference in operation. The judges became convinced that this was a viable option for helping potential patients and their families while at the same time protecting the safety of the community. They agreed that they would refuse to sign a commitment order unless the parties involved had first participated in such a conference. The judges "came to an appreciation of how the court could become a constructive collaborator toward a community reentry outcome rather than a participant in the process of alienation and deposition in a distant institution" (Hansell, 1967).

To summarize, one approach to planned social change involves consultation with social regulators. Since social regulators are the monitors of community life, one place to begin is to understand their functions. Each regulator within his or her area must find a way of coping with the strain elicited by disrupting events or groups. Regulators can contribute to the strain experienced by citizen groups by their method of operation, so that helping regulators change their perception of these groups or increasing their options in dealing with such groups can go a long way toward rectifying excessive strain.

Deciding to Use Disequilibrium Tactics: Increasing Problem Awareness in the General Community

Intervention is difficult in communities in which the majority of citizens are avoiding significant problems. In these instances, an important task is to educate the public about the problems in its midst. Here the community worker takes the role of a disequilibrium producer in that education in problem awareness produces strain in otherwise static groups. Various methods exist for accomplishing this goal, ranging from direct confrontation (marches, sit-ins, etc.) to more indirect means, such as public discussions and letter-writing campaigns. If education in problem awareness ("consciousness raising") is successful and if communities become ready for action, the job of the community worker now becomes one of working toward the constructive solution of problems and grievances, often by consultation with community regulators.

Klein (1968) conceptualizes the change process in a similar manner to that presented above, taking as his starting point the ideas of Kurt Lewin. Lewin sees the process of change as involving three steps: (*a*) unfreezing; (*b*) moving toward a new level; and (*c*) refreezing at the new level (Klein, 1968, pp. 126–136). Unfreezing, which allows a previously stable state to become amenable to change, occurs in response to some "precipitants;" i.e., events or circumstances that raise anxiety and make the status quo intolerable (*strain* in Smelser's terminology). Movement then occurs if there are "facilitants" available that remove previous obstacles to action. Unfreezing can occur through direct confrontation, so that immediate exposure to new input cannot be avoided; or through more indirect and gradual exposure and involvement, so that over time the lack of fit between previously held ideas and new information is more gradually realized.

Citizen Participation: Organizing Indigenous Groups to Solve Their Own Problems

Initially, strain is not perceived on a community-wide basis but only in those individuals and groups most affected by changing or chronically inadequate social conditions. The tendency in the community at large is to postpone dealing with "hot" issues as long as possible or to find some solution that involves the least change in the established equilibrium. Thus, education in problem awareness initially may meet community resistance. The community will become sufficiently aroused only when it is clear that the problem cannot be solved easily. When this occurs, normal channels of consultation to social institutions have some likelihood of success.

Unfortunately, attempts at education in problem awareness frequently fall on deaf ears. The community can successfully resist dealing with its problems if the strained minority is small, unorganized, and can be effectively isolated or suppressed. Both solutions, isolation and suppression, are likely to be attempted before the community will be ready to face the prospect of more massive social change.

What options are available if education in problem awareness has failed? Consultation is likely to be unprofitable because the community probably would oppose any accommodating solution in favor of continued isolation or suppression. This gives the "within system" consultant little opportunity to effect movement.

Change also can be initiated by organized citizen groups with sufficient power or resources to solve their own problems. The likelihood that indigenous groups can be organized is greater when the group is large enough, when group members share common values, or when they suffer from the same strain elicitors so that there is a reason for them to cooperate. On the other hand, indigenous citizen groups are least likely to organize when they are dispersed geographically (e.g., some rural poor groups) or share few values and traditions (e.g., differing urban ethnic groups). For example, Leighton (1959) suggests that an impediment to effective community organization in a rural Nova Scotia area was the geographic dispersion and ensuing distrust of the poor for each other. The stereotypes that poor people had of others of their own socio-economic group were the same as those held by the more affluent segments of this rural community.

Many of the major social changes that have occurred in the United States have come from pressures exerted by organized citizens groups. Social movements emphasizing civil rights, environmental concerns, and social equity for women are recent national examples. Less publicized are the numerous citizen groups and voluntary associations that organize to accomplish particular goals, such as the establishment of community hospitals and parks, the prevention of superhighway encroachment on residential neighborhoods, revitalizing local school boards, or requiring greater accountability from local officials. Citizens groups often disband after they have accomplished their goals, but occasionally they redefine their mission to encompass a broader mandate. After the Love Canal Homeowners Association won its battle for reimbursement for the homes made worthless by chemical contamination, over 1,000 telephone calls were received from other citizens throughout the country who believed they had similar grievances. In response to what was perceived to be an apparent need from other grass roots groups facing similar pollution threats, Lois Gibbs set up the Citizens' Clearinghouse for Hazardous Wastes. Since February 1981, when it was first established, members of the Clearinghouse have visited over 85 communities affected by environmental pollution, consulting with both municipal governments and citizens' groups (Lois Gibbs, personal communication).

Encouraging the Development of Alternatives

Building alternative institutions is another possible strategy for groups experiencing strain in unresponsive communities. Groups in strain may have low potential for political power but may still have untapped resources. A minority that is small both in number and potential power can develop institutional structures, perhaps even separate communities, under its own control if it can find adequate resources. For example, a little-known chapter of American history concerns the establishment of Jewish farming communities in southern New Jersey in 1882 (Brandes, 1971). These autonomous rural communities represented a divergence from the mainstream of immigration to the United States that saw East European Jews settle in the urban and industrial areas of this country. The settlers who went to the New Jersey communities hoped to avoid the corrupting influences of the big cities with the attendant likelihood of anti-Semitism. Luckily, they managed to obtain the backing of established Jewish philanthropic societies which were interested in changing the public's perception of the Jew from that of the stereotyped petty trader and peddler to that of a more noble man of the soil—a farmer. The South Jersey colonies were subsidized by the philanthropic societies that had resources but were not particularly powerful in a political sense.

Groups decide to establish their own alternatives when they believe that it is no longer possible to "work within the system" (Spector & Kitsuse, 1977). They move from protest and complaint to finding resources to solve their own problems. Often, support comes from nearby sympathetic friends. For example, communities without resources but close to universities may be able to draw upon professional talent and student manpower to develop alternatives that would be unavailable otherwise. Many communities have established their own alternative schools and community centers in this way.

Summary of Intervention Implications

We have presented a model stressing the role of equilibrium maintenance in community life and the factors likely to elicit disequilibrium and strain.[3] In any community, traditions reflecting social mores and sentiments develop as guides for action by regulatory agencies. In this sense, regulatory personnel serve to uphold and perpetuate community traditions. A second function of social regulators is to help communities accommodate to disturbing impinging events. Thus, creating an awareness among community members of the unmet needs of specific minority groups can be a first step in initiating action.

If education in problem awareness is successful, the community should become sufficiently aroused to apply pressure on personnel within regulatory agencies to deal with the disequilibrium-producing problems. These staff members, in turn, should become more open to consultation efforts. However, success is not guaranteed since community-wide strain also can lead to punitive solutions.

Education in problem awareness is unsuccessful when a significant number of citizens remain unwilling or unable to confront the issue in question. For progress to occur, everyone need not be convinced that action is necessary, but the minority must acquire a significant number of allies for the issue to remain "alive" and subject to further discussion and negotiation. Without a mandate to explore alternatives, regulators will be reluctant to act, and consultation directed at them is not likely to succeed.

The stimulus for change most often comes from indigenous citizens groups pressing officials to act on their complaints. The success of such groups depends upon a number of factors, among which are their potential for power through unified action and their access to resources. Potential power depends upon the geographic dispersion of the minority group, the number of shared values and traditions among group members, the quality of group leadership, and the size of the group and the history of its ability to form coalitions with other similar groups.

Groups with high power potential can be helped to organize unified constituencies that can compel negotiation toward problem resolution. If necessary, they can negotiate for or create their own alternative structures. Groups with low potential for the development of powerful coalitions but with good access to resources can decide to cultivate friendly relations with those controlling resources. With support from such friends, alternative structures that are more responsive to their needs become possible. However, little change should be expected for groups without organizational potential or resource access. Attention to unmet needs is least likely for such groups until significant numbers of the community at large become aware of and responsive to their plight.

---

[3] Our views are based upon theoretical discussions originally presented by Gamson (1968), Klein (1968), Rhodes (1972), Smelser (1963), and Spector and Kitsuse (1977).

We have just reviewed some factors in community life that should be considered in deciding upon an intervention strategy. Next, we turn to a discussion of some of the problems community psychologists are likely to face in the years ahead.

CHALLENGES OF THE FUTURE

While no one can predict future events with any degree of certainty, it can be useful to try to anticipate the social and psychological problems we are likely to face in the years ahead and then plan for their resolution.

There are a number of future events that can substantially influence the quality of life in the years ahead. Concerns about the likelihood of war or peace, future economic growth, the development of alternative energy sources, environmental pollution, industrial automation, and the widespread adoption of computers in homes and schools, etc., are topics that have been discussed in the popular press and in some cases have formed the basis for the development of action groups of concerned citizens. Also of importance are demographic changes occurring in American society that will influence future social life. These too deserve discussion because they represent challenges of the future for which we should be prepared.

Demographic projections allow us to gain a picture of some of the changes in the composition of society that can be expected in the next 50 years. The clearest trend can be described graphically as "the graying of America" (Storandt, 1983). In the upcoming decades, the proportion of older persons in the United States is expected to increase significantly. Table 11–1 (adapted from Morrison, 1983) shows how these changes will occur from 1982 to 2030.

TABLE 11–1
Projected Demographic Trends for 1982–2030, by Age

	1982	2000	2010	2030
Number of persons (in millions)	232	266	282	307
Age (as percent of total):				
18–24 years	12.8	9.3	10.1	9.3
25–34	16.9	13.4	13.3	12.5
35–54	22.2	29.7	27.3	25.2
55–64	9.5	8.9	11.9	10.4
65–74	6.7	6.4	6.5	10.2
75 and over	4.4	5.6	5.6	7.9

Adapted from Bureau of the Census and Social Security Administration tables reported by Morrison, 1983.

First it should be noted that the population of the United States will rise steadily during this period. The primary reason for this growth in population is the increasing life expectancy projected for both men and women (Kramer, 1982).

The anticipated aging of the U.S. population in the next 50 years is related to two trends which started some time ago. There was a large increase in the birthrate immediately after World War II as American servicemen returned to civilian life. The post-World War II babies are now mature adults, and they will continue to represent a population "bulge" as they grow older. In 1982, 11 percent of the population was age 65 or over. In the year 2030, those over 65 will represent 18 percent of the general population. Conversely, after 1960, there was a marked decline in the birthrate. Thus, from 1980 to the year 2000, there will be a decline in the adult population under 35. Furthermore, since women are entering the labor market in increasing numbers and postponing the decision to have children, the birthrate is not expected to rise in the near future. This will mean that as the post-World War II population bulge reaches age 65 and retires, there will be fewer younger workers on whom they can depend for support.

There are other population trends that are fairly certain to occur. Women have been steadily increasing their participation in the labor force. It is estimated that by the year 2000, 60 percent of adult women will be working (Morrison, 1983). Between 1982 and 2000, the proportion of working women will increase by 7 percent, while the proportion of working men will decrease by 13 percent. The reason for these projections is that while both men and women over the ages of 55 are expected to show an increased preference for leisure over work and will continue the trend toward early retirement (Flaim & Fullerton, 1978), the growing number of women entering the labor force in the next decades will increase their relative proportion.

The number of single-parent families also has been increasing. In 1970, 1 in 10 families was headed by a woman. In 1980, this ratio rose to one in seven. There were 8 million such families in 1980, and they included among them 12 million children. In 1981, 17 percent of all American children were being raised in a single-parent family headed by a woman. The reason these statistics are important is that one third of such families live below the poverty line. The median income of such families is less than half that of two-parent households (Levitan & Belous, 1981). Poverty is a risk factor for a wide variety of physical and emotional disorders (Seidman & Rapkin, 1983) as is marital disruption (Bloom, Asher, & White, 1978). For example, in reviewing the literature, Shinn (1978) found that children's cognitive development is adversely affected by father absence and concluded that low income and lack of parental attention are prime explanations for these effects. Not only is father unavailable in such families, but so too is mother if she is required to work to support the family. Parents of such families make fewer demands on their children and are seen by the children as less interested in them or their education. In one study, it was found that when both parents discussed school progress with the teacher, children's school work improved. When neither parent attended school conferences, school achievement lagged (Shinn, 1978, p. 320).

Another predictable demographic change is the increasing Hispanic population in the United States. In the five-year period from 1973 to 1978, the Hispanic population grew by nearly 14 percent, while the non-Hispanic population increased by only 3.3 percent (Newman, 1978). Unfortunately, despite our self-image as a country that welcomes all who seek relief from oppression, immigrants often are treated with suspicion and hostility, particularly those from non-white cultural or racial groups. First-generation immigrants generally fill jobs at the bottom of the labor market that are considered undesirable by native workers because of low wages and poor working conditions. Second- and third-generation children of immigrants who have assimilated into American culture have higher aspirations and expect to achieve positions at the same level as other citizens. Because of their higher birthrate, American citizens of Hispanic origin, in increasing numbers, will be competing for jobs that are valued by others. Indeed, demographers project that the American labor force will become increasingly non-white in future years (Morrison, 1983).

The current trend toward industrial automation complicates the picture. If automation increases significantly in future years, the impact will be felt most keenly by low-skilled workers. Thus, there is a serious risk that the number of chronically unemployed or underemployed individuals will increase in the future. Of concern are not only current industrial workers who have been displaced by automation from relatively high-paying factory jobs (Brenner, 1979), but also future generations for whom educational opportunity or vocational training in high technology is not available. For example, while blacks comprise approximately 10 percent of the population, they constitute 20 percent of the unemployed. They also represent 40 percent of the discouraged workers who have dropped out of the labor force and are no longer counted among the officially unemployed (Bowman, 1982). If these individuals remain chronically unemployed, never entering the labor force for a sustained period of time, they will become part of a chronic "underclass" in American society.

Implications: Planning to Meet Citizen Needs

How will we respond to these future challenges? The demographic statistics have identified segments of our population likely to be at risk for social and pyschological problems in the years ahead. We now have a choice—we could begin a program of research and demonstration projects aimed at learning how to prevent or minimize future problems, or we could do nothing. Unfortunately, there is a strong tendency in this country not to act on major social or environmental problems unless we absolutely must. There are few traditions or mechanisms that encourage social planning, in part, because we value minimal government intervention in the lives of citizens. Social programs in this country typically respond to crises *after* they occur, when there is an aroused constituency pressing for action. This is why many social scientists and environmentalists worry about our ability to respond to events that will require prior planning and research for effective action. As Brewster Smith notes:

If we were to put sensible population and environmental policies into effect now, we could perhaps stabilize the human ecosystem within the next century, but a continued no-policy of drift could lead to irreversible deterioration in the same time span. (Brewster Smith, 1978, p. 645)

Consider for a moment the anticipated aging of the U.S. population in the next 50 years. What sort of life would we like for our future senior citizens? Most of us probably do not think much about this issue, but we should because it affects us directly. Every college student reading this book in the 1980s who is still alive by the year 2030 will be at least 60 years old! Should we not be planning for our own futures?

Our fantasies of retirement probably are benign—travel, the close companionship of spouse, friends, children and grandchildren, and the freedom to follow hobbies and special interests. In reality, retirement could include these activities, but for many, aging is much less benign. While there are indeed positive features, there also are problems that must be faced—declining health, death of loved ones, declining purchasing power for many with fixed incomes, inflation, and role loss. While some of these problems cannot be prevented, only postponed (declining health and ultimate death), others are within our power to modify.

Role loss among the elderly (Rosow, 1976) is a potentially modifiable problem. In our society, the aged do not have a clear social role (Rosow, 1973). In pre-industrial cultures, the elderly are considered the bearers of traditional wisdom and are accorded a great deal of respect and status commensurate with that role. In quickly changing technological societies, the generation of new knowledge often is more important than the accumulation of wisdom. In addition, when families no longer live together as intergenerational units, the elderly are not consulted for their knowledge of child care or family relations. Thus, the elderly often find it difficult to participate meaningfully in society. As Rosow notes:

The loss of roles excludes the aged from significant social participation and devalues them . . . Role loss deprives people of their social identity. (Rosow, 1973)

Alternatives to increase meaningful social participation are possible. The answer will not be found in attempts to glamorize leisure or provide recreational diversions but will require substantial changes in attitudes and practices. We need to question some of our negative stereotypes about appropriate behavior for the elderly and consider projects that continue responsible participation for those who are able and willing. For example, full retirement at age 65 no longer fits the desires or abilities of most elderly citizens. In one survey, 79 percent of those age 55 to 69 indicated that they would prefer continued part-time work to complete retirement (Gray, 1983). There are a number of useful ways to structure part-time work that should be investigated and systematically evaluated as part of an "experimenting society" (Campbell, 1971). Consulting firms might employ semi-retired executives as consultants to those just starting out in business or professional work. "Job clubs" can be established to help older workers deal with the frustrations associated with searching for employment (Gray, 1983). The possibility of cooperative "job banks" should be investigated in which skilled work can be traded for other desired exchanges (for example, carpentry or machine work could be traded for haircuts, clothing, or reduced-cost medical care). Cooperatives of this sort exist in some localities; whether they would suit the elderly still needs to be investigated. Housing alternatives also need further study. Some elderly might do best in retirement villages, others might prefer mixed intergenerational housing if they could continue in socially valued roles (mailman, handyman, playground supervisor, cooking or sewing teacher) that recognized their particular skills but made allowances for their reduced stamina.

Up till now, federal programs for the elderly have emphasized institutional care for those unable to manage on their own. Federal expenditures for benefits to the elderly exceeded $130 billion in 1980, yet less than 10 percent of this money was directed at noninstitutional services (Gurland, Bennett, & Wilder, 1981). Furthermore, federal policies encourage *continued* institutionalization after a temporary illness or disability that requires full-time nursing care. For example, an individual entering a nursing home must cover all costs until he or she has "spent down" personal resources to a state-determined level—usually the amount needed to cover burial costs (Wack & Rodin, 1978). Thus, individuals with a "nest egg" who might have been able initially to maintain themselves in the community, soon become unable to do so. Perhaps they might become capable of discharge medically, but now they must remain institutionalized because they have become financially destitute. Statistics indicate that 47 percent of nursing home patients receiving Medicaid were not initially poor but became so after an institutional stay. The "spend down" requirement in the legislation was intended to prevent the rich from taking advantage of "free" federal care. Unfortunately, it has trapped a much larger number of persons with modest resources and has prevented their return to community living.

Alternatives that encourage independent living probably would not cost more than what is being spent on institutional maintenance; however, they will require a change in how the problem is viewed. For example, in 1975, a project called "Senior Gleaners" was started by a private citizen to combat hunger among the elderly by taking advantage of the large amount of food wasted in typical commercial food harvesting. In 1977, 400 tons of food were gathered by elderly Californians and distributed to other low-income elderly. The cost of the project was minimal because members of other community organizations helped in storing and distributing the food (Pilisuk & Minkler, 1980).

While individuals can at times create unique social roles by their own initiative alone, most often a conducive social structure is needed. Changes of this sort require problem recognition, attitude change, a willingness to try out and experiment with alternatives, commitment, and pressure (perhaps from the elderly themselves as an organized constituency) to maintain social experimentation. We are not suggesting that social problems are ever solved in any final sense (Price, 1983; Sarason, 1978), and we recognize that attempts at "solution" sometimes create additional problems (Boulding, 1983; Gerard, 1983; Rappaport, 1981). Still, forward movement is possible, even if only in small incremental steps. As Boulding notes, the solutions to problems of community life involve the ability of people to create appropriate social structures and institutions to meet their needs. While such institutions can be corrupted, they also can be changed by persons acting in unison; and "persons means us" (Boulding, 1983, p. 651.).

COMMUNITY PSYCHOLOGY AND PROBLEMS OF THE FUTURE

I first heard of Love Canal on a local television news broadcast in early August 1978. I saw people at a meeting of some sort, shouting and crying, and a number of young children, some wearing crudely lettered signs proclaiming that they did not want to die this year.

A few days later a colleague and I drove up and down 97th and 99th Streets in Niagara Falls. We saw compact homes with neat lawns, carefully tended gardens, and shade trees cooling the streets. It seemed incongruous to see plywood panels over some doors and windows, moving vans drawn up to curbs, and men and women carrying boxes and bundles out to their cars. I felt an eerie sensation that danger was lurking somewhere in this peaceful setting, and I became intrigued with the problem. After a long day spent talking with New York state personnel in hastily organized offices, with residents who were unpacking in temporary quarters, with the president of the newly formed residents' association, and with other people as well, we returned home emotionally wrung out and exhausted by the effort of making some sense of what we had just witnessed. By the next morning, I was already "hooked." Love Canal soon became my continued obsession, and the complex story continues to unfold.

In the days that followed, my immediate question was what sort of research I would do, for it was obvious that there were a number of events to examine from a sociological viewpoint. It takes resources to do any sort of research, of course, and I attempted to deal with that matter first.

After several visits, telephone calls, and written inquiries to various foundations and agencies, I concluded that little money was available for pursuing research on short notice, in new areas, and in an exploratory way. The few agencies expressing an interest required extensive detailed proposals. Therefore, rather than spending my days applying for grants, I chose to devote my time and energy to the swiftly moving and changing events.

In order to set to work immediately, I decided to use the resources readily available to me at the State University of New York at Buffalo. I organized a field-research seminar on Love Canal with five advanced graduate students, who responded to my invitation with enthusiasm. Although we initially planned to study the Love Canal families' responses to stress, we quickly realized that there was a great deal more to be learned, and we decided to find out everything we could.

. . . We prepared interview schedules based on our knowledge of the situation, interviewed families, visited the Love Canal area frequently and regularly, and attended all public meetings and other events, so that no week passed without extensive contacts between the research group members and the Love Canal people and activities.

In the first year, the students and I acted as controls for each other, checking facts and questioning the inferences that could be drawn from our observations and interview data. Several key participants met with our seminar to discuss their experiences. Although we came to understand best the views of the groups we were with in the field, we tried to keep our minds open to the various views of the different groups. We thought of our method of presenting and advocating opposing views as an "adversarial discussion method."

In the second year, . . . I continued to visit Love Canal at least weekly, talking with people at the Love Canal Homeowners Association office, talking with others by telephone, attending public and private meetings, and interviewing others as events required. I continued to collect every available document from the stream of reports, newsletters, and other information, in addition to newspapers and other published material.

. . . My university base provided immediate access to the crucial resources of ideas and advice of colleagues in several disciplines. An anthropologist joined us when we considered problems of bias in field research, and we had the advice of a social psychologist, a clinical-community psychologist, a lawyer, and others as we needed them. Thus, it was possible to do a great deal of research on an important topic, using the resources of a university, without outside support.

The creativity, knowledge, time, and energy of the graduate students who worked with me were invaluable. They benefited, too, from a wealth of real field experiences and professional participation they could have obtained in no other way. My academic base was critical, as I worked in a social setting where there is an expectation that one does research. Most important, I had the freedom to study and to describe whatever I thought important and appropriate for a sociologist to pursue, using my professional judgment. The observations and opinions of observers who are independent of official governmental or corporate efforts have been very important at Love Canal. I consider myself in that independent category and thus am able to act in the academic's traditional role of social critic. (Levine, 1982, pp. 2–4)

Adeline Levine is a sociologist, but she presents a model of research (a combination of participant observation and intensive ethnographic study) that is compatible with the community psychology orientation outlined in this book. Levine (1982) provided a detailed and objective chronicle of events, which, if studied, could provide a basis for a more informed and effective response to future environmental disasters. In its description of delay and denial of evidence in frustrating detail, Levine's account can help citizen groups prepare for similar reactions. She also documented the need for legislative reform. Her work, along with direct political action by the Love Canal citizens group itself, stimulated the recognition of the need for national legislation. The Environmental Protection Agency "Superfund" was an attempt by Congress to deal with this problem by the creation of a mechanism to clean up the most pressing hazardous waste sites found throughout the country.

In the Love Canal example, there could have been other options for action available to interested community psychologists. Such possibilities might have included lobbying for legislation that would have required industrial polluters to pay for damage or clean-up efforts, consulting with state officials to help them respond to citizen complaint more humanely, or consultation with the Love Canal residents to help them organize more effectively. Adeline Levine chose a different course of action. She decided to adopt the role of objective reporter and informed researcher to provide a chronicle that could be useful in future crises.

It is not surprising that the New York state government could not solve the Love Canal problem on its own. Many states would have similar difficulty in responding to instances of severe environmental pollution without federal help—they simply do not have the tax base to pay for massive clean-up efforts. There are other examples of problems that would require national attention for their solution. Problems involving multinational corporations, economic growth, monetary policies, the availability of imported oil, and tax incentives to businesses are influenced less by local input. Is the same true of social and psychological problems? Do they also require federal initiatives for their solution?

The Role of Federal, State and Local Governments in Responding to Citizen Need

Before the 1960s, the federal government assumed a minimal role in attending to the social and psychological needs of citizens (see discussion of historical trends in Chapter Two). For example, in colonial times it was considered the responsibility of families to care for their own (Levine, 1981). Local government units were reluctant to intervene in family responsibilities and did so only when it was clear that informal family-based care was failing. State institutions came into prominence when large-scale immigration overwhelmed local arrangements. Even so, when state institutions, such as mental hospitals, were first established, local communities initially were reluctant to send any but their most troublesome citizens. The law required localities to pay for state care, and it was cheaper to maintain people in almshouses and workhouses. The pattern of care shifted with the Industrial Revolution because localities could not cope with the sudden population growth and its attendant stresses. State institutions soon became the primary means for dealing with chronic and difficult problems. Old-age homes, orphanages, mental hospitals, schools for the retarded, prisons and reformatories became state responsibilities. However, states varied in the quality of their services. The states that experienced the largest population growth were forced to deal with citizen needs sooner than others, but in many cases, little more than custodial care was provided.

After World War II, the federal government's entry into the health and welfare arena reflected a developing consensus that the states by themselves would not respond adequately to social needs. The states appeared to be "foot-dragging" in mental health, education, and human rights, generally. Television pictures of a state governor standing in a schoolhouse door to block racial integration or local police beating and arresting peaceful civil rights protestors helped convince the public that federal solutions would be required for many social problems. In addition, Americans optimistically believed that social problems could be solved by the same technical ingenuity that was so successful on the military front (Levine, 1981). Winning the war against social injustice abroad increased national resolve to overcome social injustice at home. In this atmosphere, the petitions of needy and still disenfranchised groups met a receptive audience.

Federal responsibility expanded enormously after the death of John Kennedy in 1963 as part of the nation's commitment to continue the social agenda that he had initiated. Social programs were established as part of a national "War on Poverty" that covered a wide range of unmet needs. Preschool education, delinquency prevention, expanded mental health care, job training, medical care for the poor, and old-age assistance were some of the prominent programs.

In retrospect, it can be argued that too much was attempted too quickly and that complex problems were approached without the full realization of the time and commitment that would be required for their solution. A particularly important lesson to be learned is that, for the most part, programs were imposed on communities with little local involvement. Program priorities were set in Washington, and not much attention was given to obtaining community input or local ownership of programs. In some cases, local authorities were seen as obstacles to be overcome rather than as groups who might one day assume program ownership. State governments were not involved in program planning either, and state agencies often were relegated to the role of administrative "pass-through" bureaucracies—supervising the distribution of funds but with no voice in program development.

With a change in the political climate in the 1970s, federal funding for social services began to be phased out. Few states or localities were ready to assume financial responsibility for programs they viewed as imposed upon them. The programs that did survive were those that had taken seriously the need to establish local constituencies. In most cases, the local popularity of a program was more important than data concerning program effectiveness. Local acceptance of Head Start programs can be viewed as one example. Initial program evaluations looking at the impact on children had produced equivocal results. Only recently, in re-evaluating the data, are positive outcomes being demonstrated (Zigler & Berman, 1983). However, the programs were popular with parents, teachers, and local officials. Representatives of these groups were included on local governing boards which gave them direct, first-hand knowledge of the programs. This subjective personal involvement and ownership led to the conviction that the programs were worthwhile, even before confirmatory data were available.

Implications for Community Psychology

We have described a brief history of federal and local involvement in human services programs to overcome the misperception that progress can occur only with federal initiatives. The current overreliance on federal dollars to sustain research efforts is a relatively recent phenomenon. It is somewhat unsettling to see some of our scientific colleagues apparently willing to abandon areas of research and scholarship that are no longer favored at the federal level. A lesson to be learned from past federal involvement in the human service arena is that programs that are sustained by federal funding alone, without local involvement, are not likely to persevere. They may present an illusion of progress when in fact the more difficult task of modifying local traditions to accommodate new initiatives rarely is undertaken. The sustained research and development needed for ultimate problem resolution also is adversely affected by the sensitivity of federal funding patterns to shifting political climates.

The fate of community psychology should not be dependent upon the political atmosphere in the nation's capitol. That atmosphere is likely to be transitory (a new president is elected every four or eight years) and is not always an accurate gauge of the true state of American public opinion. For example, in the 1980 presidential election, Ronald Reagan carried every state but six in electoral votes and received 51 percent of the popular vote. That vote was a clear majority, yet a significant minority (48 percent) preferred other candidates.

To be sure, federal policy can facilitate the work of a community psychologist. New programs are established more easily when they can be supported by independent, external funding. Similarly, research in program development is aided by grants specifically designed for that purpose. Historically, states and localities have been much more reluctant to fund programs in basic research that did not have a clearly visible practical outcome. Still, the lessons of the recent past are that federal dollars alone are not sufficient to produce lasting community change. Equally important is work at the local level in which citizens come together and strive toward solving their own problems.

An example of the importance of local initiative can be seen in the problem of industrial plant shutdowns. The effect of such an action on a local community can be devastating not only in terms of the mental health of the workers involved (Buss & Redburn, 1983) but also because of its effects on other local businesses. The irony is that it is not only unprofitable plants that are closed. Large corporations sometimes close *profitable* local plants simply because a greater profit margin is desired (Blasi, 1979). In some communities, workers and community members have banded together to buy out the plant in order to save local jobs. What is particularly encouraging about these efforts is that research on worker-owned business generally demonstrates both greater profitability and increased worker satisfaction (Green-

berg, 1980; Long, 1978; Rhodes & Steers, 1981). For example, in one truck-
ing company purchased by its employees, damage claims for improperly
handled or lost freight declined by up to 60 percent, and quantity of work
output increased by 5 percent. After five years of operating with large losses,
the company became profitable (Long, 1978).

The importance of encouraging local initiatives in which local officials
and citizens groups come together to work on problems of common concern
is a key message of this book. Much can be done at the local level through
community-sponsored research, consultation, and advocacy. In this chapter, we have attempted to describe the future problems that are likely to be
pressing for solutions and the possible intervention points that are available
at the local level. We have focused upon education in problem awareness,
helping community regulators increase their options for constructive action,
supporting indigenous citizens groups in their organizational efforts, and
helping to establish alternative human service programs as demonstration
projects from which all segments of society ultimately can learn. There is
much that needs to be done and too few professionals and committed citizens with the training, foresight, and perseverance to continue despite shifting political climates. Community work can be difficult and frustrating at
times, but pressures for change are constantly occurring in a dynamic society. Opportunities for intervention are more readily available than are sometimes apparent from only superficial study. Understanding how communities
function and how to complement naturally occurring change processes can
be as important for the community worker as are dedication and good inten-
tions.

References

Blasi, J. R. Federal legislation in respect to employee ownership of firms. In L. A.
Ferman & J. P. Gordus (Eds.), *Mental health and the economy*. Kalamazoo,
Mich.: W. E. Upjohn Institute for Employment Research, 1979.

Bloom, B. L., Asher, S. J., & White, S. W. Marital disruption as a stressor: A review
and analysis. *Psychological Bulletin*, 1978, *85*, 867–894.

Boulding, K. E. Reflections on the uncertain future of social and community life. In
E. Seidman (Ed.), *Handbook of social intervention*. Beverly Hills, Calif.: Sage
Publications, 1983.

Bowman, P. J. Social psychology of discouragement among jobless Black Americans: Research agenda, preliminary analysis and implications. Paper presented
at the meetings of the American Psychological Association, Washington, D.C.,
1982.

Brandes, J. *Immigrants to freedom: Jewish communities in rural New Jersey since
1882*. Philadelphia: University of Pennsylvania Press, 1971.

Brenner, M. H. Health and the national economy: Commentary and general principles. In L. A. Ferman & J. P. Gordus (Eds.) *Mental health and the economy*.
Kalamazoo, Mich.: W. E. Upjohn Institute for Employment Research, 1979.

Brewster Smith, M. Psychology and the future. *American Psychologist*, 1978, *33*,
644–647.

Buss, T. F., & Redburn, F. S. *Mass unemployment: Plant closings and community mental health.* Beverly Hills, Calif.: Sage Publications, 1983.

Campbell, Donald T. Methods for the experimenting society. Paper presented at the meetings of the Eastern Psychological Association, Washington, D.C., April 1971.

Cumming, E. *Systems of social regulation.* New York: Atherton Press, 1968.

Cumming, J., & Cumming, E. *Ego and milieu: Theory and practice of environmental therapy.* New York: Atherton Press, 1962.

Flaim, P. O., & Fullerton, H. N., Jr. Labor force projections to 1990: Three possible paths. *Monthly Labor Review,* 1978, *101*(12), 25–35.

Gamson, W. A. *Power and discontent.* Homewood, Ill.: Dorsey Press, 1968.

Gerard, H. B. School desegregation: The social science role. *American Psychologist,* 1983, *38,* 869–877.

Gray, D. Empowering older job seekers via the job club. In M. A. Smyer & M. Gatz (Eds.), *Mental health and aging: Programs and evaluations.* Beverly Hills, Calif.: Sage Publications, 1983.

Greenberg, E. S. Participation in industrial decision-making and work satisfaction: The case of producer cooperatives. *Social Science Quarterly,* 1980, *60,* 551–569.

Gurland, B., Bennett, R., & Wilder, D. Re-evaluating the place of evaluation in planning for alternatives to institutional care for the elderly. *Journal of Social Issues,* 1981, *37,* 3, 51–70.

Hansell, N. Patient predicament and clinical service: A system. *Archives of General Psychiatry,* 1967, *17,* 204–210.

Hardin, G. The tragedy of the commons. *Science,* 1968, *162,* 1243–1248.

Klein, D. C. *Community dynamics and mental health.* New York: John Wiley & Sons, 1968.

Kramer, M. The continuing challenge: The rising prevalence of mental disorders, associated chronic diseases and disabling conditions. In M. Wagenfeld, P. V. Lemkau, & B. Justice (Eds.), *Public mental health: Perspectives and prospects.* Beverly Hills, Calif.: Sage Publications, 1982.

Leighton, A. H. *My name is legion: Foundations for a theory of man in relation to culture.* New York: Basic Books, 1959.

Levine, A. G. *Love Canal: Science, politics and people.* Lexington, Massachusetts: D. C. Heath, 1982.

Levine, M. *The history and politics of community mental health.* New York: Oxford University Press, 1981.

Levitan, S. A., & Belous, R. S. Working wives and mothers: What happens to family life? *Monthly Labor Review,* 1981, *104,* 9, 26–30.

Long, R. J. The effects of employee ownership on organizational identification, employee job attitudes, and organizational performance: A tentative framework and empirical findings. *Human Relations,* 1978, *31,* 29–48.

Monahan, J., & Geis, G. Controlling "dangerous" people. *Anals of the American Academy of Political and Social Science,* 1976, *423,* 142–151.

Morrison, M. H. The aging of the U.S. population: Human resource implications. *Monthly Labor Review,* May 1983, 13–19.

Newman, M. J. A profile of Hispanics in the U.S. work force. *Monthly Labor Review,* 1978, *101*(12), 3–14.

Pilisuk, M., & Minkler, M. Supportive networks: Life ties for the elderly. *Journal of Social Issues,* 1980, *36*(2), 95–116.

Platt, J. Social traps. *American Psychologist,* 1973, *28,* 641–651.

Price, R. H. Cooperation dilemmas. In A. Furnham & M. Argyle (Eds.), *Social behavior in context.* New York: Allyn & Bacon, 1983.

Rappaport, J. In praise of paradox: A social policy of empowerment over prevention. *American Journal of Community Psychology,* 1981, *9,* 1–25.

Rhodes, S. R., & Steers, R. M. Conventional vs. worker-owned organizations. *Human Relations,* 1981, *34,* 1013–1035.

Rhodes, W. C. *Behavioral threat and community response: A community psychology inquiry.* New York: Behavioral Publications, 1972.

Rosow, I. The social context of the aging self. *The Gerontologist,* 1973, *13,* 82–87.

Rosow, I. Status and role change through the life span. In R. H. Binstock & E. Shanas (Eds.), *Handbook of aging and the social sciences.* New York: Nostrand Reinhold, 1976, 457–482.

Sarason, S. B. The nature of problem solving in social action. *American Psychologist,* 1978, *33,* 370–380.

Seidman, E., & Rapkin, B. Economics and psychosocial dysfunction: Toward a conceptual framework and prevention strategies. In R. D. Felner, L. A. Jason, J. H. Moritsugu, & S. S. Farber (Eds.), *Preventive psychology: Theory, research, and practice.* New York: Pergamon Press, 1983.

Shinn, M. Father absence and children's cognitive development. *Psychological Bulletin,* 1978, *85,* 295–324.

Smelser, N. J. *Theory of collective behavior.* New York: Free Press of Glencoe, 1963.

Spector, M., & Kitsuse, J. I. *Constructing social problems.* Menlo Park, Calif.: Cummings Publishing, 1977.

Storandt, M. Psychology's response to the graying of America. *American Psychologist,* 1983, *38,* 323–326.

Wack, J., & Rodin, J. Nursing homes for the aged: The human consequences of legislation shaped environments. *Journal of Social Issues,* 1978, *34,* 4, 6–21.

Zigler, E., & Berman, W. Discerning the future of early childhood intervention. *American Psychologist,* 1983, *38,* 894–906.

Appendix: Training Options in Community Psychology

Students interested in further training in community psychology often are not aware of the diversity of options that are available. There is no accreditation procedure for community psychology, and hence there is no list of "approved" schools published by the American Psychological Association, as there is for clinical and counseling psychology.

Information is available that describes training opportunities in community psychology. In 1981, the Division of Community Psychology of the American Psychological Association published an issue of its newsletter specifically devoted to graduate training programs in community psychology. The information in the newsletter comes from a detailed survey conducted by Irwin Sandler and Peter Keller. However, the published descriptions, while valuable, do not represent an exhaustive list of possibilities. This is because only those programs that responded to the survey are listed, and for various reasons, a number of sound training programs chose not to be included. Also, community psychology training can occur under a number of other labels as well (e.g., social ecology, applied social psychology, or organizational psychology). With these limitations in mind, a summary and discussion of the broad options available might be useful as a guide to those considering further training.

Since community psychology evolved from clinical psychology, the *clinical-community* (or community-clinical) format has been the most frequent organizational framework. Students are trained first as clinical psychologists, with expertise in assessment and therapy at the individual and small-group level, and then acquire community concepts and skills. Community psychology often is seen as a "specialty" within clinical psychology, comparable to clinical child psychology or the study of behavioral medicine.

Proponents of the view that training in community psychology should occur within clinical psychology give both substantive and pragmatic arguments to bolster their position. They believe that theories and intervention methods in clinical psychology can be of direct relevance to community work. Furthermore, it would be a mistake not to immerse oneself in what is already known about individuals and the treatment of their psychological problems before tackling the thornier issues raised by communities and the prevention of social problems. Pragmatically, the ease of employment argument is often raised in defense of the clinical-community approach, especially in a time of economic downturn when the public sector is less likely to initiate the funding of new community projects. A second pragmatic consideration is the relative ease with which community psychology can be incorporated within existing clinical training programs, compared with the intramural battles which can be expected when the attempt is made to set up a community program independent of clinical training. Also, it is argued that the great majority of the public—including caregivers and agents of control in the community—see psychologists in clinical terms and relate to them accordingly. Rather than attempt to alter this perception, it may be more fruitful to initially accept the clinical role as a vehicle to enter community institutions; then after acceptance has been achieved, more system-level interventions can be suggested.

The problem of approaching community work from a clinical perspective is that such training could impose clinical "blinders" on students and practitioners with the result that they may tend to see social problems in individualistic and remedial terms. The critics of the clinical-community approach state that the interventions planned in such an organizational structure often tend to be basically clinical in nature, albeit applied to disenfranchised "community" groups (e.g., crisis intervention to the Spanish-speaking). Laudable and necessary as the extension of clinical services may be, the services are still clinical and, the critics charge, evince few of the hallmarks of a genuine community approach, such as an ecological perspective or an emphasis on prevention.

Those who object to community psychology's subordination to clinical work most often propose as an alternative the independence of community psychology as a distinct or *"free-standing"* area within the field of psychology. Under this form of professional organization, community psychology is a separate and co-equal branch of the field on a par with clinical, social, physiological, and other areas. Community psychologists are not trained first as clinicians. Rather, students concentrate on gaining expertise in areas believed to be of more direct relevance to understanding community functioning. According to this view, organizational psychology is a higher priority than personality theory, and environmental psychology takes precedence over psychopathology. Given the limitations of time in graduate education, the priority should go to the study and application of system-level concepts. The advocates of an independent community psychology believe that new and more system-level employment settings (e.g., in welfare systems, government planning agencies, police departments) can and will be found to provide psychologists with an opportunity to effect community change.

The advocates of community psychology as a *minor* area of study argue that community application should be seen as an aspect of the several areas of psychology already concerned with human problems. Psychologists in various relevant areas should employ the principles of community psychology or be concerned with extending the application of their work. Thus, community psychology might be of relevance to developmental psychology (Masterpasqua, 1981) or cognitive psychology (O'Neill, 1981). In this view, "community" should be the orientation of many groups rather than the defining characteristic of one. Its proponents see the creation of a loosely organized community orientation as the way to derive the most benefit for many areas of psychology with the least organizational baggage.

Proponents of one of the other modes of organizing community psychology hold that more than "interest group" meetings are necessary to forge a solid commitment to community problems in the field of psychology. Without a more tightly organized peer constellation, either as an independent area or a clinical-community specialty, the field will be little more than a hobby for psychologists whose principal commitment is elsewhere. When the choice comes between the arduous pursuit of enduring community change or retreat to the laboratory of one's "parent" discipline, those who view community psychology only as an orientation across many areas of the field may feel that following through on community intervention is, after all, somebody else's business.

The most radical view of how best to organize the field of community psychology holds that it should be organized outside psychology altogether. More precisely, it holds that understanding community processes and undertaking community change are by their very nature such complex and multifaceted phenomena that only a truly *interdisciplinary* effort has any hope of success. Psychology as a major intellectual tradition has much to offer the study of communities, but so do sociology, anthropology, urban planning, and the other behavioral sciences. While psychology may have as much to contribute as do these other areas, especially in its knowledge of individual and group behavior and its experimental methodologies, there is no *a priori* reason to assume that psychology has any more claim to community relevance than other scientific traditions. Those who view community work as an interdisciplinary endeavor believe that its organizational structure should include psychology but that it should be organized independently of any established field.

The advocates of the interdisciplinary approach believe that a science of the community will be developed best by exposing students to the relevant portions of several behavioral sciences on a co-equal basis. Only by existing independently of any established field, they state, can the biases and blinders of any one discipline be avoided. In an interdisciplinary framework, the biases of one discipline will be counteracted or compensated for by the biases of another. Thus, if psychology emphasizes the individual in the community and tends to neglect the impact of social forces, sociology stresses social forces and tends to underplay their effect on individuals. By providing education in both areas, the student should be freer to conceptualize, research, and intervene at the multiple levels necessary for community understanding and change. The organizing focuses of graduate education and professional research and practice, it is held, should be *social and community problems* rather than traditional disciplines. Thus, psychologists and others should cluster together around the problems of crime, alcoholism, or environmental quality, rather than having each discipline cluster around itself and span a variety of problems.

The proposition that community psychology training and practice are best organized outside the boundaries of the psychology profession has been criticized on a number of grounds. The detractors of this approach argue that it may produce generalists who know a little about many areas but who lack depth in any one field. They acknowledge that other disciplines may have much to contribute to community work but state that the way to achieve an understanding of the community is for each discipline to pursue community work within its own traditions, so that there would be a community psychology, a community sociology, etc., rather than a synthesized community science or profession. To the extent that knowledge from other areas is useful to the community psychologist, it can be provided in the form of "outside minors" or interdisciplinary seminars in the context of a basically psychological education. A fully interdisciplinary education, its critics argue, would leave students without a clear professional identity or a recognized peer group interested in their research and action experiences.

We have described training options in some detail to demonstrate that there is no "right" way to obtain training in community psychology. Each option has advantages and disadvantages that should be considered. From the point of view of knowledge development, the lack of orthodoxy is healthy and is likely to lead to a more vibrant and intellectually stimulating field.

What has been described in the last few pages are training options that exist at the present time. What we are likely to see in the future is a blending of the alternatives that now are distinct. This is because the field of psychology is changing. The distinction between basic and applied research is becoming blurred as fields of study begin to influence one another and become "mission oriented" (Price, 1983). What were distinct areas, such as developmental, social, organizational, and health psychology, are finding that they have much in common with a community psychology, whose themes—an ecological perspective and prevention focus—are appearing in these fields as well.

Organizational structures that pull together the various training models also are important. Organizational structures, however loosely developed, provide the reference groups and support systems needed to coordinate information flow among persons with similar interests by formally sponsoring journals and meetings and by informally facilitating the development of the social networks necessary for stimulating ideas. More symbolically, an organized interest area serves as a flag around which partisans can rally to validate themselves and to derive sustenance and support from like-minded peers when the going gets rough. The Division of Community Psychology of the American Psychological Association and the various regional community psychology interest groups have begun to serve these functions.

We should note that excessive concern with the "correct" organizational format or training model can inhibit intellectual advances in several ways. Energies that can be spent in more substantive pursuits should not be diverted to what are essentially administrative arguments. It is important that those with community interests not turn inward, spending more time debating how to organize than actually carrying out their goals. The danger is that what can begin as a social movement often can end as a guild, with a rigidity and narrowness that is as stultifying as the forms against which the movement first reacted. While we must work to separate rhetoric from theory and to supplant diatribe with data in community work, we must be careful to preserve the spirit and motivation—the social conscience—which first gave rise to the field.

References

Graduate programs in community psychology: A report from the Council of Community Psychology Program Directors. *Division of Community Psychology Newsletter,* 1981, *15*(2).

Masterpasqua, F. Toward a synergism of developmental and community psychology. *American Psychologist,* 1981, *36,* 782–786.

O'Neill, P. Cognitive community psychology. *American Psychologist,* 1981, *36,* 457–469.

Price, R. H. The education of a prevention psychologist. In R. D. Felner, L. A. Jason, J. H. Moritsugu, & S. S. Farber (Eds.), *Preventive psychology: Theory, research and practice.* New York: Pergamon Press, 1983.

Subject Index

This book has been set Linotron 202 in 10 and 9 point Times Roman, leaded 2 points. Part numbers are 18 point Times Roman Bold. Part titles are 36 point Times Roman. Chapter numbers are 14 point Times Roman Bold. Chapter titles are 30 point Times Roman. The size of the type page is 28 by 48½ picas.